MUSADDIQ,
IRANIAN NATIONALISM,
AND OIL

Modern Middle East Series, No. 14
Sponsored by the Center for Middle Eastern Studies
The University of Texas at Austin

Musaddiq,
Iranian Nationalism,
and Oil

Edited by

JAMES A. BILL and WM. ROGER LOUIS

University of Texas Press, Austin

Contents

Contents

Contributors

Shahrough Akhavi Professor of International Studies, University of South Carolina. Author of *Religion and Politics in Contemporary Iran: Clergy–State Relations in the Pahlavi Period* (1980).

Irvine H. Anderson Manager, Human Resource Development, Aircraft Engine Business Group, General Electric Company. Author of *Aramco, the United States, and Saudi Arabia: a Study in the Dynamics of Foreign Oil Policy* (1981).

Fakhreddin Azimi St Antony's College, Oxford. Author of *The Politics of Dynamic Stalemate, Iran 1944–53* (in press).

James A. Bill Professor of Government and Director, Center for International Studies, The College of William and Mary. Author of *The Eagle and the Lion: the Tragedy of American–Iranian Relations* (1988).

Richard W. Cottam Professor of Political Science, University of Pittsburgh. Author of *Nationalism in Iran* (1964).

Ronald W. Ferrier Historian, British Petroleum Company. Author of *The History of The British Petroleum Company: the Developing Years 1901–1932* (1982).

Albert Hourani Emeritus Fellow, St Antony's College, Oxford. Author of *Arabic Thought in the Liberal Age* (1962).

Homa Katouzian Former Senior Lecturer in Economics, University of Kent at Canterbury. Author of *The Political Economy of Modern Iran* (1981).

Habib Ladjevardi Director, Iranian Oral History Project, Harvard University. Author of *Labor Unions and Autocracy in Iran* (1985).

Wm. Roger Louis Kerr Professor, The University of Texas at Austin, and Supernumerary Fellow, St Antony's College, Oxford. Author of *The British Empire in the Middle East* (1984).

George C. McGhee Former US Assistant Secretary of State and Ambassador. Author of *Envoy to the Middle World* (1983).

Farhang Rajaee   Beheshti University (Tehran). Author of *Islamic Values and World View: Khomeyni on Man, the State and International Politics* (1983).

Rouhollah K. Ramazani   Harry Flood Byrd Jr Professor of Government and Foreign Affairs, University of Virginia. Author of *Revolutionary Iran: Challenge and Response in the Middle East* (1986).

Acknowledgements

This book had its origins in a conference of 26–7 September 1985 at the University of Texas at Austin that celebrated the 25th anniversary of the Center for Middle Eastern Studies. We wish to acknowledge support from the Center, the College of Liberal Arts, the Dean of Graduate Studies, the departments of Government and History, and the faculty seminar on British Studies. We are grateful for the assistance given us by the directors of the Middle East Center, Ali Jazayery and Ian Manners, and above all and most warmly, Annes McCann-Baker and Marjorie Payne. We also wish to thank Nikkie Keddie, Ali Estekhari, Anne Enayat and Jonathan Livingstone, Greg Rose and Mehdi Noorbaksh.

Note on transliteration

The system of transliteration adopted in this study is a modified version of the format recommended by the *International Journal of Middle East Studies*. We have chosen to delete all diacritical marks with the exception of the *ayn* (') and the *hamza* (') when they appear in the middle of a word, for example *shari'a*, Qashqa'i. In this system, the *e* and the *o* are not used but are replaced by the *i* and the *u*. A few common Persian or Arabic words and names are spelled in their anglicized form, for example Koran, bazaar, Khomeini.

Introduction

The purpose of this book is to reassess a critical era in Iranian and international history: the rise and fall of the government of Muhammad Musaddiq in 1951–3 and the reorganization of the Iranian oil industry in 1954. The two events were linked, and they have repercussions to the present day. The period has been clouded by controversy and misunderstanding. With the passing of time and the availability of new evidence, it is now possible to undertake a dispassionate analysis of the origins of the Musaddiq movement, the nationalization of the Anglo-Iranian Oil Company in 1951, the American and British intervention that led to Musaddiq's political demise, the part played by the Shah, and the consortium of oil companies that replaced the British monopoly.

A charismatic leader, Musaddiq mobilized the nationalist movement in the early 1950s by challenging Iran's corrupt, authoritarian political system and denouncing the economic exploitation of the British. He opposed the arbitrary rule of the Pahlavi regime by representing constitutional values and a form of democratic populism. The Musaddiq movement reached its peak at a time of increasing political discontent. Iranians demonstrated deep unease about their own form of government, and they sought to break the grip of British economic control over their resources. This struggle took place in the early stages of the rivalry between the United States and the Soviet Union, when Britain was still considered to be a major world power and was, indeed, the dominant foreign power in Iran.

The forces of anti-colonialism burst into prominence not only in Iran but throughout the non-western world following the second world war, as nationalists strongly rejected European domination and interference in their countries. 'Independence', 'neutralism', and 'non-alignment' became the slogans of the Middle Eastern and Asian leaders during the 1950s. In Iran, social and political movements developed as a result of a series of related political events that included the abrupt collapse of the Riza Shah dictatorship in 1941, the Allied occupation, and the ultimate withdrawal of the Allied troops in 1946. The fall of Riza Shah and the Allied withdrawal removed the lid from a socio-political cauldron of forces that had been simmering in Iran for decades. The late 1940s were a time of relative political freedom and wide-scale political activity.

The numerous political factions and organizations included an array of ideological forces that extended from the communist left to the religious right. The ideological centre was occupied by a shifting assortment of liberal nationalist groupings represented most prominently by a loose conglomeration formed in October 1949, the National Front (*Jibheh-i Milli*). With the minor exception of a few groups of a moderate right-wing cast, all the others shared one goal: an end to outside imperial intervention in the internal affairs of Iran. The sudden appearance of freedom of the press resulted in the publication of hundreds of Persian pamphlets, political magazines and newspapers that castigated external influence in the affairs of the country. The major target at the time, of course, was Britain, the power most directly and indirectly active in Iran for over a century. The pent-up nationalist emotions in Iran were focused, therefore, upon Britain, although the Soviet Union also came in for its share of condemnation and criticism.

There were some Iranians – 'collaborators' in the eyes of their critics – who remained wedded to the British through thick and thin in a sort of love–hate relationship.[1] Nevertheless it is the extent of the alienation that provides an essential theme for the Musaddiq years. The depth of anti-British feeling in Iran at that time is apparent in the words of the American naval attaché resident in Tehran. In a secret report on the domestic political situation in Iran in early 1953, he stated in bold and perhaps simplistic terms that were characteristic of American analysis:

> The Sickness of Iran, and the whole Middle East, is mainly concerned with an intense and overriding hatred and fear of the British. By now this should be accepted by any observer of this area. This hatred is such that it is almost unbelieveable to see, and involves intense emotions such as fear that the British will somehow, by Machiavellian operations, regain their former power . . .[2]

American officials in Iran at the time agreed that there was evidence to justify this Iranan preoccupation with British influence. The same attaché reported that, to Iranians, a recent debate in the House of Commons could be understood to mean that a partition of Iran between Britain and the Soviet Union 'would not be an unpleasant prospect to the British . . . and that such a partition might even be preferable to increased US influence in the area'.[3] Throughout the 1940s and into the 1950s, British actions in Iran reinforced Iranian preconceptions and anti-British sentiment.

The gathering nationalist storm in Iran thus broke against the British. The visible symbol of British imperial policy in Iran was the largest commercial venture in the country, the Anglo-Iranian Oil Company. Iranian nationalists recognized this powerful company as the natural target of their campaign. In so doing, they brought to bear an emotional anti-imperialism and carried with them a moral sense of righteousness that appealed to Iranians of all social and economic classes. Although deeply splintered among themselves, Iranians shared a common perception of the evil of British imperialism and a sense that they were the underdog challenging an insensitive and cunning imperial power. As mid-century approached, the positive force of Iranian nationalism linked itself with the negative force of national Anglophobia. The unifying, charismatic figure of Muhammad Musaddiq helped to bring these two forces together.

Musaddiq was born into a wealthy Iranian landowning family in May 1882. His father was a high-ranking financial administrator and man of distinction in the Qajar court. Before the turn of the century Musaddiq had acquired extensive political and administrative experience by assuming, as was customary, one of his father's posts and becoming financial administrator of Khurasan province. He pursued his higher education in France and Switzerland, obtaining a doctorate in law from the University of Neuchâtel in 1914. At the close of the first world war he campaigned effectively against British political and economic influence in Iran. In the early 1920s he served in high administrative posts in the provinces and in Tehran, and in 1924 he was elected to the Majlis, or Iranian parliament. His early administrative and parliamentary career was characterized by opposing British influence in Iran and by espousing constitutional principles. He resisted the creation of the Pahlavi dynasty, and in 1925 he voted against Riza Khan's accession as the first Pahlavi Shah.

Musaddiq upheld the principle that Iranians should manage their own affairs as independently as possible. He consistently denounced British attempts to subjugate Iran, in his view, through the Anglo-Iranian Oil Company in Abadan and the British Embassy in Tehran. His protest against the erosion of parliamentary government and his opposition to the Pahlavi regime led to his exile in the provinces in 1936. But the Allied occupation of 1941 and the forced abdication of Riza Shah (whom the British suspected of harbouring pro-Nazi sympathies) enabled Musaddiq to return as a nationalist and democratic reformer. In 1944 he was again elected to the Majlis. He enlarged his reputation as an orator of distinct ability and magnetic qualities. In December of that year he helped to enact a law aimed at preventing foreign exploitation of Iranian oil. Nevertheless in April 1946 the Iranian government consented in principle to sign an oil agreement with the Soviet Union that would create a joint Iranian and Soviet company (in which the Soviet government would own 51 per cent of the shares) in northern Iran in return for the withdrawal of Soviet troops. Musaddiq passionately denounced this arrangement in the Majlis. In October 1947 the Majlis by a vote of 102 to 2 declared that the tentative oil agreement with the Soviet Union was null and void. Musaddiq was a driving force behind the nationalist sentiment that oil, Iran's greatest natural resource, should be developed by Iranians themselves for the benefit of their own country.

Musaddiq's response to the question of exploitation is one of the major themes of this book. He believed that the Soviet Union as well as Britain wished to control Iran as a satellite state or its equivalent. Only by manipulating the 'negative equilibrium' of balancing the two rival powers against each other could Iranians preserve their independence. In Musaddiq's own mind there was no doubt that British imperialism constituted the greatest danger. Since the turn of the century, in the judgement of Musaddiq and his followers, Britain had held Iran in an unequal relationship. The D'Arcy concession of 1901, the original instrument, had granted comprehensive rights to Iranian oil (except in certain northern provinces) in return for the sum of £20,000 in cash, the same amount in shares of the company, and an annual royalty of 16 per cent of the profits. In 1909 the D'Arcy concession was taken over by (as it was then called) the Anglo-Persian Oil Company, which to the Musaddiqists became the symbol as well as the tool of exploitative capitalism.

The company also symbolized the power of the British state. In 1914, as part of the programme to convert the Royal Navy from coal to oil, the British government acquired a majority 51 per cent of the company's shares. In 1933 the Anglo-Persian Oil Company granted better terms of royalties and guarantees in exchange for, among other things, an extension of the concession up to the year 1993. The Anglo-Iranian Oil Company (renamed in 1935) offered further concessions in 1949 in an arrangement called the 'Supplemental Agreement', which would have further increased Iranian royalties but would still have kept them at a ratio unacceptable to Musaddiq and his followers. By this time the Anglo-Iranian Oil Company's refinery at Abadan had become the largest in the world. Between 1938 and 1950 world oil production had nearly doubled. The cost to the company of Iranian crude was close to the lowest in the world, and the potential seemed as yet scarcely tapped. Musaddiq's act of nationalization in 1951 was thus one of world-wide moment. His perception (accurate or not) of the international importance of Iranian oil, and its actual significance in the world market, forms another of the book's major themes.

What appeared to the Iranians to be British imperialism – a monolithic instrument of exploitation and oppression – seemed to the British themselves to be a complicated interplay of commerce, defence strategy, and political influence. To the British, moreover, their presence provided an ethical example of qualities deplorably lacking in the Iranian national life. 'It is regrettable,' wrote Sir Reader Bullard, the British Ambassador in 1946, 'but a fact, that the Persians are . . . untruthful backbiters, undisciplined, incapable of unity, without a plan.' Bullard was not condemning the Iranian people but the governing elite. Among Iran's rulers he could identify no 'civil virtues'. They did not exist: the Iranian people were simply subject to 'the mercy of a selfish, ineducable ruling class'.[4] In other parts of the world, native peoples had been able to benefit from direct British rule that could reform the ruling class and foster the development of a responsible nationalist movement. According to one of Bullard's successors, Sir Francis Shepherd, in 1951:

> The tragedy of the situation is that in the 20th century there is no country which either could or would undertake the education of Persia and its preparation for a *renaissance* which would bring it into equal relations with other Powers. But unless something is done the country is liable to sink further into corruption and to finish with a Communist revolution.[5]

The Iranians would have to be saved from themselves, morally, militarily, and economically; if they were left, according to Shepherd, 'the Oriental character' of the Iranians, which could be summed up as a combination of sloth, deviousness and suspicion, would impel them to little more than to try 'to squeeze more out of the Oil Company'.[6]

The refinery at Abadan was a source of British pride and wealth. At the time it was the greatest single British overseas enterprise. It was a distinct and self-contained enclave. Although individuals formed friendships across the cultural divide, the British community of 4,500 lived apart from Iranian society. The industrial plant functioned separately from the Iranian economy. The Anglo-Iranian Oil Company possessed its own fleet, its own hospital, and its own schools. Members of the Gymkhana Club in Abadan read the airmail edition of *The Times*. The refinery itself was a tribute to British technology. At the time of nationalization in 1951, the Anglo-Iranian Oil Company produced about 30 million tons of oil a year. After nationalization and the subsequent British evacuation, production fell to less than one million. Part of the British calculation, or hope, was that the Iranians would not be able to run the oil industry on their own. They would be forced to ask the British to return. After the creation of the consortium in 1954, Iran remained dependent on the British as well as European and American oil companies, but Musaddiq did manage to break the British monopoly.

During the time of the British Labour government 1945–51, there was considerable ambiguity in the attitude of the member of the Cabinet whose voice usually predominated in Iranian affairs, the Foreign Secretary, Ernest Bevin. Bevin wished to treat the Iranians, like the Arabs, as equals, but like most Englishmen he doubted the capacity of Iranians to manage their own affairs and he resented Iranian suspicion of British motives. Bevin also had mixed sentiments about the Anglo-Iranian Oil Company. He saw this great British industrial enterprise as critical to post-war economic recovery, yet he expected the Anglo-Iranian Oil Company to demonstrate a social conscience. He demanded that the company raise the standard of living in Iran through better wages and social services. As a socialist he could not object to the Iranian principle of nationalization:

'What argument can I advance against anyone claiming the right to nationalise the resources of their country? We are doing the same thing here with our power in the shape of coal, electricity, railways, transport and steel.'[7] Bevin was clearly troubled over the contradiction between socialism in England and British capitalism in Iran. But he was sensitive to charges of allowing the Iranians to strangle a British enterprise. When the company through the 'Supplemental Agreement' of 1949 held out better general terms, including an increase of royalties eventually up to 30 per cent, he believed that the Iranians should accept the offer as fair and reasonable.

In late 1950 the British learned that the American oil company in Saudi Arabia, Aramco, had concluded an agreement with the government of Saudi Arabia whereby the profits would be divided equally. The American–Saudi agreement became known as the fifty–fifty split, and it revolutionized the economic affairs of the Middle East. There was a world of difference in the Anglo-Iranian Oil Company's increase in *royalties*, and Aramco's *profit-sharing*. The British company would argue in vain that the difference was more apparent than real. There were psychological implications. A fifty–fifty share in the profits was a tangible concept. Nationalists could accept it as a fair basis without feeling that they were being bamboozled in the calculations of royalties. Once this basic point became clear, the British 'Supplemental Agreement' was doomed.

The State Department warned both the Foreign Office and the Anglo-Iranian Oil Company about the effect the new agreement was bound to have on the British commercial position in Iran. After first consulting with representatives of the American oil companies involved in the Middle East, George McGhee, the Assistant Secretary of State presiding over Middle Eastern affairs, went to London in September 1950 to confer with the British. He met with officials of the Foreign Office (including Sir Michael Wright, the Under-Secretary supervising Middle Eastern affairs), and with the board of directors of the Anglo-Iranian Company chaired by Neville Gass, who had prepared the 'Supplemental Agreement' of the previous year. McGhee could not reveal the precise terms of the Aramco agreement because it had not yet been concluded; but the warning was clear. Unless the British made substantial changes to meet Iranian demands, the company would be in danger of losing the concession. 'In retrospect,' McGhee wrote in his memoirs, 'the AIOC failure to act at this time can only be seen as a great tragedy.'[8]

The Fifty–fifty Agreement bore the date of 30 December 1950. Less than half a year later, on 2 May 1951, Musaddiq nationalized the oil industry. The reaction in Britain was so strong that it is important to recall the dominant sentiment in the government, in parliament, and among the public. It was one of outrage at the expropriation of a British company – *theft* would not be too strong a word to sum up the popular indictment. Sir

Donald Fergusson, a civil servant who played an important part in the subsequent negotiations with Musaddiq, expressed one of the main currents of British thought when he wrote about the dangerous precedent that Musaddiq had established:

> I feel absolutely sure that we cannot reach an agreement with Moussadec which would not have disastrous effects not only on all other British interests all over the world but on all other enterprises and trading activities in foreign countries on which the standard of living of the people of this country, and our ability to maintain our freedom and independence depend . . . In the case of a mineral like oil they [the Iranians] are of course morally entitled to a royalty. But to my mind the Asiatic idea . . . that morally they are entitled to 50% . . . is bunk.[9]

If the Iranians were allowed to get away with nationalizing the Anglo-Iranian Oil Company, what might the Egyptians do with the Suez Canal Company? Why should the Iranians be allowed to expropriate an industry that had been built and developed by British money, hard work, and ingenuity?

The British Labour government resisted jingoistic pressure to intervene. The Prime Minister, Clement Attlee, himself took control of the crisis and refused to sanction the use of force against the Iranians. One of his reasons was that the American government would not support any attempt to resolve the issue by force. Britain, now economically dependent on the United States, could not risk unilateral action in the teeth of American opposition. Attlee also had other reasons for exercising restraint. He explained to his colleagues in the British Cabinet on 12 July 1951:

> Dr Musaddiq had been able to form his Government owing to the support of Persians who were dissatisfied with former rule by a corrupt clique. We could not safely assume that if we succeeded in upsetting the present Government their successors would be less unsatisfactory, and we should risk identifying ourselves with support of an equally undemocratic régime.[10]

Attlee hoped that it might still be possible to negotiate a settlement that would salvage the situation, though he shared with many others in Britain the view that Musaddiq had crossed the Rubicon into irrationality: 'we must, in view of the present highly charged atmosphere in Persia and in particular of the emotional state of the Persian Prime Minister (who appeared to be on the lunatic fringe), agree to accept the principle of nationalization.'[11]

The belief that it would prove impossible to do business with Musaddiq led the Foreign Secretary, Herbert Morrison (Bevin's successor) to endorse covert action. The plot eventually culminated in the co-ordinated action of the British and American intelligence services, the MI6 and the CIA, in the coup against Musaddiq in 1953. This episode is another main concern of this book, and it is discussed at length in the chapters. As background, it is important here to point out that the initiative came from within the British government and not the Anglo-Iranian Oil Company. Considerable tension existed between the government and the company at this time. The Foreign Office believed that the crisis itself might have been averted if the company had been more flexible and generous in its attempt to offer a more equitable share of the profits. The chairman of the Anglo-Iranian Oil Company, Sir William Fraser, took a consistent view that the government bureaucrats, or 'West End gentlemen', as he called them, had an insufficient knowledge of both Iranian nationalism and the oil industry, and had inadequately defended the legitimate position of the company. No love was lost between the company and the government. But the responsibility for the action against Musaddiq rests with the latter.

At the outset especially, the attitude of the British and American governments diverged. The British could find no redeeming virtues in Musaddiq. To them he seemed obsessed with expropriating a British company, and by doing so bringing about the economic ruin of his own country. The American assessment was substantially different. Americans generally sympathized with Iranian nationalist aspirations. They believed that the nationalists in Iran had the ability to modernize their economy and to make their country truly independent. Above all they took a different view of Musaddiq. Like the British, the Americans held different views among themselves whether Musaddiq was rational or stable enough to come to a satisfactory agreement. But there was a major distinction between the general British and American outlook. The Americans, far more than the British, believed that a settlement might be possible.

Led by influential policy makers such as Secretary of State Dean Acheson and Assistant Secretary of State George McGhee, the Truman Administration viewed Musaddiq and his movement with considerable understanding and some sympathy. Although they were concerned about the threat of communism and the importance of Iranian oil to the western economy, they also recognized the Iranian right to nationalize and the political danger of any British attempt to force a settlement by military means. In a meeting in September 1951, for example, Secretary for Defense Robert Lovett said to Sir William Elliott, a British Air Marshal: 'what better tool could be put into the hands of the Kremlin than for the British to put troops in . . . this could give the Kremlin the excuse for moving in to Azerbaijan with the Tudeh party and other disaffected parties.'[12] In these circumstances, Acheson sought to devise a policy that would discourage British intervention and at the same time would encourage compromise on the part of the Iranian nationalists. As a part of this policy, leading American negotiators such as Averell Harriman,

Vernon Walters, Walter Levy and George McGhee spent many hours in direct contact with Musaddiq and his entourage, as McGhee relates in chapter 11.

In the end, these efforts came to naught as Musaddiq, riding the wave of Iranian nationalism, was limited in his capacity to compromise in matters concerning Iran's national autonomy and dignity. The domestic social forces of the day were strong, a fact that became quite clear to American officials during the crisis. In a meeting of the National Security Council of 18 February 1953, Secretary of State John Foster Dulles (Acheson's successor in the new Eisenhower government) remarked that Musaddiq 'could not afford to reach any agreement with the British lest it cost him his political life'.[13] The British, on the other hand, gave ground only grudgingly. The tension between Britain and the United States, especially in the early months of the crisis, was intense. In a high-level meeting held in Paris in November 1951, attended by Acheson and the British Foreign Secretary Sir Anthony Eden, these differences dominated the discussions (according to an American record):

> The British claimed that, if we had supported them, events would have been different and their policy would have been shown to be right; whereas, now we claimed that they were proved wrong because our lack of support created the very situation which we pointed to as proof. We thought that the history of the AIOC troubles in Iran, compared to the relatively happy situation of all other countries, was [the] answer to this view.[14]

The United States found itself caught between an important non-European nation which Americans believed to have legitimate national concerns, on the one hand and, on the other, an old ally with strong economic and political interests in that country.

In the latter days of the Truman Administration there had already been considerable concern in Washington about what the precedent of oil nationalization might mean to American oil companies overseas. This was moreover a time when political life in America was dominated by preoccupation with the perceived danger of a communist menace that threatened the very existence of the United States. A report submitted to the National Security Council in November 1952 held that 'in wrestling the political initiative away from the Shah, the landlords, and other traditional holders of power, the National Front politicians now in power have at least temporarily eliminated every alternative to their own rule except the Communist Tudeh Party.' According to this interpretation, 'the major United States policy objective with respect to Iran is to prevent the country from coming under Communist control.'[5] Given these concerns, it was not difficult for the British to convince the United States of the dangers of Musaddiqism. The task was made easier by the diplomatic method and bazaar bargaining techniques of the Iranians. The Iranian style, which was to prove unfathomable to Americans in future decades, left American officials at the time frustrated and exasperated. For both substantive and procedural reasons, the United States thus moved closer to the British position. The unfolding of this change in position is closely studied in this book.

Despite this shifting of position, the Democratic Administration had not been willing to sanction any direct intervention in the affairs of another sovereign state. This situation changed with the advent of the Republican Administration of Dwight Eisenhower in January 1953. At the same time the Conservative government of Winston Churchill in Britain adopted a more aggressive approach to the Iranian issue. This led to a joint intelligence operation in which Britain and the United States co-operated in an intervention in August 1953 that resulted in the fall of the Musaddiq government. The Central Intelligence Agency played a vital part in this venture and, in so doing, eventually established a reputation in Iran as the instrument of western intervention responsible for the continued rule of the Pahlavi regime.

The reasons for the success of the intervention in bringing down the Musaddiq government were both internal and external. Internally, there was discord and division; the economy was in difficulty, in part because of the effectiveness of the oil blockade imposed by the British; National Front leaders committed clumsy political errors; and the communist Tudeh Party was politically active. Psychologically, growing numbers of the Iranian people were becoming disillusioned with the Musaddiq government. This disenchantment seemed to grow proportionately to his increasingly arbitrary and personal power. As long as he was weak and exposed, outflanked and outnumbered, he was a hero, an underdog, a public figure flirting with political martyrdom. As he grew stronger and began to adopt authoritarian tactics of his own, he became vulnerable. Many observers, including Iranians themselves, have pointed out that the Iranian people sympathize with the suffering and the oppressed. Musaddiq was not unaware of this trait. He presented an image of the weak courageously battling against the strong; the oppressed had been engaged in a gallant, one-sided battle against the oppressor. Once he became prime minister, however, he had to wield power in order to maintain control over the many forces threatening him from both left and right. As he hesitantly took action against them, he saw his own image begin to deteriorate.

Still, there is considerable doubt whether the Iranian mobs would have acted to overthrow their prime minister if it had not been for the American and British intervention. The CIA operation helped to ignite the flame that enveloped the Musaddiq government. From the Iranian perspective, the internal causes of the coup became incidental to the outcome. In time the belief developed that the United States, through the CIA, was responsible, first, last and always, for the destruction of this popular political system. From the beginning many Iranians were suspicious of the part played by the CIA. This popular perception shaped attitudes toward the United States thereafter. In this case, the image is far more important than the reality. And it is this image that came to dominate Iranian political thinking, which is another theme explored in this book.

The 1953 intervention that rearranged the Iranian political system in a manner more acceptable to the Americans and the British was the major event which began the deterioration of America's reputation in Iran. In Persian, *CIA* became an epithet that implied an external evil force responsible for the social, political and economic problems that plagued the country. Thousands of Iranians of nationalist persuasion now shifted much of their criticism and attention away from the Soviet Union and Britain, towards the United States. Many Iranians were especially disillusioned since America had long been viewed as a friend and protector of the Iranian nation against the Russians and the British. With the intervention of 1953, the friend had joined the enemy. Such an action might have been expected of the British or the Russians, but not of the Americans. This was a surprise that the Iranians still bitterly discussed decades later, long after the overthrow of the Shah.

American policy in Iran increasingly identified itself with the Shah's regime after the events of 1953. Military, economic, educational, financial, industrial and political ties bound the United States to Pahlavi Iran to such an extent that it became difficult to disentangle the two parties. The world situation after 1953 did much to tighten this linkage. But the events of August 1953 represented the turning point, and, as such, remained indelibly engraved in the minds and memories of the Iranian people. During the revolution of 1978–9, the masses of Iranian opposition to the Shah's rule, whether secular or religious, were determined to see that 1978 would not be a repetition of 1953. In the process, they shouted slogans such as 'Remember Musaddiq' and 'Down with the American Shah'.

Rightly or wrongly, American leaders considered the 1953 intervention in Iran to be a resounding success. It served as a catalyst, or at least an inspiration, for other covert interventions such as the one in Guatemala the following year. In the short term, a number of important American interests did seem to be well served. American oil companies entered the Iranian fields for the first time, gaining access to 40 per cent of the production as a result of the Consortium Agreement of 1954. Over the next 25 years, the international oil industry was able to export billions of barrels of Iranian crude at prices advantageous both to the companies and to the consuming countries. Meanwhile, Pahlavi Iran avoided any possible communist takeover. If there had indeed been a serious threat in this regard, it never materialized. Specifically, the American intervention was followed by a thorough purge of the Tudeh Party, curtailing its influence in the country.

The long-term consequences of the intervention raise more serious questions about the wisdom of the operation. As the first major step on the road to locking the United States into a special relationship with the Shah, it began a process of alienating large numbers of Iranians, which climaxed in a revolution that turned not only against the Pahlavi regime but also against the United States. The intervention actually stifled the natural growth of nationalism in Iran and artificially bottled it up for 25 years. When it finally burst out in 1978, it did so with explosive force and extreme anti-Americanism. Another negative result of the intervention of 1953 involved the image of the United States generally in the third world. In the days of nationalism, neutralism, and non-alignment, the actions of the United States through the CIA flew in the face of the rising social and political forces of the day. The negative consequences are difficult to measure, but they undoubtedly hurt the reputation and credibility not only of the United States but also, to some extent, of Britain.

For the British the long-range effect of the Musaddiq crisis did not represent a watershed so much as a reaffirmation of the traditional and paternalistic attitude that the internal affairs of Iran could be influenced to the benefit of both the British and the Iranians themselves. Perhaps of greatest significance was the conclusion drawn from the intervention: it appeared to have been a success; therefore a similar operation might work elsewhere. In that sense Iran prepared the way for the disastrous intervention at Suez three years later.

At the time British officials believed that they had exhausted all possibilities of a negotiated settlement with Musaddiq, who not only had an irreversible anti-British bias but also was losing control. In this view, the intervention saved Iran from a possible communist revolution. This judgement was strongly held, then and later. 'Mussadeq remaining in power would eventually lead to a Communist takeover', one of the British participants in the planning of the coup, Sir Sam Falle, reflected later.[16] Nor could the immediate aftermath of the intervention, from a British point of view, be judged unsatisfactory. Despite abiding doubts about him, the Shah did provide political stability. Commercially, British Petroleum (as the Anglo-Iranian Oil Company became known in its new incarnation) continued to prosper despite the setback of nationalization and the loss of the British monopoly. Paradoxically Musaddiq contributed to the company's diversification at a time when the oil markets were still expanding. He thus helped to invigorate rather than to liquidate one of Britain's great industries. In terms of power politics and the international economy, the intervention of 1953 appeared to be effective. There was dissent from this view by those in American and British circles who continued to affirm a policy of non-intervention as a matter of principle, and of course by most Iranians, who from the beginning regarded intervention as a catastrophe. But on the whole the 1953 coup seemed, in western eyes, to have been a success – until the Iranian revolution of 1978 caused second thoughts.

There will probably never be general agreement, scholarly or otherwise, about the 1953 intervention, but one of the purposes of this book is to discuss it fairly from the three main vantage points of Iran, Britain, and the United States. A principal goal is to reassess, as objectively as possible, the Musaddiq era. The first section of the book analyses the nature of the nationalist movement in Iran, Musaddiq's contribution to it, his achievements, and his reputation from the perspective of today's Islamic republic as well as in its historical context.

The reassessment begins with Richard Cottam's inquiry into the nature of Iranian nationalism. He argues that, despite the Shii Islamic emphasis of revolutionary Iran today, there is a continuity in the experience of Iranian nationalism. Like the Musaddiq government, the Islamic Republic upholds the principle of national autonomy and maintains a strong antipathy to any form of outside influence. The Musaddiq movement of the 1951–3 period generally represented enlightened values as well as patriotic nationalism. By snuffing out this political movement, according to Cottam, the British and Americans weakened forces that might have prevented the advent of the royal dictatorship of the Shah and, later, might have averted revolutionary extremism. The overthrow of Musaddiq thus contributed to the radical shifts that have marked Iranian politics ever since.

The chapter by Fakhreddin Azimi assesses Musaddiq's own part in these controversial years. Was Musaddiq irrational, senile and emotionally unbalanced? Or to what extent was he, as he sometimes appeared to western eyes, a coldly rational, scheming figure whose emotions were posed? Azimi holds convincingly that within the Iranian context Musaddiq pursued his policies consistently and rationally. He faced relentless challenges and was occasionally forced to compromise democratic principles or procedures in the face of political exigency. While Musaddiq may not have grasped the intricacies of the economies of the oil controversy, he fully understood, Azimi points out, the fundamental issue: Iranians had the right to control their own resources. To him this principle was a question of 'national dignity' as well as an economic issue, and for this reason, among others, his reputation over the years has continued to grow. Today he is remembered as a revered figure in Iran's national history – as a democratic and secular nationalist – though anti-Musaddiq sentiment persists as well. Then as now judgements about Musaddiq differ, but Azimi's chapter sustains Cottam's thesis arguing the continuity of Iranian nationalism. In Azimi's judgement, the spirit of the Musaddiq movement will persist in Iranian politics.

Habib Ladjevardi reinforces many of Azimi's themes by analysing Musaddiq's social programmes and economic reforms. Musaddiq's 27-month rule has often been described by critics as not only failing to resolve the oil dispute but also doing little to improve the lot of the people. By focusing on the actual legislation of the Musaddiq government, Ladjevardi demonstrates the concrete steps taken in financial reform, education,

public health and, not least, the judiciary. Musaddiq believed that a
competent and honest judiciary was essential in promoting democratic
government. He sought to make his administration more responsive and
responsible to the public. His attempt to govern the country by law was, in
the context of Iranian history, a rare achievement. His wide-ranging
reforms, according to Ladjevardi, gave Iranians a new standard of social
justice.

The partisans of Ayatullah Khomeini have referred disparagingly to
Musaddiq while they have praised one of the principal clerics of the period,
Ayatullah Kashani, as the true leader of the anti-British movement and the
hero of nationalization. Shahrough Akhavi explains the reasons for
Kashani's rehabilitation as a 'misunderstood patriot'. Kashani was
undoubtedly the leading clerical activist of the period. He and Musaddiq
worked together toward nationalization of the oil industry, but Kashani
later broke with Musaddiq for reasons that were both personal and
political. Although cleavages existed among the clerics, the majority of
them remained aloof from national politics until about March 1953, when
Kashani finally crystallized clerical opposition by condemning Musaddiq's
alleged republicanism, communism and anti-clericalism. In examining the
clerics' part in Musaddiq's downfall, Akhavi concludes that Kashani may
have collaborated with US intelligence agents. If so, the reasons were
probably tactical; he certainly did not sell out to the West. Kashani's
political activism foreshadowed the involvement of the ulama in Iranian
politics following the revolution of 1978–9. Nevertheless, in Akhavi's
judgement, it would be a mistake to view Kashani as a precursor of
Ayatullah Khomeini. Kashani did not seek the eventual rule of the ulama.
This chapter thus helps to put into proper perspective the religious
dimension of the politics of the Musaddiq period by focusing on Kashani as
a complex figure in his own right.

The interpretation of the past by the leaders of today's Islamic Republic
of Iran emphasizes a flawed and misguided Musaddiq. Farhang Rajaee
demonstrates the deterioration of Musaddiq's historical image as the
Iranian revolution continued to unfold in the 1980s. Those who carry the
message of the revolution find it necessary to prove that nationalism is an
anachronism. But, as the preceding chapters indicate, nationalism continues to be a driving force in contemporary Iran. The leaders of the
Islamic revolution sometimes feel threatened by the Musaddiq legacy
because he was a product of the West by virtue of his education and,
perhaps, because he was a scion of the Iranian aristocracy. According to
many Iranian intellectuals, he was a charismatic, secular nationalist whose
legacy provides an alternative to the Islamic Republic.

The second section of the book concerns the oil question. Irvine
Anderson makes clear the connection between Aramco's Fifty–fifty Agreement and the nationalization crisis in Iran. The principle of an equal division

of profits had its immediate antecedents in legislation enacted by the Venezuelan government in 1948. By establishing an income tax law that guaranteed a fifty–fifty division of the profits, the Venezuelan government created a masterpiece of compelling simplicity relevant to all oil-producing countries. In turn the agreement between Aramco and the government of Saudi Arabia in December 1950 proved to be a catalyst for events in Iran. Iranians quickly grasped the advantages of equal profit sharing as opposed to royalties, which can be a complicated and confusing arrangement with hidden costs generating suspicion and mistrust. Once the appeal of equal profit sharing became clear, the Supplemental Agreement was doomed. The question now became one of whether or not Musaddiq would negotiate a comparable settlement with the British. Anderson argues that Ibn Saud's position was quite different from that of Musaddiq. Ibn Saud was willing to collaborate economically and he had total political control in his country. Musaddiq was unwilling to be a collaborator, either economically or politically, and he faced the traditional problem of political divisiveness in Iran. It was easier to rally all Iranians against the company than to unite them in favour of a settlement, even if Musaddiq had been so inclined. Anderson concludes that the Fifty–fifty Agreement between Aramco and Saudi Arabia was largely the product of post-war American policy in the region, a policy which favoured rapid development of Middle Eastern oil and shoring up Ibn Saud as a bulwark against Soviet influence. The Saudi situation was less complex than that in Iran, and the British were in no position in 1951 to duplicate the almost effortless American settlement in Saudi Arabia in 1950.

Ronald Ferrier, in a chapter which concerns the Anglo-Iranian Oil Company, argues that the experience of 1951–4 must be considered within its proper historical context. The forces of nationalism were present from the earliest days of the concession and reached a major expression in its cancellation in 1932, though the working relationship was not disturbed and the company grew in importance in a country devoid of other large-scale industrialization. In the changing post-1945 economic circumstances, the Anglo-Iranian Oil Company attempted to negotiate a revised settlement, which was agreed upon with the Iranian government in July 1949 but was never ratified by the Majlis. According to Ferrier, the subsequent nationalization of the concession at the instigation of Musaddiq brought to an end half a century of collaborative enterprise. It was followed by three years of economic and political crisis causing the dispute to become internationalized within the environment of the cold war. Ferrier argues that, for Musaddiq, the issues were primarily political, because of his phobia about the British. When Musaddiq disregarded the economic aspects of the problem, the world markets accommodated themselves to the absence of Iranian oil. Having made confident predictions about the advantages of nationalization, but having failed to achieve a settlement,

Musaddiq inevitably found himself facing increasing opposition. Ferrier concludes that it was a disaster for Musaddiq not to have built on his initial oil success and not to have achieved a more lasting transformation of Iranian society.

In the third section Homa Katouzian analyses some of the Iranian consequences of the policies pursued by the Anglo-Iranian Oil Company during the crisis of nationalization. Most Iranians assumed that the oil shortages in Britain would force a quick end to the crisis, or, at worst, that Iran could continue to export crude oil if not refined products. But the British government together with the international oil companies imposed an effective boycott. Musaddiq consistently held that the controversy was essentially political. His strategy may be described as 'non-oil economics'. His followers supported him, believing that the country's economic difficulties could be overcome if the grip of the British were broken. The loss of the oil revenues was a severe blow to the economy but, according to Katouzian, not nearly as damaging as western observers have reported. An austerity policy together with astute managing of foreign trade actually enabled the Musaddiq government to reduce its balance of payments deficit and to ensure an adequate supply of foreign reserves. There was only a slight decline in the general standard of living. Katouzian concludes that the Iranian economy bore up surprisingly well under the shocks of the boycott, but that there was a widespread belief throughout the country that 'non-oil economics' could not succeed. This public attitude contributed to the downfall of the Musaddiq government. But on purely economic grounds the fall of the Musaddiq regime was by no means inevitable. It is debatable how well Musaddiq himself grasped the economic essentials. From beginning to end he viewed the struggle as political. If Iran could assert its independence, he believed, the solution of the economic problems would follow.

The themes of the chapters by Roger Louis and James Bill have been discussed earlier in this introduction. Nevertheless a few contrasts between the British and the American responses should be emphasized in relation to Musaddiq. The British believed that his obsession with British imperialism bordered on irrationality. The question may fairly be asked, however, whether the British assumption that he was a 'lunatic' (the word used by the British Ambassador, Sir Francis Shepherd) was not also irrational. It seemed so to the Americans. The arrogance and sense of cultural superiority on the part of the British appeared to the Americans to be a fundamental part of the problem. On the other hand, it would be a mistake not to recognize the genuine insight into Iranian politics possessed by the 'orientalists' of the British Embassy in Tehran such as Robin Zaehner. To understand the reasons for British intervention in Iran, it is essential to determine what they hoped to achieve. The aim was to remove Musaddiq and to put in his place a regime that would peacefully resolve the oil dispute to the advantage of all parties concerned. The consortium created in 1954 did achieve that aim, at least from the British point of view. From this angle of vision, Musaddiq's removal served a useful purpose.

The intervention led to the achievement, a dubious one, of the United States displacing Britain as the dominant foreign power in Iran. There can be no question that, to most Iranians, the Americans have superseded the British as the foremost proponents of western imperialism. At the time, the Americans involved in Musaddiq's overthrow were quite prepared to accept all of the credit. It appeared obvious that Musaddiq's downfall benefited the United States. James Bill's chapter indicates, however, that the 1953 coup had incalculable implications for the United States as well as for Iran. In the short term it strengthened the conviction of those who believed in the effectiveness of intervention.

Over the longer perspective, the danger appears to be that the lessons of the 1953 intervention have yet to be learned. The intervention was branded on the Iranian public consciousness, and reference to it became one of the powerful and repeated rallying cries of the revolution of 1978–9. The continuing anti-western, and specifically anti-American, sentiment that has characterized revolutionary Iran had its origins in 1953. If the United States and Britain had allowed the nationalism of Musaddiq to take its natural course in the early 1950s, the extremism and anti-Americanism that accompanied the Iranian revolution might have been ameliorated.

George McGhee, as a participant in the negotiations with Musaddiq, has much to say about the policy of intervention. He believes that the Truman Administration would have opposed it, and that the officials of the Eisenhower Administration embarked on a fateful course. McGhee has stated that he would have resigned had he learned of comparable covert activity during his years in public service. This chapter also reveals much about Musaddiq's political psychology as it was perceived by the Americans. McGhee's theme is that Musaddiq was a well-educated, aristocratic, patriotic nationalist, though somewhat eccentric. His principal aim was to free Iran from foreign domination, not only from the British, whom he blamed for most of Iran's troubles, but also from Soviet influence. McGhee believes that Musaddiq thought that the West needed Iran for political and strategic reasons – in other words, that the British and American leaders would not risk the danger of a communist takeover. This chapter clarifies the western response to Musaddiq and elucidates certain aspects of the economics of the oil controversy. Above all it reiterates the principle on which the Truman Administration based its policy: though the Americans hoped to avoid nationalization of Iranian oil that was contrary to the interests of American companies, the Iranians could not be denied their legal right to nationalize with compensation and to acquire a fair share of the profits.

The last section provides intellectual and historical perspectives of the

Musaddiq era. The chapter by Rouhollah Ramazani calls attention to the relationship between Iranian culture and the Musaddiq movement, arguing that the Iranians themselves are in large part responsible for the stormy events of 1953 and their aftermath. Iranian society must bear the responsibility for the failures as well as the successes of Musaddiq. Intellectual and political elites alike, then as now, have failed to agree on the nature of a polity that is acceptable to a broad cross-section of the Iranian people, largely because of pervasive factionalism. Ramazani makes clear the historical proclivity of Iranians to look elsewhere for the causes of their own misfortune instead of engaging in constructive self-criticism based on their own philosophical heritage. Musaddiq himself for example believed that the Anglo-Iranian Oil Company was responsible for 'all the misfortunes of this tortured nation'. The tendency to place all blame elsewhere also characterized the thinking of the Shah, who accused everyone but himself for his downfall. Furthermore the leaders of the Iranian revolution envisage themselves surrounded by greater and lesser Satans. In fact, as with the *bête noires* of the United States and Britain, the causes of Iran's troubles are found both within and without.

Albert Hourani's chapter provides a conclusion to the book. In light of the other chapters, it asks whether an agreement between Musaddiq, the British and the Americans might have been possible. It poses this question on the level of national interests, of the freedom of action of the three parties and, last, of the personalities involved – their convictions, feelings and prejudices, and their characteristic modes of political action. From Hourani's discussion there emerge three basic, triangular themes linking Britain, the United States and Iran. They coincide with the arguments of this introductory essay. The links of the triangle are the themes of misperceptions. The first theme is the British confusion and misunderstanding about the nature of nationalism in Iran. In failing to understand Musaddiq, the British failed to see that he represented the hopes and aspirations of the Iranian people. The second theme is the American preoccupation with economic self-interest and Middle Eastern oil. Compared with economic self-interest, understanding of Iranian nationalism was scarcely a priority. An even more important cause of misunderstanding was the fear of communism, which Americans tended to confuse with Iranian nationalism. The third theme is the Iranian perception of British, and eventually American, imperialism. Iranians at the time tended to see the British as malevolent and the Americans as benevolent. This simplified view led to the major error of believing that the two western powers would never unite against the nationalist movement in Iran. To extend Albert Hourani's judgement, the tragedy of Iranian error and western misunderstanding is part of the greater tragedy of the Middle East and the West.

Notes

1 In his entry in his personal diary of 3 June 1950 Dr Qasim Ghani, a distinguished Iranian physician and political observer, presents a significant classification of five types of Iranian 'Anglophiles'. The categories range from those in the pay of British intelligence to Iranian patriots who believed that co-operation with the British would best preserve Iranian independence. See Qasim Ghani, *Yaddashtha-yi Duktur Qasim Ghani*, vol. II (London, 1984) pp. 188–92.

2 Office of Naval Intelligence, Information Report, 'Iran: some basic motivations of Iranians which concern the present situation', Paul O'Dwyer Papers (privately held), Tehran, 18 March 1953.

3 Ibid.

4 Sir Reader Bullard to Foreign Office, No. 1176 Secret, 15 March 1946, FO 371/52670 (Public Record Office, London).

5 Memorandum by Sir Francis Shepherd, 2 October 1951, FO 371/91464.

6 Ibid.

7 Minute by Bevin, 20 July 1946, FO 371/52735.

8 See George McGhee, *Envoy to the Middle World* (New York, 1969) pp. 322–6.

9 Fergusson to Richard Stokes, Top Secret, 'Private & Personal', 3 October 1951, FO 371/91599.

10 British Cabinet Minutes 51 (51), 12 July 1951, CAB 128/20.

11 As recorded in a minute by M. R. Starkey, 14 May 1951, FO 371/91534.

12 Memorandum recording telephone call from Lovett to Acheson and relating meeting with Elliot, 25 September 1951, President's Secretary's Files, Harry S. Truman Library.

13 'Discussion at the 132nd Meeting of the National Security Council on Wednesday, February 18, 1953', Whitman File, Eisenhower Papers, Eisenhower Library.

14 Telegram of 14 November 1951, Declassified Reference System, 1985, Fiche 72, Document No. 1046.

15 James S. Lay, Jr (Executive Secretary to the National Security Council), 'A report to the National Security Council on United States policy regarding the present situation in Iran', 20 November 1952, Declassified Reference System, 1980, Document No. 376C.

16 Brian Lapping, *End of Empire* (London, 1985) p. 218.

PART I

Nationalism and religious themes

1

Nationalism in twentieth-century Iran and Dr Muhammad Musaddiq

RICHARD COTTAM

Time magazine's choice of Muhammad Musaddiq as man of the year in 1952 and its accompanying article[1] describing the Musaddiq phenomenon are in retrospect heavily symbolic. Musaddiq was a devoted proponent of Enlightenment values and was dedicated to the task of bringing real independence and national dignity to his country. The normative system he hoped to establish in Iran was, in its central particulars, the same system that Americans and western Europeans claimed as their own. Indeed, as westerners described the cold war, then in its formative years, it was in essence a struggle to defend the very norms Musaddiq himself embraced. Yet the Musaddiq phenomenon for *Time* typified popular movements emerging in the Middle East and in the third world generally that constituted major threats to the achievement of American cold war aims.

Musaddiq without question saw western and especially British imperialism as the primary obstacle to the achievement of his goals. His hostility to Britain, a pre-eminent western power, made him anti-western in *Time*'s view. It regarded Musaddiq's nationalism as leading not to solid patriotism but to fanaticism, irrationality and irresponsibility. His movement represented a force producing instability and with it an opportunity for Soviet subversion. His refusal to suppress a communist movement that was heavily engaged in a 'Yankee go home' campaign was not a manifestation of his devotion to freedom but of innocence regarding the Soviet threat. The argument of Musaddiqists that a popular national movement, especially one loyal to liberal democratic institutions, offered the best possible obstacle to Soviet inroads through subversion was simply not heard. The logic of *Time*'s account was fully in accord with that of the Eisenhower Administration when it decided to join the British and anti-Musaddiq Iranians in a conspiracy to overturn the Musaddiq regime.

More than three decades after Musaddiq's overthrow, Iran has now another populist regime. But this regime rejects adamantly not only Enlightenment values and secularism but nationalism as well. Furthermore, throughout the Middle East secular nationalist leaders are on the defensive and liberalism virtually non-existent.

Enough years have passed for tentative conclusions to be drawn regarding the significance of that brief moment in Iranian history of secular, liberal nationalism. Was the seeming reversal of trends favouring secular nationalism in Iran and elsewhere in the Middle East foreordained? Or was the reversal of fortunes for secular nationalism avoidable? And is there likely to be in the future a shift in trends once again in favour of secular – maybe even liberal – nationalists?

The central proposition to be explored here is that western governments and western observers seriously underestimated the significance of and the prospects for not only secularism and nationalism but also liberalism in Iran and in the Middle East; that this underestimation amounted to a self-fulfilling prophesy in which western forces contributed significantly to the defeat of liberalism and the weakened position of secular nationalists; that this underestimation was a product of disguised national interest, cultural contempt and serious and persisting conceptual failures. A subsidiary proposition is that the Musaddiq phenomenon represented a critical moment in a period of exceptionally rapid change in Iran in which there was some real possibility for the institutionalization of liberal, secular and nationalist norms. The concluding proposition advanced in this essay is that, though the future of liberalism in Iran is problematic, the seeming eclipse of Iranian nationalism is illusory and the Iranian national community remains the primary identity attachment for most Iranians.

The underestimation of the prospects for liberal nationalism in the Middle East involves a disregard of substantial empirical evidence. The Musaddiq phenomenon was paralleled by a number of similar phenomena in the Middle East occurring in several countries at comparable stages of development. Sa'd Zaghlul in Egypt during the 1920s, Rashid Ali in Iraq in 1941, al-Quwatli government in Syria from 1954 to 1957 and Jordan with Sulayman Nabulsi from 1955 to 1957 are examples of similar developments which suffered defeat in large part because of external involvement. The case of the Young Turks is an important reminder, however, that the vulnerability of liberal nationalism in this stage of development is considerable and that, if there was possibility for survival, there was a considerable likelihood of failure even without external intervention. It is self-evidently true that had the Musaddiq government not been seriously vulnerable, it would not have collapsed so easily as a result of a poorly planned and executed *coup d'état*.

Perhaps a useful means for exploring the case for the above proposition is to compare the two liberal nationalist periods of recent Iranian history, 1906–11 and 1951–3. The first period, like the second, came to an end as a result of external intervention. Liberal nationalist Iranians therefore can maintain reasonably that they were denied victory in Iran by foreign powers throughout the first half of the twentieth century. Furthermore, the two periods had more in common than their arousal of external anger. In both periods the elite social support base was qualitatively, though certainly not quantitatively, similar. Three groups supported the two liberal nationalist regimes. But for two of these groups, support for the regimes was based on expectations that they would serve an important instrumental purpose. For only one, an activist, non-religious intelligentsia, liberal democracy and nationalism constituted end, rather than instrumental, political values. Muhammad Musaddiq emerged from this latter group and the brief Musaddiq era was the moment of the greatest influence of the intelligentsia.

The commercial middle class centred in the bazaar during both periods was a second support base for the regime. But merchant support depended on its vested interests. Damaged by and fearful of commercial concessions to foreigners, especially prior to the 1906 period, and desirous of the opportunity to trade without restriction throughout Iran, the commercial middle class required a government that thought in national terms and that looked with sympathy on the commercial needs of trade. The liberal nationalist regimes wished to do this but had difficulty providing the necessary order and stability.

Politically activist clergy constituted the third elite support base for both regimes. Clerical supporters of the two regimes were highly diverse. Some clearly did hold liberal values as end values and saw the Iranian and Islamic communities by and large as one. Others, however, were fearful of what they saw as secular implications of nationalism and the excessive individualism of liberalism. For them, the purpose of an alliance with the intelligentsia was to gain the strength to break the hold of Christian imperialist powers on Iran, in their view a necessary pre-condition for Islamic revival.

It was not, however, the liberalism of the liberal nationalists that gave them their potential; it was the nationalism. The set of abstract values that constitutes liberalism can attract the intense support of only a small percentage of any population; but the potential appeal of nationalism is to the overwhelming majority of the population. One of the clearest patterns of the era of very rapid change which we call developing or modernizing, is a transfer of primary community identity from parochial groups such as extended family or clan to large groups such as an ethnic, national or religious community. An intense identification with a community grants an individual a sense of security in belonging to a group. It, therefore, satisfies social needs of most individuals and, in turn, generates a fierce determination to provide for the defence, the welfare and the dignity of that community and on occasion to attend to its grandeur. The desire to

advance the interests of this community becomes one of the major
determinants of political behaviour, behaviour that we describe as
nationalistic. Liberalism is able to prevail on occasion in the early decades
of the process of rapid change in the third world because nationalist leaders
during this period frequently embrace liberalism.

The critical difference between the two periods was the percentage of
the population that was politically participant in each.[2] In the first period,
surely no more than 1–2 per cent of the population could be so
characterized and these were largely concentrated in a few urban areas,
particularly Tehran and Tabriz. By 1951 the percentage, judging from
newspaper circulation, education levels and voting, was probably in the
range of 10 per cent. Since the old traditional system had failed to contain
the challenge of pro-change elements at the turn of the century, its capacity
for doing so in 1951 was minimal. But during the period 1906–11 the tiny
support base of the pro-change leaders made it unlikely that the regime
would survive for many years. Indeed regime control of non-urban Iran at
that time was never more than partial. The support base in 1951 was much
deeper and surely consisted of a substantial majority of politically
participant Iranians. But the vast majority of Iranians were non-participant
and remained part of traditional Iran. This conclusion is easily illustrated
by the essentially free election for the Seventeenth Majlis in 1952. The
determination of the Musaddiq government not to rig that election led to a
policy of non-interference, even permitting traditional leaders to truck
uncomprehending citizens to the polls and instruct them how to vote. The
early returns painted a clear profile of the rhythm of change in the country.
In Tehran 95 per cent of the voters favoured pro-change candidates,
particularly National Front and Tudeh. In Tabriz the percentages were
similar although the Tabriz electorate differed from the Tehran electorate
in its preference for religious candidates of the National Front. But the
returns from provincial towns and rural areas reflected just as dramatically
the continued influence of traditional leaders. Since rural districts
outnumbered urban, Musaddiq was faced with the certainty of defeat once
all returns were in. To prevent this, Musaddiq stopped the elections after a
quorum of deputies in which urban centres were over-represented had
been elected. The paradox and the dilemma were obvious. A regime
dedicated to establishing liberal democratic institutions in Iran had the
support of a minority of the population, vociferous and dedicated but a
minority nonetheless. And the large majority accepted, however passively,
the authority of traditional leaders who had no interest in liberal
democratic institutions. Given this picture, can a realistic case for regime
durability really be made?

There is a strong case for the conclusion that once the process of rapid
change was underway traditional Iranian leaders could not re-establish
stable control. But between the two liberal nationalist regimes a

government did establish stable control in Iran and it was able to attract the support of major pro-change elements, especially the commercial and bureaucratic. That government was the first Pahlavi dictatorship led by Riza Shah and it, like both the liberal nationalist regimes, was terminated by external intervention. There was, therefore, a clear alternative regime type to the liberal nationalist for pro-change Iranians to turn to, one that undeniably had produced far greater change in the Iranian economy and society than had the first constitutional regime.[3] After the second world war, Riza Shah's son was more than willing to re-establish a control system in Iran much like that of his father. Can the case not be made that, given the inherent weakness of liberal democratic forces at this stage of Iran's development, the Iranian people ultimately would have turned once again to this alternative and that, therefore, the coup against Musaddiq simply hastened that day by a few months or years?

Obviously the answers to the two questions can only be tentative since they are in the category of what might have been. But the questions are not idle. They compel the analyst willing to confront them to deal with the force of nationalism as a determinant of human behaviour in our era. And the answers given should help explain the shocking reversal in momentum of growth of popular support for nationalist leaders in contemporary Iran.

There is another major difference between the first and second liberal nationalist regimes in Iran. The first period was marked by the absence of a leader who could be described as charismatic, that is, capable of attracting great and unquestioning popular support primarily by virtue of an ability to manipulate symbols. In the second period, such a leader did appear, Dr Muhammad Musaddiq. The symbols he manipulated with such extraordinary effect were those relating to the Iranian national community, its right to establish independent statehood, its welfare need, its right to be accepted as a dignified, respected and honoured member of the international community. On the negative side, the symbols he manipulated were those referring to imperialism and international oppression. Musaddiq's liberalism was manifest less in his effort to translate liberalism into sets of appealing symbols than in his avoidance of negative symbols reflecting racial or religious bigotry or those depicting the grandeur of a greater Iran. Some of his National Front colleagues were less restrained in these regards.[4]

The failure of the early constitutional period to produce a leader with a populist appeal surely has everything to do with the narrowness of the politically participant element. There was not a mass public to which a leader could address his appeal and the leaders who were able to reach an awakening urban element tended to be clerics rather than secular nationalists. In 1951, by contrast, there was a large student, young professional and middle-class element that was politically participant and quite prepared to grant an intense attachment to a leader able to articulate their sense of national humiliation and aspirations for independence.

More significant is the question of why Riza Shah failed so completely to become a populist leader. Especially in his latter years his sensitivity to affronts to the Iranian nation and the Pahlavi dynasty was so acute that a rude remark in a French newspaper could lead to a break in diplomatic relations.[5] It is difficult in looking at his behaviour to separate nation and dynasty as focuses of identity for Riza Shah; but it is also difficult to see how anyone could deny that Riza Shah's fierce attachment to Iran was anything other than a manifestation of nationalism. Yet he was never able, as Musaddiq was, to project himself as a personal symbol of Iran's struggle for independence and dignity. Even more, Riza Shah, like his son later, had difficulty establishing a claim to nationalist legitimacy.

It is not explanation enough to point to that critical moment in Riza Khan's climb to power and ultimately to the throne: his major role in the 1921 *coup d'état* that was perceived so widely in Iran as British inspired and directed.[6] The external factor in Iranian politics has been perceived to be and frequently was in the past century at the operating decisional level. As such virtually any Iranian of any political consequence, whatever his ideological persuasion, had dealings with representatives of external powers that in another setting would be deemed unacceptable on nationalist grounds. Individuals with widely accepted nationalist credibility could openly solicit external assistance without risking the loss of that credibility. For example, in the early days of the constitution British support was solicited and in the Musaddiq era American support was solicited and both acts of solicitation were widely accepted as fully patriotic. The critical variable then was one of an individual's previous reputation as a nationalist. The Democrats of the constitutional era were viewed by pro-change, politically participant Iranians as dedicated nationalists, the accepted leaders of the drive for real independence for Iran. Indeed, they and their successors saw themselves and were seen by vital elements of the interested public as the one group entitled to the appellation 'nationalist'. It follows, therefore, that an Iranian leader, such as Riza Khan, who opposed them and ultimately persecuted them would be seen as anti-nationalist. His perceived co-operation with the British in his rise to power was fully expected confirmation of this image. Musaddiq in contrast was seen as a life-long member of the group of true nationalist leaders and, unlike others such as Hasan Taqizadeh, the one senior member of the group who had never compromised his nationalist principles. The purity of his nationalism placed him in a class by himself. It was not, therefore, Musaddiq's liberalism and Riza Shah's authoritarianism that explains the granting of nationalist legitimacy to Musaddiq and its denial to Riza Shah (twentieth-century authoritarian leaders such as Ataturk in Turkey and Nasser in the Arab world achieved the status of personal symbol of a drive for national dignity just as did the liberal

Musaddiq); to the contrary, Musaddiq's nationalist legitimacy made possible the institutionalization of liberalism in Iran in his era.

In present day Iran, spokespersons for the Khomeini regime see Iranian 'nationalists' precisely as they were seen in the Musaddiq era, that is as direct descendants of the Democrats of the constitutional era. Members of the Iranian exile community who either supported Muhammad Riza Shah enthusiastically or accommodated to his rule and are now in exile and describe themselves as 'nationalists' are emphatically not accepted by supporters of Khomeini as deserving that description. To them the Shah was an agent of the oppressor powers and he and those associated with him cared nothing for Iran. But if there is an acceptance of the nationalists as a group that struggled for Iranian national independence, it is a grudging acceptance. In a very real sense the treason of the nationalists to their people was more profound than that of the royalists in Khomeini's eyes. The latter were driven to treason by their venality and the crass materialism of the weak and unprincipled. The former were truly acculturated. Their opposition to western imperialism was political and grounded in the failure of the imperial powers to act in accordance with their own principles. When western governments were true to those principles, as the American was generally perceived to be prior to 1953, the acceptance and adulation of the American culture by nationalists was enthusiastic. Nationalism and liberalism alike are manifestations of Euro-American culture and hence deserving of total rejection in the view of those supporting Khomeini.

For supporters of the Islamic Republic, it follows, the suggestion that the Khomeini phenomenon is another and not even a unique manifestation of nationalism is angrily rejected. They argue that such a suggestion is part of an effort to demean and to trivialize this most important of contemporary movements.[7] Their reaction is understandable given their view that nationalism is a secular phenomenon and 'secular' implies a rejection of the divine plan implicit in the Koran for the creation of the good society. Furthermore, most studies of nationalism tend to treat the subject as a phenomenon of regimes that are essentially non-clerical and non-religious, and hence implicitly assume that nationalism is inherently secular. But this analytic treatment is arguably an example both of historicism and reification. Definitions and descriptions of nationalism are usually based on abstractions from European experience and judgements of nationalism elsewhere are based on the extent to which they approximate this European model. The assumption is usually explicit that third world nationalists have learned to be nationalistic through their contacts with Europeans.[8] The Khomeini partisan view of nationalism and nationalists, it should be apparent, is in fact similar to the European analytic treatment of the subject. For both, nationalism is a manifestation of a deep attachment to an ethnic community organized into a state the leaders of which are non-clerical.[9]

Thus defined, however, the phenomenon should not have come to characterize the non-European and the non-Christian worlds. Few states outside Europe have the requisite ethnic homogeneity to qualify and other religions do not make a sharp church–state distinction. In these regards Iran is typical: a multi-ethnic state whose inhabitants embrace a religion, Islam, which does not accept the two-sword concept. Yet an attachment to Iran expressed in a desire for its full independence and dignity, we have seen, has been a dominant determinant of the behaviour of politically participant Iranians, including most clerics and members of a diversity of ethnic groups. It has been the basis of the populist appeal of Musaddiq and of the difficulties concerning the legitimacy of the two Pahlavi monarchs. Furthermore, it was self-evidently important in producing the intense reaction against the Iraqi invasion of Iran in 1980.[10]

Students of nationalism have long noted that when the members of a national community are in many areas highly diverse, as was surely the case in Iran, one particular element tends to become the core group of the national community and to give definition to it. In the United States, for example, the core group of a national community that is exceptionally diverse was assumed to be the white, Anglo-Saxon, Protestant (WASP) middle and upper-middle class. In Iran in Musaddiq's time it seems to have been an urban middle and upper-middle class, politically participant, Persian speaking and at least nominally Shii Muslim. But included in the core group as well were members of most or all of Iran's ethnic groups and in some cases, such as the vitally important Azarbayjani community, this included a substantial majority of their politically participant members.

A multi-ethnic national community is a fairly common phenomenon in the western hemisphere but a rarity in the eastern hemisphere. The reason for that difference is almost self-evidently the fact that the western hemisphere population is composed heavily of post-Columbian immigrants from the eastern hemisphere. Immigrants from particular ethnic communities often gathered in particular geographical areas, but very few were sufficiently strong numerically to be able to think in terms of separate statehood for their ethnic community. They tended instead, as in the United States, to adopt a new and intense attachment to a national community that embraced a wide diversity of ethnic groups. Over time, especially with intermarriage, the identity attachment of ethnic groups tended to atrophy, although the rhythm of atrophy varied depending on the ethnic group.[11]

In the rare instances where multi-ethnic national communities exist in the eastern hemisphere, for example in Belgium, there is likely to be serious problems of integration. In contrast to the western hemisphere, ethnic groups in the eastern hemisphere will frequently have a long time association with a geographical area in which they may well be the majority. Had they the capability to do so they usually would have opted for separation and for setting up an independent state organization based on their ethnic community. In all probability their history embraced many serious conflicts with neighbouring ethnic communities and the idea of joining in community with these people would be most unattractive. States that were multi-ethnic in base therefore tended not to be nation-states.

From the very beginning of the rapid change process, the largest and most significant minority ethnic community in Iran, that of the Azarbayjanis, demonstrated a strong attachment to the Iranian national community. As the inclination to become politically participant began to penetrate the Turkish-speaking population, the newly participant behaved in almost identical patterns to those of their Persian-speaking countrymen. Tabriz, second only to Tehran, became the locus of intense Iranian nationalism. There was in the Riza Shah period a sense among Azarbayjanis of relative economic and political deprivation. The Soviet effort to play on Azarbayjani separatist sentiments in 1945 and 1946 provided an excellent test of Azarbayjani community attachment. The result indicated that those Azarbayjanis who were politically participant during the 1940s identified strongly with both the Iranian national community and the Azarbayjani ethnic community. The elections of 1952 indicated as well a strong attachment to the Shii Muslim community. Pro-National Front sentiment in Azarbayjan during the Musaddiq era followed the patterns of Persian-speaking areas.

Early patterns of identity change are not necessarily predictive of the patterns that will prevail in later stages and there is much evidence to suggest that there is little inevitability in any patterning. Maltreatment of Azarbayjan by the political leadership of Iran leading to charges of discrimination could well lead to an intensification of attachment to Azarbayjan and a weakening of attachment to the Iranian national community. Indeed there are some surface indications that this phenomenon may be occurring in present day Azarbayjan because of the treatment of the late Ayatullah Kazim Shari'atmadari. But in the Musaddiq era, when tolerance prevailed, all indications were of increasing integration of Azarbayjan in the Iranian nation to the point in fact that Turkish-speaking Shii Muslims in Iran can be considered part of the core community.[12]

In most of Iran's non-Persian-speaking ethnic communities the process of change began much later than it did for the core community. There were, however, strongly contradictory trends developing among these groups during the Musaddiq era. The Kurdish ethnic community illustrated this point most clearly. As the level of political participation began to grow among Kurds, some of the newly participant followed the Azarbayjan pattern and identified fully with the Iranian nation. Indeed, several such individuals became leaders of the national movement. Karim Sanjabi, for example, remained one of the most respected of the elder statesmen of the

National Front well into the revolution. However in 1945 and 1946, the Soviets made a major effort to play on Kurdish separatism just as they had done with Azarbayjani separatism. But the results were very different. Encouraged by the Soviets to believe they had a real possibility of gaining control of Kurdish national destiny, a large proportion of politically participant Kurds, surely a majority, gave enthusiastic support to the so-called Mahabad Republic. They were able to make a claim for independence, however, only by an alliance with the traditional-minded Mulla Mustafa Barzani who provided the necessary security forces for the nascent state government.[13]

The Musaddiq era was too brief for a clear policy to emerge towards ethnic communities that were in the early stages of the change process but were already manifesting patterns comparable to those of the Kurds. Members of such communities who fully embraced the Iranian nation were accepted into governmental and political positions. But the demands for autonomy from such groups as the Turkoman, the Arabs and the Baluchis would have been opposed by the National Front. Their level of tolerance would have led to an appreciation of demands that related to basic human dignity; but their intense nationalism would have generated a fear that the demands for autonomy would lead to a weakening of the Iranian nation.

In all probability, had a liberal nationalist regime persisted, there would have been acceptance of the rights of the various ethnic groups to some cultural and political autonomy. But all signs indicate that the national community would have attracted the deep attachment of a sufficiently large majority of Iranian citizens so that strong nationalistic behavioural patterns would have prevailed in Iran.

Retrospectively it is clear that the real struggle for the nature of Iranian nationalism at Musaddiq's time revolved around the question of the identity community that would be the primary focus of nationalism. Would it be the national Iranian community, the religious community or some mix of the two? There were advocates of an exclusive focus on the national community, especially among anticlerical Iranians and members of non-Muslim sects, and there were advocates of an exclusive focus on the religious community. But behaviour suggests that among most politically participant Iranians this was a non-question and a non-issue. For those individuals who could be classified as part of the core group of the national community, politically participant Persian-speaking and Turkish-speaking Shii Muslims, conflict between the national community and the Shii community was rarely of any salience. There simply would be no reason to see the community with which they identified in other than unitary terms. Sunni Muslims and even more Christians, Jews, Zoroastrians and Bahais were far more likely to be aware of conflict, actual and potential, with Shii Muslims and hence to understand that their membership in the Iranian national community was somewhat more equivocal than that of the Shia.

But the real conflict occurred mainly at the political elite level between those who believed clerics should stay out of government and politics and those who believed that clerics had a particular and ultimately pre-eminent role to play in government and politics.

In the first days of the period of rapid change, clerics who favoured change had an advantage over their intelligentsia allies. They were able to reach and mobilize large numbers of religious labourers and employees of the bazaar, most of whom would have little comprehension of the purpose of the action. This advantage was still apparent during the post-war years in Iran. Ayatullah Abu'l Qasim Kashani and the organization Warriors of Islam could bring into the streets hundreds, even thousands of demonstrators on short notice. Trucks loaded with chanting men who revealed by their clothing their social origins were a common sight throughout the Musaddiq era. Most frequently they would be Warriors of Islam's contribution to a mass rally. But in the early 1950s the clerical advantage in mobilizing crowds was in decline. Another easily mobilized group had appeared, a large student population drawn from the high schools and colleges. The students, also easily distinguishable by their clothing, were available to secular nationalist and leftist groups. Unlike most of the Kashani crowds, they were highly politicized, well-informed and understood their political purpose. They were fully capable of sustained political interest and willing to take risks.

This was a period of rapid transition and the Toilers Party, led by Dr Muzaffar Baqa'i, was an instructive example of a political group that lived in both the traditional and the radically changed worlds. Crowds supporting Baqa'i were in part labourers who had been trucked in and in part left, nationalist students. The former were responsive to leaders very much like and sometimes identical with those in the Warriors of Islam; the latter responded to social democratic and nationalist appeals and were hard to distinguish by clothing and demeanor from Iran Party or Tudeh Party crowds. The former thus could be thought of as reflecting more an attachment to the religious community; the latter to the national community. But the fact that the close relationship persisted as long as it did illustrates the point that in the minds of Baqa'i's supporters they represented one community, national and Shii Muslim.

It was a manifestation of Musaddiq's genius as a leader with a populist appeal that he carefully avoided producing a polarization on community identity lines. He felt strongly that the movement he came to lead must remain a coalition of diverse groups who were united in dedication to the task of establishing real independence for Iran. By 1952–3 Musaddiq's appeal had become so strong within the politically participant population that anyone having the temerity to oppose him lost much of his nationalist legitimacy. This was true of Ahmad Qavam whose brilliant statesmanship had been such a vital factor in allowing Iran to emerge unified and with most of its sovereignty intact from the critical Azarbayjan crisis. Qavam's willingness to accept the premiership after Musaddiq's dismissal in 1952 led in a few days to the destruction of his reputation as a patriot.

But evidence that Musaddiq had achieved a special symbolic status is most apparent in the ease of his victory over three major National Front leaders who turned against him: Husayn Makki, Muzaffar Baqa'i and, importantly, Ayatullah Kashani. The Makki case is least important and interesting since he lacked a significant personal support base. The fate of the other two is more instructive.

Baqa'i's vulnerability was a consequence of his simultaneous membership in two worlds. Most at home in the traditional world of conservative religious leaders and non-ideological labour leaders, Baqa'i found himself quickly shorn of his social democratic support when he broke with Musaddiq. The social democrats formed the Third Force led by Khalil Maliki and viewed Baqa'i's break with Musaddiq as an act approaching treason.

Kashani's defection from the Musaddiq ranks was of exceptional significance because it had the potential for producing a major polarization of the politically active populace. As speaker of the Majlis, Kashani occupied a position of major political importance. But for him this role had to be uncomfortable. Agreeing with his friend and colleague Ruhullah Khomeini that the clerical role must be one of furnishing real, not formal, guidance to Iranian governance, he nevertheless was serving to bring religious legitimacy to a regime which seemed to prefer for the ulama the purely formal, symbolic role that had evolved from the 1906 Constitution.[14]

The Musaddiq–Kashani split, therefore, had to have been a great threat to Musaddiq's populist appeal. But in fact Musaddiq, a master manipulator of political symbols, came through this crisis remarkably well. The danger of polarization was not realized. Important clerical figures did follow Kashani's path and others such as Khomeini welcomed the split as long overdue. But the majority of the clerical deputies in the Majlis remained with Musaddiq and so did much of the bazaar.

At this point there was arguably a real possibility that the value system Musaddiq stood for could become the basis for an evolving normative system for Iran. Musaddiq had achieved a level of personal trust that led much of Iran's politically participant population to be willing to accept the institutions he was constructing. More important, though, was the impact on those beginning to enter the political system in ever-increasing numbers. This politically awakening population tended at this moment to be lower-middle-class and lower-class urban dwellers. An aristocrat and member of the intelligentsia was not a natural leader for them. But Musaddiq had achieved a status above that of any particular social group. He had achieved acceptance as the one Iranian leader able to lead his country in the battle against imperial control of Iran. His position as one who personified Iran's demands for national dignity was the basis of his leadership claims. It was his nationalist appeal, in other words, that formed the basis of his attraction. But those who followed him uncritically also accepted the institutions he believed in.

As would be true a generation and a half later when Iran had its second populist regime, western observers seriously underestimated the sustainability of a regime whose authority rested to such a degree on an ability to manipulate successfully attractive symbols. The assumption that underlies this underestimation is that fairly quickly a regime must begin to satisfy the material needs and demands of its people or lose its appeal. Muhammad Riza Pahlavi demonstrated that the opposite point also was true. If a regime which is unable to manipulate successfully attractive symbols for control purposes nevertheless does satisfy material needs and demands, it too can achieve long-term stability. Both, however, will be vulnerable and can be expected to make an effort to reduce that vulnerability. The problem was particularly acute for Musaddiq since, unlike the Shah and Khomeini, his liberalism prevented the development of a strong coercive system that could help him survive. Yet it was not Musaddiq's failures in the economic level that brought him down. It was a coup in which there was decisive American and British participation. Musaddiq and his associates were showing signs of an ability to be able to socialize newly politically participant elements into an acceptance not only of Iranian nationalism but of liberal democracy as well. It is, therefore, ironic in the extreme that the regime should be brought down by the self-proclaimed leaders of what they call the 'free world'.

There appears to have been what could be called an imperial imperative leading to the American role in Musaddiq's overthrow. Tudeh propaganda especially in 1951–2 depicted Musaddiq as the tool of if not the active agent of the United States. Whatever the sincerity in this depiction there is no denying the fact that the United States was viewed by many in the National Front as the one western power with some sympathy for Iranian liberal nationalism. Nor was that view entirely without substance. American diplomatic correspondence throughout the second world war and its immediate aftermath reflects a sympathy for Iranian nationalistic aspirations and a conclusion that Iran had been very much ill-served by British and Soviet intervention.[15] There was as well a frequently expressed preference for 'liberal' Iranians and a belief that Iranian interests would be best served by a government with liberal democratic institutions. Just who the liberal Iranians were was never clearly specified but a defensible inference can be drawn that the individuals referred to were the liberal wing of the traditional governing elite, men such as Ahmad Qavam.[16] Certainly it is true that in published documents prior to 1951 none gave anything approaching a full analysis of the national movement and the exceptional role of Musaddiq.[17]

But were these attitudes the weakly held view of an uninvolved government, easily surrendered as a strong interest in Iran began to develop? A reasonably strong case can be made that this was indeed the case. In the early days of the 1906 revolution in Iran, there were parallel views expressed by British diplomatic representatives in Iran.[18] But within a year that view had been abandoned. An explanation of the British and American change of view is easy. The liberal nationalist movement in 1906 and 1951 produced in Iran a chaotic situation which threatened the perceived strategic interests of the British and the Americans respectively. These interests, the United States and Britain believed, were best served by stability in Iran. Chaos best served the interests of their imperial rival, Tsarist Russia for the British and Soviet Russia for the Americans.

Confronted with a sharply perceived threat to their interests in Iran emanating from the actions of proponents of internal change, officials of the two governments did exactly what Fritz Heider with his psychological balance theory would expect them to do.[19] They dropped what was essentially a benevolent, complex and largely detached picture of the new government and saw instead governments and movements that deserved to be overthrown in the interests of the Iranian people. The new view, simple, judgemental and approaching the stereotypical was rooted in cultural contempt.[20] The imperial stereotype towards which the British in 1911 and the Americans in 1953 inclined is universal in its patterning. In it the political elite is seen in dichotomized form. Co-operating members of the elite, usually drawn from the traditional elements, are viewed favourably and described by such terms as 'moderate', 'responsible' or, in its early usage, 'westernized oriental gentlemen' or 'Wog'. Those favouring rapid change and thereby creating difficulties for imperial interests are dismissed as 'agitators', 'demagogues' and 'fanatics'. With regard to the public, they are 'immature', 'childlike' and, if stirred up, often by do-gooding citizens of the mentor state, they can be 'savages' and 'barbarians'. Leaders such as Musaddiq, with their liberal pretensions, are simply dismissed as incapable of such a level of comprehension. Thomas Schelling, the widely read Harvard economist and cold war bargaining theorist, clearly was fascinated by Musaddiq and saw him in the imperial stereotypical mould. He compares Musaddiq in one book[21] to a small child best handled by child psychology and in another to a puppy piddling on a floor who cannot be bargained with.[22] It is always asserted as beyond question that there is no middle class in such a state and of course no real public opinion. Publics of the 'lower races'[23] respond best, as children do, to a firm, consistent and always benign application of force.

Why did American officials agree to participate in a conspiracy with Iranian rightists and with M.I.6 to overthrow Musaddiq, the proponent of liberal democratic institutions and the symbol of his people's quest for national independence and dignity? The answer is, of course, that they made no such decision. They entered into a conspiracy, true enough, but to eliminate a demagogic agitator who was leading his immature public in a policy direction that could only enhance the Soviet subversive potential in Iran. The decision in the view of those who made it was bold and courageous and would signal to the Soviets an American determination to contain them in their own lair.[24] Those Americans, such as Henry Grady and Dean Acheson, who saw Musaddiq as a symbolic nationalist leader opposed attempting to oust him.[25]

The United States and Britain hoped that their part in the coup would not be recognized. But their hopes were fulfilled only with regard to their own publics which, even including liberals, preferred for another generation not to recognize any responsibility for Musaddiq's overthrow. Certainly, there were few if any politically conscious Iranians who failed to note the external participation. Indeed, most Iranians saw the coup as a manifestation of a brilliant application of the Anglo-American 'hidden hand'. But it was actually the lack of brilliance in application that led to the nearly universal attribution of Anglo-American complicity. The initial coup failed on 16 August 1953 and for the next three days the anti-Musaddiq effort was virtually overt.[26] The significance of this point lies in the impact of the attribution of external control and direction not only on the legitimacy claims of the Shah and his Prime Minister, Fazlullah Zahidi, but also on men such as Baqa'i and Kashani who had played a critical role in weakening Musaddiq in his last months in office. How could those who, in direct or indirect collaboration with the despised British and the – at best – naive Americans, help overturn the symbol of Iranian national dignity lay any claim to being Iranian nationalists?

It can be argued that the belief in Kashani's culpability delayed for a decade any alteration in the community identity base of Iranian nationalism. The successful coup reduced the possibility that Musaddiq and his associates could serve as the socializing agents of an Iranian population that was in the process of rapid political awakening. Operating from underground they had serious problems in gaining access to those who were newly politicized. But their primary competitors had even more serious problems. The Shah and his government carried the albatross of a still persisting, though fading, memory of the manner in which they achieved power. Furthermore, the landowning influence on the government until 1959 was considerable and these allies of the Shah did not have an interest in reaching the newly politicized nor did they have an appeal for them. The one clerical figure, Kashani, who had had a populist potential and conceivably could have altered the community base of Iranian nationalism had been discredited along with his closest associates by his advertent or inadvertent role in Musaddiq's downfall. Consequently, even though in underground, the followers of Musaddiq were in the best position to serve a socializing function.

However, a shift in balance among Musaddiqists was beginning to take place. A critical decision by the Shah in the 1950s would follow the advice of Abu'l Hasan Ibtihaj and recruit into the bureaucratic elite, particularly that associated with the Plan Organization, individuals of proven competence even if they had strong sympathy for the National Front. This decision set into motion the co-optation of young, outstanding professionals to provide the technocratic base of the Shah's regime. Seeing no real regime vulnerability, in large part because of an overestimation of the power of the external forces, and attracted by the offers of positions of influence and good salaries, this group by and large accommodated to the regime. In doing so it denied especially the secular arm of the national movement a primary base of support in a new generation of Iranians. The more religious section of the national movement, calling itself at first the National Resistance Movement and led by Mihdi Bazargan and Ayatullah Mahmud Taliqani, began to emerge as the more dynamic and resourceful of the pro-Musaddiqists. Rivalry and mutual suspicions developed between the two groups but their aspirations remained common ones and both implicitly accepted the same community identity base as had the National Front in the Musaddiq era. There was, however, a shift away from secularism in the prevailing ideology of those with nationalist legitimacy.

The June 1963 riots were a major portent of the possibility of polarization and a shift in the composition of the primary community identity. The June riots occurred less than half a year after the Shah's surprisingly easy and near total victory over the Musaddiqist leadership. Throughout 1962 the Musaddiqists clearly were expecting to return to power. They not only showed little interest in compromising with the two prime ministers who served in 1962, Ali Amini and Amir Asadullah Alam, but, though equally nationalistic, they also indulged in actional struggle regarding the role of religion in a new liberal nationalist regime. But in January 1963 the Shah struck, arresting the entire leadership and demonstrating the strength of his coercive instrument. The Shah's April referendum in which he received 99 per cent approval for his 'white revolution' symbolized the appearance of totalitarianism in Iran. The real test for the Shah's security forces came, however, in June 1963 and for a time it appeared they might not prevail.[27]

The events of June 1963 told much about the direction the forces of change were to follow in the next decade and a half in Iran. First, they provided strong evidence that clerical leaders more in tune with the thinking of Kashani than of Musaddiq were likely to serve as the primary agents for the political socialization of Iranians who were becoming predisposed to participate in politics. In this regard, the appearance of a leader with clear populist potential from this group, Ayatullah Ruhullah Khomeini, was a critically important development. Khomeini, unlike Musaddiq, could articulate the desires of this newly emerging politicized public for improved material conditions and greater dignity within the Iranian social context.[28] Khomeini's Islamic ideology, highly abstract and vague in its programmic implications, would be accepted by his followers to the same degree that Musaddiq's liberalism had been accepted by his followers. The acceptance in both cases reflected the great trust in the leader and a willingness to buy the full range of the leader's ideological convictions.

Second, the secular-minded followers of Musaddiq found it difficult to gain access to the newly politicized public and indeed had no real interest in gaining that access. They were caught entirely by surprise by the June riots and made no real effort to make contact with the individuals who led them. The lack of leadership emanating from this group both reflected and gave momentum to a strong accommodationist trend taking place among its most natural support base, the professional community. Secular-minded, nationalistic and non-accommodating youth, disillusioned with the National Front, turned to the left.

Third, the tendency towards polarization was offset to a considerable degree by the strategy followed by Mihdi Bazargan and his organization now called the Freedom Movement. Bazargan's dedication to liberal values has been demonstrated in difficult behavioural choices on many occasions. His respect for individual freedom was displayed in a disinclination to make unfavourable judgements of even his most bitter opponents, including the Shah. Yet his courage in defending his point of view was exceptional. He held deep religious convictions and his Islam was one fully congruent with his liberal values. Following his failure to achieve his goals for Iran as the first prime minister of the Islamic Republic, Bazargan was widely judged as weak, ineffectual and lacking in strategic direction. This is not the place to evaluate this harsh judgement. What is important to note here is that Bazargan was the pre-eminent strategist of the revolution and that his strategy was premised on the conviction that there must be a unity of those seeking radical change with the exclusion of those of the revolutionary left.[29] His Freedom Movement accommodated an ideologically diverse group of individuals who were united in their opposition to the dictatorship of the Shah, to the extent of external influence in Iran and to the insensitivity to the muted demands for social justice especially among the politically awakening urban poor. His co-operation with secular-minded liberals was obviously sincere since, lacking a significant base of support, the bargaining position of the secular leaders was very weak. Bazargan's acuity was demonstrated by the sensitivity with which he recognized the personal importance of Ayatullah Khomeini in any strategy to end the royal dictatorship. He and his associates moved quickly in June 1963, in sharp contrast to the secular-minded, to associate themselves with Khomeini. He maintained close contact with Khomeini in exile in Iran and then France. Bazargan's protégés, such as Ibrahim Yazdi, became among Khomeini's closest political advisers.

There is no questioning the fact that, as it has evolved, Khomeini's thinking and that of those closest to him has become anti-nationalist. But the nationalists they condemn are the direct intellectual descendants of the Democrats of the 1906–11 period and the elements of the National Front that were secular minded. In Khomeini's view these nationalists have turned their backs on the culture they were raised in, a culture intimately related to Islam, and have accepted *in toto* a Godless European culture. Their exile from the community of their birth is therefore self-imposed and it matters little whether they live in physical exile abroad or in Iran.

The nationalists then, as Khomeini sees them, have accepted an alien community. But for Khomeini the community they have rejected is neither the Iranian national community, the Persian-speaking community, nor an Aryan racial community. None of these is of any serious concern to Khomeini. They have rejected the *umma*, the Islamic community. A careful analysis of Khomeini's statements would surely reveal some ambivalence with regard to his identity attachments. There are indeed occasions when he sounds as if he identifies with the Iranian national community.[30] More frequently, however, his views have a basic consistency and reflect little understanding of the importance of attachments to ethnic, racial or national communities as determinants of behaviour. He appears genuinely to downgrade, for example, attachments to the Kurdish ethnic community and to deny that Kurdish nationalism centred on its own community lies behind demands for Kurdish autonomy.[31] Rather, he explains Kurdish rebelliousness as a consequence of a successful play on false distinctions made between the Shii and Sunni communities. A similar conclusion can be drawn regarding the Baluchis. Similarly, there seems little comprehension of the force of Arab nationalism in perpetuating the Iran–Iraq war.

As conceptualized above, nationalism is a phenomenon that occurs when a population identifies intensely with a community which should be entitled to organize as a state. Nationalistic behaviour is that which derives from an intense concern with the identity community. These types of behaviour should occur whether the community in question is national, ethnic, religious, racial or any combination of these. Hence, when Iran's President, Ali Khamaneh'i, stated recently[32] that establishing a great state based on the world Islamic community is a practical possibility, he was speaking of establishing an Islamic nation-state which, one could be confident, would be characterized by nationalistic behaviour. Khamaneh'i, of course, would not see it that way since nationalism to him, as it is to Khomeini, is identified with secularism which both find an anathema.

It is also clear that in Khomeini's view the community base is Islam. Furthermore, so defining is Khomeini's position that those governing his regime fully support this position, at least verbally. However, many deeply religious Iranians such as Mihdi Bazargan and others associated with the

Freedom Movement appear to be attached to an Islamic philosophy, to liberalism, to the Islamic community and to the Iranian national community. Indeed, the community Bazargan supports seems to be the Iranian national community and to consist at its core of Persian- and Turkish-speaking Shii Muslims.

A question of considerable importance for predicting and understanding Iranian behaviour is the extent to which Iranians in general and supporters of Khomeini in particular share the community identity attributed here to Bazargan as opposed to that of Khomeini. The answer to that question is likely to emerge as the Khomeini government places increasing demands on its people to make great sacrifices for the broad Islamic community, the *umma*. Will Iranians be willing to risk their lives and to make great resource sacrifices for the Islamic community beyond the borders of Iran? Will Khomeini and his government be able to generate great popular enthusiasm for efforts involving serious sacrifices to liberate the Arab section of the *umma* which identifies as Palestinian? Will they support a continuance of a war against a secular Iraqi government for the purpose of liberating Iraqi members of the *umma* from such leadership even when Iraq is no longer perceived as threatening Iranian state security? Will non-Persian speaking individuals who in the past appeared to identify with the Iranian national community respond negatively to Khomeini's disregard of the interests and sensitivities of their ethnic communities?

Seeing nationalism as inextricably associated with secularism, Khomeini could hardly consider seriously the contention that the ideology of his own regime, which he describes as 'Islamic', is in part a product of nationalism. Yet as conceptualized here, nationalistic behaviour is clearly manifest in the policies and the stance of the Islamic Republic. Furthermore, evidence suggests that contrary to the beliefs and expectations of Khomeini and his closest associates, the identity community base for that nationalism has not altered significantly. It remains a composite community embracing at once the Iranian national community and the Iranian Shii Islamic community. Despite Khomeini's insistence that the community he represents is an all-embracing Islamic community, there is little evidence to suggest he is having much success in persuading Sunni Muslims in Iran to accept such a community as their primary community identity base; to the contrary, there is reason to believe that the Khomeini era has seen an erosion of their identification with the Iranian national community. An explanation for this trend could be that most Sunni Muslims in Iran are members of ethnic groups, such as the Kurds, Turkoman and Baluchis, which have become increasingly concerned with preserving their own identity. The behaviour of the members of the ethnic groups suggests that their primary identity community is a conglomerate community: it is composed of the ethnic community and the community of Sunni Muslims who are members of that ethnic group living in Iran. As suggested above, Khomeini's inability to recognize the importance of ethnicity as a basis of identity has led him to misunderstand the aspirations of Kurds, Turkoman and Baluchis and to adopt policies that are deeply resented by these groups. Disaffection with and dissociation from the Iranian national community thus is a natural consequence of policies that lead to a sense of political deprivation.

What Khomeini has succeeded in doing is to have purged from the Iranian decisional process critical elements of the core group of the Iranian national community. Those purged are in fact the principal proponents of liberalism and secularism as essential features of governmental ideology. The purging of other members of the core group, such as Bazargan and the Freedom Movement, who are proponents of liberalism but not of secularism, is less complete. Their decisional role is inconsequential but their political prospects are not entirely without hope.

How lasting is the purge of these core group elements likely to be? The answer to that question should form the basis for major expectations regarding the ideological complexion of Iranian governments for the next generation. If the purge process proves to be permanent and if the new core group of the community on which these governments are based is composed of individuals who look almost exclusively to the broad *umma* and – it follows – very little to the Iranian national community, Iran may cease being a nation-state. The new core group would look at an Islamic Republic embracing many ethnic groups and several former national communities as the successor nation-state, although they would be most unlikely to describe it as such. Secularism would be totally absent and the role of liberalism problematic in the new ideology.

However, the case for arguing against this permanence is strong on two counts. First, the secular trend in Iran is a historic one and has been closely associated with technological change. Whether studying abroad or at home, Iranians who have achieved professional competence in the various technologies essential for the maintenance of the complex society Iran has become, have tended strongly to favour secularism. They favour governmental leadership that can provide organizational rationality, technical competence and a potential for innovation. Religious leaders, preoccupied with other questions, are not likely to advance the kinds of policies favoured by the technocrats. A proposition that could explain the rhythm in the change of fortunes for secularism in Iran follows from this. There were in twentieth-century Iran two trends of exceptional importance for determining the direction of change in the country. One was towards an acceptance of secularism by a growing proportion of Iranians; the other was towards active participation in politics by a growing proportion of Iranians. But the secular trend was proceeding in arithmetic progression; the political participation trend in geometric progression. Prior to Musaddiq's overthrow a substantial percentage of those becoming politically participant accepted the leadership of individuals who favoured secularism. The percentage increased dramatically during the Musaddiq era. But within a decade of Musaddiq's overthrow the majority of the newly participant were looking to clerical leaders who opposed secularism. As Khomeini's charismatic appeal grew that percentage increased dramatically. Thus, although the trend of acceptance of secularism was continuing, the trend toward politicization grew to the point that at the time of the revolution most Iranians were politicized and the majority of the newly politicized, which was a majority of the overall population, followed leaders who opposed secularism. Under the Islamic Republic, secularism is officially condemned. But religious leaders offer little guidance for the solution of highly technical problems in the advanced economy of Iran. Even though the new generation of young technocrats do not question the basic philosophical tenets of the Islamic Republic, their acceptance will have little bearing on the technical decisions they must make. In essence therefore, the secular trend is likely to continue and ultimately to produce an erosion of the anti-secular stance of the regime.

Second, if as has been contended here the primary identity community for Iranians is persistingly one that incorporates both the Shii Islamic and the Iranian national communities, Khomeini and his government with their exclusive attachment to the Islamic community are out of touch as they advance the ideals of a community with which the Iranian people do not strongly identify. This will lead to specific policies, especially foreign policies, that will place demands on the Iranian people for sacrifices in terms of lives and resources that are unacceptable. Persistence in such a course of action can lead only to erosion of support which could reach a dangerous level. Evidence thus far suggests that the transformation of the core group of that community is not likely to take place. Far more likely would be a return into the decisional process of the purged elements. Whether that return is a gradual one or one of revolutionary suddenness depends on the adaptability of the clerical regime to the realities of the community identities of the people of Iran.

Tentative answers can now be given to a question asked at the beginning of this essay: was the reversal in trends favouring secular nationalism in Iran and elsewhere in the Middle East foreordained? The case made in this essay supports a conclusion that the reversal in fortunes of secular nationalism in Iran was to considerable degree a consequence of external intervention in Iranian political affairs and not a consequence of strong internal forces. A parallel conclusion, that the political resurgence of Islam is based on a major shift of identity from national communities towards an Islamic community that incorporates a diversity of ethnic and national groups, is questionable. There was indeed a radical shift in political mobilization patterns. For the first half of the twentieth century secular nationalist leaders, and none more than Dr Muhammad Musaddiq, were able to mobilize the support of individual Iranians as they began to enter the political process. But the overthrow of Musaddiq and the subsequent royal dictatorship successfully excluded the secular nationalists from continuing this role. The Shah partly because of his lack of nationalist legitimacy and partly because of a lack of interest, failed to become a major mobilizing agent. Clerical leaders proved to be naturally suited to filling this role in large part because so many of the newly participant people came from urban lower and lower-middle classes who tended to be religious and who had habitually turned to the clerics for personal guidance. Ayatullah Khomeini was able to gain access to the newly politicized mass through the clerics and the mosque bureaucracies. Thanks to his extraordinary ability to articulate both the anguish and aspirations of this group, Khomeini was able to play a major personal role in mobilizing a mass following of unprecedented depth. But it was precisely this exceptional ability to reach the mass that led to what may well be the illusion that this mass following, like Khomeini personally, identifies exclusively with the Islamic community, rather than with one based on the Iranian national community of which the Shii Muslim commmunity of Iran is an integral part.

The general conclusion, therefore, is that identity change in Iran is less profound than it appears to be. The Iranian national community remains an object of intense loyalty, and popular regimes of the future in Iran should reflect that quality. The future of secularism and liberalism in Iran may be problematical. But the future of Iranian nationalism is far less so.

Notes

1 *Time* magazine, 7 January 1952, 59.1.
2 Carl Deutsch has written seminal works on the subject of mobilization and emerging political participation. See his *Nationalism and Social Communication* (Cambridge, Mass., 1966), and his essay with others, *Political Community and the North Atlantic Area* (Princeton, 1957). For the classic statement on value change in the developing process see Marion J. Levy, Jr, *Modernization and the Structure of Society* (Princeton, 1966).
3 Still the best evaluation of the Riza Shah era in terms of change induced is Amin Banani, *The Modernization of Iran, 1921–41* (Stanford, 1966).
4 The National Front included elements, particularly of the Pan Iranist persuasion, that in important respects resembled European fascist movements.
5 For the break in relations with France see *United States Foreign Relations*, vol. II (1938) pp. 746–7.
6 Documentary accounts of the actual role of Britain in the 1921 coup are still unavailable. For a summary of what is known on the subject see Richard Ullman, *Anglo-Soviet Relations, 1917–1921*, vol. 3, *The Anglo-Soviet Accord* (Princeton, 1972).
7 For an article advancing this theme strongly see the July 1985 issue of *Crescent*.

8   For a statement on nationalism advancing the view of nationalism as a badly digested European import see the introductory essay in Elie Kedourie, *Nationalism in Asia and Africa* (Cleveland, 1970).

9   See Ernest Gellner, *Nations and Nationalism* (Ithaca, 1983). The thesis of nationalism as a phenomenon associated with ethnic identity is presented in this brilliant essay.

10   For a more developed effort reconceptualizing nationalism see R. W. Cottam, 'Nationalism and the Islamic Republic of Iran', *Canadian Review of Studies of Nationalism* 9.2 (autumn 1982).

11   The point of a decline of ethnicity as an identity focus in the United States is a matter of some controversy. See Nathan Glazer and Daniel P. Moynihan eds, *Ethnicity: Theory and Experience* (Cambridge, Mass., 1975); and Michael Novak, *The Rise of the Unmeltable Ethnics* (New York, 1972).

12   The historical case for Azarbayjani association with Iranian nationalism is easily presented. Explanations for the lack of a more strongly developed Azarbayjani nationalism requires a carefully empirical study that cannot be made without an atmosphere permitting free inquiry.

13   The Mahabad Republic deserves more attention than it has received. See William Eagleton Jr, *The Kurdish Republic of 1946* (London, 1966).

14   See Yann Richard, 'Ayatollah Kashani: precursor of the Islamic Republic', in *Religion and Politics in Iran*, ed. Nikki Keddie (New Haven, Conn., 1983). Also see Shahrough Akhavi, *Religion and Politics in Contemporary Iran: Clergy–State Relations in the Pahlavi Period* (Albany, 1980).

15   See for example *United States Foreign Relations*, vol. VI (1945) p. 501.

16   See *United States Foreign Relations*, vol. V (1947) p. 998.

17   For an example of typical reporting on the National Front see *United States Foreign Relations*, 1950, vol. V, p. 501. This report consists of a description of the Shah's views of Musaddiq without any serious embassy comment.

18   See for example the 27 February 1907 statement of Sir Cecil Spring-Rice, *State Papers*, 1909, Persia, No. 1.

19   The seminal work on psychological balance theory on which the theory of cognitive consistency rests is that of Fritz Heider, *The Psychology of Interpersonal Relations* (New York, 1958).

20   For a full development of the view of cultural distance as a determinant of perceptual tendencies see Richard Cottam, *Foreign Policy Motivation* (Pittsburgh, 1977).

21   Thomas Schelling, *The Strategy of Conflict* (New York, 1969) p. 13.

22   Thomas Schelling, *Arms and Influence* (New Haven, Conn., 1966) p. 38.

23   John A. Hobson refers ironically to the common usage of the term 'lower races' by the imperial-minded in his *Imperialism: a Study* (London, 1902).

24   For a revealing picture of how Musaddiq was perceived by those who authored the coup against him see Kermit Roosevelt, *Counter Coup: the Struggle for Control of Iran* (New York, 1979).

25   Henry Grady made clear his view that American opposition to the Iranian national movement would be a historical mistake in a series of lectures and interviews in 1951. See for example the *New York Times*, 18 October 1952, 5.5. Dean Acheson's views are recounted in his *Present at the Creation* (New York, 1969).

26　Kennett Love, in an unpublished account of his own experiences in this three-day period as a *New York Times* correspondent with no connections with the CIA or the United States government, describes the overt quality of the embassy activities, including the direction of Ambassador Loy Henderson.

27　Among the neglected areas of recent Iranian history is the 1960–3 period. A comparison of 1960–3 with 1977–9 would be most revealing of the Shah's *modus operandi*.

28　For a development of the theme of mass mobilization applied to revolutionary Iran see Jerrold D. Green, *Revolution in Iran: the Politics of Countermobilization* (New York, 1982).

29　For an impressively developed and inclusive picture of the Iranian left in Iran see Ervand Abrahamian, *Iran Between Two Revolutions* (Princeton, 1982). Still needed is a study relating the relationship of the left and the national movement.

30　For a typical case see Khomeini's address to the Friday Imams at the Jamaran Mosque on 6 May 1985. The mix of references to Iran and to Islam suggests some identity to Iran but with much less intensity than that to Islam. Tehran Domestic Service in *FBIS* 8.088 (7 May 1985), South Asia.

31　President Khamaneh'i on 7 May 1985 continued a theme Khomeini developed in 1979 to the effect that the Kurdish rebellion is a product of those playing on Sunni–Shia differences for their own interests. Tehran Domestic Service, *FBIS* 8.089 (8 May 1985), South Asia.

32　President Khamaneh'i has been advancing this theme very explicitly for the past several months. For one example, see his Friday sermon, Tehran International Service in Arabic, *FBIS* 8.130 (5 July 1985), South Asia.

2

The reconciliation of politics and ethics, nationalism and democracy: an overview of the political career of Dr Muhammad Musaddiq[1]

FAKHREDDIN AZIMI

During his trial before the military tribunal in the autumn of 1953, Musaddiq gave the following account of his aims and ideals as well as of the reasons precipitating his downfall and eventual prosecution:

> In the course of the history of Iranian constitutionalism, this is the first time that a legal prime minister of the country has been subjected to imprisonment and accusation . . . They attribute many sins to me but I know I have committed only one, and that is my refusal to capitulate to the demands of foreigners, thereby depriving them of the sources of our nation's wealth. Throughout my premiership I had only one aim in both domestic and foreign policy, which was to ensure that the Iranian nation had control over its own affairs and that the will of the nation determined the destiny of the country. After fifty years of contemplation and experience I have come to the conclusion that it is only the attainment of freedom and full independence which will enable the Iranian nation to overcome numerous obstacles in the path of its prosperity and greatness. I have done my utmost in this regard . . . The Iranian people know that in certain respects my situation is not dissimilar to that of Marshal Petain. I am also old and have served my country. Like him I have also been put on the stand of the accused at the end of my life, and perhaps I will also be convicted like him. But not everyone knows that there is a salient difference between the two of us. Petain was tried by the French nation for having collaborated with the enemy of France. I am being tried by the agents of foreigners for having struggled against the enemy of Iran.[2]

His assessment is intensely and nostalgically attested by the bulk of the intelligentsia in particular, and in general by large sections of the urban population of Iran, for whom Musaddiq as a national hero and as the architect of the nationalization of the Anglo-Iranian Oil Company (AIOC)

– the most significant event in Iranian history after the Constitutional Revolution – has grown in esteem over the years. The memory of Musaddiq has in fact come to constitute a rich and inspiring repository of democratic nationalist mythology. This paper attempts to explain the significance of Musaddiq in the context of the political development of Iran after the Constitutional Revolution and to provide an account of his character, aims and achievements which will, it is hoped, help to render his political vocation more understandable; the concept of understanding in this context should be conceived in terms of the Weberian notion of *verstehen*. Emphasis here is placed on certain salient aspects of Musaddiq's political experience, as a full account would be beyond the scope of this paper.[3]

Musaddiq was born in 1882 into a wealthy and prominent *mustawfi* family; his father was a financial administrator during the reign of Nasir al-Din Shah Qajar and his mother a granddaughter of Abbas Mirza, the reformist Qajar prince.[4] He was in his teens when his father died and when, as was then customary, he assumed his father's post and was assigned the task of managing the finances of Khurasan, a task which, aided by elder officials, he learnt to tackle with skill and which enabled him to experience at first hand the chaos of Qajar bureaucracy.

Like other children of privileged families, Musaddiq not only had the opportunity of acquiring a good education but was assured of access to high office. Yet from an early age his traits of character distinguished him from many of his peers; an account of the young Musaddiq's personality – perhaps the earliest available assessment – describes him as follows:

> despite his youthfulness, he has reached the peak of experience and maturity and is endowed with knowledge, learning, intelligence, and in this he is exemplary . . . professionally he has now become the *mustawfi* and accountant of Khurasan, yet the status, talent, learning, and knowledge of accountancy and administration of this child outstrips [the honour of] becoming a chief provincial accountant . . .
>
> Any capable person can buy himself a position, such as that of accountant of a province but [Musaddiq] has other qualities which add to his greatness (*uzm*) . . . among men of intelligence and learning [Musaddiq's] courtesy and decorum cannot be surpassed. He talks with, behaves, and receives people and extends respect to them in such a way that without undermining his own eminence and dignity, he sincerely shows utmost humility and courtesy towards them.
>
> In his relations with his equals he may have treated some finance ministers and high bureaucrats with contempt, yet in his dealings with other people he has, sincerely and not fraudulently, displayed humanity (*insaniyyat*), pleasantness and humility. A person who stands out so brilliantly in his youth, should in the future become a great examplar [*bayad az ayat-i buzurg gardad*].[5]

Musaddiq was in his early twenties when the Constitutional Revolution, which he ardently supported, took place. He was elected to represent Isfahan in the first Iranian Majlis (national assembly), but could not take up the position, being at the time below the minimum age for parliamentary membership. When Muhammad Ali Shah Qajar turned against the constitutional government, Musaddiq joined the ranks of his active opponents.

Musaddiq went to Europe to study at l'Ecole des sciences politiques in Paris (1909–10) but was forced to return to Iran because of illness. Soon he resumed his studies in Neuchâtel, Switzerland, where he received his doctorate in law in May 1914[6] – the first Iranian to obtain a doctorate in this subject.

He returned to Iran on the eve of the first world war to begin teaching at the School of Political Science and preparing a number of publications in the fields of law, politics and finance. He also engaged in political activity through the membership of various societies and was invited by Ali Akbar Dihkhuda, a life-long friend, to join the I'tidal (Moderate) Party. He then entered state service, becoming an under-secretary at the Ministry of Finance. However, he soon found himself in self-imposed exile in Europe, residing at Neuchâtel where his children were then studying. From Neuchâtel he launched a campaign against the 1919 Agreement between Iran and Britain, which provoked extensive opposition in Iran.[7]

Following the collapse of the Cabinet of Hasan Vusuq (Vusuq al-Dawleh) which had concluded the abortive Agreement, Musaddiq was invited to assume the portfolio of Justice (1920). Upon his return to Iran, however, local dignitaries of the southern province of Fars, through which he was passing, invited him to become governor of the province. He resigned the governorship upon formally hearing of the coup of February 1921 launched by Sayyid Zia al-Din Tabataba'i[8] and Riza Khan. He took up residence in the safe Bakhtiyari area until the collapse of the government of Sayyid Zia three months later.[9]

Upon assuming office, Sayyid Zia's successor, Ahmad Qavam, invited Musaddiq to accept the portfolio of Finance but he refused, objecting that a British citizen was then advising the Finance Ministry. Musaddiq eventually became Finance Minister with plenary powers, following the departure of the British adviser. In this capacity, *inter alia*, he reduced the budget of the royal Court. His vigorous anti-corruption drive, however, antagonized the elite, including many Majlis deputies.[10] Qavam's successor, Hasan Pirnia (Mushir al-Dawleh), despite his own preference failed to retain Musaddiq in his Cabinet and efforts were renewed to invite foreign advisers to manage the Iranian finances.[11]

Subsequently, actively supported by the War Minister Riza Khan, Musaddiq assumed the difficult task of governing Azarbayjan. But when Riza Khan instructed the military commander in Tabriz not to co-operate

with him, Musaddiq resigned (July 1922).[12] Later he was assigned the
portfolio of Foreign Affairs, a task which impressed upon him further the
unacceptable consequences of the capitulatory rights enjoyed by European
powers,[13] and therefore of the necessity – despite clerical opposition – of
serious efforts to modernize, secularize and codify the Iranian legal
system.[14]

The political and intellectual impact of Musaddiq was felt in a wider
arena from the time he first entered parliament in February 1924. His
primary concern as a deputy in the 5th and 6th Majlises (1924–8) was to
elaborate his views on the necessity of strengthening parliamentary
arrangements and of national self-assertion. In the course of his vigorous
criticism of Vusuq al-Dawleh he asserted:

> If bringing prosperity to the country through the work of other nations were
> of benefit to the people, in accordance with the economic principle of
> avoiding loss and gaining benefit, every nation would have invited foreigners
> into its home. If subjugation were beneficial, no subjugated country would
> have tried to liberate itself through bloody wars and heavy losses.[15]

The theme of Iran for the Iranians was repeatedly emphasized by
Musaddiq, as was the necessity of the Iranians themselves managing their
own affairs. Musaddiq's main concern was always the promotion and
preservation of democratic values, or more broadly the interests of the
people as he perceived them.[16]

Above all, Musaddiq insisted on the necessity of free elections and of
enriching parliamentarianism through patient and steady practice. He
spoke out against the gradual erosion of parliamentary rule, legality and
justice which accompanied the rise of Pahlavi authoritarianism. He was
bold enough to advocate the construction of factories rather than the
renovation of royal palaces[17] and to castigate the activities of the army in
stage-managing the elections.[18]

The consolidation of Pahlavi rule led to the exclusion of Musaddiq from
active politics. From 1936 onwards he was forced to lead the life of an exile
on his family estate at Ahmadabad, some 90 miles to the north-west of
Tehran, occupying himself with agriculture, amateur medicine and
carpentry, as well as pursuing private studies.

In June 1940 Musaddiq was summoned unceremoniously to Tehran and
exiled to Birjand, a desolate town in southern Khurasan. According to his
own account, in the course of his journey to Birjand he twice attempted to
commit suicide but failed;[19] he was maltreated and confined to a cell
shared with common criminals. He was eventually returned to Ahmadabad
six months later as the result of the intervention of the then Crown Prince,
Muhammad Riza.[20] This episode aggravated Musaddiq's hatred of royal
authoritarianism and deepened his belief in democracy. The experience of

exile, whether in Ahamadabad or Birjand, was accompanied by physical disability resulting in his often being unable to walk unaided.

For Musaddiq the source of many of the adversities suffered by the nation was the coup of 1921. He was convinced there had been active British involvement,[21] and oblivious of the domestic socio-political conditions which accounted for its genesis and success. He believed the consolidation of authoritarianism in Iran was related to British domination over the country, which had been secured to the detriment of the Russians. He was of the opinion that dismantling authoritarianism did not simply require the termination of the inordinate British influence in Iran, but the establishment of a polity in which the great powers were equally deprived of undue influence over Iranian affairs. This belief constituted the essence of Musaddiq's later advocacy of 'negative equilibrium' as the optimal paradigm for Iranian foreign policy.

The Allied occupation of Iran in 1941 resulted in Musaddiq's return from exile and in the abdication and exile of Riza Shah. Despite the fact of foreign occupation, the circumstances of the post-Riza Shah era were far more congenial to the mode of political thinking and activity advocated by Musaddiq. The emergence of a semi-modern state structure, the expansion of urbanization, literacy and national culture, and the development of a secular ethos as well as of a political culture with strong anti-authoritarian and anti-imperialist components, were all conducive to the expansion of Musaddiq's political constituency.

The years of exile, on the other hand, had not only failed to obliterate the memory of Musaddiq in the public mind but had enhanced his prestige – a fact well demonstrated by his election as Tehran's first deputy in the 14th Majlis (1944–6). Musaddiq was undisputedly the most prestigious and popular deputy in the Majlis and his parliamentary activities revealed his evolving but consistently firm democratic and nationalist beliefs. His opposition to the parliamentary credentials of Sayyid Zia signified not only avowed opposition to the rise of pro-British politicians but also his outright condemnation of the 1921 coup and, by implication, his denial of the legitimacy of Riza Shah's rule.[22] His successful campaign against the Millspaugh mission of 1943–5, largely warranted by Millspaugh's unimpressive record, indicated his growing belief in the necessity of an exclusively Iranian management of the country's affairs.

Behind Musaddiq's vigorous opposition to the Cabinet of Muhsin Sadr (June–October 1945) was his belief in the need to recognize the pluralistic configuration of the existing parliamentary structure, and to include the opposition in the decision-making process. Similarly, Musaddiq's force-fully argued opposition to grants of oil or any other concessions to foreigners, provoked by the American, British and, later, Russian concessionary demands, derived from his unwavering insistence on national sovereignty and a foreign policy of negative equilibrium. His strong opposition to the abortive Bevin-sponsored Tripartite Commission of 1946 and his unqualified rejection of any kind of foreign tutelage over Iran were motivated by the same convictions.[23] Musaddiq was also fully aware of the grim consequences of the ideological polarization of Iranian political culture into pro-western and pro-Soviet strands; his own brand of nationalist and democratic reformism was a potentially viable counter-vailing force *vis-à-vis* foreign-oriented ideologies.

On the eve of the elections for the 15th Majlis, which took place throughout the first half of 1947, it was certain that Qavam al-Saltaneh's Democratic Party of Iran would effectively stage-manage the elections. Musaddiq raised his voice in opposition, writing open letters to the Shah, Qavam and the press,[24] and even took sanctuary in the royal palace along with a number of other politicians. Qavam, however, did not concede; the elections were conducted as planned, and Musaddiq was denied a seat in the Majlis. He was subsequently inclined to view himself as having unwillingly retired from active politics, but one major development not only necessitated but facilitated his resumption of political activity and further prepared the ground for the realization of his ideals.

In October 1947, upon rejecting the Qavam–Sadchikov draft oil agreement of 1946, the Majlis passed a law assigning the government the task of redeeming the impaired rights of the nation regarding its southern oil resources. The British at that moment failed to appreciate the significance of this law and regarded it as merely a tactical move.[25] However, this act marked the beginning of the domination of the oil issue over the entire spectrum of Iranian politics. An abortive assassination attempt on the Shah (4 February 1949) resulted in suppression of the opposition and provided an opportunity for the monarch and his supporters to convene a Constituent Assembly which formally enhanced royal prerogatives by, *inter alia*, granting the Shah the right to dissolve parliament. This development constituted a temporary setback for the vocal but small parliamentary opposition which nevertheless succeeded in thwarting the Gass-Gulsha'iyan oil agreement, which was considered by the British as just and adequate and by the Iranians as grossly iniquitous.[26]

Meanwhile, the government was trying to control the elections for the 16th Majlis in such a way as to prevent the election of Musaddiq and other vocal opposition deputies. This once more impelled Musaddiq, along with a number of his followers, to take sanctuary in the royal palace with the aim of forcing the Court publicly to uphold the cause of constitutionalism, thereby restricting its opportunity openly to condone non-constitutional measures. The efforts of Abdul Husayn Hazhir, the Court Minister, to enlist the support of the British Embassy in order to arrest the protesters failed,[27] but Musaddiq and his co-protesters were obliged to leave the palace when the Shah refused to heed their criticism. The protesters, however, did not abandon their efforts; they formalized their group, calling it Jibheh-i Milli (National Front). Hoping to minimize ideological conflicts and factional strife, Musaddiq and his followers regarded a 'front' as a more appropriate framework than a party and emphasized ideals which could command broad support. They demanded free elections, a free press and an end to martial law – objectives which were organically linked to the crucial issue of oil.

The Musaddiq-led National Front effectively maintained that by rigging the elections the government aimed to create a Majlis that would conclude an oil agreement favourable to the British. In the face of their campaign, the government found it increasingly difficult to tamper with the elections, at least in Tehran and eventually, following the assassination of Hazhir (4 November 1949), felt unable to prevent the election of Musaddiq and a small number of his followers. The National Front deputies, despite their small number, soon utilized the hegemony of their movement to establish themselves as the most effective parliamentary group and began to exert a drastic influence on the political process. On the floor of the Majlis Musaddiq vigorously objected to the interference of the Court and the army in politics and to the setting up of the Constituent Assembly.[28] He succeeded in thwarting and frustrating all royal bids for increased power. Meanwhile the oil issue – repeatedly described by Musaddiq as 'Iran's most vital question'[29] – continued to assume further significance.

The oil issue was a tangible instrument around which popular demands and national aspirations could be focused, through which the pro-western and Court-sponsored government of the hard-line General Hajji Ali Razmara could be challenged and the Court restrained. The National Front, moreover, perceived the nationalization of the Anglo-Iranian Oil Company as a goal which symbolized the real decolonization of Iran, and an ideal inseparable from the consolidation of constitutionalism. In the words of Husayn Fatimi, Musaddiq's loyal supporter and colleague, the oil issue was 'as significant for Iran as was independence for Indonesia, India, Syria, and Lebanon'.[30] Against the advice even of some of their close Iranian friends, the British, however, continued to insist that the Gass-Gulsha'iyan agreement was fair.[31] Assuming intimate knowledge of the workings of the 'Persian character' they maintained that further concessions would only stimulate the appetite of the Iranians while 'decisiveness' would eventually force them to capitulate. When the Agreement was rejected by the Majlis Oil Committee, the government of Razmara was forced to withdraw it (December 1950) amid increasing National Front demands for the nationalization of the AIOC. The British, assured of the co-operation of Razmara, pressed the Shah to dissolve the Majlis.[32]

The Shah, however, dared not dissolve the Majlis on account of its firm position over oil. The National Front intensified its demand for nationalization, relying on the growing movement which relentlessly upheld this ideal. What Musaddiq had deemed impossible during th 14th Majlis[33] had now, as he himself had hoped, proved irreversible. By this time, no one could meaningfully step forward to oppose a movement which aimed to assert national sovereignty. About a month before his assassination (on 7 March 1951) Razmara and the British had seriously considered the fifty–fifty principle,[34] but the opportunity for this had already been lost; the National Front would settle for nothing less than nationalization.[35]

Following the death of Razmara, British efforts were concentrated on securing the premiership of Sayyid Zia; however, it was Musaddiq who assumed office. Musaddiq made his acceptance of the position conditional upon parliament approving the principle of nationalization, and in the first year of his premiership, his main aim was to implement this.

It has been argued that Musaddiq and his advisers were not adequately aware of the complex implications of nationalization – that they over-estimated the extent of the western and particularly of the British need for Iranian oil, and failed to grasp adequately the problems involved in the production and marketing of Iranian oil.[36] Musaddiq and his advisers may indeed not have fully grasped the intricate international and commercial aspects of the oil issue; they apparently failed to appreciate the potential extent of concerted and determined Anglo-American efforts to thwart any measure of success on the part of Iran. Their primary concern, however, relying on a favourable moral and legal judgement of their course of action internationally, was to cultivate the political and symbolic significance of the oil question domestically for the purpose of changing the prevailing pattern of Iranian politics. They knew that they had embarked on a formidable task and saw no easy victory. Musaddiq had not even ruled out the possibility of losing his own life in the process. He perceived the oil nationalization movement as a movement whose primary purpose was the realization of suppressed Iranian national aspirations and the spiritual revitalization of the nation. It was a cause which required dedication and justified sacrifice.[37] Even if it did not result in a tangible material victory for Iran, the positive political and moral consequences of the struggle, in his view, overshadowed instrumental calculations.

On the other hand, by the time Musaddiq assumed power, the nationalist movement had acquired such autonomous dynamism that neither his personal preferences nor those of his advisers could have affected the course of events. Musaddiq was the architect of the oil nationalization movement, but as prime minister he was himself its product. He owed his privileged position not only to his leadership of the movement but to his successful grasp and articulation of its underlying objectives – objectives which would in no way be meaningfully reduced to the mere dictates of a leader.

Moreover, as prime minister, Musaddiq lacked sufficient room for manoeuvre. The configuration of his supporters, the nature of his power base as well as the tactics resorted to by his opponents meant that he could only make moves which would not be readily branded as contravening the nationalization principle. The charge of 'compromise' – unhesitatingly invoked by opponents of both left and right – would have undermined his parliamentary and even his popular power base. Yet the movement for oil nationalization was not simply aimed at consolidating the substance of Iranian nationalism; it was also meant to result in the financial and economic improvement of the country. Only a settlement of the oil dispute could procure sufficient revenues to finance Musaddiq's reformist objectives; and the oil industry had indeed been nationalized in the name of the well-being (*sa'adat*) of the nation.

Musaddiq was, therefore, deeply interested in an honourable settlement of the issue. Although he could not, in view of his delicate power base, appear to be taking the initiative in negotiations, he did not ignore any viable scheme. He was sceptical of British readiness to come to an agreement with him, but he welcomed American mediation efforts, and was prepared to accept reasonable solutions. One such scheme was worked out in October–November 1951 with George McGhee, the US Assistant Secretary of State, but was in the event rejected by Anthony Eden, the British Foreign Secretary.[38] The officials who advised British politicians were on the whole unwilling to comprehend or recognize the force, authenticity and legitimacy of Iranian nationalism,[39] or to view the Iranians as morally entitled to own and manage their British-created oil industry.[40] They were particularly reluctant to give credit to Musaddiq as the articulator of Iranian national aspirations. For their part, Musaddiq and his colleagues – being preoccupied primarily with moral and legal questions and the sovereign rights of Iran – were similarly unprepared to take account of the British loss of revenue and, more significantly, of prestige. They did not appear to be concerned about the various political and strategic factors which could shape British reactions to the act of nationalization and its implementation.

Musaddiq's avowed preoccupation with the ethico-legal aspects and implications of the oil question and the issues pertaining to Iranian national sovereignty helped him to make a favourable impression at the Hague and the United Nations. It did not, however, prove congenial to the thinking and calculations of multinational oil companies which understandably revolved exclusively around 'business'; nor did it correspond to the idiom and conventional stipulations of *realpolitik*. In Egypt, which he visited in November 1951 to a warm welcome, Musaddiq's message and aims were immediately understood. In the West, however, for all its familiarity with the ideals and objectives which Musaddiq propounded, he could not elicit a sympathetic hearing. Indeed the preconditions for mutual intelligibility between Musaddiq and his British opponents were fundamentally lacking. He suspected them of harbouring insidious designs against the independence and prosperity of Iran, while they viewed him as a 'lunatic', displaying the worst aspects of the 'Persian character' and bent on ruining his country. They appeared ready to negotiate with him, but simultaneously spared no effort in attempting to destabilize his position.

The British initially intended to use force in southern Iran, but for a variety of reasons the idea was abandoned.[41] They also tried, through covert means, and especially through the manipulation of parliamentary tactics, to undermine the government, and with this aim in mind Robin Zaehner was sent to Iran soon after Musaddiq assumed office. Musaddiq's opponents, including the parliamentary opposition and the opposition press, came to enjoy extensive British support. To the destabilizing efforts of the British and their domestic supporters and agents were added the pressures of the Court and its clientele although the fears and indecision of the Shah, meant that he was unable to muster enough courage to confront Musaddiq and the oil nationalization movement openly. On the other hand, Musaddiq's own popularity, the power of the movement he personified, and the relative cohesion in the ranks of his immediate entourage, frustrated the activities of the opposition, including the Tudeh Party and the Fida'iyan-i Islam.

Musaddiq was convinced that domestic opposition to his government could only be sustained with British support. This was bound to intensify the anti-British mood and campaigns in the country which from the outset of the oil nationalization movement had facilitated the task of mass mobilization. Although an ardent anti-imperialist, Musaddiq did not harbour instinctive anti-British sentiments. He made use of anti-British rhetoric at home and in conversation with foreigners he suspected to be anti-British, yet he had on several occasions expressed admiration for the British people and their democratic traditions:[42] he consistently maintained that Iran was in dispute not with the British people or even the government but with the AIOC.[43] For him the operations of the AIOC had for 50 years overshadowed the economic and political life of Iran; the company had exploited the country and undermined its autonomy. His aim was to bring prosperity to the people and establish a meaningful national sovereignty: 'If we are to be deprived of freedom of action in our own home and to be subjugated by foreigners . . . death is preferable to such an existence.'[44]

Musaddiq's attitude was bound to aggravate British reactions, which he and his colleagues hoped partly to contain by enlisting American favour. The Iranians thought that the Americans, in welcoming the decline of the British Empire, would help Iran or at least not act against it. Events soon proved that this was a mistaken assumption.[45] Henry Grady, the American ambassador (1950–1), showed some sympathy with the Iranian cause, but his successor, Loy Henderson, soon found himself in agreement with the policy of the Conservative government which proved increasingly unwilling to come to terms with Musaddiq. Much to the delight of Musaddiq's

domestic opponents, the British now began to maintain more systematically that a settlement with Musaddiq was impossible, and the danger of a
communist takeover of Iran was imminent; Musaddiq and his colleagues,
on the other hand, maintained that it was only the weakening of his
government which would benefit the communists. In tune with the
prevailing conventional wisdom, Musaddiq also believed that fear of a
communist takeover in Iran would lead the Americans to support his
government despite British pressure. To this end he or some of his
supporters would occasionally invoke the communist threat, clearly a
counter-productive tactic the implications of which they did not at that
time fully appreciate.[46]

Eventually, in July 1952, the extensive destabilizing activities of the
British and the domestic opposition appeared to bear fruit when
Musaddiq, whose demand for personal assumption of the War portfolio
had been rejected by the Shah, handed in his resignation. Ahmad Qavam,
who had for months been engaged in intensive behind-the-scenes efforts to
replace Musaddiq and who enjoyed full Anglo-American support, was
appointed premier. However, his short-lived government ended in fiasco
and Musaddiq returned to power as the result of the popular uprising of
21 July which conferred unprecedented legitimacy upon his leadership. He
assumed the War portfolio (renamed Defence) as well as control of the
army and acquired plenary powers from the parliament for a period of six
months; his opponents retreated and the Court was further marginalized.
Musaddiq's augmented power gave him an opportunity to begin implementing various significant reform projects;[17] it also provoked the
opposition of some of his own supporters. Resentful primarily of what they
saw as an incommensurate share of the political spoils, given (as they saw
it) their role in bringing his government to power, Ayatullah Abu'l Qasim
Kashani, Husayn Makki and Muzaffar Baqa'i, among others, turned
against Musaddiq. They soon invoked 'the Constitution' against him and
began to encourage the anti-Musaddiq opposition.

The desertion of these figures enhanced the homogeneity of Musaddiq's
loyal followers, who far outnumbered his disgruntled ex-supporters. The
pro-Musaddiq National Movement Faction in the 17th Majlis increasingly
assumed the functions of the virtually defunct National Front. Yet the
Majlis, in which an absolute majority was behind Musaddiq, succumbed to
factionalism and gradually became the main anti-government platform.
Musaddiq succeeded in renewing his plenary powers for a further 12
months, but his vulnerability in parliament increased and mutual enmities
were further aggravated. As was the case during his first year of office,
Musaddiq was criticized from all sides both for flexibility and inflexibility in
regard to the oil question: he was accused of readiness to compromise with
the British and yet criticized for having failed to resolve the issue. In such
circumstances, and in view of his delicate popular power base, his growing

scepticism of British willingness to reach a settlement with him, as well as his insistence on the irreversibility of nationalization, his negotiating position was unlikely to soften. The main issue of contention in the oil negotiations during this period was the question of compensation. The Iranians appeared ready to pay compensation only for the physical assets of the company, while the British, with American support, demanded unspecified compensation for the act of nationalization and the loss of revenue caused by the cancellation of their oil concession.

The Republican victory in the US presidential elections of November 1952 enhanced open American backing for the British and contributed to the intensity of exhaustive overt and covert anti-Musaddiq activities. Propaganda was increasingly concentrated on the spectre of communism; financial, economic and political pressure and the continued British embargo on the purchase of Iranian oil aggravated the domestic crisis, while ideological strife, personal intrigues and jealousies, and factional discord added to Musaddiq's problems, weakening the possibility of national solidarity *vis-à-vis* Britain. Musaddiq had hoped to reverse the strategy deployed by the British against him by resisting until they made further concessions, but this proved impossible. He had already closed down British consulates and suspended diplomatic relations; he had also dissolved the Senate and stepped up his efforts to restrict the Court. His main difficulty, however, was with the Majlis and this increased the hopes of the British and the Shah in the imminent collapse of his government.

Musaddiq must have envisaged the numerous problems, including relentless parliamentary opposition, which he was to encounter as prime minister during a most critical period in the history of Iran. His political experience as a parliamentarian had largely consisted of leading the opposition against successive governments and championing the unrestrained power of the parliament. Yet, as prime minister, he had to recognize that the same tactics which, as a deputy, he had readily deployed against various governments could also be used against his own.

Musaddiq had always maintained that free elections would result in a parliament of 'real' representatives of the people who would not defy the 'national interest', and who would therefore support the policies he advocated. However, within the framework of the existing electoral law, and in the face of the persisting influence of the Court, the army, and the pro-British local magnates, free elections for the 17th Majlis had not chosen deputies predominantly sympathetic to his aims. The elections were therefore suspended pending a revision of the electoral law; only 79 deputies were elected, instead of the usual 136, including some who were distinctly hostile to the National Front.

Faced with this situation, towards the end of his first year in office Musaddiq contemplated measures aimed at the consolidation of his position. During his second year in office he acquired plenary powers to reduce his vulnerability *vis-à-vis* the Majlis. He also attempted to assume real control over the army in order to strengthen his position *vis-à-vis* the Court. Moreover, he imposed martial law on Tehran, and utilized measures such as the 'Public Security Act' to prevent violent clashes between extremist left-wing and right-wing groups, and to contain the activities of saboteurs. His other measures, including the revised press law, did not bear immediate fruit while in the event his new electoral law was never implemented.

Indeed none of the measures taken by Musaddiq – some of which were condemned as non-democratic – greatly reduced the institutional fragility and vulnerability of the government.[48] Musaddiq did not succeed in creating a viable executive apparatus and in fact his opportunity to do so was drastically constrained by the very structure of the existing parliamentary arrangements. He had no effective means of consolidating his government or sustaining the movement on which it was based: the army resisted far-reaching civilian control; the police, the intelligence services and the judicial apparatus were inadequate and incapable of either effective law-enforcement or of containing anti-government activities; and the effects of many firm governmental measures were vitiated by a barrage of press campaigns castigating them as 'dictatorial'. Moreover Musaddiq's own dispositions and his restrictive civic and moral concerns considerably reduced his options in dealing with – by comparison – unprincipled opponents.

With the active support of the Court, the opposition used the Majlis to discredit and paralyse the government. Eventually Musaddiq was forced to call a referendum to dissolve the Majlis, but fears of violent disruptive activities meant that the referendum was conducted in clear contravention of proper electoral procedures. Musaddiq was in principle committed to those fundamental democratic ideals and values which he believed enriched and sustained the spirit of constitutionalism. But in the prevailing critical situation, he could not respect and abide by all the existing constitutional rules, particularly those which were evidently manipulated to the clear detriment of the basic prerequisites of a democratic political arrangement. Indeed Musaddiq's move against the Majlis, though in part an indication of his increasing populism, also resulted from his realization that the vocal opposition deputies had no objective other than his downfall. In his view, the Iranian national movement would suffer gravely were his government to be toppled by ostensibly parliamentary means. However the referendum, portrayed by the opposition as a grave anti-constitutional measure, gave anti-Musaddiq forces a new impetus, while the cumulative impact of extensive destabilizing activities against his government eventually led to the coup of August 1953, a coup which owed its conception, as well as its success, to active Anglo-American backing.

Had existing parliamentary arrangements not inevitably resulted in a

succession of impotent governments, the Court could not have easily
sustained its influence, nor would a small minority have been able to
manipulate parliamentary rules and procedures. If the energy of the
government had not been so chronically vitiated by domestic opposition
and if the loyal followers of Musaddiq had had the chance to mobilize
themselves in an effective organization the clumsily executed coup of 1953
could not have so easily succeeded. In this case Musaddiq, or his followers,
relieved of the intrinsic constraints of the existing mode of constitutional
monarchy, might have acquired an opportunity to create a more effective
parliamentary system.

From the beginning of his political career, Musaddiq had come to realize
that, although not formally a colony, Iran was dominated by Britain. The
British Embassy was an effective institutional component of the Iranian
polity and the AIOC the main pillar of British domination. For Musaddiq
colonialism – whether formal or informal – was not only an instrument of
economic and political backwardness and dependence, but also brought
spiritual and cultural decay. Anti-imperialism, however, did not in his eyes
mean obscurantist anti-westernism, impetuous xenophobia or a return to
the *gemeinschaft* of anachronistic 'authentic' local traditions.

Musaddiq was a prudent secular reformist and in his doctoral thesis he
had adopted an essentially rationalist jurisprudential position, maintaining
that reason should prevail over other sources of the law. He had,
concomitantly, advocated a modernist interpretation of Shii Islam and a
qualified secularization of the Iranian legal system.[49] He admired western
cultural values, and was deeply sensitive to the charge of anti-
westernism.[50] He was constantly concerned to gain the respect and enlist
the support of world opinion; he dreamed of an Iran which, benefiting
from freedom and independence, would one day achieve a level of
prosperity and a status comparable to that of western countries. He was
equally convinced of the need for a critical appreciation of the specific local
conditions of Iran and of its culture. He avoided wounding popular
religious sensibilities; mainly through his association with Kashani he
benefited for a period from the mobilized religious sentiments of the
people, and when he broke away from Kashani he astutely defused the
efforts of Kashani and others to utilize religion against his government.

Musaddiq held intellectuals in high esteem and appreciated the value
and significance of academic institutions. He was the first politician to
instigate a bill for the financial independence of Tehran University,[51] and
many of his close associates were university lecturers. He greatly valued
educational merit[52] and conceived of the university as a place for scientific
inquiry and the advancement of learning, rather than as a vehicle for
indoctrination. Musaddiq's *idée fixe* was the 'real' interests of the nation or
the people, to be identified by consensus reached through disinterested

rational argument and enlightened free debate. He was, however, self-righteously dismissive of those who disagreed with his ideals and seldom doubted his own understanding of the 'real' national interests. Musaddiq's nationalism embodied firm beliefs in both independence and democracy; it aimed not only at creating a genuinely Iranian state to rule the nation, but also an autonomous and credible democratic polity. It entailed a firm conviction that the Shah should, in the spirit of the Constitution, reign and not rule.

Musaddiq's efforts to clarify the vexed ambiguities of the Constitution in regard to the nature of royal authority aggravated his protracted conflict with the Court and its parliamentary supporters and were eventually frustrated.[53] Yet he never ceased to insist that the realization of freedom and independence required a government independent of the Court. He persistently barred the Shah and his family from intervening in governmental affairs: indeed no politician in the constitutional era of Iranian history succeeded to such a degree in marginalizing the Shah and containing the Court. Characteristically, in the course of his trial he defiantly asserted: 'even if I am hanged I will not accept that in a constitutional country the king has the right to dismiss the prime minister'.[54] In Musaddiq's view, the Shah's only hope of political survival was to observe constitutional principles. In May 1950, he had warned the Shah to behave in such a way as never to have to face the prospect of fleeing the country; the future of the monarchy would be bleak if the Shah lost popular support.[55] Musaddiq maintained that, with the triumph of royal authoritarianism, not only would real political development cease but foreign domination would be facilitated – for by dominating the Shah, foreigners could subjugate the entire nation. The victory of the coup of 1953, which aimed at forestalling the rapid decline of western influence in Iran as well as consolidating royal authority, fully demonstrated the relevance of Musaddiq's insight.

Musaddiq's vision of the desirable polity had clear ideological overtones and was not without an apocalyptic tinge. His political outlook, however, did not amount to an elaborate ideological system and there were no coherent and detailed doctrinal guidelines to define and regulate the activities of his supporters. Musaddiq's politics was above all a politics of conviction, enthusiasm and spontaneity, not an ideological politics. This was both a source of strength as well as weakness. On the one hand, clearly no dogma or entrenched set of commanding principles could be invoked to legitimize moral absolutism and justify suppression of dissent and other oppressive measures; on the other hand, the goals, and particularly the methods and means of attaining them, were not systematically specified.

Consequently the vital question of how, against all odds, to sustain meaningful national sovereignty, embodied in truly representative institutions, had not been adequately tackled. The lack of an elaborate programme, the constraints of an essentially legalistic frame of mind, a residue of old-fashioned liberal beliefs,[56] together with the repeated failure of previous efforts to create parties in Iran – which had succeeded only in unleashing intense factionalism and rivalry – all contributed to Musaddiq's failure to organize a party of his own. In addition Iranian political culture was not, it seems, wholly congenial to the emergence of large-scale, sufficiently cohesive, disciplined and durable associations committed to a clear programme and policy. Nor, in fact, were efforts to create corporate organizations viewed favourably.

Musaddiq had conducted his oil nationalization campaign within the framework of the National Front, which was both organizationally and ideologically amorphous. But following his assumption of power he made no attempt to transform the Front into a cohesive party; indeed he virtually abandoned it.[57] Concerned to maintain his untarnished public image and to speak on behalf of the entire nation Musaddiq did not want to entangle himself in factional disputes or sectional affiliations and concerns. He therefore refused to be identified with the parties and groups organized by his followers or even adequately to cultivate their support and utilize them.

Musaddiq did, of course, make use of the radio and press to communicate his views to the people. There were also vehicles such as the Iran and the Toilers' parties,[58] guilds such as those of restaurant owners and tea house owners, and other formal and informal bazaar-based associations which liaised with the public on his behalf. However, the absence of an effective large-scale party organization behind Musaddiq and his failure to appreciate the need for such an organization hampered the consolidation of public support for his government. Indeed, several years later in September 1962, in a letter to Dr Ali Shayigan, one of his close associates, Musaddiq – then living in confinement in Ahmadabad – made the following significant confession:

> The backwardness of we Iranians is due to the absence of political and social organizations and it was because of this defect that our beloved Iran lost its freedom and independence without anyone being able to make the slightest protest.[59]

Clearly Musaddiq innocently placed his main hope for success and for political survival as prime minister in the continued momentum of the nationalist movement and the spontaneous support of the people, as did the majority of nationalists. Musaddiq was aware that it was primarily his own personality which provided the main focus of inspiration for popular support. Resisting the cult of personality, however, he did not submit to the temptations of artificial self-aggrandizement. He made very little use of state rituals to promote his own image, and opposed the erection of any statue of himself.[60] He showed no desire for self-sanctification and soon after he took office he issued an order forbidding the radio to use ceremonial titles when referring to him, and affirming that no newspaper would be suppressed for publishing even defamatory material about him.[61]

Musaddiq believed that it was not propaganda and spurious image making which would assure him of popular support, but an unblemished political record coupled with moral courage and dedication. In his view the people were perfectly capable of recognizing and, in congenial circumstances, rewarding their genuine servants.[62] Moreover, in a society with a low degree of political institutionalization, loyalties were oriented not towards the invariably precarious collectivities, but towards individuals. Musaddiq's main leadership strategy was to rely on unmediated, intimate and frank communication with the people, and in this respect the dynamism of his own character is crucial for an understanding of his political significance.

Endowed with personal charm and appeal, Musaddiq was capable of generating respect and conviction. He consistently adhered to lofty principles and was a man of undisputed honesty and integrity. He made no use of office for nepotistic ends or to maximize material gain; as a deputy in the 16th Majlis and as prime minister, he refused to collect a salary, donating it to charity. He personally met many of the expenses he incurred in an official capacity, transferred to the state whatever gifts he received, greatly reduced the ceremonial expenses of the prime minister's office, and cut its secret budget. During the greater part of his term of office he carried out his duties from his own home, often lying on his metal bed, clad in his so-called 'pyjamas'.

Musaddiq's life was under threat from the Fida'iyan-i Islam and perhaps others and therefore it was safer for him to stay indoors. It had become customary for Cabinets to meet in the royal presence and Musaddiq terminated this practice by holding Cabinet sessions in his own house. Musaddiq's personal idiosyncracies constituted important elements of his political style which, on occasion, comprised consciously self-monitored performances. Musaddiq's expression of strongly held sentiments or opinions was often accompanied by tears,[63] his physical frailty and his humility and compassion, however, were accompanied by remarkable mental vitality and decisiveness. In his view, a politician needed courage and dedication, as well as the ability to take firm and prompt decisions.[64] Yet Musaddiq's resolve, even obstinacy, coupled with his reluctance to trust others, sometimes resulted in serious unease among his followers, who viewed him as insufficiently attentive to their expectations, arguments or problems. Musaddiq's opponents, on the other hand, were scarcely treated with firmness. What perhaps above all distinguished Musaddiq from many other statesmen of his stature was his genuine attempt to combine political activity with consistent adherence to moral standards.

It remains to be determined what Musaddiq's enduring achievements were. In defiance of purely Machiavellian or pragmatic concerns, he was not intent on ensuring his own political survival at any price. His main aim was to lay the foundations of a polity which was qualitatively different from and superior to that which had existed before. Musaddiq succeeded neither in creating his envisaged autonomous parliamentary system, nor in bringing about a desirable and lasting settlement of the oil dispute. Among other things, however, by systematically restraining the Court, and by attempting to consolidate the powers of the executive, reform the parliamentary electoral laws and procedures, and create a responsible press, he provided indispensable guidelines. Moreover, by elaborating the notion of the 'oil-less economy' and attempting to implement it, Musaddiq forcefully challenged the assumption that the survival of Iran depended entirely on its oil revenues. Above all, he irrevocably put on the agenda of Iranian politics the salient issues of the credibility and legitimacy of the state as well as the integrity and competence of its office holders. He brought to public attention sharply focused questions of constitutionalism, national sovereignty and the government's position in relation to foreign powers. He seriously undermined British influence in Iran, accurately maintaining that royal authoritarianism could not sustain itself without foreign backing. He set in motion a process that eventually eroded the legitimacy of the non-constitutional, foreign-backed political arrangements which succeeded his government.

Any explanation of Musaddiq's immediate political failure should be attempted partly in terms of circumstances which were beyond his control, and partly in terms of his personality. Yet even Musaddiq's character, his perceptions, beliefs and other traits were to a considerable extent a product of the exigencies of Iranian society and political culture. Musaddiq's mentality was moulded by his background, the entrenched orientations of his generation, the repercussions of constant foreign encroachments, as well as the political milieu of both the Qajar and Pahlavi eras of Iranian history. Musaddiq was an heir to the intellectual traditions of the nineteenth-century reformists, and of the Constitutional Revolution and embodied in himself the strengths and weaknesses, as well as the antinomies of such traditions. These traditions encouraged the cultivation of western liberal values and the defiance of western or foreign political domination; yet they provided no solid ground for an elaborate theoretical and organizational framework for the realization of an effective parliamentary system and a modern polity.[65] Moreover, Musaddiq's own personal characteristics and qualities did not perhaps equip him for the difficult tasks which he, as prime minister, took upon himself. Yet had he not had such characteristics and qualities, he might have behaved very differently, may not have gained significant prominence, and, in all likelihood, he would not have become the much respected figure he is today.

Following the coup of 1953, Musaddiq and his colleagues were imprisoned but his fortitude remained unshaken. He skilfully utilized the platform provided by the military tribunal to condemn his accusers, reject the legitimacy of royal authoritarianism and communicate his views to the people. If he shed tears and showed any sorrow it was, he contended, not for his lost position, his ruined and looted house or the hardship inflicted upon his family and friends, but because of his worries and fears for the future of Iran, 'the beloved one'.[66] In the course of his trial, remaining true to his attachment to Shii mythology, he asserted:

> My creed is the creed of the Lord of the Martyrs [Imam Husayn]. That is, whenever right [*haqq*] is at stake I will oppose any power; I dispense of everything, I have no wife, no son, no daughter, nothing, I see only my homeland before my eyes.[67]

Musaddiq was condemned to three years imprisonment and subsequently confined to Ahmadabad, to lead a lonely life until his death in March 1967 at the age of 84.[68] The spectre of Musaddiq, whether imprisoned or in exile, continued to haunt the Shah; Musaddiq remained a very significant factor in Iranian politics even after his death, a factor which his opponents – including the Shah – could not afford to disregard. Despite all restrictions and constraints, and in defiance of his advanced age, Musaddiq never relaxed his efforts to promote his ideals. For a variety of complex reasons his efforts to revive the National Front ended in failure but up to the very end of his life his insistence on liberty and independence was reiterated in all his letters and messages.[69]

For many, Musaddiq became a legend in his own lifetime. After his death his popularity continued to increase, culminating in meetings and processions in Tehran and Ahmadabad during and immediately after the revolution of 1979, in commemoration of his life and career. Of course, zealots of various ideological dispositions, namely ultra-monarchists, extreme leftists and religious fundamentalists, have understandably been, and continue to be, opposed to Musaddiq. Regarding as distasteful and dangerous his spiritual heritage, especially his secular nationalism and advocacy of liberal democracy, the religious fundamentalists in particular have encouraged a relentless campaign to undermine his image and the appeal of his ideals.[70] In a milieu in which only his opponents are allowed to express themselves, there is no reason to suppose that Musaddiq's public support and his significance – indicated by the extent of animosity towards him – has crucially dwindled. Indeed, it is not implausible to suggest that democratic Iranian nationalism has no myth or symbol more potent and more capable of transcending ideological and factional strife than Musaddiq.

Notes

1 The author would like to thank Iraj Afshar, James Bill, Mark Gasiorowski, John Gurney, Albert Hourani, Roger Louis and Marvin Zonis who have commented on various drafts or parts of this paper.

2 Jalil Buzurgmihr ed., *Musaddiq dar mahkameh-i nizami*, book I, vol. 1 (Tehran, 1985) pp. 166–7.

3 For a detailed account of Musaddiq's political activities in the post-1941 era see F. Azimi, 'The politics of dynamic stalemate, Iran 1944–53', D.Phil. thesis, Oxford, 1984. See also Bahram Afrasiyabi, *Musaddiq va tarikh* (Tehran, 1981); Ali Janzadeh, *Musaddiq* (Tehran, 1979).

4 Afrasiyabi, *Musaddiq va tarikh*, pp. 25–6.

5 Afzal al-Mulk, *Afzal al-tavarikh*; quoted in Iraj Afshar, 'Sanadha'i chand bara-yi karburd dar tarikh', *Ayandeh* 11.8 (1985) pp. 557–8.

6 Iraj Afshar ed., *Taqrirat-i Musaddiq dar zindan*, recorded by J. Buzurgmihr (Tehran, 1980) pp. 31–6. (Hereafter referred to as Musaddiq, *Taqrirat*); Afrasiyabi, *Musaddiq va tarikh*, pp. 26–38.

7 Ibid., pp. 41–50; Afrasiyabi, *Musaddiq va tarikh*, pp. 47–9; on the 1919 Agreement see William J. Olson, 'The Genesis of the Anglo-Persian Agreement of 1919', in Elie Kedourie and Sylvia G. Haim, *Towards a Modern Iran* (London, 1980) pp. 185–216.

8 Hereafter referred to as Sayyid Zia.

9 Musaddiq, *Taqrirat*, pp. 66–9.

10 See further, Abdullah Mustawfi, *Sharh-i zindigani-yi man*, vol. III (Tehran, 1945) pp. 370–470; Musaddiq initiated a number of such reforms when he served as under-secretary in the same ministry. For a criticism of him by an official who had himself suffered on account of these measures see Abu'l Hasan Buzurg-Umid, *Az mast keh bar mast* (Tehran, 1956) pp. 271–80.

11 Musaddiq, *Taqrirat*, pp. 70–7.

12 Afrasiyabi, *Musaddiq va tarikh*, p. 74.

13 He had been the first Iranian who succinctly argued against such rights. See Musaddiq, *Kapitulasion va Iran* (Tehran, 1914); repr. in I. Afshar ed., *Musaddiq va masa'il-i huquq va siyasat* (Tehran, 1979) pp. 19–55.

14 Musaddiq, *Taqrirat*, pp. 96–100.

15 Musaddiq, speech in the Majlis, September 1926; text in *Nutqha va maktubat-i Duktur Musaddiq dar dawrehha-yi panjum va shishum-i Majlis-i shawra-yi Milli* (Tehran, 1979) pp. 33–51.

16 See further: *Nutqha va maktubat*.

17 Musaddiq, speech in the Majlis, 4 January 1928, text in ibid., pp. 152–66.

18 Musaddiq, speech in the Majlis, 17 February 1928, text in ibid., pp. 167–78.

19 Musaddiq, speech in the Majlis, 7 March 1944, text in Husayn Kay-Ustuvan, *Siyasat-i muvazineh-i manfi dar Majlis-i Chahardahum* (Tehran 1949), vol. 1, pp. 23–35.

20 The Crown Prince had been persuaded by his companion, the Swiss citizen Ernest Perron, who had received medical treatment from Musaddiq's son, to intervene on Musaddiq's behalf. Perron subsequently played a significant role in the court of Muhammad Riza Shah and actively liaised on the Shah's behalf with Musaddiq's opponents and with British agents in the country.

21 Musaddiq, *Taqrirat*, p. 102.
22 Even in the course of his trial, Musaddiq reiterated his refusal to recognize the legitimacy of Riza Shah's rule; see Buzurgmihr ed., *Mahkameh-i nizami*.
23 See further, Husayn Kay-Ustuvan, *Siyasat-i muvazineh-i manfi dar Majlis-i Chahardahum*, 2 vols (Tehran, 1949–51).
24 *Jibheh*, 28 November 1946, 4–7 January 1947.
25 Minute by Pyman, 24 October 1947, FO 371/61974.
26 Kazim Hasibi's articles in *Shahid*, 22, 28 December 1949.
27 Lawford to FO, 13 October 1949, FO 371/75466.
28 Musaddiq, speech in the Majlis, *Muzakirat-i Majlis*, 25 May 1950.
29 Musaddiq's letter to the National Front, *Ahang-i Sharq* (*Shahid*), 31 December 1949.
30 Husayn Fatimi's editorial in *Bakhtar-i Imruz*, 13 December 1950.
31 Minute by Furlonge, 11 August 1950, FO 371/82375.
32 Minute by Furlonge, 5 January 1951, FO 371/91452.
33 Ghulam-Husayn Rahimian's article in *Umid-i Iran* 11 (17 April 1979), repr. in Mahmud Tafazzuli ed., *Musaddiq, naft, kudita* (Tehran, 1979) pp. 161–3.
34 Shepherd to FO, 11 February 1951, FO 371/91522.
35 Musaddiq's message to the nation, *Bakhtar-i Imruz*, 6 March 1951.
36 See for instance Mustafa Fateh, *Panjah sal naft-i Iran* (Tehran, 1956) p. 523.
37 Musaddiq, message to the nation, *Bakhtar-i Imruz*, 22 July 1953.
38 See George McGhee, *Envoy to the Middle World: Adventures in Diplomacy* (New York, 1983) pp. 393–403.
39 See for instance: Shepherd, 'A comparison between Persian and Asian nationalism', 11 October 1951, FO 371/91464; Wheeler's letter, 29 October 1951, FO 371/91464; R. E. G. Sarell of the Foreign Office's Eastern department, however, concluded that 'for the time being at least [Iranian nationalism] represents a force in Persia which must be reckoned with'. Sarell, 'Nationalism in Persia', February 1952, FO 371/98596.
40 Fergusson to Stokes, 3 October 1951, FO 371/19607.
41 Wm Roger Louis, *The British Empire in the Middle East 1945–1951* (Oxford 1984) pp. 657–78; further on British policy towards Musaddiq see Roger Louis's chapter in the present volume.
42 Musaddiq, speech in the Majlis, *Muzakirat-i Majlis*, 23 July 1927; speech in the Majlis, 25 May 1950.
43 Musaddiq, press conference, *Bakhtar-i Imruz*, 7 April 1951.
44 Musaddiq, speech in the Majlis, *Muzakirat-i Majlis*, 12 July 1951.
45 Musaddiq's speech in the Majlis, *Muzakirat-i Majlis*, 11 December 1951.
46 On the attitude of the US government towards Musaddiq see James Bill's chapter in the present volume.
47 These reforms included a variety of measures, such as steps towards some degree of land reform; new bills for land tax and income tax; various measures to facilitate exports; an increase in the educational budget; the modification of rents; the construction of roads; the nationalization of telephone installations; the creation of a uniform bus service in Tehran; and a comprehensive scheme for workers' social insurance. There were also steps for the reform of the administration and particularly of the judiciary, and new press and electoral laws were also promulgated. See further F. Azimi, 'The politics of dynamic stalemate', pp. 344–7.

48   See further, F. Azimi, ibid., pp. 283–418.
49   M. Mossadegh, *Le Testament en droit Musulman (secte Chyite)* (Paris 1914).
50   Musaddiq, speech in the Majlis, *Muzakirat-i Majlis*, 20 June 1950.
51   Musaddiq, speech in the Majlis, *Muzakirat-i Majlis*, 23 January 1943.
52   The testimony of Mahmud Nariman in the court; text in Buzurgmihr ed., *Mahkameh-i nizami*, book I, vol. 2, pp. 584–95.
53   Musaddiq demanded that the Majlis approve the report of an eight-man parliamentary committee set up to investigate the relations between the Shah and the prime minister, which emphasized the ceremonial nature of royal authority. His opponents, however, procrastinated and successfully utilized a variety of tactics to thwart the approval of this report. For further details see F. Azimi, 'The politics of dynamic stalemate', pp. 383–97.
54   Buzurgmihr ed., *Mahkameh-i nizami*, book I, vol. 2, p. 597.
55   Musaddiq, speech in the Majlis, *Muzakirat-i Majlis*, 29 May 1950.
56   Khalil Maliki, 'Sarnivisht-i tarikhi-yi libiralism', *Ilm va Zindigi* (August–September 1952) pp. 580–4, 652–67; Maliki, 'Alami az naw bibayad sakht', in ibid. (January–February 1953) pp. 769–78; Maliki, 'Mubarizeh ba buzurgtarin khatari keh nahzat-i milli ra tahdid mikunad', in ibid. (May–June 1953) pp. 203–6, 291–5.
57   See further, Ahmad Maliki, *Tarikhcheh-i Jibheh-i Milli* (Tehran, 1953).
58   In October 1952 the Toilers' Party (Hizb-i Zahmatkishan) split into two opposing branches: one – known as the Third Force – loyal to Musaddiq and led by Khalil Maliki, and the other opposed to him and led by Muzaffar Baqa'i.
59   Text in *Mukatibat-i Musaddiq: Talash bara-yi tashkil-i Jibheh-i Milli-yi Sivvum* (n.p., 1975) p. 103.
60   Musaddiq's message to the nation, *Bakhtar-i Imruz*, 8 July 1951.
61   Ibid., 2, 3 May 1951.
62   Musaddiq, speech in the Majlis, *Muzakirat-i Majlis*, 20 June 1950.
63   See for example Afrasiyabi, *Musaddiq va tarikh*, pp. 48–9.
64   Musaddiq, *Taqrirat*, p. 130.
65   See further, R. K. Ramazani's chapter in the present volume.
66   Musaddiq, *Taqrirat*, p. 142.
67   Buzurgmihr ed., *Mahkameh-i nizami*, book I, vol. 2, p. 413.
68   The extent of the entrenched royal fears of and vindictiveness towards Musaddiq can be gauged from the fact that the Shah allowed neither a public funeral procession for Musaddiq nor burial in Ibn Babavayh, the burial site of those who had lost their lives in the pro-Musaddiq uprising of July 1952 and the place which Musaddiq had specified in his will.
69   See further, *Mukatibat-i Musaddiq*.
70   See for instance Hasan Ayat, *Chihreh-i haqiqi-yi Musaddiq al-Saltaneh* (Qum, 1981). Arguments similar to Ayat's can also be found in Bahman Isma'ili, *Zindiginameh-i Musaddiq al-Saltaneh* (n.p., n.d.). For a more balanced view by a one-time influential group among the supporters of the Islamic Republican regime in Iran see Sazman-i Mujahidin-i Inqilab-i Islami, *Nigarishi kutah bar nahzat-i milli-yi Iran* (Tehran, 1979). See also F. Rajaee's chapter in the present volume.

3

Constitutional government and reform under Musaddiq

HABIB LADJEVARDI

Dr Muhammad Musaddiq's 27-month rule from April 1951 to August 1953 is one of the more controversial periods in contemporary Iranian history. Much of the writing about this period has concentrated on Musaddiq's handling of the oil dispute between Britain and Iran. A good many other works contain generalities about his personality and idiosyncrasies. Some depict him as a well-meaning democrat who was too incompetent to govern. Others accuse him of practising a double standard: a constitutionalist while out of office and a dictator while in office. For example, one British official involved in the oil dispute has observed that Musaddiq was 'incapable of bringing any form of stability or prosperity to Persia. He could not govern, and the sooner that he left power, the better for Persia. Not for us, for Persia.' Another British official has observed: 'We didn't think he would do any good for Iran. The two years he was there was too long for our thinking. He did nothing for Iran.' A third critic reported: 'Mussadeq's megalomania is now verging on mental instability.' And a British intelligence officer stated that 'Mussadeq was leading the country to hell on a wheelbarrow.'[1] Musaddiq's most vehement critic within Iran was Muhammad Riza Shah whose description of the former prime minister is a good example of the type of criticism levelled against him.

> Mossadeq, the orator, is difficult to judge as a politician because of the perpetual contradiction between his words and his acts, and because of his sudden changes of mood from elation to depression before one's very eyes. His absolute certainty, violently expressed in hysterical speeches, would turn to tears and sobbing. He had frequent 'diplomatic' illnesses and he played out macabre comedies in which he would exclaim: 'I am a-dying . . .' and so forth. He has been compared to Robespierre, to Rienzi, and even to characters from the *Commedia dell'Arte*. He was certainly a completely irrational being . . .[2]

Musaddiq was further accused of interfering in Majlis elections, 'overruling' the parliament, dissolving the 16th Majlis and 17th Majlis, using martial law, and seeking and misusing limited legislative powers.

This chapter will examine two aspects of Dr Musaddiq's administration: first, to what extent his government adhered to democratic principles; and second, to what use Musaddiq put the legislative powers granted him by the Majlis. It is hoped that this work will clarify some of the misunderstandings surrounding this important period of Iranian history.

Musaddiq came to power as a result of the movement to nationalize Iran's oil industry. On 7 March 1951, Prime Minister Razmara was assassinated by Khalil Tahmasibi of the Fida'iyan-i Islam. The next day the Oil Committee of the Majlis voted unanimously to nationalize the oil industry, and on 15 March the Majlis voted, also unanimously, to approve the committee's report.

The Cabinet of Husayn Ala, the veteran statesman, after a brief term as a caretaker government, was replaced by that of Dr Muhammad Musaddiq. On 28 April the Majlis nominated Musaddiq by 79 out of 100 votes cast to assume the post of prime minister. The Senate confirmed the appointment on the following day. Musaddiq presented his first Cabinet to the 136 members of the 16th Majlis and stated that his government would have only two goals: implementation of the oil nationalization law and revision of the electoral law. On 6 May Musaddiq received a vote of confidence from the Majlis with 99 votes in his favour (*Ittila'at*, 25 November 1951). Thus, Musaddiq came to power in accordance with Iran's Constitution and with the full blessing of a Majlis and Senate which he had had no part in electing.

Elections for the 17th Majlis

One of the erroneous charges made against Musaddiq is that 'at his insistence' the 16th Majlis was 'dissolved early in 1952 and elections held in an effort to secure a more pliant parliament'.[3] The fact is that, according to article 5 of the Iranian Constitution, the term of the Majlis was limited to two years. In October 1951, while Musaddiq was defending Iran before the Security Council of the United Nations, a number of his opponents in the Majlis were promoting a plan to lengthen the term of the Majlis from two to four years, and thereby prevent the popular prime minister from solidifying his support in the Majlis through the impending elections. When he returned to Iran in November, Musaddiq reported on his trip to the United States and then requested a vote of confidence. Once reconfirmed by the Majlis, Musaddiq told the deputies that in accordance with his constitutional duties he would proceed to hold elections immediately (*Ittila'at*, 25 November 1951).

Prior to the 1960s, Iran's parliamentary elections were held in various electoral districts over a period of several months. Thus, on 7 January 1952, balloting for the 17th Majlis began in Tehran and a number of other districts while the 16th Majlis was still in session. As an indication of the relative importance of the Majlis *vis-à-vis* the executive branch of government during that period of Iranian history (in stark contrast to the 1960s and 1970s), two of Musaddiq's senior Cabinet ministers, Dr Karim Sanjabi, Minister of Education, and Mahmud Nariman, Minister of Finance, resigned their Cabinet posts in order to stand for election to the Majlis. On 27 January the counting of votes from Tehran was begun at the Sepahsalar Mosque. On 18 February the two-year term of the 16th Majlis came to an end, and on 27 April the 17th Majlis was inaugurated. Thus, Musaddiq did not dissolve the 16th Majlis; it completed its full term.

Another charge directed against Musaddiq is that he 'halted the electoral process, when only 80 out of 132 deputies had been elected . . .' (*Shah's Story*, p. 55). This statement as it stands is essentially correct. However, a review of the facts is essential to an understanding of the circumstances.

The elections for the 17th Majlis were conducted with far less government interference than any election in Iranian history since the 1920s. This is borne out by the fact that few charges were made by the opposition that the elections had been manipulated by the Musaddiq government. For one thing, the elections were supervised by the Ministry of the Interior headed by the conservative and independent landowner, Muhammad Ibrahim Amirtaymur, and subsequently by Allahyar Saleh, whom even the Shah described as reasonable. Moreover, the army, the chief source of interference in previous elections, was still controlled by the Shah and not by the Musaddiq government. According to Richard Cottam:

> Dr Mossadeq insisted that these would be the first free elections in Iran's history, and by and large he succeeded. But the question arises, what is a free election in a country of Iran's economic and social development? Does freedom require that the landowners be free to instruct their peasants how to vote and to herd them to the polls? Dr Mossadeq apparently believed it did. The results for the Nationalists were disastrous.

Musaddiq did not believe the practice of coercion described by Cottam represented free elections. As far back as the 14th Majlis he had urged passage of a new election law giving greater weight to the votes of the urban literate population. He was well aware that if the Ministry of the Interior remained neutral in provincial elections, the results would be determined by the army commander, under the control of the Shah, and the local landowner. In Tehran, however, with a large literate population, and under the watchful eye of the central government and a free press, popular candidates would be elected. Consequently, while Tehran elected Musaddiq supporters, in rural provincial areas 'district after district saw the election of men who, though willing to give lip service to Mossadeq, were known to want nothing more than the destruction of his government.'

Once a majority of Majlis deputies had been seated, the 17th Majlis, in accordance with the Constitution, was inaugurated by the Shah and began its deliberations on 27 April 1952. 'Confronted with the inevitability of defeat unless he utilized the traditional rigging devices of his predecessors and successors,'[4] Musaddiq halted the elections rather than let them continue – with or without interference. The decision to suspend the election was announced on 19 May. A government spokesman stated that elections in the remaining areas would be postponed until the return of the Iranian delegation who were about to depart for the International Court of Justice at the Hague to present Iran's side of the oil dispute (*Ittila'at*, 19 May 1952). The promised elections, however, never took place. At his trial, two years later, Musaddiq defended his action: 'In view of the Royal Court's flagrant interference in the electoral process, we had to suspend the remainder of the Majlis elections.'[5] Nevertheless, although it is true that 40 per cent of the Majlis deputies were not elected, the Majlis itself was far from unrepresentative – or pliant.

Whether Musaddiq was justified under the extraordinary circumstances of the time in halting the elections is a matter of debate. While it is clear that he did not follow the letter of the Constitution, it is likely that, if he had completed the elections, deputies representing the privileged elite – who were opposed to his non-aligned foreign policy and domestic reforms – would have gained a majority in the Majlis, even though (as will be seen in the July 1952 uprising) the overwhelming majority of the literate urban population of Iran supported his policies.

An analysis of the election results[6] indicates that 80 of the 134 seats, or 60 per cent, were filled when the elections for the 17th Majlis were halted. Moreover, important regions such as east and west Azarbayjan, Kirmanshah, Zanjan, and Yazd elected 100 per cent of their deputies, while the Kirman Province and the Central Province elected 83 and 76 per cent of their deputies, respectively. Cities for which all the allotted deputies were elected included Kirman, Kirmanshah, Qazvin, Tabriz, Tehran, Yazd, and Zanjan. On the other hand, the provinces of Khuzistan, Mazandaran, Fars, Khurasan, and Kurdistan (some with large tribal populations under military control) had none – or only a small percentage – of their seats filled. As a result, the major cities of Ahwaz, Isfahan, Hamadan, Mashhad, Rasht, Sari, and Shiraz had no representatives at all in the 17th Majlis.

Opponents of the government were not alone in their dismay at the way the elections were conducted; two ministers of the Interior had resigned over policy disagreements regarding the elections, and Dr Musaddiq himself was unhappy about the results. Instead of preventing the entry of his opponents to the Majlis, as has been suggested by his critics, he followed the proper constitutional procedure, and on 30 April 1952, *asked* the Majlis Election Committee to reject the credentials of a number of deputies he believed had acquired their seats illegally (*Ittila'at*, 30 April 1952). The Majlis majority, however, wishing to avoid the use of delaying tactics by government opponents in the Majlis, confirmed the election of these deputies.

Even though one scholar has asserted that 'by October [1952], Mossadegh felt strong enough to dissolve parliament entirely',[7] the 17th Majlis continued to function until the summer of 1953, when it was dissolved as the result of a controversial referendum. In October 1952, however, Musaddiq did dissolve the 60-member Senate, half of whose members were appointed by the Shah and the other half elected through a complicated two-stage process.

Musaddiq and his liberal colleagues were not enthusiastic about restoring the Senate. Although this legislative body, along with a five-member board of Islamic jurists, had been envisioned in the Constitution of 1906, neither body had actually been formed at that time. In a wave of popular sympathy after an assassination attempt in February 1949, the Shah decided to proceed with his long-held desire to revise the Constitution. A constitutional assembly was hastily and undemocratically called into session to take measures to increase the power of the Shah, among them the formation of the Senate, half of whose members the Shah would appoint.

In the 17th Majlis, members of the privileged elite, composed of army officers, landowners, leading businessmen, and some clerics, either joined the handful of loyal Musaddiq supporters or opposed him cautiously. In the Senate, members of the elite held nearly all the seats and continuously criticized Musaddiq's unyielding aversion to British influence in Iran, as well as his liberal domestic programmes. As Zabih has written,

> Unlike the Majlis, where opposition to Dr Mossadegh did not show any disposition to criticize the government's oil and foreign policy, the opposition in the upper house overtly and daringly attacked these policies and charged the government with isolating Iran and leading it to economic and political suicide.[8]

On 23 October 1952, a week after diplomatic relations with Britain had been severed, a group of National Front deputies in the Majlis submitted a motion which interpreted article 5 of the Constitution to mean that the term of *both* the Majlis and the Senate was two years. This motion was promptly approved on the same day by the majority of the deputies and sent to the Imperial Court for the Shah's signature. According to Zabih,

'His endorsement was secured within two days, after the prime minister had an audience with the Shah, during which Dr Mossadegh promised to hold an election for a new Senate in the near future.'[9] This was confirmed by a government spokesman, who stated that, following reform of the election law, new elections for the Senate and the remaining seats in the Majlis would take place (*Ittila'at*, 23 October 1952).

The Musaddiq administration can be blamed for not living up to its pledge to reform the electoral law and hold new Senate elections. While lack of interest in reopening the Senate is understandable, it is not clear why Musaddiq did not revise the electoral law which he had always considered so important. The question is especially puzzling when we see that with the limited legislative powers granted him by the Majlis he could have single-handedly rewritten the election law for the Majlis.

21 July uprising: indication of popular support

Because of Iran's flawed electoral law and the interference in elections by the military, Musaddiq declared that ultimate political power rested not in the legislature but with the Iranian people, especially the literate public who continued to give him support through rallies, demonstrations, and other means. The first major test of actual public support for Musaddiq's leadership and policies occurred in July 1952. On 5 July, following the formation of the 17th Majlis, Musaddiq resigned as prime minister in accordance with constitutional procedure. The next day, the same Majlis that was elected during Musaddiq's premiership gave him only 52 out of the 80 votes cast, another indication that elections for the 17th Majlis had been little influenced by the government. On 9 July the Senate, which had been elected to office before Musaddiq's rise to power, confirmed him, not because he was their choice but because of the vast support Musaddiq enjoyed among the public. Consequently, on 11 July the Shah reluctantly invited Musaddiq to form a new Cabinet.

Musaddiq, who had long believed that the Shah's control over the military was unconstitutional, had become even more convinced of this point during recent elections, when military commanders interfered in provincial elections. Upon his reappointment, Musaddiq insisted on the prime minister's constitutional prerogative of selecting the Minister of War, subject to Majlis approval. For the Shah, who was unwilling to relinquish his hold over the military, this was the last straw. He recalled that in July 1952

it seemed to me that I could no longer credit [rely upon] a man who was leading the country to its downfall. We had sold no oil since nationalization, there was no agreement in sight . . . we were heading towards ruin. A desperate Mossadeq, beaten on all fronts and excited by his entourage, wanted to remain in power, so he asked me for the war portfolio. I refused point blank. On July 17 he resigned. (*Shah's Story*, p. 55)

There is every indication that Musaddiq's resignation was not a ploy to pressure the Shah into submission, but rather a decision to return to retirement and rural life at Ahmadabad. This is borne out by the fact that his senior associates began assessing their own chances for the premiership.[10]

In the meantime, the remaining members of the Majlis, meeting without a quorum and following the Shah's directive, nominated the veteran politician, Ahmad Qavam, as prime minister.

Oil workers in Abadan and Khurramshahr were among the first to protest, by stopping work and conducting demonstrations in response to the news of Musaddiq's resignation (*Ittila'at*, 17 July 1952). On 19 July there was a major pro-Musaddiq demonstration in Tehran. At the same time, National Front deputies in the Majlis declared 21 July (30th of Tir) a day of public protest (*Ittila'at*, 19 July). On that day bloody confrontations took place across Iran between the military and unarmed civilians. The Shah conceded later that a vast majority of the people supported Musaddiq, and that a 'popular uprising' had taken place. Nevertheless, he allowed the army to fire on the demonstrators even though he has written, 'I refused to give the troops the order to fire' (*Shah's Story*, p. 55). After approximately 30 people had been killed and a number of officers and soldiers had joined the demonstrators, the troops were withdrawn. On the afternoon of 21 July, the Majlis formally nominated Musaddiq as prime minister, with 61 out of 64 votes in his favour (*Ittila'at*, 21 July). Immediately afterwards, a delegation from the Majlis met with the Shah, urging him to reappoint Musaddiq. The Shah begrudgingly yielded to the popular will. 'The threat of civil war', the Shah wrote, 'obliged me to call back Mosaddeq and to accept his conditions. As a victim of his own demagogic conceit, his xenophobia and his incompetence, he had become the prisoner of his allies to the right and the left' (*Shah's Story*, p. 55). Two days later, also yielding to public pressure, the Senate confirmed the Musaddiq Cabinet, with 33 favourable votes out of 41 (*Ittila'at*, 23 July).

On 26 July Musaddiq presented his Cabinet to the Shah, and himself temporarily assumed the post of Minister of War (*Ittila'at*, 26 July). A few days later, Musaddiq requested from the Majlis limited legislative powers, for a period of six months, to carry out necessary reforms – a move which has received as much criticism as any of his other political measures.

Musaddiq's limited legislative powers

On 3 August, following the 21 July uprising, the Majlis passed a bill delegating to Musaddiq for a period of six months limited legislative powers based on the programme his administration had presented. The following week, the Senate, which had been elected prior to the selection of Musaddiq as prime minister and half of whose members were appointed by the Shah, chose a ten-man delegation to ascertain from the prime minister what he meant to do with the legislative powers granted by the Majlis (*MEJ* 6 (1952) p. 49). On 11 August, the Senate approved the bill containing the following provisions (*MQ*, pp. 1–2):

> Single article: authority is given for a period of six months from the date of the passage of this law to the person of Dr Muhammad Musaddiq, the prime minister, to prepare bills that are necessary for the implementation of the following nine-point programme of the government that was approved in the 7 Murdad 1331 [29 July 1951] meeting of the Majlis and in the 11 Murdad 1331 [2 August 1952] meeting of the Senate and, after a trial period, to present them to the two houses [of parliament] within six months. Until the time when the two houses have acted upon them they are binding.

1 Reform of the electoral law of the Majlis and the municipalities.
2 Reform of financial affairs and revision of the budget by reducing expenses and establishing direct taxes and, if necessary, indirect taxes.
3 Reform of the economy through increasing production, creation of additional employment, and the [revision of] monetary and banking laws.
4 Exploitation of the country's oil resources, in accordance with the nine-point law regarding the implementation of the nationalization of the oil industry, and preparation of articles of association for the national oil company.
5 Reform of administrative organizations and civil, judicial, and military employment laws.
6 Establishment of local councils in villages for the purpose of social reform through enactment of taxes.
7 Reform of the laws relating to the judiciary.
8 Reform of laws governing the press.
9 Reform of educational affairs, public health, and means of communications.

The limited legislative powers granted to Dr Musaddiq by both houses of parliament and signed by the Shah have come under frequent attack by his critics. They regard the means by which he secured these powers as unconstitutional, and consider the purpose for which these powers were used as detrimental to the national interest. For example, the *New York Times* wrote at the time: 'What he proposes is in effect a legal coup d'etat that smacks of Hitler's tactics';[11] and the 18th Majlis in November 1954 declared all bills approved by Dr Musaddiq to be unconstitutional and thus null and void.[12]

In an attempt to assess these charges, the first question to be posed is why Musaddiq found it necessary to seek these powers. He has responded to this question in various statements.[13] As noted earlier, when he became prime minister he limited his programme to just two goals: the implementation of the oil nationalization law and reform of the electoral law. Aware of the difficulty of dealing with a powerful foreign state over the oil dispute, Musaddiq did not wish to create domestic dissension. At a time when he needed internal unity, he realized that each prospective reform would bring him into conflict with a different interest group. However, by the summer of 1952, it had become clear that the oil dispute would not be resolved in the near future and that demands for domestic reform could no longer be postponed.

In considering the process by which reform was to be accomplished, Musaddiq faced a monumental challenge familiar to democratic leaders in developing countries. Although he was supported by the vast majority of the urban population of the country (as evidenced by the 21 July uprising), the major centres of power – the Imperial Court, the military, the Senate and the upper echelon of the bureaucracy – were dominated and controlled by the privileged elite, who favoured the status quo and accommodation with Britain. Musaddiq was well aware that previous attempts at reform since 1941 had been frustrated, not only by other power centres but also by the majority of the deputies in the Majlis: landowners, prominent businessmen, and army oficers, who rarely represented the wishes of their electoral districts. It was clear that attempts at electoral, land and tax reform would be opposed by these deputies and therefore by the Majlis.

The 17th Majlis was controlled by supporters of Musaddiq who backed his reforms. However, the Majlis minority, in alliance with the Imperial Court, the Senate, the military and the conservative clergy, had demonstrated its ability to block Musaddiq's reform bills through parliamentary manoeuvres. Thus, Musaddiq was left with difficult choices: he could proceed through ordinary parliamentary channels, in which case few, if any, of his reforms would even reach the floor for debate; alternatively he could ask the Shah to dissolve the parliament so that he could rule by decree, as Ahmad Qavam had done in 1946–7 and Dr Ali Amini would do in 1961–2. It was clear, however, that the Shah would not give such an opportunity to a prime minister with whom he disagreed so intensely. Moreover, Musaddiq himself, by word and deed, had shown that he opposed government without the participation of the Majlis, even if that body were not totally representative of the electorate.[14] With public support as his main leverage, Musaddiq convinced the Majlis to give him limited legislative powers, which would serve as a new experiment in reform through constitutional means.

The limited powers granted to the prime minister did not represent a legal *coup d'état* for the following reasons. First, the authority was given for a period of six months – not indefinitely. Second, Musaddiq was not granted power to *enact* laws in the usual sense, but was authorized to prepare bills, implement them on a trial basis for a period not exceeding six months, and then to present them to the Majlis for revision, approval, or rejection. Third, this authority was granted to Musaddiq legally after considerable debate and criticism by an independent legislative branch, and was signed by the Shah. Moreover, neither Musaddiq nor the Majlis suspended any part of the Constitution. The press remained unhampered. A review of the many opposition newspapers of the time, including *Shahid*, indicates the degree to which political rights were respected. Most important of all, the independent Majlis continued to remain in session, and to monitor Musaddiq's actions, and was in a position to dismiss him from office at any time by a vote of no confidence.

As a democratic prime minister, Musaddiq sought periodic votes of confidence from the Majlis. For example, on 16 September 1952, a little over a month after being given limited legislative authority, Musaddiq received a vote of confidence from the Majlis with 60 out of 61 votes cast in his favour (*Ittila'at*, 16 September 1952); the next day he received a vote of confidence from the Senate (*Ittila'at*, 17 September 1952).

On 7 January 1953, when Musaddiq requested an extension of his limited legislative powers for another year, Ayatullah Abu'l Qasim Kashani, speaker of the Majlis, declared that the request conflicted with the Constitution (*Ittila'at*, 7 January 1953) – another indication that opposition had not been suppressed. Nevertheless, on 19 January the Majlis approved Musaddiq's request with 59 votes in favour and seven against out of 80 possible votes (*Ittila'at*, 19 January).

A review of the bills approved by Musaddiq during the first six-month period, from August 1952 to March 1953, gives the impression of a man running out of time and in a great hurry to carry out a carefully thought-out agenda. In that relatively short period he approved 122 bills. A count, or analysis, of the bills approved from March to August 1953 was not carried out by the author because the Zahidi administration, which took power in August 1953, did not publish Musaddiq's bills, which it considered illegal, in the annual collection of laws.

Martial law and public security laws

A major charge of Musaddiq's opponents is that he curtailed political freedom through the imposition of martial law and enactment of public security bills. Martial law had seen frequent use in Iran's major cities ever since the Anglo-Russian invasion in August 1941. As a matter of fact, during most of the period between 1941 and 1951 Tehran was under martial law. As recently as 20 March 1951, Tehran had been placed under martial law by Prime Minister Husayn Ala. It is true that Musaddiq and the other constitutionalists had always opposed indiscriminate use of martial law, contending that it was often used by the government on the pretext of maintaining public order but in fact to suppress opposition and political freedom.

On 12 August 1952, as one of his first acts after being granted limited legislative powers, Musaddiq lifted martial law in Tehran (*MEJ* 6, p. 459). As noted in other chapters of this book, calm and normalcy were not desired by Musaddiq's foreign and domestic opponents, who actively instigated domestic chaos in order to discredit him and destabilize his government – a campaign that finally succeeded in bringing down Iran's last attempt at constitutional monarchy. Within a few days after the lifting of martial law, disorder broke out in the streets of Tehran. On 18 August, clashes took place between members of what were described as the Tudeh and neo-fascist Sumka parties. The next day 'Moslem combatants' were reported to have joined the clashes (*MEJ* 6, p. 459). Only recently, we learned that many of these clashes were staged by agents of the British and, later, American intelligence services.[15] On 20 August Musaddiq reinstated martial law (*MEJ* 6, p. 459).

Although Musaddiq was forced to fight on both domestic and foreign fronts, he continued to respond legally. When necessary, his government introduced new *laws* in order to meet new situations with judicial recourse rather than resorting to arbitrary action outside of the law.

On 10 October Musaddiq, using his limited legislative powers, outlawed the carrying of weapons in public thoroughfares and the disruption of public order, including harassment of women (*MQ*, pp. 69–70). Four days later, Musaddiq approved penalties against anyone disrupting the vital oil industry by strikes or sabotage (*MQ*, p. 73). On 23 October, a week after breaking diplomatic relations with Britain, Musaddiq approved a temporary public security bill which was to remain in effect during an emergency period of three months (*MQ*, p. 85). The bill, much criticized by his opponents, provided that anyone inciting others to strike, or to create insurrection or disorder would be arrested and subject to internal exile for a minimum of three months to a maximum of one year. At the same time, the bill confirmed that public assembly remained legal, while demonstrations in public thoroughfares that resulted in clashes, public panic or disorder were forbidden. Implementation of these regulations was given to the military governor and the military courts wherever martial law was in effect. In November, Musaddiq approved a bill penalizing the disruption of or damage to communication and electrical facilities (*MQ*, pp. 116–17).

On 14 February 1953 he approved a bill which prohibited strikes by civil servants and established monetary fines and possible dismissal for violators (*MQ*, pp. 237–8).

At a time when Iran was in a state of emergency, the Majlis continued to play the decisive role in determining the degree to which the need for public security required curtailment of political freedoms. Martial law was not only freely discussed in the press but was under periodic review by the Majlis. For example, on 6 November 1952, parliament approved the extension of martial law in Tehran for a period of two months (*Ittila'at*, 6 November 1952). Moreover, while martial law was in effect, the vocal and independent Majlis continued to evaluate Musaddiq's conduct by periodic votes of confidence. As late as 6 January 1953, for example, the Musaddiq administration received a vote of confidence from the Majlis with 64 out of 80 votes in its favour (*Ittila'at*, 6 January 1953).

It had been known for some time that General Fazlullah Zahidi was the key figure in a plan to overthrow Musaddiq. It is instructive to review the way in which Musaddiq dealt with this major adversary. On 24 February 1953, General Zahidi was arrested on charges of inciting opposition to the government (*Ittila'at*, 24 February). In less than a month, however, he was released from prison (*Ittila'at*, 17 March). As part of a concerted plan to disrupt Musaddiq's rule of law, the head of the national police, General Mahmud Afshartus, was kidnapped in Tehran in April. He was later taken outside the city, kept in a cave for 48 hours, and murdered (*Ittila'at*, 20 April). General Zahidi was strongly suspected of being a leader of this conspiracy, yet on 4 May he was allowed to take sanctuary in the Majlis by Ayatullah Kashani, the speaker, and Musaddiq did nothing to prevent it (*Ittila'at*, 4 May). General Zahidi remained under the protection of the Majlis until July, when he was allowed to leave and go into hiding in preparation for his successful overthrow of the Musaddiq government.

Improving the lot of the peasants, urban poor and labour

As the first exercise of his newly granted powers, on 13 August 1952, Dr Musaddiq approved a bill abolishing feudal dues and forced labour in the villages (*MQ*, pp. 24–5). The following week, he approved a bill which enabled the Ministry of Finance to sell government land in Tehran in small lots to those needing housing (*MQ*, p. 26). During the same month, the government announced that sugar, an essential commodity to the Iranian masses, could not be kept in storage in excessive amounts, and that hoarding would be subject to confiscation (*MQ*, p. 33).

The following October, Musaddiq approved a bill which deducted 20 per cent from the landowners' share in agricultural products. Half of the proceeds were distributed among the peasants who had produced the commodity and the other half were placed at the disposal of the newly established local development fund. This fund was to be used to provide for drinking water, pest control, education, assistance to the elderly, loans to needy farmers, construction and maintenance of mosques, public baths, low-cost housing, mortuaries, laundry facilities, bridges, warehouses, rural roads, schools, electric power plants, and promotion of cottage industries. In each village a local council composed of five members would be elected. The members included the legally elected village headman, a represent-ative of the local landowners, and three representatives of the local peasants (*MQ*, pp. 60–7).

On 24 November 1952, Musaddiq approved a bill placing a tax on domestically consumed gasoline, to provide aid for the unemployed and the needy (*MQ*, p. 115). The following January he approved a bill reducing by 10 per cent rents on all residential and commercial buildings that were rented for less than 3,000 rials per month. At the same time, real estate taxes on such buildings were increased by 10 per cent. The proceeds from this tax were placed at the disposal of the newly organized Construction Bank for the purpose of building low-cost housing on government land. The new units would be rented or sold with long-term financing to qualified buyers (*MQ*, p. 200). The articles of association of the Construction Bank were approved the following week (*MQ*, pp. 204–8). Subsequently, two housing projects were completed in Tehran, one in Narmak and the other in the Naziabad district.

A major step to improve the lot of the workers was taken on 21 January 1953, when Musaddiq approved a comprehensive and progressive workers' social security bill containing 96 articles (*MQ*, pp. 35–56). This bill, which established the Workers' Social Security Organization, obliged all factories and firms covered by the labour law to insure their employees with the organization. As a result of this bill, workers and their immediate families would be eligible to receive insurance benefits in case of accident, illness, physical disability, marriage, pregnancy and delivery, retirement, burial, and unemployment. All workers were also to be given a medical examination before employment and once every two years thereafter. Those workers found to be ill would be given treatment by the Social Security Organization.

The organization's 11-man council included not only government representatives but also two representatives each from the employers' associations and the labour unions. As a means of reducing bureaucratic inefficiencies, the bill provided for the payment of certain benefits by local Settlement Councils. The Social Security Organization was funded by fees paid by the workers and employers (4 per cent and 8 per cent, respectively, of the workers' wages).

Economic development

Critics have accused the Musaddiq administration of bringing Iran's economy to ruin. There is no question but that the nationalization of the oil industry and Britain's unwillingness to negotiate in good faith to resolve the dispute with Iran eliminated the country's main source of foreign exchange and reduced government revenue. Nonetheless, it is important to note that the economy was in dire condition even before Musaddiq became prime minister.

For some time the Iranian public had been told that the Seven-Year Economic Development Plan, devised with the assistance of an American firm, Overseas Consultants Inc., was the cure for Iran's economic ills and that General Razmara's administration possessed the political will to carry it out. Yet on 8 January 1951, five months before Musaddiq took office, it was announced that Iran's contract with the consultants had been cancelled. In response, Overseas Consultants Inc. issued a statement asserting that the plan was 'doomed from the start' because of Iranian political interference (*MEJ* 5 (1951), p. 204). A month before Musaddiq assumed power, the government's financial condition had become so desperate that the Majlis ordered the National Bank (Bank-i Milli) to call in all 500 and 1,000 rial notes to raise enough money to pay civil servants and soldiers. The parliament also met to discuss special measures that could be taken to deal with the financial crisis developing in the country.[16] On 20 October 1952 Musaddiq approved a five-year plan for the construction, improvement, and maintenance of the country's highways (*MQ*, pp. 80–1). And on 30 October he approved a bill providing for compulsory third-party insurance for drivers of all motor vehicles (*MQ*, pp. 89–90).

Musaddiq took an even more important step when, on 26 November, he approved the articles of association of the National Iranian Oil Company that would own and operate Iran's oil industry. A few of the features of this document clarify Musaddiq's views on two important points: the role of the Majlis in government and the place of foreign nationals in Iran. The articles of association stated that the company was run by a board of directors which was to be selected by its High Council. The council was composed of two ministers, the president of the Bank Milli, and four representatives of the legislative branch (which Musaddiq was accused of wanting to dominate). Regarding the place of foreign nationals in Iran, the articles of association stated that, while the chairman of the board of directors and the managing director had to be of Iranian nationality, the other four members of the board could be from other countries, provided that the Council of Ministers and the legislative branch approved their appointments (*MQ*, pp. 118–22). Musaddiq was, therefore, not a blind xenophobe; he merely opposed foreign domination in Iranian affairs.

In order to properly administer, expand and support the nation's industries, the Central Industrial Supervisory Board was established in Tehran on 26 November 1952, to be headed by the minister of the National Economy, representatives of the Ministry of Labour, the Plan Organization, the Bank Milli and an expert in industrial matters. Local boards could also be established in other cities. The boards were charged with supervision, support and guidance of factories and workshops in technical, financial, productional and administrative matters. In the future, local supervisory boards would have to approve financial assistance to industrial enterprises. Government assistance would be limited to those firms that followed the guidelines of the central and local boards. All cutbacks in production and plant shutdowns had to be approved by the local board; otherwise, the board was empowered to take over management of the factory. The board, on the other hand, was obliged to familiarize all firms under its supervision with industrial and cost-accounting techniques (*MQ*, pp. 130–2).

The following month, Musaddiq approved the bill governing mining, which dealt with discovery, ownership, exploitation and fees for mines. A High Council of Mines was established to determine policy and to supervise implementation of the regulations (*MQ*, pp. 149–55).

With the shutdown of the oil industry and termination of oil revenues, Musaddiq launched his 'Economy without oil' programme. As a part of that programme, on 20 January 1953, Musaddiq approved a bill promoting exports. Accordingly, exporters were provided with various incentives, including discounts on domestic transportation, as well as tax and tariff exemptions. Another step was the establishment of an organization to control the quality of exported items (*MQ*, pp. 144–7). The following month the Export Promotion Bank was established to expand exports, compare local export items with international standards, and advise exporters about foreign markets (*MQ*, pp. 242–8).

Financial reforms

Lack of oil income not only affected Iran's foreign exchange earnings, it also reduced government income. In order to deal with this reduction, the government attempted to increase revenues by collecting unpaid taxes, simplifying regulations, and making the employees of the Ministry of Finance more responsive to the taxpayers. To this end, on 21 August 1952, Dr Musaddiq approved a new regulation for the settlement of unpaid taxes (*MQ*, pp. 34–5). This was followed by the establishment of criminal penalties for those officials refusing to issue tax clearance certificates to taxpayers who had settled their accounts (*MQ*, pp. 32–3), thereby dealing with one source of corruption. To raise new revenue from those who could afford it, on 12 December Musaddiq approved a land tax equal to 3 per cent of the value of land over a certain minimum size in all major cities (*MQ*, pp. 133–5). This was followed in February with a bill that simplified certain sections of the income tax law (*MQ*, pp. 217–21).

Education

One of the nine points in Musaddiq's programe was the improvement of Iran's educational system. On 8 January 1953 Musaddiq approved a bill establishing the High Council of Education, to improve and expand all aspects of education throughout the country. The composition of this council included the minister of Education, the chancellor of Tehran University, and the director-general of the Ministry of Education. However, in order to involve the legislative branch in important educational affairs, the chairman of the Education Committee of the Majlis was also included. As an indication of respect for religion, a member of the clergy, selected by one of the senior clergy of Tehran, was also appointed. Moreover, a number of council members – all of high rank – were to be *elected* by members of their professions: three members of the faculty of Tehran University by the university council; a physician by the physicians of Tehran; an engineer by the engineers of Tehran; a jurist by the General Council of the Court of Cassation (Hayat-i Umumi-yi Divan-i Kishvar); three Tehran secondary school teachers by the representatives of the secondary school teachers; and, finally, two Tehran primary school teachers by the representatives of the primary school teachers (the bill also prescribed the procedure by which representatives of the teachers would be elected).

Like the board of directors of the National Iranian Oil Company, the High Council of Education could include foreign nationals. The bill stipulated that the council could invite as honorary members foreign scholars who specialized in education or in the field of Middle Eastern studies – further evidence that Musaddiq was not a xenophobe, but a patriotic Iranian who wanted to improve his country without foreign domination.

Among its duties, the council was authorized to approve all school regulations and curricula, and to encourage scholarship. It would also approve the organizational structure of the Ministry of Education, issue licences for new kindergartens, primary and secondary schools, and assess the credentials of foreign experts to be employed in Iran's education system (*MQ*, pp. 192–6).

The independence of universities from government interference has been an important issue in Iran's educational as well as political history.

Although the goal of independence was stated in the 1934 law establishing Tehran University, the enabling legislation had not been approved. On 11 January 1953, Musaddiq approved a bill giving financial independence to Tehran University (*MQ*, pp. 201–2).

Public health

To improve public health, Musaddiq took a number of steps. On 20 October 1952, he reorganized the Razi Institute, which produced vaccines (*MQ*, pp. 78–80). The following February he approved a bill revising the 1943 law regarding establishment of the state pharmaceutical organization (*MQ*, pp. 216–17). To facilitate the employment of graduates of nursing schools, a bill specifying civil service grades for them was passed on 1 January 1953 (*MQ*, p. 164), and a week later Musaddiq approved a bill with respect to the education and employment of public health workers (*MQ*, pp. 196–8). Perhaps the most significant health programme of the Musaddiq administration was the one dealing with the eradication of malaria from Iran.

Judiciary

Musaddiq believed that a competent and honest judiciary was an essential element in promoting democratic government in Iran. Hence, reform of the judicial branch and rooting out of corruption was a high priority. On 9 September 1952, using his limited legislative powers, Musaddiq revised the law pertaining to employment of judges. According to article 1 of this law, a commission composed of high-ranking jurists would review the records of judges considered incompetent or corrupt by the Ministry of Justice and would rule on whether they should remain in office. Article 15 of the law required that new employees of the judiciary be approved by a special commission composed of the president and two elected members of the Court of Cassation. Judges were given back the security of remaining in their post regardless of the popularity of their judicial decisions as they could no longer be transferred at the will of the minister of Justice (*MQ*, pp. 28–32). At the same time, Musaddiq abolished the special courts (*mahakim-i ikhtisasi*) (*MQ*, pp. 27–8), and reorganized the court system (*MQ*, pp. 73–8). As a result, disputes would no longer be heard in special courts, often held outside of the court's jurisdiction, but in ordinary courts within the judiciary itself. He also abolished the Department of Supervision of the Ministry of Justice, and in its place created the Office of the Disciplinary Prosecutor of Judges (Dadsara-yi Intizami-i Quzat), which would prosecute alleged misconduct of jurists before the High Disciplinary

Court (Dadgah-i Ali-yi Intizami), providing for judicial rather than administrative review of alleged wrongdoing by jurists (*MQ*, pp. 71–3). Later in September, he approved the bill regarding the reorganization of the administrative structure of the Ministry of Justice (*MQ*, pp. 90–2). On 11 November 1952, as part of his anti-corruption drive, he empowered the minister of Justice to replace within five days the presiding officers of the judicial branches of the Court of Cassation and the disciplinary courts (Divan-i Kishvar va Dadgah-i Intizami) (*MQ*, pp. 111–12). This measure has been misrepresented by some critics as the dissolution of the Supreme Court. Finally, on 2 January 1953, he approved a bill revising certain provisions of Iran's civil code of 1939 (*Ayin-i dadrasi-yi madani*) (*MQ*, pp. 169–92).

Building democratic institutions

Building and strengthening democratic institutions were given high priority by Musaddiq. On 2 November 1952 he approved comprehensive legislation with 90 articles regarding municipalities (*MQ*, pp. 92–111). According to this bill, each village and town would be governed by a local council with between nine and 30 members (men or women) who would be elected by secret ballot. An important innovation, which Musaddiq had supported for many years as a means of preventing election fraud, was that only those who could write were eligible to vote. Another important provision was that women were no longer ineligible as electors. A third feature of the law was that the executive officer of each village or town would be a mayor *elected* by the local council rather than *appointed* by the central government. The council would also have the authority to question and discharge the mayor.

On 24 December 1952, Musaddiq approved a bill revising the law of 1942 regarding the establishment of chambers of commerce (*MQ*, p. 156). Again, to ensure proper and democratic elections, the board of directors was to be elected by secret ballot in general meeting of all members of the chamber. It is worth noting that in later years voting was carried out by proxy: the candidates would all collect as many membership cards as they could and deposit an equivalent number of ballots for themselves.

While the Tehran Chamber of Commerce was to have 30 members, provincial chambers would have only 10 to 18 members. However, at least one member of various categories of business, such as manufacturing, transportation and insurance, had to be represented on the board. In addition, representatives of registered guilds would also have seats on the board: eight in Tehran and two or three in the provinces. Once again, it is important to note that in later years the guilds were no longer associated with the Chamber of Commerce and thus a rift was created between the more traditional and more modern segments of the business community. The Chamber of Commerce had one function of particular importance: the Ministry of National Economy was obliged to consult it before the enactment of laws and regulations affecting the business community.

Another important bill provided for the independence of the legal profession from the Ministry of Justice. This was accomplished by the establishment of an independent Bar association (*MQ*, pp. 239–42), with 12 board members elected by members of the profession. There would also be branches in provincial centres with boards of five members elected by the local lawyers. The duties of the association included issuing licences to new lawyers, supervision of lawyers' conduct, and investigation of possible misconduct. No member of the Bar could be discharged from his duties without the vote of the Lawyers' Disciplinary Court (Dadgah-i Intizami-yi Vukala).

The Press

Before Musaddiq became prime minister, the 16th Majlis had taken an important step towards freedom of the press when, on 9 January 1951, the deputies approved a bill repealing all previous press laws except for the liberal law of 8 February 1908 (*Ittila'at*, 9 January 1951). The bill received Senate approval on 18 January. On 4 February 1953, Musaddiq approved a new comprehensive press bill containing 64 articles under which the Ministry of the Interior would issue permits for the publication of newspapers and periodicals (*MQ*, pp. 224–33). A commission composed of the director-general of the Ministry of the Interior, a representative of the Ministry of Education, and the public prosecutor of Tehran would comprise the decision-making body.

All newspapers had to submit annual financial statements in order to identify their sources of funding. The press was also obliged to print responses made by those mentioned in their publications, whether newspapers or periodicals. A penalty of six months to three years in prison was set for inciting sabotage, arson, murder, robbery, or military disobedience. Publishing military secrets meant imprisonment of two to five years in wartime and six months to two years in time of peace. Statements injurious to Islam were punishable by prison terms of three months to one year. No insult to the Shah was permitted. Any private or public individual who was in any way defamed by the press could take his complaint to the public prosecutor, who could stop publication of the offending paper. The publisher, on the other hand, could protest to the city court.

In accordance with article 79 of the Constitution, press trials were to be conducted in the presence of a jury composed of representatives of the following seven groups: scholars and writers, members of the legal profession, businessmen, teachers, landowners and farmers, workers, and craftsmen and members of the guilds. Musaddiq himself took the lead in promoting the freedom of the press when, on 2 May 1951, he instructed the national police to disregard all derogatory statements about him.[17] A review of the opposition press of the time, which was full of critical comments regarding the prime minister, demonstrates that this order was not a public relations gesture, but a genuine attempt to give the press the courage to exercise their rights.

Conclusion

Although Musaddiq's adherence to democratic procedure was not absolute, *greater effort* was made by his administration to make laws more democratic, to make government more responsive to the public, and to govern the country by the rule of law than by any other administration in Iranian history. Moreover, Musaddiq's reforms were well conceived and far-reaching, although his administration was overthrown before they were fully implemented.

There were, however, a number of occasions when Musaddiq ignored democratic procedure. He can be faulted for promising to reopen the Senate and not doing so, and for failing to reform the electoral law, which was at the heart of his democratization programme. But his most serious mistake, and one that marked his administration, occurred during his last month as prime minister, when he held a referendum on the question of ending the 17th session of the Majlis and holding new elections for the 18th Majlis. The method adopted for voting on this question was blatantly undemocratic and left the validity of the electoral results in doubt: supporters and opponents voted at separate polling places.

Musaddiq's critics have attempted to overshadow unique accomplishments of his administration by concentrating on a handful of faulty decisions. The impression has been created that Musaddiq's methods were not unlike those of the Shah; a few distinctions between the Musaddiq administration and those of subsequent governments during the rule of the Shah should be drawn.

During the post-Musaddiq years, lofty goals were presented by successive administrations as pretexts for the systematic constriction of democratic procedures. More specifically, during this period the Shah employed authoritarian means to increase his personal power while reducing the power of independent democratic institutions. A review of the bills approved by Musaddiq demonstrates that during his administration a reverse course was followed: power was transferred from the Royal Court, the military and the privileged elite, not to Musaddiq but, in keeping with the Constitution, to the judiciary, local councils, professional associations and the public. It should also be remembered that Musaddiq's programme for reform was attempted without oil revenue in an atmosphere of constant domestic and foreign intrigue to overthrow his administration.

One of the first measures adopted by the Zahidi administration after Musaddiq was overthrown was to reinstate all civil servants and military personnel that had been discharged or retired because of incompetence or corruption.[18] Then the military courts were re-established. The 18th Majlis, hand-picked by General Zahidi, declared all bills approved by Dr Musaddiq to be unconstitutional and thus null and void.[19] Nevertheless, Musaddiq's initiatives were too popular with the public and too substantive in content to be totally disregarded. As a result, the Zahidi Majlis was obliged to approve revised and truncated versions of a large number of Musaddiq measures. Zahidi and the succeeding administration then proceeded to pay lip service to many of these laws (particularly those with political implications), but in practice to ignore their implementation.

The workers' social security law is a good example of a Musaddiq initiative that could not be officially ignored since the International Labour Office had aided in its preparation, and hundreds of thousands of workers counted on its implementation. The bill approved by the Zahidi Majlis, however, no longer contained the provision regarding modest unemployment benefits provided in the Musaddiq version.[20] Althought the social security bill was approved with little delay, more than ten years passed before even the major employers in the modern sector of industry were forced to pay their share of the premium.

Musaddiq is still blamed for introducing the public security law used during the Shah's rule to silence protest. A comparison of the bills approved by the Musaddiq and Zahidi administrations is instructive. While the Musaddiq bill was aimed exclusively at banning strikes and civil disorder for a period of three months, the Zahidi law, which was made permanent, expanded the jurisdiction of the law to peasants refusing to pay their dues to the landowners. Musaddiq's bill brought the accused before the regular courts for judgement except in regions under martial law, as approved by the Majlis (*MQ*, pp. 84–5). The Zahidi law created permanent regional public security commissions, composed of the local governor, head of the local court, the public prosecutor, chief of police, and chief of the gendarmerie, which could sentence the accused to internal exile. Judicial review provided by the Zahidi law was possible only after the sentence had begun and the accused had no right to be present at the hearing.[21]

Another important bill approved by Musaddiq which could not be set aside by Zahidi had established local councils and municipalities.[22] While keeping most of the provisions of this bill intact, the Zahidi Majlis dropped the important provision, designed to reduce corruption and fraud, requiring all electors to be able to write the names of the candidates of their choice.

The area on which Musaddiq placed the most emphasis was that of building and strengthening democratic institutions. This included framing bills which reformed the judiciary, encouraged the formation of various professional associations, and set up local councils. Musaddiq correctly believed that once a democratic base was created in Iran, measures dealing with social and economic improvements would be more effective.

The Musaddiq administration provided Iran with its first government dependent on popular support. During the difficult time they held office, Dr Musaddiq and his colleagues made a genuine effort to govern the country and reform it in accordance with the Constitution. Not always successful, the Musaddiq administration nevertheless presented Iranians with a standard of social justice and political participation they had never experienced before or since.

Notes

The following abbreviations have been made in the text: *Middle East Journal* to *MEJ*; *Majmu'eh-i qavanin 1331* (Tehran, 1953) to *MQ*.

1   Brian Lapping, *End of Empire* (London, 1985) pp. 213, 214, 215, 214.
2   Muhammad Riza Pahlavi, *The Shah's Story* (London, 1980) p. 53.
3   *Iran Yearbook* (Tehran, 1977) p. 17.
4   From Richard W. Cottam, *Nationalism in Iran* (Pittsburgh, 1964) p. 100.
5   Sepehr Zabih, *The Mossadegh Era* (Chicago, 1982) p. 112.
6   Ataullah Farhang-Qahramani, *Asami-yi namayandigan-i Majlis-i Shawra-yi Milli az aghaz-i mashrutiyyat ta dawreh-i 24 qanun-guzari va namayandigan-i Majlis-i Sina dar haft dawreh-i taqninieh az 2508 ta 2536 shahanshahi* (Tehran, 1977) pp. 221–31.
7   Barry Rubin, *Paved with Good Intentions* (New York, 1980) p. 73.
8   Zabih, *Mossadegh Era*, p. 77.
9   Ibid., p. 78.
10 Interview with Dr Muzzafar Baqa'i, New York, 24 June 1986.
11 Cited Rubin, *Good Intentions*, p. 73.
12 *Majmu'eh-i qavanin-i sal-i 1333* (Tehran, 1955) p. 74.
13 *Nutqha va maktubat-i Duktur Musaddiq*, vol. 2, book 3 (Paris, 1971) pp. 121–7.
14 Ibid., pp. 155–8.
15 See chapter 10 of this book.
16 *Le Monde*, 20 March 1951.
17 Buzurgmihr, Jalil, *Musaddiq dar mahkameh-i nizami*, vol. I, p. 15.
18 *Majmu'eh-i qavanin 1333*, p. 75.
19 Ibid., p. 74.
20 *Majmu'eh-i qavanin-i sal-i 1334* (Tehran, 1956) pp. 114–57.
21 *Majmu'eh-i qavanin 1334*, pp. 179–80.
22 *Majmu'eh-i qavanin 1333*, p. 185.

4

The role of the clergy in Iranian Politics, 1949–1954

SHAHROUGH AKHAVI

Introduction[1]

Since the Iranian revolution, the Islamic Republic has encouraged reassessments of the clergy's role in politics. Generally, the Khomeini view stresses clerical activism and participation during the 1949–54 period. Specifically, Ayatullah Abu'l Qasim Kashani (d. 1962) has been lionized as the leader of the anti-British movement and spearhead of oil nationalization. Kashani is exonerated of having collaborated with the monarchists to overthrow Musaddiq's government on 19 August 1953. He is now seen as the true hero of the nationalist movement who boldly challenged the British and Americans. Musaddiq has become something of an unperson. Khomeini, if he alludes to him at all, is said to refer to him as 'that nationalist man'.[2]

Kashani's rehabilitation has advanced also in the West.[3] Without following in this tradition, the present paper addresses the ulama's role during the Musaddiq era in the context of Kashani's activism. I do not accept Tehran's revisionist views of Kashani as the misunderstood patriot who tried to save Iran from imperialism *despite* Musaddiq's authoritarianism at the end of his tenure. In fact, pieces of evidence are emerging to suggest that the Americans offered Kashani – and he may have accepted – funds to take an anti-Musaddiq position during the coup of August 1953. It is possible to argue that by receiving such money Kashani was making a tactical move, and it did not mean that he had *strategically* aligned himself with western interests. Certainly Kashani stood to gain if Musaddiq fell. But to argue that Kashani broke with Musaddiq, that the West engineered Musaddiq's downfall after this break, that the West retained its oil interests, and that therefore (sic) Kashani was a western agent is indeed to argue in a *post hoc ergo propter hoc* fashion.

My conclusions are more mundane. These are:

1 Cleavages existed among the clergy.
2 The majority of the ulama remained aloof from politics until about March 1953.
3 Kashani was undoubtedly the most important clerical actor in national politics.
4 The clerics finally opposed Musaddiq because they feared republicanism, communism, anticlerical policies, neglect of the clergy and religion in public life.

In consequence, the ulama – with some exceptions – supported monarchy, conservative economic values, and respect for Islamic norms, law and institutions in social relations. They spoke of Iranians not as the religio-political community (*ummat*) of Islam but as the *people* (*millat*) of Iran. They rallied around oil nationalization, although major figures chose silence over engagement. They also opposed female enfranchisement, urged a ban on alcohol and attacked the press for carrying articles critical of religion. Neither Kashani nor the ulama generally justified their political activism or aloofness from politics in terms of doctrinal principles of the imamate or *vilayat* (rule exercised by the Imam).

The years between 1949 and 1954 can be divided into five periods. The first begins a month before the attempted assassination of the Shah in February 1949 and ends in April 1951 when Musaddiq became prime minister. The second coincides with the time of Musaddiq's first government, ending with his dramatic resignation and the Shah's failure to replace him with a viable alternative. This was a time of good feelings between Kashani and Musaddiq. The third covers a time of increasing tension between the two leaders, ostensibly due to Kashani's anger over Musaddiq's requests, in August 1952 and again in January 1953, for emergency powers. The fourth is notable for the final rupture between the Ayatullah and the prime minister and the *coup d'état* that overthrew the Musaddiq's government. The final period takes us from the coup to the year 1954.

January 1949–April 1951

At the beginning of this period anti-British sentiment was growing rapidly in the country in response to the so-called Gass-Gulsha'iyan supplementary agreement on oil. This agreement, which was a weak effort to revise the one-sided 1933 Oil Agreement between the Anglo-Persian Oil Company (APOC) and Iran, was introduced at the end of the 15th Majlis (January 1946–June 1947). The pro-British government of the time tried to force its ratification through the parliament, but the opposition destroyed it with filibusters.

The main group of the Iranian clergy, led since 1946 by Ayatullah Muhammad Husayn Burujirdi (d. 1961) was more concerned with strengthening Shii institutions than trafficking in politics. Following the attempt on the Shah's life in early February 1949 telegrams expressing indignation and regret were sent. Burujirdi wrote: 'May God Almighty preserve [your] kingdom.' Other ulama, including Ayatullah Fayz of Qum, Ayatullah Muhammad Bihbihani of Tehran and Ayatullah Abdul Karim Zanjani of Najaf similarly sent messages. Perhaps the most effusive reaction was that from Najaf by Ayatullah Hibat al-Din al-Shahristani: 'a curse on every abominable criminal who makes an attempt against this crown, this throne and this young shah.'[4]

Approximately a week later some 2,000 clergymen, ranging from grand *mujtahids* (Burujirdi, Fayz, Muhammad Hujjat, Sadr al-Din Sadr and Muhammad Taqi Khvansari) to lesser ranking ayatullahs, preachers and students, convened a conference in Qum. Its resolutions forbade clergymen from joining political parties or otherwise engaging in politics. Disobedience would result in defrocking, although no mechanism for this exists in Shii Islam (*Ittila'at*, 19 February 1949). The failure to define political activity was to allow not only Kashani's consistent political involvements, but also that of others on issues ranging from oil nationalization to women's suffrage.

The National Front was formed in the fall of 1949, with Kashani in exile, when Musaddiq and some 20 partisans protested against election fraud, martial law and the press law.[5] The 16th session of the Majlis began in February 1950, and Kashani was elected *in absentia* as a representative of Tehran. The National Front deputies immediately began to press for the nationalization of (what was now called) the Anglo-Iranian Oil Company (AIOC). At approximately the same time, a member of the Fida'iyan-i Islam – a militant fundamentalist group – assassinated the former prime minister and then minister of Court, Abdul Husayn Hazhir in November 1949.

It is said that Kashani's allies in Qum, most particularly Ayatullah Khvansari, urged Burujirdi to pressure the regime for Kashani's return from exile. Eventually, the government relented, and he arrived on 9 June 1950 from Lebanon, where he had been dispatched by the Shah after the abortive assassination attempt against the ruler in February 1949. He was welcomed by two senior Tehran clerics with strong ties to Burujirdi, namely ayatullahs Muhammad Bihbihani and Baha al-Din Nuri. Musaddiq and his associates also went to the airport to greet the returning cleric.

Although a member of parliament, Kashani chose not to attend Majlis sessions but instead issued public proclamations and messages to Musaddiq. For example, he publicly condemned those who had exiled him for their cowardice on the oil issue (*Ittila'at*, 18 June 1950). Another time, Musaddiq read his letter to the Majlis condemning the government's oil policy and rebuking the Senate for strengthening the Shah's powers[6] (half of its membership was to be appointed by him). A month later, Musaddiq read another Kashani missive to the Majlis, this time attacking the bill on provincial councils, as it was tantamount to a British plot to weaken the central government and fragment the country.[7]

Kashani also attacked Prime Minister Razmara, who had been Chief of General Staff when the Shah was wounded in the February 1949 assassination attempt, for having behaved 'repressively'. As prime minister, Razmara in June 1950 had ordered the forceful dispersal of anti-government crowds in Parliament Square. Kashani further charged Razmara with trying to borrow secretly £30 million from the AIOC, in contravention of article 25 of the Constitution (*Ittila'at*, 6 August 1950).

The clerics of Qum, by contrast, abjured the political scene. Qum had been economically devastated during the second world war. The founder of Qum's theological seminary, Ayatullah Abdul Karim Ha'iri Yazdi (d. 1936) had had to deal with Riza Shah's severely anticlerical policies. Upon his death a caretaker regime of triumvirs administered the seminary for a decade: ayatullahs Muhammad Taqi Khvansari (d. 1952), Muhammad Hujjat Kuhkamarah'i (d. 1953) and Sadr al-Din Sadr (d. 1954). In 1946, Burujirdi found Qum in deep trouble. He appealed for private-sector financial assistance to the seminary and attributed the city's economic condition to the stagnation of commerce following the war, which had led to a drop in *khums* contributions by bazaar merchants to the clergy (*Ittila'at*, 6 June 1950).

Clerical affairs thus seemed encapsulated by Qum's financial worries and abstinence from politics and Kashani's preference – supported by a few important clerics such as Khvansari and Muhammad Khurramabadi in Qum – for political activism. But after Razmara's death at the hands of a member of the Fida'iyan-i Islam, other important clerics tentatively entered the political arena, and increasing numbers of higher clergymen began to issue *fatvas* on the need to nationalize the AIOC. Among these clerics were ayatullahs Khvansari, Muhammad Riza Kalbasi, Baha al-Din Mahallati, Mahmud Ruhani Qummi and Abbas Ali Shahrudi. All but Kalbasi referred to Kashani by name, and Shahrudi mentioned Kashani's political acumen, while Mahallati declared it a 'religious duty' to co-operate with Kashani. All five were senior clerics. In addition to their *fatvas*, letters in support of Kashani came from ayatullahs Khalil Kuhkamarah'i and Muhammad Baqir Kuhkamarah'i.[8]

Indeed, it seems that the death of Razmara, who had publicly stated that Iranians could not even run a cement factory, much less the oil industry, released the floodgates of ulama *fatvas*. But clerical activism could be discerned even before his departure from the scene, as in the speech in Parliament Square of Sayyid Ja'far Gharavi on 29 December 1950 and the open letter by theological seminary students published on 7 January 1951 (*Ittila'at*, 30 December 1950; 7 January 1951); and more spectacularly the simultaneous *fatvas* by seven *mujtahids*: ayatullahs Husayn Chahar Suqi, Muhammad Husayn Mallaz Rawza'i (*sic* Rawzati?), Mihdi Najafi, Husayn Khadimi, Murtaza Mudarris Ardakani, Mustafa al-Araqayn, and Muhammad Baqir Rasuli.[9]

April 1951–July 1952

After Razmara's death the parliamentary Oil Commission voted on 8 March 1951 for nationalization, the Majlis approved it on 15 March, the Senate on 20 March, and enabling legislation was enacted on 26 April. Meanwhile, a strike among Khuzistan workers was met by British war ships showing the flag in the Persian Gulf, while Musaddiq and Kashani tried to end the strike. On 27 April Husayn Ala resigned as prime minister, and the next day the Shah named Musaddiq to replace him.

Meanwhile, Kashani's influence began to increase. Shortly after the Majlis approved the nationalization, Kashani was asked if he was more popular than the Shah: 'Naturally, the people are normally inclined to those who serve them in a self-sacrificing way . . . I also have influence in Iraq. My influence there is even greater than in Iran.' Kashani declared Razmara's assassin to be an agent of the people of Iran and urged his release. But he denied he had any links to the Fida'iyan. When asked what if the Shah had been found to be a collaborator of Razmara, Kashani replied: 'The Shah has absolutely no responsibility in the national government, and beyond that I cannot say anything more' (*Ittila'at*, 17 March 1951). This statement contrasts with Musaddiq's views of the Shah's control over the military and with Kashani's own unhappiness with the Shah's increased powers when, after the February 1949 assassination attempt, he had martial law declared and convened a Constituent Assembly which vested him with the right to dissolve the Majlis.

Upon Musaddiq's appointment, Kashani thanked the Majlis for its decision to nationalize the AIOC and also declared:

> so that . . . Dr Muhammad Musaddiq be completely at liberty in choosing his aides, from the very beginning I am refraining from giving any advice to him *and shall abstain from doing so hereafter* so that he will not feel any constraints in carrying out his responsibilities. [Emphasis added] (*Ittila'at*, 5 May 1951)

But Kashani *did interfere* in Musaddiq's appointments, as will be seen. Ironically, Musaddiq wanted Kashani to adhere to Burujirdi's line of clerical political quietism, whereas Kashani iterated and reiterated that politics and religion in Islam are inseparable. Islam has no curia, he noted; clerical activism in politics means to attend to the affairs of the Muslims – a clear religious duty (*Ittila'at*, 17 March; 5 June). Personality conflicts were perhaps possible. Musaddiq was the aristocrat who nevertheless aspired to speak for the common people and was seemingly areligious, if not a secularist. Kashani was from a lower social class background, and grandly declared about his own role: 'My rising up in Iran against oppression and misery has today caused the entire world of Islam to appreciate our movement . . .' (*Ittila'at*, 5 June).

With Musaddiq in power, did the Burujirdi clerics become 'more political'? It seems that during Musaddiq's first government, from 28 April 1951 to 20 July 1952, they remained well in the background. Occasionally, they demanded more attention to public morality and the *shari'a*. For example, Ayatullah Bihbihani in early May 1951 appealed for public vigilance against attempts to subvert religious teachings: attend the mosques, he admonished. 'All classes should get close to Almighty God and, *in accordance with religious precepts*, put aside class conflict' [emphasis original] (*Ittila'at*, 5 June). Bihbihani, unlike Kashani, had direct access to the Court and publicly praised the Shah for ordering the closing of liquor stores on the eve of Ramadan (*Ittila'at*, 5 June); he regularly met with the minister of Court during religious holidays.[10] Interestingly, Bihbihani at one point requested the press to desist from writing about him so much and asked that the ulama as a whole be covered instead; the attention was causing him embarrassment, he said (*Ittila'at*, 23 November).

Meanwhile, elections were set for the 17th Majlis. A group of clerical deputies was elected to the Majlis that was to form a nucleus of clerical support for Musaddiq's policies. Of course, not all clerical deputies were pro-Musaddiq, and some early backers later defected. Pro-Musaddiq clerics in parliament were: Shams al-Din Qanatabadi, from Shahrud (a defector from Musaddiq's ranks after January 1953); Ahmad Safa'i, from Qazvin (also to defect); Baqir Jalali Musavi, from Dāmavand; Hajj Sayyid Javadi, from Qazvin; Ibrahim Milani, from Tabriz; Muhammad Ali Angaji, from Tabriz; Murtaza Shabistari from Tabriz. Another cleric, Husayn Ali Rashid, the well-known preacher, was elected but seemingly never attended the Majlis.

This group was not cohesive. Only Qanatabadi was politically vocal. Others, such as Milani and Javadi, sometimes spoke out on minor issues (such as alcohol) or served on reconciliation committes in the Musaddiq–Kashani and Musaddiq–Shah disputes. Outside the Majlis, the strongest clerical supporters of Musaddiq were ayatullahs Abu'l Fazl Zanjani and his brother, Riza Zanjani. Of lesser importance was the younger Sayyid Mahmud Taliqani. The latter claims to have tried to mediate the dispute between Musaddiq and the Fida'iyan-i Islam but attributes his failure to 'enmity' (*khusumat*).[11]

As the crisis with Britain deepened, Kashani's publicly expressed support for Musaddiq kept pace in the first seven or eight months. He issued a veritable blizzard of manifestos on sundry topics, usually declaring his loyalty to the regime. With time, however, these proclamations became fewer and fewer, as did the warmth of his references to Musaddiq. A monthly count since the start of Musaddiq's government reveals the following pattern: May 1951: four; June: four; July: two; August: two; September: six; October: three; November: three; December: four; January 1952: none; February: one; March: one; April: none; May: none; June: none; July (prior to 30 Tir/22 July); one. Even if one were to count his interviews and telegrams, the decline in the Kashani–Musaddiq relationship can be documented before the 30 Tir/22 July events.[12]

At first Kashani urged steadfastness and resolve against the British, and he threatened to call a jihad in case of military hostilities. Accusing the British of seeking a pretext to intervene, he appealed constantly for unity of ranks at home. On the threat of communism, he either denied Soviet ulterior motives in Iran or else, somewhat inconsistently, declared that communism could only succeed due to British and American policies (*Ittila'at*, 12 August 1951), which would push Iranians to seek Soviet help.

Kashani urged patience while the government sought internal reforms. Musaddiq's Cabinet enjoys the support of the people, he claimed, and avowed his 'total backing' for him. He declared a 'financial jihad', urging Iranians to transfer accounts from the Imperial Bank (under British control) in Tehran to an Iranian bank in order to show solidarity against imperialism (*Ittila'at*, 31 July 1951). Kashani equated internal strife with warring with the Hidden Imam. His tactics included mass meetings in Parliament Square, one-day general strikes, telegrams communicating his views, etc. In a rare call for an Islamic government, he noted that it would end poverty, upon which communism thrives. We do know that he privately importuned Musaddiq to establish an Islamic system; the prime minister replied that his first task was to solve the oil crisis and then there would be time for the other.[13] On one occasion Musaddiq told Sayyid Mahmud Taliqani, 'I am not a man who calls for an Islamic government . . .'[14]

In late September 1951 Kashani declared that no foreign plot had been able to oust Musaddiq from the political arena. Two months later, he told Stewart Alsop of the *New York Herald Tribune* that no one could topple Musaddiq and rejected the American's suggestion that Qavam al-Saltaneh might be the next prime minister: 'I and the whole Iranian people fully favour and support [Musaddiq]' (*Ittila'at*, 25 November). And again, to a Japanese journalist: 'Since the only nationalist government is that of Dr Musaddiq, and he is working with total seriousness for the progress and glory of this country, I will *always* support him' [emphasis added] (*Ittila'at*, 19 December).

Toward the end of the honeymoon period between the two, on the first anniversary of the nationalization law, Kashani defended Musaddiq at a time of rising dissatisfaction with the state of the economy. He characterized as 'unfair' criticisms of the Cabinet for ruinous conditions which the British had caused (*Ittila'at*, 20 March 1952). But his enthusiasm had waned, and by March 1952 he was subdued. Noting Musaddiq's distress at the turmoil accompanying the 17th Majlis elections, Kashani argued that not even the prime minister could fight on all fronts at once. Some three weeks later, Kashani felt moved to deny to citizens of Fars province that the regime was seeking to rig the elections there.

The month of Ramadan was between May and June 1952. Riots occurred in the Shah Mosque of the Tehran bazaar against the sermons of Muhammad Taqi Falsafi, a preacher. Falsafi's anti-Musaddiq line led to crowd efforts to silence him. Some believe Kashani was at that time opposed to Falsafi's statements, although there is no convincing evidence to indicate this. In any case, the anti-Falsafi actions by the partisans of Musaddiq led to an outpouring of indignation by the Society of Preachers of Tehran, and even by Burujirdi himself. Falsafi had to hide several hours in the mosque's library until security forces came to rescue him. Some clerics felt that the government had not acted fast enough to rescue Falsafi. A telegram from Qum clerics and bazaar merchants referred to Falsafi's work as 'always in the service of . . . preserving the country's independence and the concerns and greatness of the monarchy'. Alleging that the Shah was a 'propagator of religious slogans', they implored 'the beloved Shah' to prevent recurrences of this sort of disturbance (*Ittila'at*, 1 June 1952).

Calling upon the Shah seemed to suggest that the clergy had little confidence that Musaddiq's government could rebuff anticlericalism. Kashani did not say anything publicly, and this omission may have hurt Musaddiq's standing somewhat. Yet, Kashani's sermon on the day of Musaddiq's return from the Hague in late June 1952 is worth noting as an act of support at a difficult time. Musaddiq's resignation on 17 July led to a meeting between the minister of Court and Kashani, presumably to probe the depth of Kashani's support for Musaddiq. Rumours were rife that Kashani had ordered the reopening of the Tehran bazaar, which had closed in support of Musaddiq. Another rumour had it that Kashani had been arrested on the 18 July by the government of Qavam al-Saltaneh, which itself lasted only three days. Neither rumour was substantiated, but Kashani was hardly ready to abandon Musaddiq at this time.

July 1952–January 1953

The Shah's opposition to Musaddiq came virtually out into the open at the start of this period. Musaddiq had Majlis support but the Senate refused to back him prior to the Shah's appointment. Ultimately, though, it gave in and 14 out of 36 votes were cast for Musaddiq, 19 were blank, one was for General Fazlullah Zahidi, and two ballots were invalidated. The Majlis gave Musaddiq 52 out of 65 votes cast (*Ittila'at*, 6 July 1952; 9 July). The Shah thereupon appointed Musaddiq, who then met with the ruler for three and a half hours (*Ittila'at*, 12 July; 16 July). They must have discussed Musaddiq's demand to appoint the War minister, and possibly Musaddiq raised the issue of placing the crown's endowed properties under the office of the prime minister. The Shah's refusal led to Musaddiq's resignation, but three days later he returned to power when Qavam al-Saltaneh failed to form a government. Musaddiq received a unanimous vote of confidence with 68 votes in the Majlis.

What role had Kashani played in Musaddiq's return to power? Could the prime minister have been returned without the ayatullah's support? The answer cannot be given with certainty. Kashani mobilized great crowds to protest Qavam's appointment, while Musaddiq retired from public view those few days. Presumably, had he wanted to do so, Kashani could have made it very hard for Musaddiq. But if Kashani had remained aloof, in my opinion, Musaddiq could undoubtedly have succeeded without him. As it was, a number of Kashani's devotees, along with non-Kashani people, were killed in the uprisings of 30 Tir. The prosecution of those responsible would be a rallying call for Kashani and his supporters against Musaddiq for many months.

Conflict began to emerge immediately over Musaddiq's appointments. In a letter to the prime minister, the cleric objected to the following appointees: General Ahmad Vusuq, who had been commander of the gendarmerie in the three-day government of Qavam al-Saltaneh and appointed as Deputy Minister of Defence after 30 Tir; Dr Ali Akbar Akhavi, Minister of Economics; Nusratullah Amini (post uncertain); General Muhammad Daftari, a relative of Musaddiq, Razmara's chief of the national police and appointed after 30 Tir commander of the Customs Guard. Vusuq had been the one to order the troops to open fire on demonstrators after Musaddiq's sudden resignation. Akhavi had spent time in the United States and was, according to Kashani, 'pro-American' and, in any case, 'not good for this job'. Amini was 'spineless'. And Daftari not only had served the hated Razmara but was personally responsible for Kashani's arrest and internal exile to Falak al-Aflak, a remote old citadel, upon Razmara's assassination.

Kashani thus retracted his earlier pledge to stay out of Musaddiq's way in regard to appointments. 'If things go on this way', he admonished, 'I will be forced to leave Tehran and perhaps Iran . . .' Musaddiq's reply reminded Kashani that Vusuq and Akhavi had agreed to work without compensation.

> I do not know what shortcomings and faults you see in them . . . If you want reforms to take place, you must abstain from interfering in matters for a while, especially since no sort of reform is possible unless the person undertaking them is completely independent . . .[15]

Despite Kashani's protests, the Majlis unanimously approved the new Cabinet (*Ittila'at*, 29 July 1952). The rejection of Kashani's views by clerical members of parliament can be seen in Hajj Sayyid Javadi's expression of 'good will' toward the new Cabinet ministers (*Ittila'at*, 27 July).

Nonetheless, Kashani's influence remained powerful among pro-Musaddiq deputies in the parliament. An eight-man committee, including a number of nationalist movement deputies, was designated to persuade Kashani to accept the speakership. Did the offer to Kashani stem from Musaddiq's desire to soothe his feelings? Possibly, although when the voting took place, Kashani received 47 votes, Mu'azzami (a senior aide of Musaddiq) 10, and four were blank ballots (*Ittila'at*, 7 August; 9 August). It was a strong showing for Kashani, but it could have been stronger.

These events set the stage for a torturous and finally bitter struggle for the leadership of the nationalist movement between the two men. The next benchmark came with Musaddiq's request for emergency powers. This request was granted by the Majlis on 12 August 1952 (*Ittila'at*, 13 August). As far as I am aware, Kashani did not publicly object to this original request for emergency powers. Yet he could not have been pleased, and when Musaddiq sought an extension five months later, Kashani opposed it. No doubt Musaddiq's immense popularity in July 1952, returned to power at the same time that the World Court ruled it lacked jurisdiction in the oil dispute, ruled out any opposition by Kashani to Musaddiq's original request for emergency powers. But he continued to carp in private. For example, in late August 1952 one of his letters was handed to the prime minister by an intermediary who, while claiming harmony between the two leaders, added: 'The only expectation that exists [i.e. Kashani's expectation] is to expedite [the process] of legal decision making in order to secure political results' (*Ittila'at*, 25 August).

Still, in public Kashani continued to urge support for Musaddiq. Noting that reforms were lagging, he said, 'For us to succeed on this path, my opinion is that everyone must support Dr Musaddiq' (*Ittila'at*, 23 September); and, for good measure, Musaddiq 'is impartial' and would take good advice on how to attach 'greater seriousness' to reforms (*Ittila'at*, 23 September).

But Kashani's partisan, Shams al-Din Qanatabadi, was more blunt. Reforms require tools, the ministries are the tools, but the ministers themselves are the problem, he argued. Waste, oppression and chaos are the legacies respectively of the minister of Finance, the minister of Justice and the minister of Economics, in his words. Yet, unaccountably Qanatabadi recommended non-interference by the Majlis in governmental appointments and suggested open-armed co-operation, instead (*Ittila'at*, 23 September). Two days later, Kashani met Musaddiq for half an hour, but they failed to resolve their differences.

Problems between Musaddiq and the Shah continued to sharpen, and his negotiations with Washington, London and the World Bank seemed to be going nowhere. It is clear that the army was not securely behind Musaddiq. For example, in October 1952 the government announced the arrest of retired General Abdul Husayn Hijazi, along with the notorious Rashidian brothers (wealthy merchants) for plotting with a foreign embassy to overthrow the regime. Others, including those who enjoyed parliamentary immunity (a veiled reference to General Zahidi, then a senator) were also under suspicion (*Ittila'at*, 13 October).[16] Zahidi, though not specifically mentioned, nevertheless made a speech in which he angrily protested his innocence (*Ittila'at*, 15 October).

In the meanwhile, Kashani departed for the pilgrimage to Mecca. Upon his return he learned of the death in Qum of Ayatullah Khvansari, an ally whose prominence provided Kashani with the greatest support he could receive from the backing of any one cleric. Kashani went directly to Qum and stayed at the late Khvansari's home, where he was visited by Burujirdi (*Ittila'at*, 22 September).

Returning to Tehran, he told the *New York Herald Tribune* that he had no conflicts with Musaddiq. Asked about the Shah, Kashani replied: 'The Shah of Iran has followed the inclination of the people in the movement against imperialism, and he is supporting Dr Musaddiq's government and the people's movement with all his might' (*Ittila'at*, 1 November). Whether Kashani believed this or was trying to improve his poor image in the Court is not clear.

When asked about communism, Kashani had a range of answers. One was to blame the British for any appeal it might have in the country. Another was that religion and nationalism would prevent its spread. As to the threat posed by Iranian communists, he replied that he regarded all Iranians as brothers fighting the common enemy, imperialism (*Ittila'at*, 13 September). He denied the Tudeh (communist) Party would seize power and rejected the possibility of Tudeh deputies becoming ministers in the Cabinet (*Ittila'at*, 1 November 1952). Asked if a beleaguered Iran would accept Soviet military help, Kashani answered that the regime would look to Islamic countries but allowed that the Soviet–Iranian Treaty of 1921 permitted the Soviets to send their troops into the country were the

British to invade (*Ittila'at*, 5 June 1951). Later, he again answered a question on Soviet military assistance by saying Iran would seek the best interests of the people, but 'As long as such a situation has not arisen, one cannot say what method the government would choose . . .' (*Ittila'at*, 5 November 1952).

Another argument on clerical opposition to Musaddiq is that the ulama feared his 'leftism'. The land question is normally a good indicator of whether policy is 'leftist' or 'rightist'. Musaddiq was hardly radical in his approach to the land problem, with his proposal that landlords increase peasant income by 20 per cent. The Qum establishment opposed land reform, but Kashani was more pragmatic. He once argued that land reform was not necessary because lands in Khuzistan, once freed from the control of the AIOC, could be brought under cultivation in an unprecedented way (*Ittila'at*, 17 March 1951). To a French journalist he returned to this theme and added: 'I am very hopeful that in the next Majlis beneficial laws will be approved for the reform of agriculture and its full improvement' (*Ittila'at*, 10 February 1952). But seven months later, he seemed to advocate out-and-out land redistribution:

It is true that Islam has accepted the principle of property ownership. But at the same time, in order to protect the homeland and observe the general interests of the Muslim people, the state can expropriate the property of people in order to avert the accumulation of wealth and property which has been brought together against the [principles of] social justice and declare such possessions to be *haram* [forbidden]. (*Ittila'at*, 5 November 1952)

Kashani thus appeared flexible on issues of internal communism, Soviet policy towards Iran, and leftism. In this he differed from the Qum establishment which was very sensitive about these matters. Additionally, one notes that Kashani's discourse was laden with *nationalist* themes and symbols. In the citation above, it is significant that he refers to the 'homeland' (*vatan*) and the 'Muslim people' (*millat-i islam*), rather than to the 'community of believers' (*ummat-i islam*). Indeed, Mihdi Bazargan, whose religious credentials have always been deemed proper by most clergymen, has argued – somewhat hyperbolically, in my judgement – that the clerics' activities in the Musaddiq period 'were free of a religious character' (*khali az da'iyeh-i dini*).[17]

This is not to say Kashani was areligious, of course. He once said, for example, that 'the wellsprings of all the problems, poverty, backwardness and misery of the people is the lack of religious belief . . . all moral corruption and misery stem from irreligion . . .' (*Ittila'at*, 6 August 1952). And when asked by a reporter for the Italian newspaper *Oggi* which government was best for Iran, he replied that Musaddiq's was; but then, on reflection, he answered: 'If you mean the type of government, I must reply a government of real democracy that is in accordance with the true religion of Islam' (*Ittila'at*, 11 October 1952).[18]

Still, current reassessments of Kashani by the Khomeini regime that he believed in clericalism (*vilayat-i faqih*) are unacceptable. After all, many clerics of that period lamented that the mosques were half empty and people were in danger of forgetting Islam;[19] but it could not be said of them that they were precursors of Khomeinism. Moreover, Kashani used the word democracy, a term that the followers of Khomeini have tried to exorcise from the vocabulary of Iranian politics. Additionally, Kashani welcomed American Point IV (the US aid programme) assistance, urged an American loan of $100 million to Iran and met with American Ambassador Loy Henderson at least once for two and a half hours.[20] These were not actions consistent with a putative precursor of the Islamic Republic.

Kashani's greater pragmatism did not lessen his problems with Musaddiq. By November 1952 people were asking if he wanted to replace the prime minister. On at least two occasions he or a spokesman was forced to deny this (*Ittila'at*, 1 November 1952; 13 November). As late as mid-November 1952, Qantabadi flatly stated: 'Ayatullah Kashani is a true and total supporter of Dr Musaddiq's Cabinet (*Ittila'at*, 13 November) – hardly believable in view of Kashani's already stated opposition to certain Cabinet officials. Yet, two weeks later, Kashani himself declared:

> No sort of conflict – old or new – exists between myself and Dr Musaddiq. There is perfect, comprehensive and total agreement. For a conflict to exist there must be a reason, whereas both myself and Dr Musaddiq have one purpose. When the purpose is the same, in no way will a difference of views be found. (*Ittila'at*, 17 November 1952)

But it was not to last. Just three days later, after dozens of iterations about his agreement with Musaddiq, Kashani's defences broke down. Now, he declared: 'It is nothing serious. If we can call it a disagreement [*kudurat*] it will be taken care of . . . In any case, I cannot say anything further in this regard' (*Ittila'at*, 30 November). And what was the problem? This was left unclear. But among the domestic policy issues were the following: the bill to nationalize the telephone company, which Kashani opposed; a bill to ban alcohol, which other clergymen, but not so much Kashani, pushed; a new press law; a bill on employment; a bill on judicial reform; and a highly controversial bill on electoral reform, which sought to enfranchise women and was roundly denounced by the clerics[21] (but again not so much by Kashani). Finally, there were appointments by Dr Mihdi Azar, Minister of Education, to his ministry, which Kashani strongly opposed on grounds that the appointees were western trained.

Musaddiq became embittered over *ad hominem* attacks that

Qanatabadi, Ha'irizadeh, Baqa'i and others were directing at his ministers. But Kashani tried to modulate the dissonance:

> It's nothing important. A rift has appeared and will be dissipated. I am sure that the words of those who spoke in the Majlis on [25 November 1952] were not spoken with ulterior motives. For everyone supports Dr Musaddiq and the current government. (*Ittila'at*, 1 December 1952)

About this time local problems in Qum provided a rare opportunity for Burujirdi's followers to interact with the government. The first issue involved the regime's decision to fire the administrator of the shrine at Qum, Abu'l Fazl Tawliyyat, the Majlis deputy from that city. The power to remove him lay not with Burujirdi, but with the regime. Of course, Burujirdi's opinion would be weighed. Musaddiq sent a close collaborator, Husayn Makki, to Qum to talk with Burujirdi over the Tawliyyat affair and acquainted the cleric with the charges that Tawliyyat had violated his responsibilities by failing to send receipts of expenditures and income to Tehran. The regime had to declare martial law in Qum because Tawliyyat's supporters refused to accept his dismissal peacefully (*Ittila'at*, 6 November 1952; 10 December). Kashani, too, urged Tawliyyat's termination and, in view of the probable support Tawliyyat would have from Burujirdi, this is further evidence of no love lost between the two clerics. In the event, Tawliyyat managed to stay at his post – a clear rebuff to both Musaddiq and Kashani.

A second issue had the potential to damage Musaddiq's image in Qum. This was the Burqa'i affair, involving the leftward leaning cleric Ali Akbar Burqa'i. The press referred to Burqa'i by the title of Ayatullah, but there is some doubt as to his actual rank. Allegedly, Burqa'i and associates entered Qum after having returned to Iran from Vienna, where they represented Iran at the Soviet-sponsored World Peace Conference. Some of them apparently provoked the city's religious circles by shouting 'long live Stalin' and issuing invectives against the top *mujtahids*. Respondents attacked communism and female suffrage, which led to clashes, crowd actions and rifle fire by the security forces. Qum was shut down for a week, police officials were transferred at the insistence of Burujirdi, who sent his thanks to Musaddiq for acting quickly to end an ugly incident (*Ittila'at*, 13 January 1953). Tawliyyat, the deputy for Qum, declared: 'Ayatullah Burujirdi has full regard and concern for the person of Dr Musaddiq. If government officials in Qum did not undertake their duties, that has nothing to do with the prime minister' (*Ittila'at*, 13 January).

January 1953–August 1953

Qum, in fact, was not really challenging Musaddiq. Kashani's opposition was much more serious. Musaddiq's request for a year's extension of his emergency powers in January signalled the actual breakup of his coalition, with the departure of Ha'irizadeh, Baqa'i, Qanatabadi and Makki.

Musaddiq could probably have survived their defections, but not when these were combined with the foreign policy pressures. Makki had already temporarily resigned in late December 1952 because Musaddiq had appointed Riza Fallah as head of the executive committee of the Abadan refinery, rather than him (*Ittila'at*, 26 December 1952).[22] The others accused Musaddiq of trying to prorogue the Majlis and collaborate with the United States (*Ittila'at*, 4 January 1953). The new election bill raised the number of parliamentary deputies to 172. But more than 80 members were yet to be elected to the 17th Majlis. Therefore, Baqa'i and others claimed that Musaddiq would nevertheless make the election bill law by invoking his already existing emergency powers. The Majlis would then be perpetually without a quorum, giving Musaddiq the pretext to dismiss it and to rule by decree. Yet, when Musaddiq demanded a vote of confidence, 64 voted in his favour, and only one (Ha'irizadeh?) opposed him (*Ittila'at*, 6 January).

Kashani characterized Baqa'i's speech as 'helpful' to the government, but then he paradoxically said that he 'has not and does not' have conflicts with Musaddiq (*Ittila'at*, 8 January). The next day, Kashani declared that he wished to retire from politics. Musaddiq's partisans must have viewed this with some alarm and tried to dissuade him, since it would have left a disaffected mass of his partisans whose support Musaddiq still would have wished to attract. Afterwards, Ahmad Razavi, a Musaddiq stalwart and a deputy speaker of the Majlis, claimed that 'Kashani's opinion is that if the government truly needs the emergency powers . . . the Majlis must help and co-operate with it' (*Ittila'at*, 9 January).

But Razavi was wrong. Kashani wrote an open letter condemning the idea as a violation of articles 11, 13, 24, 25 and 27 of the 1906 Constitution and articles 7, 27 and 28 of the Supplementary Fundamental Law of 1907 (*Ittila'at*, 18 January). The prime minister's supporters noted Kashani's silence in August 1952 with irony as, in January 1953, he protested the harm such powers would inflict on the 'interests of the country and the state'. Enactment of emergency powers would be a concession to dictatorship, argued Kashani, and in any case 'without legal value . . . if the deputies previously erred [in granting emergency powers] that is no reason to repeat that [error]' (*Ittila'at*, 18 January).

Kashani's position was repudiated by the Majlis. Of 67 deputies, 59 voted in favour of extending emergency powers, five abstained (Baqa'i,

Qanatabadi, Ha'irizadeh, Zuhari, Bahaduri), one voted against (Mir Ashrafi) and one ballot was left blank (*Ittila'at*, 20 January). In the meanwhile, Ayatullah Sadr from Qum telegrammed Makki to encourage him to retract his resignation: 'Your resignation has caused concern. It is opportune, nay imperative, for you to . . . retract it so that . . . you bring to fruition the struggles of the Muslim people [*millat*] of Iran' (*Ittila'at*, 14 January). It seemed that the clergy was uniting against Musaddiq. Even Hajj Sayyid Javadi, a pro-Musaddiq Majlis cleric, had signed Baqa'i's resolution against emergency powers – although it is true that he almost immediately repudiated his signature (*Ittila'at*, 4 January). But the 12-man leadership committee of the Majlis, which included some of the prime minister's strongest critics, respectfully noted to Kashani that the granting of emergency powers was constitutional and lay within the prerogatives of parliament. The Majlis, it noted, had in the past granted such powers to its own commissions and to individuals. Such grants could always be revoked and are not unconstitutional; nor do they violate the principle of national sovereignty or Majlis procedures (*Ittila'at*, 19 January).

These events took some of the wind out of Kashani's sails, and to make matters worse for him the bazaar of Tehran struck in support of Musaddiq, and telegrams began to pour in from all the provinces on his behalf (*Ittila'at*, 19 January). Faced with these trends Kashani backed down a little, reiterating his support for Musaddiq but still criticizing his quest for emergency powers.

Musaddiq's problems with Kashani on the one side, and the Qum establishment on the other, were accumulating. True enough, his regime had survived the change in the administrator of the Qum shrine and the Burqa'i affair. But would Qum remain satisfied? If not, would it openly challenge the government?

Ahmad Safa'i, a mulla who had close ties to ayatullahs Burujirdi and Bihbihani, probably reflected their views when he argued in the Majlis that two factors had saved Iran in the past from imperialism: the clergy and nationalist political leaders. They had been equally important, said Safa'i, just as man needs both a spirit and a body. 'Just as for politics a stable centre is necessary – and that is the monarchy – in the same way for religion there must be a stable centre . . . and that is the *marja'iyyat-i taqlid* of the Shia, as exemplified by Ayatullah Burujirdi' (*Ittila'at*, 8 January).

Musaddiq's partisans could not have quarrelled with the first part of Safa'i's statement, since they would naturally assume that the nationalist political leader referred to was their own man; it must have come as an unpleasant surprise to hear Safa'i mention the monarch, instead. Several weeks later the clerics strongly backed the Shah against Musaddiq in what was to become known as 'the affair of the 9th of Isfand' (27 February 1953).

Kashani and Musaddiq tried to reconcile their differences in late

January 1953. A joint communique referred to the 'unjust interpretations' put by the media on the 'letter which [Kashani] had sent to the Majlis in protest against the bill on emergency powers'. Both sides pledged they would continue to 'march in step' with one another and to 'spare no effort at co-operation . . .' (*Ittila'at*, 28 January). But the effort failed. Kashani did not retract the substance of his criticisms. The differences were too deep. As Makki once said, 'the truth is these differences . . . have existed for two years' (*Ittila'at*, 27 January).[23]

By now, Musaddiq was fending off pressures from the British, the Majlis opposition, and the Shah. In late February, the Shah suddenly declared his intention to leave Iran with Queen Suraya, a move that Musaddiq claims was orchestrated by the British, who hoped to rally the population on the monarch's behalf and humiliate the government.[24] One thing is certain: the Qum-based clerics and Kashani both vehemently opposed the Shah's departure.

Kashani warned that the trip 'could possibly have a profound and undesirable impact throughout the country . . .' (*Ittila'at*, 27 February). The headline in the main Tehran daily read: 'If the people and Ayatullah Bihbihani had arrived ten minutes later, the Shah and Queen would have left the palace [for the airport]' (*Ittila'at*, 28 February). In fact, Bihbihani and Ayatullah Baha al-Din Nuri both arrived at the royal palace just as Musaddiq and his ministers – who had come to say goodbye to the Shah – were about to leave the palace grounds. It is not inconceivable that the crowds would have set upon Musaddiq and killed him had he not escaped by another door. Burujirdi himself, ever apolitical in public, wrote:

> Expressing regret over the recent incident [of 9 Isfand], since I am entirely confident that His Majesty and His Excellency, the Prime Minister, are fully committed to the independence and greatness of Iran, I hope and expect that – as in the past – they will preserve unity of views, so that deviant and trouble-making elements do not have the chance to cause disorder and turbulence in the country. (*Ittila'at*, 4 March 1953)

Bihbihani protested his desire to stay out of politics, but he claimed that bazaar merchants and artisans had urged him to dissuade the Shah from his trip (*Ittila'at*, 28 February).

At this time, Kashani met with a group of retired military officers, one of whom asserted:

> The charges that are being levelled at us [in connection with the events of 9 Isfand] are absolutely untrue. Apart from love of the Shah, we had and have no views, and we have complained to the Ayatullah on this issue. (*Ittila'at*, 1 March 1953)

Kashani, it will be noted, had also met with military officers after the events of 30 Tir to exonerate the army in general of charges of culpability in the deaths of demonstrators during the riots of that time. Did Kashani and the officers, who had come to appreciate his support of them, now discuss the idea of General Zahidi replacing Musaddiq? All we know for sure is that Kashani found himself in a position of having publicly to deny as 'groundless and mendacious' rumours that he supported Zahidi for prime minister (*Ittila'at*, 1 March).

Musaddiq, of course, was rumoured to have desired the end of the monarchy. In his *Prison Memoirs* he wrote that he advised the Shah against leaving but did not ultimately insist.[25] His feelings about monarchy were revealed in a Majlis speech in September 1951, when he admitted his refusal to take the oath of allegiance to Riza Shah but had sworn this oath to Muhammad Riza Pahlavi. Then he had added: 'So that the Shah can rest assured, I say that I shall *never* be prepared for this country to become a republic' (*Ittila'at*, 9 September 1951). Had he now changed his mind? The answer must remain unclear. He did deposit $9,000 in a European bank account for the Shah and ordered that he be given $1,000 in cash for his trip (*Ittila'at*, 28 February 1953). But it may be that he actually believed the trip would be a short one. Most believe the Shah himself made the decision to go.

At any rate, republicanism was becoming a troublesome charge for Musaddiq. He could certainly not afford to allow it to become combined with anticlericalism. When boldly anti-religious pamphlets began to circulate in early spring 1953, Musaddiq warned of legal prosecution of anyone who slandered Ayatullah Burujirdi.[26]

Kashani's unpredictable gyrations from criticism to promises of support were beginning to take their toll on the prime minister. Musaddiq could tolerate Kashani's cavils on his appointments, but broad attacks on general policy was another matter. An example of Kashani's inconsistent statements can be seen in a three day stretch in January. One day, he proclaimed his support, and affirmed 'if necessary I shall not stint in the advancement of the objectives of His Excellency'. But the next day he demanded that the prime minister refrain from making 'illegal demands' and cautioned: 'If you do not return from the path of straying and set aside the goal of violating the people's rights, you will be sorry some day . . .' Kashani for the first time used Islamic discourse against Musaddiq when he quoted the Koran: *wa amruhum shura baynahum* ('for their affairs are a matter of counsel', an ironic reference to the need for an independent-minded parliament). Yet, the very next day, he had the temerity to say that 'there is no conflict between myself and the prime minister' (*Ittila'at*, 19 January; 20 January; 21 January).

The internal situation by spring 1953 had deteriorated so much that reconciliation commissions were established to work out the differences between Musaddiq and Kashani and Musaddiq and the Shah. At one point a four-hour marathon meeting took place between the prime minister and the ruler, and at the very same time, Kashani offered to leave politics 'if my presence causes problems for the work of the government'. Qanatabadi, for his part, offered to resign his post in the Majlis (*Ittila'at*, 23 February; 24 February). Finally, at this time, the government announced the arrest of General Zahidi on charges of conspiring with the 'Organization of Retired Army Officers' (*Ittila'at*, 24 February; 25 February). Kashani's ties to Zahidi again were suspected, especially in the light of his efforts to keep the Shah in Iran on the 9th of Isfand (27 February). But the cleric explained this action as follows:

> Since I had no knowledge of the truth of the matter [despite his meeting with the Minister of Court on 21 February 1953, a few days before the 9th Isfand], when the question of the Shah's departure suddenly came up, I did not think this trip was in the interests of the country. My opposition was based on the principles of the Constitutional Revolution. You are all witnesses to the fact that up to now I have neither seen the Shah nor had any dealings with the Court [but he had]. But since I felt that this trip could tear the fabric of this country apart, I opposed it. (*Ittila'at*, 3 March 1953)

The next day the Shah made the following statement: 'I personally support the implementation of the Constitution and extend to Dr Musaddiq's government every kind of support' (*Ittila'at*, 4 March). Then, Musaddiq made his own statement on the Shah: 'Not only am I an adherent of constitutional monarchy, but I am sincerely loyal to Muhammad Riza Pahlavi' (*Ittila'at*, 13 March). Clearly, someone was hiding the truth of his real feelings among these three leaders.

In his search for support among the ulama Musaddiq met with eight leading Tehran clergymen, who thanked him for seeking to ban the sale of alcohol and urged him to subject the operation of the Endowments Department to the *shari'a*. On the same day Zahidi was released from police custody (*Ittila'at*, 16 March)

After the Persian New Year, Musaddiq acknowledged his deep disagreements with the Shah, disagreements he termed 'fundamental . . . and related to the Constitution, nothing more' (*Ittila'at*, 30 March). But Kashani was at this time defending the Shah to a visiting Egyptian reporter: 'Our Shah is very different from [Egypt's King] Faruq.' The reporter noted that Kashani had seemed previously to be a strong opponent of the Shah and wondered why he was now defending him. Kashani avoided a direct answer and instead said:

> The thing is that the Shah's trip, with those conditions which Dr Musaddiq wanted to lay down, would have caused dissidence and corruption in Iran.

This would have caused dangerous conditions to come to pass . . . The Shah
of Iran is neither corrupt nor capricious, like Faruq, nor is he a dictator and a
tyrant. The Shah is an educated and reasonable man. (*Ittila'at*, 30 March
1953)

What conditions he had in mind is not clear, nor the sort of corruption he
feared were the Shah to have left. But the Shah could not have missed the
message behind the words. Qum, in a last effort to reconcile Musaddiq and
the Shah, sent Ayatullah Bihbihani to try his hand, but the results
remained fruitless (*Ittila'at*, 11 April).

Then, in early May 1953 an incident occurred that was to have a lasting
impact on the country's political direction. Zahidi, although earlier
released from custody, was now wanted for the kidnapping and murder of
the chief of the national police, Afshartus; the regime alleged that this
was the preliminary to a *coup d'état*. Zahidi disappeared and then took
sanctuary at the Majlis. Kashani's supporters say that, as speaker, he had
no choice but to allow Zahidi to take refuge, since this was part of the
national traditions, and Musaddiq himself had done the same thing at an
earlier time.

However, Kashani's detractors argue that although Kashani may not
have been able to throw Zahidi into the arms of the police, he did not have
to meet with him. But this is precisely what Kashani chose to do.
Accompanied by some of Musaddiq's bitterest enemies – Muhammad Zu
al-Faqari, Mir Ashrafi, Bahaduri, Ha'irizadeh and Qanatabadi – Kashani
told Zahidi: 'I have given orders that as long as your freedom has not been
secured, you will be received here with welcome.' Then, turning to the
commander of the Majlis guard, he said: 'My wish is that as long as
General Zahidi abides here, you will take care of our dear guest' (*Ittila'at*,
4 May). Such effusive words, together with Kashani's several previous
meetings with military officers, have led many observers to believe that he
was even then aligning with those who eventually overthrew the government.

The final issue between Kashani and Musaddiq was the latter's plan for
a referendum on proroguing the parliament and holding new elections for
that body. Musaddiq sought thereby to overcome the tactics of the
opposition deputies, whose deliberate absenteeism prevented the necessary quorum for the sessions to take place. In late July Kashani condemned
Musaddiq's authoritarian conduct in trying to stage-manage the plebiscite
and refusing to give him air time over the state-run radio. Kashani berated
Musaddiq for having 'played along with the nationalist movement simply
to gain power'. He now ridiculed Musaddiq for not having taken a single
beneficial step in all his 28 months as prime minister – a favourite criticism
of Baqa'i, Ha'irizadeh and company. The only thing that has happened is
'the nationalization of oil, which occurred with the general uprising and

sacrifice of the noble people of Iran'. Kashani was thereby minimizing Musaddiq's role in the issue that in the minds of many Musaddiq seemed to symbolize.

Kashani satirized Musaddiq for calling his opponents foreign agents and warned that the prime minister was 'consolidating his dictatorship, personalistic government and self-enhancement'. Musaddiq's referendum, at 'bayonet point', was a fraud, he charged. Worse, to pay for it he had ordered the government to print up 450 million tomans. The dissolution of parliament would be an act of treason, and the request for emergency powers from the people in the absence of the Majlis a facade for tyranny. Separate ballot boxes for ayes and nays was the height of deceit, charged Kashani. He condemned the regime's willingness to pay compensation to the AIOC and for having cut the price of oil by 50 per cent. Dramatically, he added: 'A plot against my life has been hatched.' He characterized the regime as 'this government, which has acted against the holy law of Islam, the Declaration of the Rights of Man and the Charter of the United Nations, has undertaken abuse and torture in the gaols' (a reference to those arrested and held in custody over the murder of Afshartus) (*Kayhan*, 29 July). This marked Kashani's irrevocable and public split with Musaddiq.

The next day, Safa'i gave a speech at Kashani's house condemning the upcoming referendum (*Kayhan*, 30 July). In my opinion, this was a final sign, if one is needed, that many Qum and Tehran ulama were falling in line with Kashani on Musaddiq's rule. But Musaddiq still had supporters in the streets, and a mob burst into Kashani's house and wounded Safa'i. Kashani responded by ordering his supporters to boycott the referendum and the next day resigned as speaker (*Kayhan* 1 August; 2 August). Earlier, his threatened resignation had caused Musaddiq's supporters concern about losing the support of such an important figure; this time his resignation made it possible for them to elect Abdullah Mu'azzami as speaker and then to have Zahidi escorted out of the Majlis precincts. He went underground. The regime responded by placing a price upon his head. As is well known, Zahidi's ability to elude capture was probably decisive for the success of the *coup d'état*.

Of the clerical deputies in the parliament, only Qanatabadi and Safa'i seem to have been opposed to the referendum. The press showed pictures of Ibrahim Milani, Hajj Sayyid Javadi, and even the non-clerical deputy from Qum, Abu'l Fazl Tawliyyat, voting in favour of the referendum (*Kayhan*, 10 August; 11 August). But such gestures, even if they were sincerely felt, were insignificant when compared to the clerical opposition to Musaddiq at this point.

Kashani's supporters have recently contended that they have 'found' a letter he had written to the prime minister on the 27 Murdad, a day before Musaddiq's overthrow, warning of his impending arrest by Zahidi. There are three possible interpretations of this incident. Either Kashani did write the letter and was sincere, which seems improbable given the animus he had towards Musaddiq. Or he did write it but to protect himself were the coup to fail. Or the letter is a forgery, written after the coup presumably by one of the cleric's sons, with a view to vindicating his role during this period of Iranian politics.

In my opinion, the letter is a forgery. Had such a letter indeed been written and delivered to the prime minister on the alleged date, it would not seem possible it should have escaped the knowledge of Musaddiq's close aides, such as Kazim Hasibi, Ahmad Razavi, Ali Shayigan, Abdullah Mu'azzami, or his attorney during his trial, Jalil Buzurgmihr. In any case, Musaddiq was certainly aware of the danger that Zahidi represented, and he did not need a letter from the opposition to alert him to it. Kashani's supporters claim that Musaddiq had ordered Kashani out of the country after the referendum.[27] Moreover, how did the letter get into the hands of members of Kashani's family? They claim the cleric ordered a copy of it to be kept, but this only begs a whole series of other questions. The only 'evidence' provided by pro-Kashani elements is a copy of the letter, presented by those who have an interest in maintaining a revisionist view of Kashani's role in the coup.

A growing body of evidence tends to support the view that Kashani's followers accepted money from the Americans to bring the crowds out in opposition to Musaddiq. In particular, scholars doing research in this period are underscoring the role played by Ahmad Aramish, a partisan close to Kashani, as a go-between for the United States and Kashani.[28]

After the coup d'état of August 1953

After Musaddiq's overthrow, clerical support for the Shah intensified, but Kashani almost immediately dropped from sight. The coup ushered in a period of harmony between the Qum clergy and the Court that was to last six or seven years. In my view, the quid pro quo between Qum and the Court was that Qum would remain quiet on the defeat of the nationalist movement, Iran's impending entry into the Baghdad Pact, and the continued presence of the western oil companies in Iran; the Court would provide a general atmosphere of security, pledge to uphold religious shrines and provide moral and financial backing for religious causes, such as public morality, anti-Bahaism, respect for the high clergy, etc.

Ayatullah Burujirdi, having received a telegram from the Shah in Rome, cabled back – *after* Musaddiq's overthrow – 'To His Royal Majesty, may God protect his kingship', and expressed his 'joy' to have received the Shah's message. 'It is hoped that Your Majesty's return to Iran is blessed [by God] and will be the cause of the improvement of religious objectives, the glory of Islam and the tranquility of the Muslims' (*Ittila'at*, 23 August).

Bihbihani met with the bazaar merchants in the presence of the military governor of Tehran. The government wanted the bazaars to open their shops in order to make a public show that Musaddiq did not have any supporters in that influential quarter. Bihbihani, who undoubtedly had played a major role in bringing the crowds out in favour of the Shah, was there to reinforce the government's interest in a general opening of the shops (*Ittila'at*, 22 August). In my judgement his role here was crucial in rendering the idea of a counter-coup more difficult.

Shortly after the coup, General Zahidi, 'by virtue of the courtesies [*in ihtiramat*] that Ayatullah Kashani had observed toward him during his refuge in the Majlis', asked to meet with the cleric. The meeting was also attended by the inevitable Qanatabadi and Ha'irizadeh. Zahidi claimed he would never give in to the British on the oil issues and would not allow compensation to be paid to the AIOC (*Ittila'at*, 22 August). But Zahidi apparently found Kashani troublesome. Three days later, one of Kashani's supporters announced the ayatullah's departure from the political arena because of the people's 'indifference' and his resultant 'disappointment' (*Ittila'at*, 25 August). It is striking how quickly Kashani's star sank and Bihbihani's rose in the immediate aftermath of the *coup d'état*.

No doubt the Shah felt that he owed much more to Qum and Bihbihani than to Kashani, despite Kashani's role in the coup and latter-day encomiums about the ruler. After all, Bihbihani had collaborated too (and received bribe money from the Americans).[29] Others contend that Bihbihani organized the ulama of Tehran at his own house to write letters to all the important clerics of the country, using red ink and the insignia of the Tudeh Party in a lurid effort to totally discredit the left. According to these observers, the letters contained grisly threats to hang all the mullas from the lamposts of various Iranian cities.[30]

A few clerics, such as ayatullahs Abu'l Fazl Zanjani and Riza Zanjani, as well as some junior figures, such as Sayyid Mahmud Taliqani, remained loyal to Musaddiq after the coup. A significant pro-nationalist demonstration is said to have occurred at the Masjid-i Hidayat in Tehran in 1954;[31] but there is no information on the details of this episode. Taliqani's biographers contend that he regarded Kashani as 'standing in the corner of Zahidi and the Court'. They note that Taliqani had been a candidate in the elections for the 17th Majlis in the north (the districts of Chalus, Nawshahr, Shahsavar). But the government had cancelled the elections there because of unrest or, perhaps, fear that pro-Musaddiq candidates would lose. In any case, although barred from running, Taliqani threw in his lot with the Musaddiqists until the end.[32] Later, we now know, he helped found the Freedom Movement with Mihdi Bazargan, an organization which carried the imprimatur of the old nationalist movement and National Front.

Conclusions

I have argued that the clergy during the Musaddiq period played a varied role but ultimately coalesced in opposition to him. Although the core of the parliamentary clerics did not abandon Musaddiq, the fact is that they simply did not participate significantly inside or outside the Majlis in the politics of the time. Certainly, Qum's channels to the Tehran ulama did not pass through Angaji, Jalali, Javadi, Shabistari and Milani.

There seems to have been three main clerical tendencies – not groups, which implies more coherence than evinced by the ulama. One may perhaps be called the dominant clerical tendency, led, of course, by Burujirdi. Quietist, it ultimately became activist on behalf of royalism and against Musaddiq. A second may be termed the militant clerical tendency, under the leadership of Kashani. Far more activist in the beginning, it seemed to have support from few grand mujtahids, although certain of them may have been more vocal behind the scenes. The third would be the pro-Musaddiq clerical tendency, which included the six deputies of parliament and the non-Majlis cleric, Taliqani. These were lower ranking mullas. But Musaddiq did also have the support of important *mujtahids*, including the Zanjani brothers and Ayatullah Baha al-Din Mahallati.

The Fida'iyan-i Islam, which was mentioned in connection with the pre-April 1951 period, has not received much attention in this paper. In part this is due to lack of information. But, although Kashani broke with them and supported the Society of Muslim Strugglers – an amorphous organization notable more for holding rallies than anything else – the inclusion of the Fida'iyan in the militant category seems warranted. Of course, the members of the Fida'iyan were not clerics, or at any rate not clerics whom Burujirdi recognized.

I believe that Kashani turned against Musaddiq for a combination of reasons. These are not listed in any order of priority but include the following. First, Kashani thought he was the rightful leader of the nationalist movement. He was not averse, as we have seen, to specifying his leadership role to reporters. There existed, then, a personality conflict between him and Musaddiq.

Secondly, Kashani was encouraged to sharpen his differences with Musaddiq by the Qum clerics. The decisive event here, in my judgement, was the incident of 9 Isfand 1331/27 February 1953. People like Burujirdi, Bihbihani, Fayz, Nuri and others became frightened of the possibility of the monarchy coming to an end, and they probably urged Kashani to do something in his capacity as speaker of parliament.

Thirdly, Musaddiq irrevocably alienated Kashani with his arbitrary behaviour over the referendum. Although Kashani had criticized Musaddiq many times before that point, the referendum was in a sense the point of no return, since it was the occasion for his charge that the prime minister was a traitor to his country. Yet, in my view this was a tactical reason for Kashani's hostility. The man was no democrat, himself – certainly not in any categorical sense. We must remember his contacts with the military, contacts which probably led him to think that he had sufficient support in the event of a showdown with Musaddiq. The referendum merely provided the pretext for the final rupture.

Through his contacts with the military, Kashani collaborated with Zahidi to overthrow the prime minister. I do not say this lightly, because I realize that so far the evidence is circumstantial. This is suggested by his behaviour when Zahidi took sanctuary in the Majlis. Moreover, Kashani must have been fully aware of the logical consequences of his support for the general, given the government's overriding concern about what it perceived as Zahidi's conspiratorial actions.

On the other hand, charges that Kashani in backing Zahidi was *ipso facto* a British agent should be rejected. Yes, the British were sponsoring Zahidi's conspiracy, but they had different purposes in mind. For them Musaddiq's overthrow meant the return to a status quo under a pro-British monarchy; Kashani was seeking Iran's independence from Britain under a monarchy subject to a particular brand of Shii politics and as a state representing an 'Islamic internationalism', as it were, in the global arena.

Since Kashani talked about *millat* (people) as much as he ever did about *ummat* (community of believers), I see little ground to view him as a precursor to Khomeini. As far as I can tell, none of these clerics argued for clerical rule, which is certainly the argument of Khomeini since 1971. If anything, the dominant wing of the ulama urged abstention from day-to-day politics. True, they supported oil nationalization. But in this they were behaving more as the legatees of the clerics in the time of the Reuters and Tobacco concessions than as the forerunners of *vilayat-i faqih*.

Finally, Kashani had no particular plan of procedure and action after Musaddiq. Unlike Khomeini, who revealed his programme in 1971 with his set of lectures on the governance of the jurisprudent (*pace* Bazargan and others who claim to have been 'misled' by him), Kashani seemed to operate from week to week with only a vague notion, at best, of what he wanted. Musaddiq received Kashani's ire partly because he saw the prime minister as a 'negative' leader, his supporters maintain. Ironically, though, it would not be far off the mark to say of Kashani that he knew far more assuredly what he did not want than what he wished to accomplish.

In that sense, too, Kashani must not be seen as an early version of Khomeini. As far as Khomeini himself is concerned within the context of the subject of this paper, one is impressed by his sheer absence from the arena of clerical politics during the Musaddiq period. Perhaps he was biding his time behind the scenes. But he abjured social action. Yet, today he has made Musaddiq – the activist *par excellence* of the period – a virtual non-person by referring to him as *an mard-i milli* (that nationalist man).

Notes

1 The author would like to thank the following colleagues for reading the original draft and their helpful comments, some of which have been incorporated here: Ervand Abrahamian, Fakhreddin Azimi, and Homa Katouzian.

2 Khomeini is said to have referred to Musaddiq and his efforts on one occasion: *'yek mard-e melli bud, va yek karha'i-ra mikhvast bekoneh'* (once there was a nationalist man who wanted to do something [for the country]). Personal communication to me from a source who must remain anonymous, based on one of Khomeini's television statements shortly after the seizure of power.

3 Yann Richard, 'Ayatullah Kashani: precursor of the Islamic Republic?', in *Religion and Politics in Iran*, ed. Nikki R. Keddie (New Haven, Conn., 1983) pp. 101–24.

4 *Ittila'at*, 10 February 1949; 13 February 1949.

5 Jalil Buzurgmihr ed. *Taqrirat-i Musaddiq dar zindan* (Tehran, 1980) pp. 114–17.

6 S. M. Aliev, ' 'Antiimperialisticheskoe Dvizhenie 1949–1953 gg.', in *Iran: Ocherki Noveishei Istorii*, ed. Z. Arabadzhian (Moscow: Izdatel'stvo 'Nauka', 1976) p. 183.

7 *Kayhan*, 23 July 1950.

8 *Ittila'at*, 13 February 1951; 8 March 1951; 14 March 1951; 17 March 1951; 18 March 1951; 8 April 1951. Khvansari cited the *hadith* attributed to the Prophet, that he who upon wakening without concerning himself with the affairs of the Muslims is not himself a Muslim. Ruhani Qummi cited the Koranic verse: *Lan yaj'al Allah al-kafirin 'ala al-muslimin sabilan* (God shall not open a way for the unbelievers against the Muslims).

9 *Ittila'at*, 28 January 1951; 9 September 1951 identifies Chahar Suqi and Ardakani and Rawzati as Isfahan ulama.

10 For example, during Ashura, as reported in *Ittila'at*, 12 October 1951.

11 Bahram Afrasiyabi and Sa'id Dihqan, *Taliqani va tarikh* (Tehran, 1981), p. 140.

12 The following six paragraphs are summarized from *Ittila'at*, 5 June 1951; 11 June; 13 June; 16 June; 21 June; 31 July; 12 August; 13 August; 5 September; 24 September; 21 September; 30 September; 22 November; 25 November; 12 December; 19 December; 24 December; 20 March 1952; 12 April; 26 May; 27 May; 31 May; 1 June; 7 June; 6 July; 19 July.

13 Personal communication based on statements made by Dr Ghulam Husayn Musaddiq, the prime minister's son, made known to me by a source who must remain anonymous.

14 Afrasiyabi and Dihqan, *Taliqani va tarikh*, p. 140.

15 'Mujahid' [pseud.], *Ayatullah Kashani va nameh-i Muhandis Hasibi* (Tehran, n.d.) pp. 12–15.

16 That the Rashidian brothers were actually plotting with the British against Musaddiq has been recently confirmed by an M.I.6 agent in an interview with Granada Television in Britain. Naming Robin Zaehner, later professor of Eastern religions at Oxford, as the chief M.I.6 operative in Iran during the

Musaddiq era, this individual links Sayfullah, Qudratullah and Asadullah Rashidian to the British effort. One wonders how different things might have been had Hijazi, Zahidi and the Rashidians been convicted.

17 Mihdi Bazargan, 'Inqilab-i Iran dar daw harakat: Ruhaniyan-i Fatih-i Sivvum', part 25 of his book, *Inqilab-i Iran dar daw harakat*, cited in *Iran Times* (Washington, DC), in Persian, 14 July 1985.

18 Compare his statement, to a reporter of *Ittila'at*, 30 September 1951, that an Islamic government is the best in the world.

19 For one example, Ayatullah Muhammad Bihbihani, *Ittila'at*, 5 June 1951.

20 *Ittila'at*, 1 November 1952; 5 November; 8 November. Indeed under Khomeini, when Bazargan met with US National Security Advisor, Zbigniew K. Brzezinski, he was forced to resign. Henderson was a key player in the coup that overthrew Musaddiq in August 1953.

21 The only cleric I have found who did not condemn the election bill was the popular Tehran preacher, Husayn Ali Rashid, who denied that sufficient reason existed in the *shari'a* to ban women's suffrage. See *Ittila'at*, 29 December 1952.

22 In his *Prison Memoirs* Musaddiq hints at Makki's weakness as an administrator and at his narcissism. See Musaddiq, *Taqrirat*, p. 136.

23 Makki did claim the differences to be 'trivial', however.

24 Musaddiq, *Taqrirat*, pp. 126–30.

25 Musaddiq, *Taqrirat*, p. 126.

26 *Kayhan*, 30 April 1953.

27 'Mujahid', *Ayatullah Kashani*, p. 34.

28 On Aramish's ties to Kashani and to the Americans, who gave him money to turn over to Kashani in exchange for Kashani's mobilization of anti-Musaddiq crowds, see the important forthcoming paper by Mark J. Gasiorowski, 'The 1953 *coup d'état* in Iran,' pp. 27–8, 48. Gasiorowski also reports that after the coup, the Iraqi ambassador in Tehran faithfully reported to the British that the Shah and Zahidi personally visited Kashani to thank him for his role in the overthrow of Musaddiq.

29 Richard W. Cottam, *Nationalism in Iran* (Pittsburgh, 1964) p. 226.

30 Afrasiyabi and Dihqan, *Taliqani va tarikh*, pp. 121–2.

31 Ibid., p. 151.

32 Ibid., p. 144.

5

Islam, nationalism and Musaddiq's era: post-revolutionary historiography in Iran[1]

FARHANG RAJAEE

If, at that time [1951–3], one of the statesmen, one of the religious leaders or a group of people had ever cried that they would not want this dynasty . . . the course of Iranian history would have been different and we would have had no need for this revolution . . . Musaddiq could have achieved it. He gained power, but committed many mistakes. He wanted to serve the country but fell in error. One of his mistakes was that when he gained power he did not execute *this man* [Muhammad Riza Pahlavi] to put an end to the issue; not a great task at the time. He had the army as well as all other powers in his hand. Besides, this man was nobody then . . . This is a big mistake that the Doctor committed. [Emphasis added]

Ayatullah Khomeini (1978)[2]

We have suffered because of this nationalism quite often. I do not want to express how at the time of nationalism – the time of *that man* [Dr Muhammad Musaddiq], whom they exalt so much . . . the Faiziyeh school was machine-gunned . . . All these groups should be dissolved. We cannot tolerate the nationalists to do and say as they wish . . . I want the nationalists to be Islamic . . . We want Islam. [Emphasis added]

Ayatullah Khomeini (1981)[3]

How have the elites of the Islamic Republic of Iran treated Dr Muhammad Musaddiq and the popular nationalist movement for the nationalization of the oil industry since the revolution? This paper argues that the ascent of an Islamic world view has entailed a gradual change in the attitude of the ruling elite with regard to Musaddiq and that this change is related to the degree to which Islamic revolutionaries consolidated their power. The paper will attempt to capture this change in the interpretation of Musaddiq and the nationalist movement, as the revolution unfolded, in newspapers,

118

journals, pamphlets and books. Because the transformation in the elite's perception was gradual, the approach taken here is chronological as well as topical.

The Islamic Republic claims to be an ideological as well as a revolutionary state in that it perceives events, phenomena and developments through a doctrinal perspective. While the revolution was in the making, the objective of overthrowing the monarchy overshadowed ideological demarcations. The opposition to the Shah's regime proved so deep rooted that it united even opposing political propensities. The very rapid demise of the monarchical regime also provided very little opportunity at the time for various political groups to emerge and gain acceptance or popularity. Only after the revolution did their opposite world views surface.

The discussion here concentrates on two of these world views, one based on Islam and the other on nationalism. Indeed, it appears that nationalism imposes the most serious threat to the ruling Islamic regime of Ayatullah Khomeini. It was the residue of the Musaddiqist National Front that formed the provisional revolutionary government. For a while, some of the ideas and policies of the original National Front were, in fact, pursued. Even after six years of Islamic rule the nationalists seem to present a serious political challenge: in the presidential election of 1985 the most serious opposition candidate to that of the ruling Islamic Republican Party (IRP) (founded 19 February 1979) was Mihdi Bazargan, who openly declared himself to be a Musaddiqist on numerous occasions. Many argue that the fact that the Council of Guardians dismissed Bazargan's candidacy was an indication that the government was fearful of the return of the nationalists.

The struggle between the nationalists and the ruling elites of the Islamic Republic is only a symptom of a broader and deeper clash between Islam and nationalism. Islam claims universality, meaning a comprehensive way of life both in terms of membership and aspects of life; nationalism recognizes the primacy of one particular group of people with respect to a particular piece of territory. In practice, in the early days of the advent and expansion of the European-based states system to the Islamic world, the primacy of nationalism was accepted. Even the more religiously-minded Muslims approved of it in terms of patriotism and love for one's homeland – an idea which is accepted and encouraged in Islam, since 'the love of homeland stems from the faith.'

The resurgence of Islam has brought the debate to the fore by giving rise to 'political Islam', or Islam as a political ideology. This is the most significant after-effect of the revolution in Iran. 'Political Islam', as interpreted by Ayatullah Khomeini, serves as both the philosophical foundation of the regime and the guiding principle for the policy-making apparatus. Its central doctrine, known as the guardianship of the theologian jurisconsult (*vilayat-i faqih*), is theoretically based on the Shii theory of the imamate,[4] and claims to be a revival of the practices of Mirza Hasan Shirazi (the protagonist of the Tobacco Protest of 1891), Shaykh Fazlullah Nuri (the leader of anti-constitutionalism), Sayyid Hasan Mudarris (an opponent of Riza Shah), and Ayatullah Kashani (a leading figure during oil nationalization). These figures are characterized by their anti-foreign attitude. This is clearly in contradistinction to the nationalists, particularly Musaddiq whose central political idea was that of consti-tutionalism, a European concept. Naturally, the Islamic Republic perceives Musaddiq and what he stood for as a threat.

Those views which are in accordance with Ayatullah Khomeini's theory are in accordance with the views of the Islamic Republic. Support or lack of support for the theory of the guardianship serves as a screening device in hiring or firing state employees and as the criterion of good or poor citizenship. Such terms as *ta'ahud* (commitment), *maktab* (doctrine), *khatt-i* Imam (the line of the Imam) and *vilayat-i faqih* (the guardianship of the theologian jurisconsult) are used with amazing frequency. And all denote allegiance to Ayatullah Khomeini's doctrine. In an interview with key figures of the Islamic Republic, 'the line of the Imam' was defined as absolute faith in the views of Ayatullah Khomeini. The following definition by Hujjat al-Islam Khu'iniha was typical:

> The line of the imam [Ayatullah Khomeini] means that we accept the interpretation of Islam presented by the imam in political, economic and social areas and [for solving] our various problems . . . I have suggested that the line of the imam be taught as a unit of study in educational establishments.[5]

It appears that his suggestion has been put into practice, because Khomeini's interpretation of Islam is the one most widely taught at schools. Moreover, that interpretation has become the political foundation of the regime governing Iran today. Article 5 of the Constitution of the Islamic Republic recognizes the supreme jurisconsult as the sovereign in the country.

The followers of 'the line of the Imam' only acceded to power after considerable struggle. They were on the defensive from the actual downfall of the monarchy, in February 1979, until the March 1981 crisis and the subsequent impeachment of the first elected president of the republic. During this time they were busy consolidating their power and legitimizing their rule. The image of Musaddiq and the historiography of his era has changed through the years, as Islamization progressed. Musaddiq as a person, as a politician and as the leader of the nationalization movement is treated differently depending on whether one is referring to the early days of the revolution or the more recent years.

The ascendancy of the followers of Musaddiq

Having assumed power on 11 February 1979, the new provisional government, many of whose members were from the National Front, began preparation for the anniversary of Dr Musaddiq's death (5 March 1967). It was the first time this hitherto forbidden event could be openly discussed. The ceremony was performed with splendour. For the first time, special ceremonies were held everywhere to honour the former prime minister; schools were either closed or held special meetings. The newspapers gave extensive coverage to the life and personality of Dr Musaddiq. One article stated that Musaddiq was buried in his private estate, Ahmadabad, in defiance of his last wish,[6] because 'the Shah's regime was frightened even of Musaddiq's corpse', and would not allow a public burial.[7]

On 5 March 1979 people rushed toward Ahmadabad by the thousands. With the exception of the IRP, all the major political parties and groups participated in the ceremony. Ayatullah Taliqani (d. 1979) delivered a long speech in honour of Dr Musaddiq. Hidayatullah Matin-Daftari declared the formation of the Democratic National Front, the primary objective of which was to implement Musaddiq's philosophy and policies. The proceedings were later published.[8] In contrast, there was no sign of any official memorial ceremony for Ayatullah Kashani, who had died on 14 March 1962. Apparently, private ceremonies were held by his supporters, but no report of them appeared in the pages of any of Tehran's daily papers.[9] Only Ayatullah Taliqani referred to Kashani in his long eulogy of Musaddiq, but did so in a critical tone.

This public display of respect and deference for Musaddiq was repeated on 20 March, in memory of the day when the bill nationalizing the oil industry had been ratified by the parliament (Majlis) in 1329/1951. Dr Musaddiq was presented as the man who alone stood up to the British. He was also portrayed as the prototype of an Iranian nationalist, the protagonist of law, democracy and pluralism, and the precursor of the revolution of 1977–9.[10] This perception of Musaddiq was to persist until March 1981. As in the ceremony of 5 March, little attention was paid to Ayatullah Kashani.

Even on 22 July 1979, on the commemoration of the anniversary of the July 1952 uprising in support of Musaddiq, Kashani's name was rarely mentioned. Neither in his talk, nor in the official press release from the Freedom Movement of Iran on the occasion, did Bazargan make any reference to Kashani.[11] Ayatullah Taliqani merely referred to the unity between the National Front and Ayatullah Kashani as the leading factor in the victory of the people in reinstating Musaddiq to his position as prime minister.[12] One notable event was the protest against the speech of the spokesman of the National Front: a group shouted *hizb faqat hizbullah* (the only party is the party of God), indicating that nationalistic emphases were not welcomed in all quarters.

Mention should be made, however, of a series of articles by Hasan Ayat which appeared in August 1979 in *Jumhuri-yi Islami*, the organ of the IRP, dealing with the contemporary history of Iran. In its part two (18 August 1979), the series criticizes Musaddiq and considers him responsible for the coup of August 1953.[13] Interestingly, however, the newspaper published the piece with an editorial note stating that the views of the article did not reflect those of the editorial board. This is very significant in that it shows the defensive mood of those who represented the views of the Islamic Republic at this time. The situation soon changed dramatically. In a few months Bazargan's government fell (8 November 1979). It was claimed that he had to resign because he had contacted the American National Security Council Advisor while attending a national ceremony in Algeria. But, the facts point to the fundamental clash referred to earlier: Bazargan was seen as the symbol of nationalistic sentiment.[14]

The newly elected president, Abu'l Hasan Bani-Sadr, added to the problem because he, like Bazargan, displayed certain nationalistic propensities, and even saw himself as a new Musaddiq. In a memorial ceremony in March 1980, Bani-Sadr paid tribute to Musaddiq. One could, however, detect a slight shift in the tone. Musaddiq was portrayed not as the guarantor of Iranian nationalism but, as Bani-Sadr put it, 'the symbol of our Irano-Islamic identity'. One newspaper portrayed Musaddiq as an anti-imperialist hero and 'the vanguard of the struggle against western colonialism'.[15] The shift may have been a response to the radicalization of society in the wake of the occupation of the American Embassy in Tehran a few months earlier, and the introduction of the 'line of the Imam' as the prevalent way of thinking in the country.

Although the 'followers of the Imam' had made inroads, they were still on the defensive. In a public and relatively large memorial ceremony honouring Kashani, held by the teachers of Qum seminaries and the Revolutionary Guards, one speaker thanked the organizers for breaking 'the conspiracy of omission and neglect which heretofore has been exercised with regard to Ayatollah Kashani' and to the role he played in the nationalization of the oil industry.[16] The same speaker also attacked what he labelled liberals, nationalists included, for their revision of history. This attack was significant for two reasons. First, all non-leftist propensities which did not heed the theory of the guardianship of the theologian jurisconsult, came under the banner of 'liberals'. Second, it moved the followers of the Imam to the offensive. As an example, one may note an article which appeared in *Jumhuri-yi Islami*, on 31 March 1980, dealing with memorial stamps issued by the government since the revolution. All stamps are introduced along with their picture except the one issued in

1979 honouring Musaddiq.[17] One may also note an editorial dealing with the July 1952 uprising, published a few months later, which was even more indicative of the shift to the offensive. While questioning the validity of many of Musaddiq's judgements, it argued that the glorification of Musaddiq is a means of undermining the followers of the Imam and 'is tantamount to undermining Islam'. It continued:

> The root cause of the disagreement is not the fight between a specialist [*mutakhassis*] and a religious [*mazhabi*] mind . . . rather it is the problem of outlook; the latter views Islam as a comprehensive scheme with ordinances for every problem . . . and the former regards Islam as a religion which should be separated from social life.[18]

Soon the schism between nationalism and Islam came to be associated with Bani-Sadr on the one hand, and the newly appointed prime minister, Muhammad Ali Raja'i, whose crusade was to institutionalize the primacy of *commitment* (*ta'ahud*) over *specialization* (*takhassus*), on the other. The final showdown came in the crisis of March 1981, during which the followers of·the Imam won the war.

So far, only the newspaper account of the treatment of Musaddiq has been discussed. For a more comprehensive account one must examine the relevant books or pamphlets which were published during 1979–81. The most notable ones containing the views of the Islamic Republic are as follows:

1 *Ruhaniyyat va asrar-i fash nashudeh az nahzat-i milli shudan-i san'at-i naft* (The religious leaders and the unrevealed secrets of the national movement for the nationalization of the Iranian oil industry);[19]
2 *Nigarishi kutah bar nahzat-i milli-yi Iran* (A short account of the national movement of Iran);[20]
3 *Guftari kutah dar bareh-i vaqa'i-yi 28 Murdad* (A short chapter on the events of the August 1953 coup);[21]
4 *Qiyam-i millat-i musalman-i Iran dar 30 Tir* (The uprising of the Muslim people of Iran, 22 July 1952).[22]

Prepared by a group of Iranians in West Germany, calling themselves 'the supporters of the Islamic movement of Iran in Europe', the first book is very significant. It was the first work to defend Ayatullah Kashani and exhalt his role in the nationalization of the oil industry. It also served as an important source for subsequent books on the topic. Moreover, the followers of the Imam in Qum welcomed it immediately; hence it was published there. The book contains a long introduction and more than 60 documents to prove that Ayatullah Kashani played an important role in the nationalization of the oil industry in Iran. In the introduction, the authors note that during the Shah's reign one could not talk about Musaddiq's period because of censorship. They continue:

> Unfortunately even this year (1979, the year of revolutionary democracy and the absence of censorship), those speakers who spoke on the anniversary of the oil nationalization spoke only of Dr Muhammad Musaddiq – which was a good and proper thing to do – and honoured him alone. Either unintentionally or on purpose, they did not reveal many of the undeniable facts of history. (*Ruhaniyyat*, p. 6)

According to the book, the most significant of these 'undeniable facts' was that the religious figures were not given due credit for the role they played in the nationalization of the oil industry.

The work also suggests that some of the policies of Musaddiq suffered from naivity and false optimism. These criticisms, however, are presented in an apologetic manner. One important passage begins by saying that the government of Musaddiq 'always enjoyed the unequivocal support of the religious apparatus . . . on the oil nationalization issue and foreign policy', but continues that this was so even when religious leaders disagreed with him on many issues. According to the book, the most outstanding areas of disagreements included Musaddiq's disregard for the separation of the branches of government; his appointment of ill-suited persons to sensitive posts; his failure to enforce the anti-alcohol law; and his enactment of the public security bill (*Ruhaniyyat*, pp. 29–30).

In short, while Musaddiq's policies are criticized, the perception of Musaddiq as the protagonist of oil nationalization is not challenged. Even on the sensitive issue of the Musaddiq–Kashani relationship, the book blames 'enemies' for destroying the alliance. But the thrust of the argument is in Kashani's favour. According to the book, the enemies' objective was to undermine the power of the religious leaders and their followers because it was obvious that they were the only force 'which could mobilize all the people for fighting any kind of foreign domination' (*Ruhaniyyat*, p. 56). More explicitly, the book defends Kashani by calling attention to the many documents which, it claims, prove Kashani's positive contribution to Musaddiq's efforts.

The second work is an essay published in the summer of 1979 by the Mujahidin-i Inqilab-i Islami (The Mujahids of the Islamic Revolution, not to be confused with the leftist Mujahidin-i Khalq). Less apologetic than the first book, the preface makes it clear that this is another document proving Kashani's important role in the nationalist movement. It begins with the following passage:

> For a long time a review of the contemporary history of Iran, particularly the movement for nationalization of the oil industry, has been our special

concern. In view of the opportunistic groups that are using the era to their own advantages and by their effort usurp its anti-imperialistic heritage, a realistic and documented account of that period is warranted. (*Nigarishi*, p. 7)

But this stated goal of presenting a 'realistic and documented account' does not reveal the whole purpose of the book. It seems that it aimed to achieve the following: (1) to defend Kashani and Fida'iyan-i Islam (the Devotees of Islam);[23] (2) to criticize the left; and (3) to criticize the short-lived provisional government of Mihdi Bazargan. Similar to the first book, it speaks of Musaddiq in a respectful manner. 'One of the vanguards . . .', states the book, 'was Dr Muhammad Musaddiq who . . . along with Mudarris, rose against internal despotism and external colonialism' (*Nigarishi*, p. 25). The key word in this passage is *one*: Musaddiq is seen only as one of the vanguards. The book assigns leadership of the nationalization movement to Musaddiq and the nationalists but only within the parliament, and to Kashani and the Devotees in society as a whole. 'From within and outside the parliament', the book states, 'Musaddiq and Kashani led the anti-imperialist struggle of the Muslim people' (*Nigarishi*, p. 28). Such a middle road seems to be a prudent way of defending Kashani without at the same time antagonizing the nationalists.

Musaddiq, however, is indirectly criticized. The criticisms of the first book are reiterated here, but the emphasis is upon two areas which have less to do with Musaddiq's policies and more with his personal character. The first is that Musaddiq was not a 'revolutionary' leader; the second that his struggle lacked ideological underpinnings. Musaddiq is blamed for not acting firmly against those responsible for the killings of the uprising of July 1952, and not supressing the left who 'were obviously supporting Musaddiq hypocritically' (*Nigarishi*, pp. 46–9).

But the most important point in this book, so far as the thesis of this paper is concerned, may be its criticism of Musaddiq for not allowing the 'doctrine' to guide him (*Nigarishi*, pp. 50–1). According to the book, in their social and political positions, Muslims are of three kinds: They are either *mazhabi-yi mazhabi* (religiously religious), or *siyasi-yi mazhabi* (politically religious) or *mazhabi-yi siyasi* (religiously political). The majority of Muslims, who do not form any particular opinion about social issues, comprise the first group. The second are those who give priority to politics, and are subdivided into those who use religion for political ends and those who innocently believe that religion should not play an important political role. The third refers to those who follow their religious beliefs in their social and political life. According to the author, Musaddiq was a 'politically religious' individual who, while being a good Muslim, lacked an 'ideological world view' and thus could not utilize 'the standards of the doctrine in his social policies' (*Nigarishi*, pp. 114–17). This criticism is a very shrewd one in that it points to the heart of the problem (i.e. the confrontation of Islam and nationalism). It is more than a criticism of Musaddiq; it was at the time a criticism of Bazargan as well as the policies and practices of his provisional government. Indirectly, Bazargan was portrayed as a 'politically religious' person. In fact, the concluding section of the book clearly states this point.

> A dangerous effort which may harm the revolution would be to follow Musaddiq and his government as a model and standard. Despite their weaknesses and deviations, the efforts of Musaddiq and the national movement were glorious and praiseworthy, but to try to adopt them in a different historical epoch is non-revolutionary and impractical. (*Nigarishi*, p. 81)

In spite of the deference towards Musaddiq, these criticisms go far deeper than before. They become much sharper and less tactful in the next two works, published in late summer of 1980. The timing was crucial in that the 'second revolution' (the name given to the fall of Bazargan and the capture of the United States Embassy) was making headway, and the new candidate for premiership, Muhammad Ali Raja'i, had assumed office.

The third work, *A short chapter on the events of the August 1953 coup*, is a pamphlet that re-evaluates the events which led to the August coup. Like the previous works, it presents a positive picture of Ayatullah Kashani. It begins by stating that 'the conspirators want to repeat their inauspicious plans in our glorious Islamic revolution' (*Guftari*, p. 5). In order not to experience another 1953 coup, the work argues, one should understand the way in which the glorious uprising of July 1952 was transformed into the miserable failure of August 1953 (*Guftari*, p. 7). The author blames Musaddiq for this reversal. The book reiterates the criticisms of other works but with more vigour and less deference to Musaddiq. Furthermore, the author claims that Musaddiq developed close ties with the communists after July 1952, which in the author's mind turned out to be 'one of the significant factors contributing to the failure of the movement' (*Guftari*, p. 25). In short, the work attempts to reverse the perception of Musaddiq from being a victim of the coup to an agent who contributed to it, and that of Kashani from being a supporter of the coup to its victim.

The fourth work is the most direct in its criticism of Musaddiq. *The uprising of the Muslim people of Iran* was written by Mahmud Kashani, Ayatullah Kashani's son and one of the candidates in the 1985 presidential election campaign. Similar to the other works, it begins with the complaint that the realities of the modern history of Iran have not been objectively explained due to the censorship of the Pahlavi regime in the past and the intentionally revisionist attitude of certain groups, particularly the nationalists, of today:

Under the banner of nationalism, and at times due to a peculiar intention and occasional lack of knowledge, these people insist on undermining the role of Islamic forces, particularly the leadership of the religious apparatus. (*Qiyam*, p. 89)

What distinguishes the line of reasoning in this book, as compared with the other three works, is the way in which its author relates the issue to contemporary political developments in Iran. He sees the honouring of Musaddiq and his era by the nationalists as a 'cynical way of weakening the leadership of the imam [Ayatullah Khomeini] and his clear path of neither East nor West' (*Qiyam*, p. 10).

Mahmud Kashani's criticisms of Musaddiq can be summarized as follows. First, Musaddiq is taken as a member of the aristocracy, and thus, by the author's account, was only interested in securing the interests of his own class. Second, Musaddiq practiced a policy of the separation of religion and politics. Third, 'Musaddiq did not respect the parliament and the laws.'

To substantiate his first accusation, the author points to Musaddiq's membership in a political association (the Anjuman-i Adamiyyat) during the Constitutional Revolution (1905–11) which he claims to be one branch of Freemasonry in Iran (*Qiyam*, p. 9).[24] He also refers to Musaddiq's inaction against the four-day government of Ahmad Qavam, which is widely believed to have been responsible for the killings of 22 July 1952, and also his appointments of 'ill-suited individuals' to high positions. 'Following the bloody uprising of the people,' the author writes, 'the most urgent demand of the people was . . . to take revenge on the thieves and murderers who had sucked the blood of the nation' (*Qiyam*, p. 84). Not only did Musaddiq arrest no one, he helped Qavam escape punishment by failing to implement the law which permitted confiscation of his properties, and appointed people who had been close to Qavam to high positions without even consulting Ayatullah Kashani (*Qiyam*, pp. 101–12). When Kashani objected to such appointments, Musaddiq wrote back asking him 'not to interfere with the affairs of the government for some time' (*Qiyam*, p. 115). The author interpreted this, not as a division of labour in the interests of good governance, but as evidence of Musaddiq's belief in the separation of religion and politics, a view which contradicts the prevalent view in Iran today.

This bring us to the second charge against Musaddiq, namely, that he and his supporters chose to forget that 'the movement was in fact an Islamic one' (*Qiyam*, p. 3). They followed a policy of 'the separation of religion and politics, thereby alienating gradually the religious arm of the movement' (*Qiyam*, p. 4). Other occurrences which, in the author's view, alienated Musaddiq's supporters were his resignation on 17 July 1952, without any prior consultation with Ayatullah Kashani; that he did not pay

attention to Kashani's letters to him throughout his rule, particularly prior
to the coup of August 1953; and his opposition to Kashani's election as the
speaker of the Majlis (*Qiyam*, p. 4). On the issue of Musaddiq's
resignation, the author suggests that outside powers played a role, but he
does not clarify this (*Qiyam*, p. 23).

The third accusation against Musaddiq contradicts what is widely
accepted as his greatest virtue, namely his respect for law. In the author's
view such reputation is not justified. He believes that Musaddiq's failure to
enforce the law prohibiting the consumption of alcohol and his insistance
on special executive power demonstrate his disrespect for legislative power
(*Qiyam*, pp. 151–65). This objection is not as serious as the other two.

The author does not explain his accusation that Musaddiq was a
Freemason, and his citation of Musaddiq's oath of membership to
Anjuman-i Adamiyyat (the Association for Humanity) and his passing
comment are unconvincing.[25] Moreover, his account of Musaddiq's
resignation is very vague. Is this vagueness due to the fact that at the time
the followers of the Imam were unsure what position to take concerning
Musaddiq? The answer seems to lie in the fact that they had not achieved
complete control of power as yet. Following the March 1981 crisis from
which the followers of the Imam emerged victorious, they expressed their
position with regard to Musaddiq with much greater vigour and clarity.

The crisis of March 1981

What transpired in March 1981 was the final showdown of the internal
struggle for power in Iran, manifested in the persons of President Bani-
Sadr and Prime Minister Raja'i.[26] Its importance for the discussion here
stems from the fact that Bani-Sadr came to represent the nationalists' point
of view and in fact was referred to by some as the 'new Musaddiq'. Raja'i,
on the other hand, came to represent the followers of the Imam.

In September of 1980, at a gathering for the memorial ceremony of
'Bloody Friday' (7 September 1978), Bani-Sadr criticized the government
for what he called 'the use of religion for political ends'.[27] His speech came
under attack by key religious figures in the government. The first official
response came in the form of a vote of confidence (169 in support, 14
against and 10 abstentions) for Muhammad Ali Raja'i to assume the post of
premiership, with the mandate of following the line of the Imam. Later the
speaker of the parliament, Hujjat al-Islam Ali Akbar Hashimi-Rafsanjani,
voiced his opposition to the speech. Interestingly enough, he went beyond
personality by saying,

In short, as they are afraid of a doctrinaire [*maktabi*] government, we
similarly are afraid of the government of liberals. We cannot tolerate

liberalism to rule the country after the revolution, thereby ruining the revolution altogether.[28]

The uneasy relationship continued, and the crisis culminated in the first week of March. On the invitation of four members of the Majlis (Mihdi Bazargan, Yadullah Sahabi, Ibrahim Yazdi and Hashim Sabbaqiyan) a gathering was held on 30 February 1980. While reiterating their commitment to 'Irano-Islamic identity', the speakers voiced their concern about the way in which the revolution was losing its popularity and the country was moving towards one party rule.[29] Bazargan even went so far as to say that 'the slogan of the revolution, "Freedom, independence, and the Islamic Republic", has in fact evolved from the same philosophy [Musaddiq's] under the leadership of the great revolutionary the Grand Ayatullah Khomeini.'[30] As he tried to link Musaddiq and the nationalist movement to the revolution, the 'followers of the Imam' found the view offensive that Ayatullah Khomeini had followed Musaddiq's path. During the first week of March thousands of pictures of Musaddiq kissing the hand of one of Muhammad Riza Pahlavi's previous wives were distributed to defame him.

The climax came on 5 March 1981, which coincided with the anniversary of Musaddiq's death.[31] Throughout the country special ceremonies were held, but only by the followers of Bazargan and Bani-Sadr. In Tehran, where Bani-Sadr spoke, the ceremony turned bloody as a result of a clash between various factions in the audience. The organ of the IRP blamed 'the president's special guards' for attacking the members of the party of God (Hizbullah); while Bani-Sadr blamed the 'thugs of the government' for attacking the 'innocent participants'. A significant editorial was published on the same day in *Jumhuri-yi Islami*, entitled 'Musaddiq and the end of the ideology of nationalism and Tudehism',[32] which marked the beginning of a new phase in the Islamic Republic's attitude to Musaddiq. 'Nationalism does not suffice,' it argued.

> The nation . . . has learned that 'national aims' and their attainment, even if very grand – such as oil nationalization – cannot in themselves pave the way for the emergence of a just, free and popular regime . . . If only independence and the downfall of the monarchy, the slogans of the old and new nationalists, without any ideological commitment . . . constitute the aim, the success will be temporary . . . *Indeed these types of mentality were buried with the late Musaddiq.* This, in no way, means any contempt for the positive contribution of that great man . . . The point to be made here is that what has happened in Iran is clearly a revolutionary movement, in the full sense of the term, based on the [Islamic] doctrine . . . whose criteria is absolute servitude to God, the Koran, the imams and the religious leaders under the leadership of Imam Khomeini.[33] [Emphasis added]

According to the passage, Musaddiq was good but only for his time, which is long gone. Those who exalt him are anachronistic. The theme of this editorial became the central topic of debates in the aftermath of the crisis of 5 March. The followers of the Imam celebrated their victory a few days later on 14 March when the first country-wide official ceremony was held to commemorate Ayatullah Kashani's death. Clearly the nationalists had lost the upper hand. The impeachment of Bani-Sadr a few months later (by a resolution of the Majlis on 21 June 1981) marked the end of the active role of the Iranian nationalists, at least inside Iran, and the beginning of intensive Islamization in the country.

The ascendancy of the followers of the Imam

The first sign of Islamization is seen in the statement of the prime minister on 20 March 1981, in commemoration of the 1951 nationalization of the oil industry. The statement, *inter alia*, read:

> This day is a reminder of the struggle of our heroic nation to secure our rights and the removal of international colonialism from our country . . . Those who are familiar with the events of the period and the problems which led to the nationalization of the oil industry know very well that . . . the victory in that movement came only because of unity and the constructive teachings of Islam.[34]

There is no mention of Musaddiq or his role. A member of parliament, Bazargan did at this time talk about Musaddiq and his role in an interview published in his own newspaper *Mizan* (5 March 1981). But his was the only mention of Musaddiq. Henceforth, the focus of attention turned to the religious wing of the movement, particularly Kashani and the Devotees.

A memorial stamp was issued honouring Ayatullah Kashani on 21 July 1981.[35] A few months later, for the first time, the anniversary of the death of the leader of the Devotees of Islam, Navvab Safavi, was commemorated officially. One magazine devoted a special issue to him[36] and so did some newspapers.[37] The contributers to the magazine argued that it was Navvab Safavi who should be credited for the nationalization, and not others. The fact that no mention of Musaddiq is made on 5 March 1982 points to the intensification of the Islamic trend. On 14 March in commemoration of Kashani's death, special ceremonies were held everywhere and the newspapers ran special stories. The newspaper *Kayhan* even had one full page for three subsequent days (15–17 March) showing how Kashani had supported Musaddiq but the latter had betrayed him by 'implementing the thesis of the separation of politics from religion and making constant efforts to undermine the religious leaders who were the leaders of the religio-political currents' (17 March). It further suggested that it had been 'Kashani's influence which encouraged Musaddiq in his struggle against the British and in the withholding of Iran's recognition of Israel' (16 March). In other words, there was a conscious attempt to revise the historiography of that period and replace Musaddiq with Ayatullah Kashani and Navvab Safavi.

The following years witnessed the repetition of ceremonies for Kashani and Safavi, with Musaddiq pushed into further obscurity. The commemorations of January and March of 1985, however, are worth noting. There is no mention of Musaddiq, and Ayatullah Kashani and Navvab Safavi are portrayed as the real heroes of the nationalization period. President Hujjat al-Islam Khamaneh'i said on the occasion: 'Following the late Mudarris who started a parliamentary struggle against the ruling regime, we know of no one who like Navvab Safavi presented the necessity of Islamic struggle.[38] He emphasized the Islamic aspect of the struggle without ever mentioning its nationalistic aspect. Those newspapers which dealt with the nationalists' movement, only spoke of Kashani and his role. 'It was because of public opinion, Ayatullah Kashani's struggle and the unequivocal support of Islamic religious leaders', one paper suggested, 'that the nationalization bill . . . was passed . . . *Musaddiq, who happened to be present along with Kashani during the nationalization movement*, became prime minister' [emphasis added].[39]

While the review of the daily papers, especially the organ of the ruling IRP, shows the general perception on Musaddiq's era and the way in which it has been greatly Islamized since the crisis of March 1981, the crudest and the most direct treatment of Musaddiq is found in the works of Hasan Ayat. No individual in Iran could represent the views of the Islamic Republic better than Ayat. He was one of the founders of the IRP; the secretary of the Assembly of Experts which approved the new Constitution (and is thought responsible for the principle of the guardianship of the theologian jurisconsult being incorporated into the new Constitution); a vocal member of the first parliament until his assassination in August 1981; and the most adamant critic of Musaddiq and Bani-Sadr.[40]

Ayat's treatment of Musaddiq and his era, outlined below, is taken from two of his works: one published by the IRP in 1984, entitled *Darsha'i az tarikh-i siyasi-yi Iran* (Lessons from the political history of Iran); the other published by the theological teachers of Qum in 1982, entitled *Chihreh-i haqiqi-yi Musaddiq al-Saltaneh* (The real face of Musaddiq al-Saltaneh).[41] It should be pointed out, however, that even Ayat's criticisms of Musaddiq changed as the society experienced greater Islamization. Before the March 1981 crisis, Ayat was more tactful and reserved. Two of the works treated earlier, *Nigarishi kutah bar nahzat-i milli-yi Iran* (A short account of the national movement of Iran) and *Guftari kutah darbareh-i vaqa'i-yi 18 Murdad* (A short chapter on the events of the August 1953 coup), that had been published in the name of various organizations turned out to be Ayat's.[42] A new book published in 1983 in his name, by the theological teachers of Qum seminaries, entitled, *Fasli az tarikh-i siyasi-yi Iran: Nigarishi kutah bar nahzat-i milli-yi Iran* (A chapter of the political history of Iran: a short look at the national movement of Iran) includes the two earlier works.[43] This is significant in that it precisely shows the shift referred to earlier. Even Ayat who, as will be shown, makes the crudest attacks on Musaddiq, had a more moderate view of the events of Musaddiq's period before the March 1981 crisis.

Ayat begins by arguing that two trends of thought have been dominant in Iran during the past two centuries. On the one side, there is what he calls 'the line of colonialism' (*khatt-i isti'mar*), and on the other side, there is 'the line of anti-colonialism' (*khatt-i zidd-i isti'mar*) both of which are easily identifiable (*Darsha'i*, pp. 274–5). The line of colonialism includes those elements which have had direct connections with foreign powers (i.e. the Tudeh Party), and those who are inspired by outside ideologies (i.e. the constitutionalists). Ayat implies that Musaddiq belongs to the latter group. Furthermore, he equates those who follow Musaddiq today as the followers of the line of colonialism. In his view, followers of that line commemorate 5 March (Musaddiq's death), whereas those who follow the anti-colonial line commemorate 14 March (Kashani's death) (*Darsha'i*, p. 176). Ayat's primary objective in his lectures on the modern political history of Iran was to identify and combat the protagonists of the line of colonialism. According to the preface, provided by the IRP, Ayat spent all his life trying to achieve this objective.

> It was during these years [post 1953] that western colonialism portrayed him (Dr Musaddiq) as a victimized individual, a patriotic politician and a man of high political stature. Moreover, through widespread propaganda he was even presented as a martyr, thereby obscuring the bad record of his career. Many political parties and groups whose roots are linked with the obvious and not so obvious agents of Britain and America (e.g. the National Front), the Socialists [i.e. Khalil Maliki's Third Force party, later the Socialist League] and ten other groups had one thing in common which was their praise for Musaddiq . . . The martyred Ayat never walked the misguided path of the nationalists. Since his early youth, because of his correct identification of this satanic path and his familiarity with the real character of Musaddiq, Ayat launched a staunch struggle against Musaddiq and his followers. (*Darsha'i*, pp. 3–4)

Ayat's treatment of Musaddiq and his era qualitatively differs from those presented earlier. He reiterates almost all the criticisms raised by others presented here, but the language he uses is different. First, he is very aggressive and offensive in his tone. Second, he emphasizes those criticisms which undermine the image that people have formed of Musaddiq throughout the years. Third, while others acknowledge Musaddiq's contribution to the era, he tries to prove that Musaddiq made none. And finally, his approach to Iranian contemporary history is the most revisionist. The most effective way of presenting his account is identifying his answers to three questions: who was Musaddiq? who was responsible for the nationalization of the oil industry? and what was Musaddiq's role in the coup of August 1953?

The answer to the first question is found in the first chapter of his book entitled *Chihreh-i haqiqi-yi Musaddiq al-Saltaneh* (The true face of Musaddiq). He begins with the following words:

A review of *Payam-i Jibheh-i Milli* (the organ of the National Front), *Junbish* (the organ of Ali Asghar Hajj Sayyid Javadi's group), and *Payam-i Mujahid* (the organ of the Mujahidin), shows that they all cry that the 'revolution should follow Musaddiq's path'. What we see so clearly in Musaddiq's path is the manifestation of colonialism. Without any doubt, Musaddiq has been one strong element (of foreign powers) in Iran in the past hundred years . . . In a careful analysis, the conspiracy of August 1953 [the coup] was the defeat of the uprising of our oppressed nation and not the fall of Musaddiq. In this conspiracy, he played his role well and was greatly rewarded for it; imperialism made him a national figure by its widespread propaganda. (*Chihreh-i*, p. 27)

Thus, according to Ayat, far from being a nationalist, Musaddiq did nothing but to secure 'the interests of the foreign powers' and he did that because he was a member of the Iranian aristocracy who has 'always paid allegiance to outside sources'. To substantiate his claim, the author points to Musaddiq's family background and his association with the British. 'Contrary to common belief,' he writes, 'Musaddiq was not from a poor or even a middle-class background. Rather, he was a descendant of the Qajar family which is responsible for the majority of our calamities and miseries' (*Chihreh-i*, p. 28). While it is not clear what he means by 'common belief', he concludes from his statement that this brought Musaddiq enormous wealth and influence. How else, Ayat asks, could he spend his time 'in Europe or live a completely complacent and secure life in his green and beautiful village, Ahmadabad', whenever he was out of political office (*Chihreh-i*, p. 32). Moreover, because of this background, Musaddiq was given such an important position as the governor of Fars province at a very young age, a province where Musaddiq's uncle, Farmanfarma, had committed 'many crimes and the people hated this family there' (*Chihreh-i*, p. 32). Then, the author wonders whether such a person could serve the oppressed people or be a model for a 'revolution which has made Imam Ali's justice its guiding principle' (*Chihreh-i*, p. 29).

More than family background, in Ayat's mind, Musaddiq's 'close ties with the British' stopped him from serving the Iranian people. To begin with, Ayat dwells on the issue of Musaddiq's membership of the Adamiyyat association, seen as the Iranian Masonic lodge. He quotes Musaddiq's oath of joining the society as a proof; but he sees Musaddiq's support for Mirza Malkam Khan (1833–1908), the founder of Freemasonry in Iran, as a stronger proof (*Chihreh-i*, p. 31). The other evidence he gives of Musaddiq's close ties to Britain are:

1 Musaddiq took refuge in the home of the secretary to the British delegation at the time the constitutionalists had to escape the royalists by rushing to the compound of that delegation (*Chihreh-i*, p. 28).
2 He became the governor general of Fars province when that part of the country was under British domination, and served the British by suppressing the Tangistani uprising (*Chihreh-i*, pp. 32–4). Subsequently, when due to the change of administration in the capital he lost his post, the British delegation supported his reinstatement (*Chihreh-i*, p. 35).
3 He participated in many Cabinets which 'were definitely pro-British'. Also Ayat argues that Musaddiq supported Riza Shah and, in fact, helped him to gain power by joining his Cabinet and later serving him as an advisor when he became the king (*Chihreh-i*, pp. 37–42). His response to the question of Musaddiq's opposition to Riza Shah is that Musaddiq wanted a constitutional monarchy and Riza Shah was an autocrat. In Ayat's view, Musaddiq had no philosophical disagreement with this secular leader; his opposition was over tactics (*Chihreh-i*, p. 80).
4 He defended the interests of Britain on more than one occasion. For example, Musaddiq's introduction and successful lobbying for the bill which limited Millspaugh's authority (in Ayat's analysis Millspaugh was undermining British interests) (*Chihreh-i*, p. 48). Musaddiq also defended British policies, Ayat argues, by trying to show that British interference in the internal affairs of Iran was the function of certain individual diplomats and not the conscious policy of that country (*Chihreh-i*, pp. 49–51).

As further sign of foreign ties, Ayat cites Musaddiq's relations with the United States. He claims that Musaddiq is responsible for the American involvement in Iran. Musaddiq's third power foreign policy is interpreted as a way of inviting the Americans into Iran. Musaddiq's letter to President Harry Truman for assistance, according to Ayat, was written when Ayatullah Kashani was trying to eradicate all involvement of foreign powers in Iran (*Chihreh-i*, pp. 66–7). He also cites Musaddiq's understanding with the Americans in 1953, which Ayat argues 'established the

American nest of spies under the rubric of the office of the Point IV', as indicative of Musaddiq's favourable inclination towards foreign forces (*Chihreh-i*, p. 71).

Exaggerations and over-statements in Ayat's argument are readily apparent. For example, his claim, based on contradictory sources,[44] that Musaddiq simultaneously served British and American interests leads to one conclusion only: Ayat deploys an ideological approach in his bid to undermine the image of Musaddiq as an anti-imperialist and the prototype of an Iranian nationalist. This may be linked with Ayat's close ties with the Toilers' Party, which after parting from Musaddiq became his arch-enemy, as well as a further attempt to consolidate the power of the Islamic Republic.

Ayat's objectives become even more evident when the second question, Musaddiq's role in the nationalization of oil, is examined. He questions the common perception which equates nationalization with Musaddiq's name. He claims that far from the hero of oil nationalization, Musaddiq was a latecomer to the game. Ayat begins by arguing that 'the 14th Majlis, whose majority were elements of British colonialism, played the role of defending the British interest and keeping Russians and Americans out' (*Chihreh-i*, pp. 45–6). In other words Musaddiq's proposal, ratified by the 14th Majlis, forbidding the granting of any concession to foreign powers was, according to Ayat, a way of achieving exactly that goal; Musaddiq's bill, forbidding any future concession to any foreign power, amounted to preserving the monopoly of the British concession. If Musaddiq had been interested in limiting foreign influences he would have called for the retroactive cancellation of all standing concessions as well. As further proof of Musaddiq's support of the British, Ayat cites Musaddiq's refusal to sign the proposal of Ghulam Husayn Rahimian (a member of the parliament), during the 14th Majlis (1944–6), calling for oil nationalization (*Chihreh-i*, p. 47).

According to Ayat, the real heroes of the oil nationalization are the following: members of the parliament who 'blocked the passage of Gass-Gulsha'iyan's Supplemental Agreement in the 15th Majlis'; Ha'irizadeh, a member of the special committee dealing with oil in the 16th Majlis; Kashani, 'the first person who made it an issue outside the parliament'; and the Devotees of Islam who assassinated Hajj Ali Razmara (*Darsha'i*, pp. 166–8). In Ayat's view, Musaddiq did his utmost to undermine these people's efforts. As the supplementary agreement was debated in the 15th Majlis, Musaddiq, who was inactive politically, only sent a note on Makki's request which *inter alia* said, 'if the proposal has to pass', make sure that the royalty is paid in gold instead of British pounds. Ayat takes this phrase to mean that Musaddiq implicitly approved the agreement (*Chihreh-i*, p. 56). and he points to the message Musaddiq sent to the head of the Anglo-Iranian Oil Company in Tehran, N. R. Seddon, on 21 June 1950, informing him of the formation of the special committee to handle the oil dispute, as another reason for Musaddiq's support of the British. Since Musaddiq's note included the names of the members of the committee, Ayat regarded this as an indication that the committee was formed with the consent of the British (*Chihreh-i*, p. 60). 'Basically,' Ayat writes, 'Musaddiq's mission in this committee was to delay the resolution of the oil issue by wasting time' (*Chihreh-i*, p. 61). Only Razmara's assassination saved the oil for Iranians. Ayat's shrewd manipulation of facts and documents, in the face of the lack of any challenge to his account, produces a great deal of confusion about that period in Iranian history which might prove hard to disentangle. His treatment of Musaddiq's role in the coup is even more striking.

Ayat's arguments on this issue are encapsulated in his account of Musaddiq's resignation on 17 July 1952, after Musaddiq's failure to secure the post of the minister of Defence. According to Ayat, since Musaddiq 'wanted to deadlock and destroy the struggle of the Iranian nation', he used the issue of the Ministry of Defense as an excuse (*Chihreh-i*, p. 77). If this had not been the case, Ayat argues, Musaddiq would have consulted Ayatullah Kashani or his colleagues when his negotiations with the Shah proved futile; or at least, after his resignation, he would have talked to the Iranian people. But instead he went directly to his home and did not receive anyone until he was returned to his position by the uprising of 22 July, under the leadership of Kashani (*Darsha'i*, pp. 217–18). Moreover, after his triumphant return he not only did not punish the responsible individuals in the four-day government of Ahmad Qavam, but allowed certain officials to continue in their high positions (*Darsha'i*, pp. 218–22). Musaddiq alienated himself further by demanding emergency temporary executive power of legislation, thereby undermining the Majlis and enacting unpopular laws such as the public security bill (*Darsha'i*, pp. 192, 251–5). This kind of behaviour, in Ayat's mind, prepared the way for the coup.

Ayat argues that Musaddiq supported the coup in order to leave office as a 'hero', so that 'they [possibly foreign powers] could use him or his name to defeat future movements' (*Darsha'i*, p. 305). The strongest evidence Ayat presents to demonstrate his thesis is a letter by Ayatullah Kashani to Musaddiq, supposedly written the day before the coup. In the letter the ayatullah warned Musaddiq of the coup and even named the general involved.[45] But Musaddiq made no response, which Ayat takes as a sign that he approved of the coup. The authenticity of the letter has been questioned by some people.[46] Furthermore, he bases his argument on a book published by the Tudeh Party which is an apologetic account of its role in the nationalization movement.[47]

Conclusion

To the proponents of the Islamic Republic of Iran, Musaddiq is not simply an individual, but a trend, and a very controversial one. Historically, nationalism originated in Europe but, like the states system itself, nationalism expanded its horizon by becoming an international ideology. In fact, many Islamic countries used it effectively to free themselves from colonialism. But as the editorial of the IRP organ suggested, the age of nationalism may have passed; at least, this is what the resurgence of Islam and the effective defeat of the nationalists in Iran seem to suggest. There is a paradox, however, which would question this assumption: if the age of nationalism has long passed why do the same people who make this declaration continue to find it necessary to prove that nationalism is an anachronism.

Following the setback of the nationalists after the fall of Bazargan's government and the impeachment of Bani-Sadr, the perception of Musaddiq as the hero of nationalism has been constantly under attack. To some extent, this is a response to the challenge of the nationalists and their activities. But there may have been other motives behind it after the March 1981 crisis. For by then the nationalists had already lost the battle for control of the revolution and their last survivor, Mihdi Bazargan, had been subject to constant criticism and even physical assault. He was even accused of holding un-Islamic views and his candidacy for presidency was dismissed, because he was considered to be a 'liberal'.

Were such criticisms due to the ideological difference between Musaddiq's political philosophy and 'juridical Islam' (*Islam-i fiqahat*) (the interpretation of Islam ruling Iran today)? On the level of theoretical discourse, the answer seems to be strongly affirmative; but in practice this is less so because, if philosophical discussion was the central concern, a careful examination of Musaddiq's works would show that he would not have approved of the concept of the guardianship of the theologian jurisconsult. Neither personal attacks nor detailed analyses of the relationship between Musaddiq and Kashani were necessary.

Such great concern results from the political dynamics of a revolutionary state trying to legitimize its rule and consolidate its power. In other words, the revisionist historiography is a way of demystifying the image of Musaddiq while exalting Kashani. In short, though there is always the potential of an ideological clash between Islam and nationalism, it has been proven that they can coexist; but when the existence of one is threatened by the other the two can no longer coexist and the clash becomes inevitable. The defensive attitude of the pre-March crisis and the shift of focus from the nationalists to the liberals point to such an assertion. Even the more Islamic National Front members like Bazargan, whose views do not concur with juridical Islam, are now under attack. When nationalism threatened the regime it came under attack; and now that a more liberal interpretation of Islam is threatening the regime, with the exception of Musaddiq personally, liberalism comes under attack.[48]

A more remote reason for the revisionary treatment of Musaddiq's era and his image may be due to the authoritarian tradition of Iranian politics. The absolute authority of the leader cannot be questioned by any other rival source, whether a living political leader or a previous charismatic leader alive in people's consciousness. The cases of Riza Shah Pahlavi and his son Muhammad Riza are two very recent examples: neither could tolerate a rival political leader, though both had to deal with Dr Musaddiq. Is not the intolerance of Musaddiq and his followers today, in part, a manifestation of the same tradition?

Notes

1   I would like to thank greatly professor R. K. Ramazani who allowed me to use his valuable private collection of books and newspapers of Musaddiq's era and discussed some of the issues raised in this paper with me. Professor James Bill originally suggested the topic and made insightful comments on an earlier draft. My wife, colleague and friend Fatemeh Givechian, herself a social scientist, read the chapter carefully; Dr John Kelsay, professors H. L. Seneviratne, M. R. Ghanoonparvar, Dr Lowell Gustafson, and Dr F. Azimi read an earlier draft. Hassan Farahnakiyan, Yann Richard, and Mehdi Noorbaksh helped me to procure some of the primary sources. Needless to say, I assume full responsibility for errors of interpretation or facts.

2   Sermon delivered on 7 November 1978. See *Kalam-i Imam; saltanat va tarikh-i Iran* (Tehran, 1984) p. 83.

3   Sermon delivered on 22 July 1981. See *Kalam-i Imam; Milligara'i* (Tehran, 1983) p. 49.

4   See Farhang Rajaee, *Islamic Values and World View; Khomeyni on Man, the State and International Politics* (Lanham, Md, 1983), and sources cited therein.

5   *Jumhuri-yi Islami*, 22 December 1981.

6   On 22 July 1952, following Musaddiq's resignation on 17 July there was a popular uprising in his support. Those who died in the incident, known as the 30 Tir uprising, were buried in the Ibn-Babarayh cemetery. It was Musaddiq's wish to be buried there, but the government withheld permission and he was interned at Ahmadabad.

7   *Ittila'at*, 4 March 1979.

8   *Chardah-i Isfand-i 1357: Yadbud-i Dr Muhammad Musaddiq* (Tehran, n.d.).

9   The IRP held a private ceremony for him in which one of its principal and vocal founders, Hasan Ayat, spoke.

10 For example, in his account of the revolution, Bazargan takes the oil nationalization episode and its aftermath as the beginning of the revolution. By contrast, the official historiography in Iran takes June 1963 as the

beginning. See Mihdi Bazargan, *Inqilab-i Iran dar daw harikat* (Tehran, 1984).

11   *Ittila'at*, 22 July 1979.

12   *Jumhuri-yi Islami*, 22 July 1979.

13   See 'Tahlili mustanad az kudita-yi 28 Murdad', *Jumhuri-yi Islami*, 18 August 1979.

14   For Bazargan's account of the story see his *Shawra-yi inqilab va dawlat-i muvaqqat* (Tehran, 1982).

15   'Musaddiq pishva-yi mubarizat-i zidd-i isti'mari-yi gharb', *Ittila'at*, 4 March 1980.

16   *Jumhuri-yi Islami*, 17 March 1980.

17   Ibid., 31 March 1980.

18   Ibid., 22 July 1980.

19   (Qum, 1979). Hereafter cited in the text as *Ruhaniyyat*.

20   (Tehran, 1979). Hereafter cited in the text as *Nigarishi*.

21   Pamphlet 2 (Tehran, 1979). Hereafter cited in the text as *Guftari*.

22   By Mahmud Kashani (Tehran, 1980). Hereafter cited in the text as *Qiyam*.

23   Fida'iyan-i Islam were an Islamic 'integralist' group who adopted political assassination as an official policy. For a sympathetic account of their activity see Riza Gulisurkhi, 'Fida'iyan-i Islam, Aghazgar-i junbish-i musallahaneh dar Iran', *Ittila'at*, 30 April 1979; and Husayn Khushniyyat, *Sayyid Mujtaba Navvab Safavi: Andishiha, mubarizat va shahadat-i U* (Tehran, 1981). For the political views of the group see *Rahnama-yi haqayiq* (Tehran, 1950); a translation of this work is found in Adele K. Ferdows, *Religion in Iranian Nationalism* (Ph.D thesis, Indiana University, 1970).

24   See also Appendix 1 which includes Musaddiq's oath of membership to the Adamiyyat association.

25   On Dr Musaddiq's membership of the Adamiyyat association and or a Freemason Lodge see *Asnad sukhan miguyand: aya Musaddiq Feramason bud?* (Tehran, 1980–1); and Isma'il Ra'in, *Feramasoniri dar Iran*, vol. 1 (Tehran, n.d.). The first work was prepared by the National Front to disprove the claim that Musaddiq was a Freemason. On the formation and the philosophy of the Adamiyyat association see Firaydun Adamiyyat, *Fikr-i azadi va nahzat-i mashrutiyyat* (Tehran, 1961) pp. 199–332.

26   For a revealing account of the relation between the two men see *Chigunehgi-yi intikhab-i avvalin nakhust vazir-i Jumhuri-yi Islami-yi Iran* (Tehran, 1981).

27   *Ittila'at*, 8 September 1980.

28   Ibid., 10 September 1980.

29   For a detailed account of the day and the text of the speeches see *Mizan*, 9 Isfand 1359/1 March 1981.

30   Ibid., p. 3.

31   The daily papers gave complete coverage of the whole crisis. See for example *Ittila'at*, 5–11 March 1981.

32   'Musaddiq va payan-i ideolozhi-yi milligara'i va Tudeh'igara'i', *Jumhuri-yi Islami*, 5 March 1981.

33   Ibid., pp. 1ff.

34   The text of the message is found in *Mizan*, 14 Isfand 1359/5 March 1981.

35   *Jumhuri-yi Islami*, 21 July 1981.

36   'Vizheh nameh-i Shahid Navvab Safavi', *Surush* 3.130 (16 January 1982).

37   See for example *Kayhan*, 17 January 1982.

38   *Jumhuri-yi Islami*, 17 January 1985.

39   Ibid., 14 March 1985.

40   A sympathetic profile of Ayat, prepared by the IRP, is found in Hasan Ayat, *Darsha'i az tarikh-i siyasi-yi Iran* (Tehran, 1984). Hereafter cited in the text as *Darsha'i*.

41   Hasan Ayat (Qum, 1982). Hereafter cited in the text as *Chihreh-i*.

42   See *n*.20 and *n*.21.

43   Hasan Ayat, *Fasli az tarikh-i siyasi-yi Iran: Nigarishi kutah bar nahzat-i milli-yi Iran* (Qum, 1983).

44   The first is a book by Dr Bahman Isma'ili, *Zindiginameh-i Musaddiq al-Saltaneh* (Tehran, n.d.), which portrays Musaddiq as an agent of British interests and the second is by Mihdi Bahar, *Miraskhar-i isti'mar* (Tehran, 1978), which portrays Musaddiq as an agent of American interests.

45   For the text of this letter in English as well as Musaddiq's response see Yann Richard, 'Ayatollah Kashani: precursor of the Islamic Republic?', in *Religion and Politics in Iran*, ed. Nikki R. Keddie (New Haven, 1983) pp. 114–15.

46   Ibid., p. 115.

47   M. F. Javanshir, *Tajrubeh-i 28 Murdad: nazari beh tarikh-i junbish-i milli shudan-i naft* (Tehran, 1980).

48   For an example of such a criticism see Mihdi Marubi, *Ifshagari darbareh-i Nahzat-i Azadi* (Tehran, 1983).

PART II

Oil

6

The American oil industry and the Fifty–fifty Agreement of 1950

IRVINE H. ANDERSON

On 30 December 1950, Fred A. Davies, executive vice-president of the Arabian-American Oil Company, and Shaykh Abdullah Sulayman al-Hamdan, Finance minister of the Kingdom of Saudi Arabia, signed an agreement dividing Aramco's profits equally with Saudi Arabia through the medium of a Saudi income tax. The exact phrase was a tax equalling 'fifty percent (50%) of the gross income of Aramco, after such gross income . . . [had been] . . . reduced by Aramco's cost of operations, including . . . income taxes . . . payable to any foreign country' (i.e. the United States).[1] This Fifty–fifty Agreement of 1950 had the practical effect of transferring revenue from the American government to King Abd al-Aziz ibn Saud of Saudi Arabia, much to his pleasure, but much to the dismay of the Anglo-Iranian Oil Company – which found itself faced with demands for a similar arrangement in Iran. Other chapters in this volume deal with the influence of the Fifty–fifty Agreement on subsequent events in Iran; this chapter focuses on the origins of the Aramco–Saudi agreement, and the role that the American government did or did not play in its formulation. There was much rhetorical smoke surrounding the subject in the late 1970s, and the intent here is to blow some of that away and examine what really happened.[2]

This analysis will present three different versions of the same story – all technically correct, but each focused on a different aspect of the same sequence of events, and each leading to a different conclusion. Karl Mannheim pointed out long ago that different world views focus attention on different aspects of complex situations, and can lead to radically different interpretations because they 'do not merely deflect thought from the object of observation, but also serve to fix attention upon aspects of the situation which otherwise would be obscured or pass unnoticed'.[3] The three versions presented here provide a classic illustration of Mannheim's point. The first I have chosen to call the Church–Blair version, because it summarizes the manner in which the episode was described in the final report of Senator Frank Church's Subcommittee on Multinational Corporations in 1975,[4] and in John Blair's subsequent book on *The Control of Oil*.[5] The second is a micro-version detailing the actual sequence of events at the working level. The third is a macro-version viewing the same set of facts from a much broader perspective. To the question of whether the United States government was the major force behind the Fifty–fifty Agreement, the three versions provide the answers yes, no, yes. This argument will favour the third perspective.

The broad context within which the episode occurred is as follows. By the late 1940s, increasing domestic demand had converted the United States from a net exporter to a net importer of petroleum. Not only did American oil companies have an interest in continuing to develop overseas sources of supply, but the Joint Chiefs of Staff and the Department of State had concluded that American strategic interests were best served by expanding eastern hemisphere production and conserving western hemisphere resources for potential use in wartime.[6] This strategic viewpoint, coupled with a growing concern over containing the spread of communism, focused attention on Saudi Arabia, where Aramco held an exclusive petroleum concession, and where an Islamic fundamentalist ruler, Abd al-Aziz, stood in staunch opposition to communism on both religious and royalist grounds.

Aramco was a jointly owned subsidiary of Standard Oil of California (Socal), The Texas Company (Texaco), the Standard Oil Company (New Jersey) (later Exxon), and the Socony-Vacuum Oil Company (later Mobil). It had staked its claim in 1933, discovered oil in commercial quantities in 1938, and begun a full-scale production buildup immediately after the second world war. Prior to oil, Abd al-Aziz's only real sources of income were custom duties and the annual Muslim pilgrimage to Mecca. He had therefore been delighted with the prospect of growing revenues from oil, but became increasingly discontented with the slow rate of production buildup and the royalty of only four shillings per ton to which he was entitled by the original concession agreement of 1933.

It was in response to this demand for increased revenue that Aramco consulted with the Department of State in 1950 and renegotiated its arrangement with Abd al-Aziz so that each party would henceforth receive 50 per cent of the profits made by Aramco. But subsequent critics have charged that the party behind this was really the executive branch of the American government, which used the foreign tax credit provision in American tax law as an 'ingenious way' to subsidize Saudi Arabia 'without ever needing [an] appropriation or authorization from the Congress'.[7] The charges were based on testimony and data collected for hearings conducted in 1974 by Senator Frank Church's subcommittee of the Senate Foreign Relations Committee investigating the influence of multinational corporations on American foreign policy. Based primarily on the testimony of George C. McGhee, who in 1950 had been Assistant Secretary of State for Near Eastern Affairs, the subcommittee concluded in its final report that the decision to allow Aramco to use a foreign tax credit to offset a Saudi income tax was made by the Treasury Department on the specific recommendation of the National Security Council.

The tax credit idea was a complicated one which requires some explanation. Some type of foreign tax credit had been a part of the American tax code since 1918, to avoid double taxation and help American companies compete overseas. What was at issue was whether under the circumstances the Internal Revenue Service would interpret the increased payments to Saudi Arabia as a *de facto* royalty (which would have been an operating expense) or as a legitimate Saudi tax on Aramco profits. Counting the payment as a tax permitted it to be deducted in full from Aramco's American income tax; whereas counting it as an operating expense would decrease Aramco's American tax bill by less than half of that amount.[8]

In his book, *The Control of Oil*, Blair made this clear with excerpts from an exchange between Senator Church and Ambassador McGhee:

Senator Church: Upon the recommendation of the National Security Council, the Treasury made the decision to permit Aramco to treat royalties paid to Saudi Arabia as though they were taxes paid to the Arabian government . . . The effect of the decision was to transfer . . . [funds] . . . out of the US Treasury and into the Arabian Treasury . . . to give Arabia more money . . . Isn't that correct?
Ambassador McGhee: Yes, that is one way of looking at it.[9]

This is the Church–Blair version of the origin of the Fifty–fifty Agreement.

The Saudi viewpoint

What I have chosen to call the micro-version is much more intricate. To examine the episode in depth requires a look at the motives, leverage, and actual behaviour of each of the specific participants mentioned above: Abd al-Aziz, Aramco, Aramco's four parent corporations (Socal, The Texas Company, Jersey and Socony-Vacuum), George McGhee and the Department of State, the Treasury Department's Internal Revenue Service, the Joint Chiefs of Staff, and the National Security Council.

Let us start with Abd al-Aziz. As we know, he was a shrewd and charismatic ruler of what was then an impoverished desert country, who used liberal financial subsidies to prevent his Bedouin tribesmen from raiding one another and to keep them loyal to himself. He had an aversion to modern bookkeeping, and, as one observer put it, 'his income never matched his generous conception of his functions and obligations as a ruler.'[10] He maintained steady pressure on his Finance minister, Abdullah Sulayman, for more income, and both were heavily influenced by four events which occurred in the late 1940s.

The first event concerned a fight among Aramco's parent companies and a change in the way Aramco's books were kept. As a result of this rather arcane squabble, the United States government received more in taxes from the Aramco operation than Abd al-Aziz received in royalties – a fact which the king felt to be grossly unfair.

The problem began in 1947, immediately after Socal and The Texas Company completed the sale of a 40 per cent interest in Aramco to Jersey and Socony-Vacuum. Eventually output would be shared on the same basis as ownership, but for the first two years an interim Off-take Agreement split output 74 per cent to Socal and Texas and 26 per cent to Jersey and Socony. Book profits made by Aramco were therefore shared 60–40, while production was shared 74–26 for the first two years.[11] Jersey and Socony stood to gain from whatever profit Aramco made in selling the extra 14 per cent to Socal and Texas, and Jersey and Socony therefore had a vested interest in setting the transfer price as high as possible. This was normally a matter of routine bookkeeping, since the parent could take its profit either upstream or downstream, and the transfer price between the two parts of the business was an arbitrary bookkeeping decision. But under these circumstances, the difference in a transfer price of $1.02 per barrel (which Socal and Texas wanted to retain) and $1.48 per barrel f.o.b. Ras Tanura (which Jersey and Socony demanded in the first meeting of the Aramco Board after the sale) made a difference of $14 million going to one or the other set of parent companies.[12]

After a long and acrimonious debate, including a threat of legal action if the Aramco board did not live up to its obligation to run the company 'for its own benefit as a separate entity',[13] the issue was finally resolved in July 1948, by raising the transfer price to $1.40 per barrel.[14] It was assumed that this price would still be competitive with west Texas and Venezuelan oil on the eastern seaboard of the United States. But it had the effect of increasing the taxable income of Aramco itself, and resulted in the American government receiving $44 million in taxes from Aramco in 1949 compared with the $39 million received by Abd al-Aziz in the same year.[15] Aramco's books were not open to the Saudis, but Sulayman deduced all of this from information he was able to collect. Abd al-Aziz's royalties were still tied to production rather than profit, at the rate of four shillings (or $0.33) per barrel under the original concession agreement of 1933.[16] The price increase proved to be a significant catalyst for the events that followed.

The second event was a slowing in the rate of increase in Saudi production as a by-product of British economic problems in the late 1940s.

The central issue was a shortage of dollar earnings as Britain struggled to rebuild its war-torn economy. In the late 1940s increasing restrictions were placed on purchases in dollars, and this led to a policy of purchasing 'sterling oil' from affiliates of British companies rather than 'dollar oil' from companies like Jersey and Socony. Since the 'sterling bloc' at the time included Sweden, Denmark, Norway and Finland, the impact was significant. In addition, total free-world production of petroleum temporarily caught up with demand in the late 1940s, and Jersey and Socony found their European market severely curtailed.[17]

The immediate effect in Saudi Arabia was a slowdown in the rate of increase in production well below the figures originally targeted for 1949. The Aramco board decided to slow its expansion programme from seven drilling strings in the field in January 1949 to five in July.[18] Since Abd al-Aziz's royalties were still tied to production at the time, it was clear to everyone that the slowdown would have an immediate impact on the rate of growth of the king's income. A State Department position paper in December 1949 pointed out that 'the current dollar–sterling crisis in oil could reduce the Saudi Arabian annual income by 25 million dollars' or one-quarter of its anticipated level.[19]

With the backing of the American government, Jersey's Howard Page finally negotiated a complicated but satisfactory settlement of this issue directly with the British Treasury in 1950. The British ended petrol rationing; Jersey agreed to supply all of the additional petrol required with payment in sterling; and instead of remitting profits to the United States in dollars, Jersey agreed to purchase necessary equipment in Britain with sterling. This and some additional agreements essentially solved the 'dollar oil' problem.[20] But all of this made Abd al-Aziz acutely aware of how closely his income was tied to Aramco's rate of production, rather than to its profits.

The third event involved the wealthy American entrepreneur J. Paul Getty, and the Saudi–Kuwait Neutral Zone.[21] In June 1948 the American Independent Oil Company (Aminol) acquired a concession from Shaykh Ahmad al-Sabah of Kuwait for half-rights in the Neutral Zone, at a fairly high price for 1948. Rather than try to match that, Aramco decided to relinquish its preferential rights in the Neutral Zone in return for Saudi recognition of a claim that its original concession included offshore rights in the Saudi portion of the Persian Gulf. This put Abd al-Aziz in the position of being able to auction off his half-rights in the Neutral Zone to the highest bidder.

The highest bidder proved to be J. Paul Getty's Pacific Western Oil Company – at an exceptionally high price for the time. Getty agreed to a royalty of $0.55 per barrel, an initial payment of $9.5 million, an annual payment of $1 million, and Saudi rights to purchase shares in Pacific Western and to receive one-eighth of its production profits and one-quarter of its refinery profits. The sale was concluded in January 1949 and convinced Abd al-Aziz that oil companies could afford to be somewhat more generous than Aramco had been thus far.

The fourth event occurred in Venezuela in November 1948, but it had repercussions that reached Saudi Arabia. Five years earlier, in 1943, the Venezuelan government had enacted a complicated set of tax laws intended to divide profits equally with the oil companies. It is interesting that the original laws had been proposed to the Venezuelan government by the State Department's petroleum adviser, Max Thornburg, as a way to increase Venezuela's oil revenue in a measure to offset severe curtailment due to wartime tanker losses. At the time, all parties clearly understood that under the United States Internal Revenue Act of 1918 the tax portion of these payments was deductible from corporate taxes normally due to the American government by Jersey and Gulf Oil.[22]

Unfortunately, the complicated 1943 statutes did not work out exactly as planned, and inadequate oil revenues became a major issue in post-war Venezuelan politics. Largely in response to left-wing pressure on this issue, the government in late 1948 enacted an income tax law that guaranteed a fifty–fifty division of profits. This one was a masterpiece of simplicity. It provided that if oil company income exceeded the combined total of government taxes and royalties, the surplus would be subject to an additional tax of 50 per cent.[23]

The new law was widely discussed in oil circles and well known to the Saudi government. A minor Saudi official went so far as to ask an American Treasury representative sent to Saudi Arabia to advise on monetary policy, 'what kind of arrangements' existed 'throughout the world' for governments to 'participate in the income from the production of oil', and the discussion included 'the difference of the effect on the company between a royalty and an income tax'.[24] The Venezuelan precedent for the fifty–fifty agreement was well established and well understood two years prior to its appearance in the Middle East.

From all of this it should be clear that by 1950 Abd al-Aziz and his Finance minister had ample incentive and precedent to press Aramco for a renegotiation of its concession agreement. The immediate pressure, however, was for additional revenue in whatever form it could be provided – loans; payment for the cost of harbour piers and railroads; contributions to a Saudi 'welfare fund'; royalties on oil used in refinery operations, and so on.[25] 'Each time the company agreed to one thing, there was always just one more' to be discussed.[26] By 1950, these pressures began to converge on a settlement modelled after the Venezuelan income tax to produce a fifty–fifty split.

The Aramco viewpoint

The conduit through which this pressure was transmitted to the four owners of Aramco was Aramco itself – headed by William F. Moore, originally from Texaco, as president, and Fred A. Davies, originally from Socal, as executive vice-president.[27] Aramco's headquarters were still in New York City in 1950 (later moved to Dhahran), but its field operation had grown to 16,000 people in Saudi Arabia (2,300 Americans, 10,700 Saudis, and 3,700 others), and a production rate of 546,000 barrels per day.[28] Most of the buildup had occurred immediately after the second world war, but oil in commercial quantities had been located as early as 1938. Full-scale drilling and construction of a refinery at Ras Tanura had been delayed by the onset of war in Europe, and the result was a period of three years from 1941 until 1944 when a contingent of Americans (later termed 'the hundred men') sat out the war in Saudi Arabia learning Arabic, becoming acquainted with Islamic ways, and engaging in various service projects (such as drilling waterwells) for Abd al-Aziz. This combination of being strictly a production operation and becoming well acquainted with the Saudi government gave Aramco a unique character.[29]

It is important at this point to emphasize the close relationship which existed between Aramco and the Saudi government. Abd al-Aziz was an unusual individual: an absolute ruler, astute, charismatic, and keenly aware of the Islamic sensitivities of the fundamentalist Wahhabi and the Bedouin people; he was, on the other hand, dedicated to the improvement of his own and his country's fortunes through the use of modern technology and western money. From his point of view, the Aramco operation was an instrument to those ends, and Abd al-Aziz provided the framework for cultural accommodation within which Aramco could thrive. One small incident illustrates the point. When challenged by a fundamentalist Shaykh for having Aramco personnel drill water wells in land belonging to the people of Allah, the king permitted the issue to be decided by an Islamic court and argued that even the Prophet Muhammad had used foreigners to help his people. The king won the case, the Shaykh was ultimately pacified, and Aramco continued to drill water wells.[30]

Aramco personnel were equally aware of the importance of avoiding cultural conflict and accommodating the wishes of the king in every way that they could. When construction workers began to arrive in large numbers in 1944, the original 'hundred men', with the tacit agreement of the Saudi government, developed a policy of immediately discharging and shipping out of the country by night barge to Bahrain any worker that publicly breached Islamic law, in order to avoid an arrest which might lead to an attempt by the worker's colleagues to release him by force.[31] Both parties wanted to avoid incidents that might stand in the way of production.

To the field personnel production was their entire *raison d'être*. The Aramco staff had objected violently to the post-war decision by H. C. Collier, board chairman of Socal, and W. S. S. Rodgers, board chairman of Texaco, to sell a 40 per cent interest in Aramco to Jersey and Socony. Collier and Rodgers were conservative businessmen who wanted both cash and additional marketing outlets for Saudi oil in order to satisfy Abd al-Aziz's interest in increased revenue. But the Aramco staff were sitting astride one of the greatest petroleum discoveries in history, and they were adamant in wanting to go it alone. They lost the argument, but echoes of it were sounded again in 1949 and 1950 when the 'dollar oil' crises curtailed Jersey and Socony's sales and led to a slowdown of growth in Aramco production. Field personnel blamed 'lack of aggressive selling' on the part of Jersey and Socony.[32]

It was Aramco personnel, of course, who bore the brunt of Sulayman's constant pressure for more revenue, and businessmen though they were, they were not unsympathetic to the king. The profit margin on Saudi oil was a healthy one; there was an admitted inequity in the Saudi government receiving less from Aramco operations than did the American government; and above all, it was important to keep good relations with the king. There is never an exact answer as to what is a fair price, but by mid-1950 Aramco officers had reached the conclusion that the time had come to retreat – and to retreat along the lines of the Venezuelan precedent. Hopefully a fifty–fifty split would appear so simple and so eminently fair that it would end the petty bickering for a long time to come.[33] This later proved to be a false hope, but at the time it appeared to Aramco personnel to be the eminently sensible thing to do. The principal spear-carrier for the point of view was Fred Davies, one of the original Socal geologists who had been with the Saudi venture from the very first, and who was now Aramco's executive vice-president.[34] All that he had to do now was to convince the four parent companies to agree.

Companies seldom yield to demands for higher prices from their suppliers unless there are very good reasons to do so, and in 1950 Socal, Texaco, Jersey and Socony initially saw few reasons to agree. There was an indirect factor, however, which appears to have entered into the picture in 1950. The officers of all four parents had become rather edgy over their relationship with the United States government, which they wanted to be very careful not to offend.[35] 'Big oil' had been under attack in American society since the turn of the century around the issue of monopolistic practices, and this charge had raised its head again immediately after the second world war. Several congressional hearings took place on various aspects of the subject, and the Federal Trade Commission (FTC) in 1949 decided to extend its investigation of alleged cartels (which it had been conducting since 1944) to the international petroleum industry.[36] Its report, entitled *The International Petroleum Cartel*, was issued in 1952 and led to a lengthy Justice Department anti-trust unit against the major American oil companies. The point for our purpose, however, is that in 1950 the FTC investigation was in full swing, and executives of the major oil companies were well aware of it. No documentary evidence has been found directly linking this concern with the fifty–fifty decision, but corporate and government documents for the period reflect great care by the companies to check major actions overseas with the appropriate agency, especially Justice and State, to be sure not to act contrary to government policy. Based on what happened in this instance it is a logical inference that a corporate desire to act in accord with government wishes was at least one consideration in the fifty–fifty case. Whether by accident or by design, this gave Davies additional leverage to win approval for renegotiation of the 1933 Saudi Concession Agreement along the lines of the Venezuelan precedent.

The American government

The principal government official with whom Davies had contact during the 'fifty–fifty' discussions was George McGhee, Assistant Secretary of State for Near Eastern, South Asian and African Affairs. McGhee's viewpoint was shaped in part by a number of events during and after the second world war which left their imprint on State Department policy. The end result was solid support for Davies's recommendation in discussions with officers of the four parent companies – a factor which appears to have tipped the scales in favour of acquiescence; but the events which led to the State Department's position deserve examination for the light they shed on its policy at the time.

As early as 1943, petroleum experts within the Department of State had developed a basic policy *vis à vis* foreign oil which continued to be the essential guideline for over a decade. An internal position paper, dated 1 December 1943, argued for 'orderly development of all of the resources of the Middle East, both British and American-controlled, to attain the fullest possible production . . . as soon as possible'. For security reasons, it was 'advisable that Middle Eastern oil be developed to the maximum and that supplies in this hemisphere be . . . conserved' because American and Caribbean reserves would be far easier to defend in time of war. In addition, maximum development was critical to retention of the Anglo-American concessions in general and the Saudi concession in particular because it would assure economic benefit 'to the . . . countries which contain the resources'. The paper went on to argue that 'proper proportioning of output . . . between countries in the area on the basis of their economic need' was essential.[37] The means changed significantly between 1943 and 1950, but the ends were the same: conservation of western hemisphere reserves and adequate income for Abd al-Aziz to keep the Saudi concession in American hands.

The instrument of policy decided upon by the State Department in 1943 was an Anglo-American Petroleum Commission to regulate post-war Middle Eastern oil production for the benefit of all concerned.[38] The domestic model for this was the oddly named Texas Railroad Commission, an elective body that regulated Texas oil field production to keep it roughly equal to market demand in the interest of both conservation and price stability.[39] Stripped of all the legal and diplomatic verbiage surrounding them, these were both government-controlled cartels, but they fared different fates depending on 'whose ox was gored'. The Texas Railroad Commission received adequate support to survive because it served the interest of the so-called Texas independents. The proposed Anglo-American Petroleum Commission was perceived as running counter to their interests and died a painful death. The State Department succeeded in negotiating an agreement with the British in late 1944, and it received solid support from both the British and American companies already established in the Middle East. But the Texas independents saw this as a thinly disguised effort to obtain government support for increased production and potential importation of cheap Middle Eastern oil into the United States. The result was a fire storm of criticism in the industry and in Congress which caused the Agreement to be withdrawn for renegotiation in early 1944. A much watered-down version was renegotiated in late 1944, but ultimately died as the Senate failed to ratify it.

What the State Department learned from all of this was not to take any action which appeared to favour one segment of the industry over another. Post-war oil policy was therefore carried out with a minimum of overt government action, but with quiet support at every opportunity for private initiatives consistent with the objectives of conserving western hemisphere reserves and ensuring adequate income for Abd al-Aziz.

This strategic viewpoint received a considerable boost from post-war military planning. Many civilians are unaware that standard military planning procedure starts with an assumed threat and works from these to determine what equipment to develop and purchase, what strategies and tactics to adopt, and what training and mobilization plans to prepare. With the Soviet Union the only other credible military power left in the world after 1945, it was logical for it to be the assumed enemy for planning purposes – even before the onset of the cold war. The tensions which developed following the second world war served to sharply accelerate a process which was already in motion. By early 1947 a full-scale Joint Logistics Committee study concluded that access to oil was so critical in a major future war that everything possible should be done for conservation of 'domestic and United States controlled foreign crude petroleum resources other than in the . . . Middle East by maximum importation in peacetime of crude petroleum from the . . . Middle East, consistent with the maintenance of a healthy petroleum industry in the United States, South America, and the East Indies'.[40]

And the State Department continued its direct interest in Saudi oil. A position paper prepared in 1948 pointed out that it was

> essential that the development . . . [of this oil] . . . be allowed to continue and that the United States and other friendly nations have access to it. For this to occur, it will be necessary to keep the good will of the King . . . and to prove to . . . [him] . . . that American business initiative is developing the oil of Saudi Arabia in the best possible way for the Government and people of the country.[41]

Middle Eastern experts within the Department became increasingly concerned that American support of the new state of Israel would alienate the Arab world in general and Abd al-Aziz in particular, and they looked to the oil companies as a vehicle for remedying some of the damage that they believed was being done. An internal memorandum in August 1948 deplored 'the recent setback suffered by all American interests in the Near East as a result of our stand on Palestine', but went on to note that, 'it may well be that the oil companies are in a position to recover lost ground . . . sooner than the US Government.'[42]

Woven through all of this post-war policy discussion was the mounting tension of the cold war. By 1950 extreme distrust of the Soviet Union and a real sense of urgency had developed within the American government. Debate over how to proceed was intense, and was not resolved at a policy level until April 1950 when Truman approved NSC-68, a National Security Council policy paper prepared by an *ad hoc* joint State and Defence Department study group; the paper defined national policy as rapid creation of adequate forces-in-being to deter the Soviet Union from aggression.[43] Outbreak of the Korean War in June 1950 helped create the political will to implement this policy, and defence expenditures tripled between 1950 and 1952.[44]

Within this framework, Abd al-Aziz became not only the keeper of a strategic resource, but also a staunch anti-communist ruler in an area critical to the defensive arc being constructed around the Soviet Union, and his wishes were well known to personnel in the Department of State. A position paper drafted in September 1950 noted that with 'the threat of Communist aggression increasing throughout the world, the Middle East . . . [was] . . . highly attractive to the USSR because of oil, its strategic location . . . [and] . . . its vulnerability to attack from without and within'. It was important to encourage economic progress, political stability, and western orientation, and the oil companies were well positioned to contribute in this regard. The paper went on to note that a number of

Middle Eastern states were now pressing for changes in their concession agreements similar to 'the Venezuelan sharing of profits arrangement'. However, since this would take tax revenue away from the US Treasury, the paper argued that the State Department would be ill-advised to actively press for such a settlement. A company retreat along these lines should be viewed with favour, but not overtly promoted.[45]

The negotiations

Such was the climate of opinion within the Department of State on 6 November 1950, when Davies and an Aramco delegation met with McGhee and several of his advisers to discuss the problem of Saudi oil. Davies was now clear that a fifty–fifty split was the appropriate decision, and found McGhee in agreement. The topic of whether or not the Internal Revenue Service would treat such an arrangement as a legitimate foreign tax came up for discussion, but McGhee would take no position. Although he was privately convinced that the foreign tax credit did, in fact, apply in this case,[46] his official position was that this was a legal matter 'which could only be handled by the Treasury'. One of Davies' Aramco colleagues pointed out that – while he felt confident that the tax credit would be granted – 'the Bureau of Internal Revenue would not take a position on a theoretical case'.[47] It should be noted that the resolution contemplated would neither add to nor subtract from the bottom line of Aramco's balance sheet, since whatever was paid to the Saudis as an income tax would simply be deducted from Aramco's American tax bill. The amount of money which would be transferred from the American to the Saudi Treasury in one year at that time was approximately $70 million.[48] The meeting ended with tacit agreement on a retreat along the lines of the Venezuelan arrangement, even though the tax credit issue could not be definitively settled in advance. The next step was to deal with the parent companies.

On 13 November Davies arranged a meeting between McGhee and three senior officers of the parent companies – Gwin Follis, vice-chairman of Socal, Orville Harden, executive vice-president of Jersey, and Brewster Jennings, president of Socony – to convince them to go along with what Davies and McGhee had already agreed was the best course of action.[49] By this time, the decision-making process had been partially overtaken by events. Saudi Arabia had declared a 20 per cent income tax on all companies within its jurisdiction – despite a provision in the original Aramco concession agreement exempting it from such taxes.[50] There was general agreement in the meeting that despite the words in the concession agreement, no valid objection could be raised against the Saudi action because 'a sovereign cannot sign away his sovereign rights' of taxation.

McGhee said that he 'agreed with the Aramco evaluation of the necessity of negotiating changes in their contract in the present circumstances'; and Davies stated that 'from a psychological point of view . . . [the Venezuelan] . . . formula sounded fair and would be considered fair in Saudi Arabia.' The question of whether or not the Saudi tax would be deducted from Aramco's American tax was touched upon, but *no assurances of any kind were given to the company representatives on how that issue might be decided by the Internal Revenue Service.*[51]

This meeting tipped the scales with the parent companies and Davies, Aramco general counsel George W. Ray, Jr, and financial vice-president Robert L. Brougham flew out to Jidda to open talks with Sulayman and Prince Faysal.[52] After a month of intense negotiations, an agreement was finally signed on 30 December 1950. From a legal point of view, it came in two parts. A Saudi Royal Decree issued on 27 December created an additional income tax on companies (i.e. Aramco) engaged in the production of petroleum in an amount equal to 'fifty percent (50%) of the net [sic] income' of such companies, but provided that all other 'taxes . . . royalties, rentals, duties and all other sums . . . payable to the Saudi Arab government' would be applied against this tax.[53] The document signed by Davies and Al Sulayman on 20 December referenced this decree, agreed to cancellation of the clause in the original concession agreement forbidding an income tax on Aramco, and spelled out a number of details regarding interpretation of the Royal Decree.[54] Taken together, these two documents constituted the Fifty–fifty Agreement of 1950.

It will have been noted that the issue of deducting this new tax from Aramco's American income tax had not yet been decided, and no mention at all had been made of National Security Council involvement in the incident. Careful research into the episode reveals that not only did the IRS not give advance rulings on hypothetical cases, but its practice at the time was to accumulate several years of corporate tax returns and audit them all at once. In this instance, Aramco's 1950 tax return was not audited until 1955. The only question remaining was whether Aramco's acquiescence in the Saudi decree, which negated the provision of the 1933 agreement exempting it from Saudi taxes, made the money an 'agreed payment' equivalent to a royalty rather than a tax. The counter-argument was that a sovereign power cannot contract away its taxing power and the 1933 clause had been invalid in the first place. The IRS New York office ruled in Aramco's favour in May 1955, *four and a half years after the Fifty–fifty Agreement.*[55] A staff report of the Joint Congressional Committee on Internal Revenue concluded in 1957 that the decision was a perfectly correct interpretation of a law that had been in effect since 1918.[56]

As for a National Security Council directive to the Treasury, there is simply no evidence that such an intervention ever took place. Two searches of NSC records failed to produce any indication that the tax question itself was ever even considered by that body.[57] In retrospect, it appears that the exchange between Senator Church and Ambassador McGhee in the 1975 hearings took place without the benefit of documentary evidence or knowledge by either party of how the final tax decision had actually been made. A careful reading of Ambassador McGhee's full testimony reveals he was defending the overall wisdom of the State Department position – not affirming the correctness of Senator Church's charge.[58] Unfortunately, the authors of the committee report used the original exchange to infer NSC pressure on the IRS to bend the law out of shape, and Blair and others picked up the charge and repeated it.[59] Sceptics of this conclusion should recall that all parties were virtually positive that the foreign tax credit would apply, and since the action was consistent with established American policy in the region, there was no need to refer the matter to the NSC. Had such a need existed, it would be a matter for conjecture what the decision might have been. The question here is the historical fact as to whether or not such an intervention took place, and all of the available evidence points to the fact that it did not.

Viewed from this perspective, the Fifty–fifty Agreement was a purely commercial transaction, initiated by the government of Saudi Arabia on the basis of the Venezuelan precedent. It was acquiesced to by Aramco because the company really had little choice due to its relatively high profit rate, its recognition of the basic inequity involved, its determination to maintain a sound relationship with Abd al-Aziz, and its lack of legal recourse against an income tax of first 20 per cent, then 50 per cent. The State Department's policies *vis-à-vis* Saudi Arabia happened to support the direction of the settlement, and Davies used this fact as a lever to convince the parent companies to agree. The prime mover was Abd al-Aziz, not the National Security Council.

Conclusions

This is the micro-version; now let us look at the episode from a broader viewpoint, a macro-version. This can be brief, because it examines the same factual material from a different perspective. Viewed in a broader context, it can be argued that the Fifty–fifty Agreement was indeed the product of American governmental policy, though not in the manner charged by Senator Church. There are at least five points where government policy influenced the episode and created the context within which the Fifty–fifty Agreement emerged.

The first point was the foreign tax credit enacted by Congress in 1918. The purpose, of course, was to avoid double taxation, and to help American companies compete overseas. But it did create the circumstances within which increasing the king's revenue through a tax rather than a royalty payment had the effect of tapping into the United States Treasury rather than the company's profits. This, in turn, made it considerably easier for the parent companies to agree to increased payments to Abd al-Aziz than would have been the case if the money had come from their own accounts.

The second was the so-called Venezuelan precedent. As we have seen, the Venezuelan use of a tax to split revenues with petroleum companies was originally suggested by the State Department's petroleum adviser, Max Thornburg, in 1943. The intent in that instance was to shore up the finances of the Venezuelan government at a point when that country was an indispensable supplier of a critical wartime resource, and when its revenue was being severely curtailed by loss of tankers to Axis submarines. Even though the specific Venezuelan law used as a precedent by Saudi Arabia was enacted several years later, in 1948, the basic idea clearly originated with the American government itself. In effect, the State Department invented the idea of subsidizing an important ally through the foreign tax credit, and George McGhee stoutly defended this concept in his testimony before Congress as late as 1975.

Third was the post-war State Department policy of avoiding direct participation in the politics of foreign oil, but attempting to guide private initiatives in directions compatible with the department's concept of the national interest. This posture grew out of the State Department's disastrous experience during the second world war of negotiating a Petroleum Agreement with the British which greatly pleased the major companies with their extensive interests overseas, but angered the Texan independents whose income came from domestic oil. After that, the department carefully kept its distance from situations where it might be seen as offering direct assistance to any specific company as opposed to another, but tried to guide private initiatives in appropriate directions. Ambassador McGhee's actions in this case were perfectly consistent with this policy.

Fourth is the question of the national interest as defined by the appropriate branches of the American government. There is no question but that strategic planning by agencies of the Joint Chiefs of Staff supported the rapid development of Saudi oil as a means of conserving western hemisphere reserves, and that they also considered it important to retain the Saudi concession in American hands. In addition, the National Security Council through NSC-68 defined the national interest as containing the spread of communism and Soviet influence – an objective which automatically added strategic significance to Saudi Arabia because of its geographic location and its staunch anti-communist ruler. When it came time to convert this broad interest into specific action, the climate of opinion within the government made State Department support of a fifty–fifty profit-sharing arrangement with Abd al-Aziz almost a foregone conclusion.

Finally, there was the role of Assistant Secretary of State George McGhee. As we have seen, he certainly collaborated with Davies in winning the parent companies' approval for proceeding with the agreement. Seen in the above context, it took only a sophisticated final nudge by him to get the companies to do what had already been determined to be in the national interest.

From what has been recounted, it is clear that the Church–Blair version of the episode is incorrect. The National Security Council did *not* direct the Treasury to bend the tax laws out of shape to accommodate Abd al-Aziz. Whether overall the prime mover was Abd al-Aziz, since it was his pressure for more revenue that led directly to the agreement, or the United States government, since it created the framework within which the idea and desirability of such a settlement arose, remains a matter of opinion.

My own view favours the broader interpretation. Regardless of the definition one chooses for the term 'foreign policy', it can now be argued with considerable force that the Fifty–fifty Agreement was, in fact, the product of American foreign policy. Defining the term narrowly as 'the enunciated policy of the Executive Branch of Government on matters outside the national boundary', it is clear that a consistent policy had been in place for a long time supporting exactly the type of action which was taken here. Defining the term broadly, as 'the *de facto* cumulative thrust of all competing interest groups within a nation-state (both governmental and private) outside the national boundary', makes the assertion even more clear. Including Aramco and the parent companies in the equation leaves little doubt that the Fifty–fifty Agreement was the product of American foreign policy.

While it is outside the scope of this chapter to assess the adeptness of Sir William Fraser, the Anglo-Iranian Oil Company and the British Foreign Office in dealing with the situation in Iran, it is appropriate to point out that the AIOC's position in Iran in the early 1950s was very different from that of Aramco in Saudi Arabia. To begin with, Aramco was a relative newcomer in Saudi Arabia, and due to the quirk of a wartime hiatus in production, its 'hundred men' had become quite skilled at cultural accommodation. Far more important, however, was the fact that Abd al-Aziz was an absolute monarch not faced with the internal political strife which had to be reckoned with by the Iranian government. His prime interest was revenue, and in 1950 he had no problem using an American company as an instrument toward this end. This was quite different from the situation in Iran, where the central issue in 1950 was not revenue but the termination of British control.

There was also a difference in the legal situation in the United States and Britain. American tax laws made it relatively painless for American companies to come to an agreement – it cost them nothing. British tax law had no such provision, and any settlement would have had to come out of company profits. In addition, the American government was in the business of subsidizing its allies in 1950, and the British government was not. Still recovering from the second world war, the British needed all of the cash that they could get.

None of these factors in themselves account for the breakdown in negotiations between the British and Iranian governments, but they were complications which made the problem faced by the British more difficult than that faced by the Americans in 1950.

The four parent companies involved in the Aramco–Saudi Fifty–fifty Agreement (Jersey, Socony, Texas and Socal) were the same American companies (along with Gulf) involved in negotiations for the Iranian consortium four years later. The symbiotic relationship between the Saudi and American governments during their negotiations was also evident in the negotiations with Iran when, however, the stakes were much higher, the issues far more complex, and the roles quite different. Instead of the gentle nudge which George McGhee used to finalize the Saudi arrangement, the American government was much more overt, proactive and forceful in its efforts with the Iran settlement. The oil companies, for their part, had neither need for, nor interest in obtaining extra supplies from Iran, but they were worried that the Soviets might gain control of those supplies and flood the world market. Despite this, they used the lever of State, Defense, and – in this case – National Security Council concern over potential Soviet expansion to exact anti-trust immunity in Iran and a downgrading of the Justice Department's pending anti-trust suit from a criminal to a civil case as the price of their participation in the consortium.[60] By comparison, the Aramco–Saudi Fifty–fifty Agreement was a far simpler affair.

Notes

1   '1950 Agreement', US Congress, Senate, Committee on Foreign Relations, Subcommittee on Multinational Corporations, *Multinational Corporations and United States Foreign Policy, Hearings*, parts 4, 7 and 8 (28 January–28 March 1974), 93rd Cong., 2nd sess. (Washington, DC: Government Printing Office, 1974), part 8, pp. 372–4.

2   The original research underlying this essay was done for my study of *Aramco, the United States, and Saudi Arabia* (Princeton, 1981), but further reflection and more rigorous analysis have produced different conclusions than appeared in the original work. For an excellent overview of the impact of the Aramco–Saudi Fifty–fifty Agreement on relations between the oil companies and other Middle Eastern states, see William Roger Louis, *The British Empire in the Middle East, 1945–1951* (New York, 1984) pp. 595–600. On its impact

within Iran, see Nikki R. Keddie, *Roots of Revolution: an Interpretative History of Modern Iran* (New Haven, Conn., 1981) pp. 132–4.

3 Karl Mannheim, *Ideology and Utopia: an Introduction to the Sociology of Knowledge* (New York, 1936); the quotation is from the Preface by Louis Wirth, p. xxi.

4 US Congress, *Multinational Oil Corporations, Report*, Committee Print, January 1975, 94rd Cong., 2nd sess. (Washington, DC, 1975) pp. 81–6.

5 John M. Blair, *The Control of Oil* (New York, 1976) pp. 196–9.

6 J.C.S. (Joint Chiefs of Staff) 1741, 'Problem of procurement of oil for a major war', 29 January 1947, pp. 1–7, file: CCS463.7 (9-6-45) sec. 6, J.C.S. Decimal File, 1946–7, Record Group 218, National Archives, Washington, DC; and State Department position paper prepared in advance of the 'Pentagon Talks' with representatives of the British government in October and November 1947, US Department of State, *Foreign Relations of the United States* (Washington, DC: Government Printing Office, 1852–), volume V for 1947, p. 553 (hereafter cited as *FR ([year])*, [volume]).

7 US Congress, *Multinational Corporations, Hearings* (hereafter cited as *MCH*), part 4, p. 89. The charge was made by Senator Church.

8 For a detailed explanation of the computation which leads to this conclusion see Blair, *The Control of Oil*, pp. 199–201.

9 Blair, *Control of Oil*, p. 198, quoting from US Congress, *MCH*, part 4, pp. 88–99.

10 H. St John B. Philby, *Saudi Arabia* (London, 1955) p. 333.

11 'Aramco Offtake Agreement – 1947', US Congress, *MCH*, part 8, pp. 169–76; and Letter, Olmsted to MacGaregill, 22 March 1947, US Congress, *MCH*, pt. 8, pp. 176–8.

12 'Exxon Paper – 7/25/47', US Congress, *MCH*, part 8, pp. 205–7.

13 Letter, Harden to Jennings, 25 November 1947, US Congress, *MCH*, part 8, pp. 237–8.

14 Letter, Coleman to J. A. Cogan (Jersey), 12 July 1943, and memorandum, Coleman to J. W. Connally (Jersey), 19 July 1948, US Congress, *MCH*, part 8, p. 278.

15 These figures are calculated from data in Zuhayr Mikdashi, *A Financial Analysis of Middle Eastern Oil Concessions: 1901–65*, pp. 120 (Aramco's 1949 net profit), 122 (payments to Saudi Arabia); and telegram, [Ambassador J. Rives] Childs to Secretary of State, 13 June 1950, *FR(1950)*, V, 52 (Aramco's tax rate).

16 The figure of $0.33 is based on an exchange rate of $0.12 to the British pound agreed upon by Aramco executives and Sulayman in 1948; *FR(1950)*, V, 238, n.2.

17 Henrietta M. Larson, Evelyn H. Knowlton and Charles S. Popple, *New Horizons 1927–1950*, vol. 3 in *History of Standard Oil Company (New Jersey)* (New York, 1974) pp. 701–6; interview with Howard W. Page, former Exxon director, in New York, 2 May 1977.

18 'Working paper, Near East Conference' 20 December 1949, file: 'Near East Oil', box 2, Records of the Petroleum Division, Record Group 59, General Records of the Department of State, National Archives, Washington, DC; letter, McPherson to Moore, 22 June 1949, US Congress, *MCH*, part 7, pp. 95–7.

19 'Working paper, Near East Conference', 20 December 1949, file: Near East Oil, box 2, Records of the Petroleum Division, RG 59.

20 Page interview; Larson et al., *New Horizons*, pp. 710–13; and telegram, Douglas (American ambassador in London) to Secretary of State, 3 July 1950, *FR(1950)*, V, 60–1.

21 This discussion of J. Paul Getty's acquisition of a concession in the Neutral Zone is based on Stephen H. Longrigg, *Oil in the Middle East: its Discovery and Development* (New York, 1968) pp. 214–16.

22 Stephen G. Rabe, 'Energy for war: United States oil diplomacy in Latin America during World War II', in David H. White ed., *Proceedings of the Conference on War and Diplomacy, 1976* (Charleston, South Carolina, 1976) pp. 125–32; and Larson et al., *New Horizons*, pp. 479–84. For comment on Thornburg's brief government career see Anderson, p. 42, *n*.17. He was a former Socal official who joined the State Department in 1941 and resigned under probably false charges of conflict of interest in 1943.

23 Leonard M. Fanning, *Foreign Oil and the Free World* (New York, 1954) pp. 71–110.

24 US Congress, Senate, Subcommittee of the Committee on the Judiciary and the Committee on Interior and Insular Affairs, *The Emergency Oil Lift Program and Related Oil Problems, Joint Hearings* (27 February–22 March 1957), part 2, 85th Cong., 1st sess. (Washington, DC: Government Printing Office, 1957), pp. 1444–6.

25 Telegrams, Childs to Secretary of State, 23 June and 25 July 1950, *FR(1950)*, V, 58–60, 62–8; see also Arthur N. Young, *Saudi Arabia: the Making of a Financial Giant* (New York, 1983) pp. 20–1.

26 Interview with George W. Ray, Jr, former general counsel of Aramco, by telephone to East Thetford, Vermont, 11 February 1978.

27 Letter, Francis E. Meloy, Jr (Dhahran) to Secretary of State, 12 December 1948, 890F.6363/12–1248; RC 59. Senior Aramco positions were divided in this manner to give both Socal and Texaco a direct hand in the business; loyalty to their original companies ran strong and produced considerable friction from time to time within Aramco, but not in its primary role as a production organization.

28 Roy Lebkicher, *Aramco and World Oil* (New York, 1952) p. 55; and *Aramco Handbook: Oil and the Middle East*, rev. edn (Dhahran, Saudi Arabia, 1968) p. 135.

29 Interviews with Thomas C. Barger, who took part in Aramco's government operations during the second world war and later become board chairman, in La Jolla, California, 26 August 1977; Floyd W. Ohliger, Aramco's resident manager in Saudi Arabia during the second world war, in Pineville, Pennsylvania, 22 July 1977; Ambassador James S. Moore, Jr, minister resident in Jidda from 1942 to 1944, in Washington, Kentucky, 21 April 1977; and Ambassador Parker T. Hart, American consul in Dhahran from 1944 to 1946, in Washington DC, 15 July 1977.

30 Letter, William A. Eddy (Jiddah) to Secretary of State, 4 December 1944, 890F.001 Abdul Aziz/12–444, RG 59.

31 Letter, Hart to Secretary of State, 20 December 1944, 890F.00/12–2044, RG 59; Ohliger interview; Wallace E. Stegner, *Discovery: the Search for Arabian Oil* (Beirut, 1971).

32 For a full discussion of the Aramco viewpoint, see Anderson, *Aramco, the United States, and Saudi Arabia*, pp. 108–23, 149–50, 185.

33 Ray interview; telegram, Secretary of State to embassy in London, 31 August 1950, *FR(1950)*, V, 75–6.

34 Lebkicher, *Aramco and World Oil*, p. 42.

35 The following discussion of the Federal Trade Commission investigation of the petroleum industry is based on Burton I. Kaufman, *The Oil Cartel Case* (Westport, Conn., 1978).

36 Ibid., p. 29.

37 'Memorandum on the Department's position . . .', 1 December 1943, folder: 'Petroleum Reserves Corporation Activities, 7/3/43–1/1/44', box 1, Records of the Petroleum Division, RG 59.

38 This account of the Anglo-American Petroleum Agreement is based on Anderson, *Aramco, the United Sates, and Saudi Arabia*, pp. 68–107, and Michael B. Stoff, *Oil, War, and American Security* (New Haven, Conn., 1980) pp. 151–95. For a broad view of all American policy *vis-à-vis* Saudi Arabia during the second world war, see Aaron David Miller, *Search for Security: Saudi Arabian Oil and American Foreign Policy, 1939–1949* (Chapel Hill, 1980).

39 Harold F. Williamson, et al., *The American Petroleum Industry*, vol. 2 (Evanston, Ill., 1959–63) 543–4.

40 J.C.S. 1741, 'Problem of procurement of oil for a major war', 29 January 1947, pp. 1–7, file: 'CCS463.7 (9–6–45) Sec. 6', J.C.S. Decimal File, 1946–7, Record Group 218. Those familiar with the politics of petroleum will recall that this J.C.S. State Department policy was effectively overridden by the imposition of import quotas on foreign oil in 1957 as a result of political pressure from the oil industry; see Kaufman, *Oil Cartel Case*, pp. 64–76.

41 State Department position paper, *FR(1947)*, V, 553.

42 Memorandum, [Acting Director of Near Eastern and African Affairs Raymond A.] Hare to Lovett, 25 August 1948, *FR(1948)*, V, 39–40.

43 NSC-68, 'United States objectives and programs for national security', 14 April 1950; copy held by the Modern Military Branch, Military Archives Division, National Archives, Washington, DC, pp. 64–5.

44 Samuel P. Huntington, *The Common Defense: Strategic Programs in National Politics* (New York, 1961) pp. 25–64.

45 Memorandum, 'Middle East oil', September 1950, *FR(1950)*, V, 76–96.

46 Discussion with Ambassador George C. McGhee, former Assistant Secretary of State for Near Eastern, South Asian and African Affairs, in Austin, Texas, 27 September 1985.

47 Memorandum of conversation, McGhee, Davies, et al., (6?) November 1950, *FR(1950)*, V, 106–9; interview with Robert L. Brougham, former financial vice-president of Aramco, by telephone to La Jolla, California, 2 December 1977; and McGhee testimony, US Congress, *MCH*, part 4, pp. 85–92.

48 The figure of $70 million is derived by extrapolating backwards from Aramco's Consolidated Balance Sheet for 1962 and 1963, located in US Congress, *MCH*, part 8, p. 443, to match the figures for Aramco's 1950 royalties and net earnings after taxes given in Anderson, *Aramco, the United States, and Saudi*

Arabia, p. 121. The precise method for computing the Aramco tax was quite complex, but the relevant figures are as follows:

Table A *Aramco's royalties paid, tax and net earnings for 1963, 1962 and 1950 in millions of dollars*

	1963	1962	1950
Royalties paid to Saudi Arabia	135.4	126.4	56.7
Saudi Arabian Income Tax	317.6	280.2	*
American Income Tax	0.2	0.2	*
Net Earnings After Taxes	445.7	405.5	127.4

* If the ratios existing in 1962 and 1963 were equally valid for 1950, the amount potentially shifted from the US Treasury to the Saudi Treasury would be about $70 million.

49 Interview with Ambassador McGhee in Washington, DC, 7 July 1977; McGhee testimony, US Congress, *MCH*, part 4, p. 91; and George McGhee, *Envoy to the Middle World* (New York, 1983) pp. 324–5.
50 Saudi Arabian Royal Decree of 4 November 1950, US Congress, *MCH*, part 8, pp. 374–7.
51 Memorandum of conversation, McGhee, Harden et al., 13 November 1950, US Congress, *MCH*, part 8, pp. 345–8.
52 *FR(1950)*, V, 118, *n*.1.
53 Saudi Arabian Royal Decree of 27 December 1950, US Congress, *MCH*, part 8, pp. 377–88.
54 '1950 Agreement', US Congress, *MCH*, part 8, pp. 372–4.
55 Bureau of Internal Revenue Ruling 55–296, 16 May 1955, No. 20, US Congress, *MCH*, part 8, p. 358; Brougham interview; interview with Douglas Erskine, former tax counsel for Aramco, by telephone to Portola Valley, California, 28 December 1977.
56 Report by the staff of the Joint Committee on Internal Revenue Taxation (undated), US Congress, *MCH*, part 8, pp. 350–78. The date of this report is given as 1957 in US Congress, *Multinational Oil Corporations, Report*, p. 91.
57 Letter to the author from Beverly Zweiben, Freedom of Information, National Security Council, 18 May 1979.
58 McGhee testimony, US Congress, *MCH*, part 4, pp. 84–99.
59 Blair, *Control of Oil*, pp. 196–9; Stephen D. Krasner, *Defending the National Interest: Raw Materials Investments and US Foreign Policy* (Princeton, 1978) pp. 205–13; and Louis Turner, *Oil Companies in the International System* (London, 1978) pp. 47–8.
60 Kaufman, *Oil Cartel Case*, pp. 55–60.

7

The Anglo-Iranian oil dispute: a triangular relationship

RONALD W. FERRIER

Ce qui inspirait la politique Britannique . . . c'etait évidemment la volonté de s'assurer la propriété exclusive de notre pétrole . . . L'emprise se fit par la compagnie concessionaire, L'Anglo-Iranian Oil Company . . . devenue un Etat dans l'Etat, détermina les destinées du pays.

Muhammad Musaddiq, 1952[1]

The historical perspective, 1901–47

Dr Musaddiq's testimony before the International Court of Justice indicates his main motivation in the Anglo-Iranian oil dispute. It also expresses an aspect of twentieth-century Iranian nationalism which has been represented by many as a struggle to eradicate inimical British presence from the country, exemplified by the Anglo-Iranian Oil Company (AIOC).[2] It is often forgotten that most of the accusations made against AIOC in the post-war period had already been raised against it earlier, particularly prior to the cancellation of the D'Arcy concession in 1932. Even a cursory glance at the press coverage in the late twenties and early thirties, much of it organized by Ali Dashti in *Shafaq-i Surkh*, shows a marked similarity to that mounted by Husayn Fatimi in *Bakhtar-i Imruz*. Just as Musaddiq criticized Riza Shah's action in negotiating a new oil concession as simply another example of the British government's unscrupulous hold over Riza Shah, by claiming that the 1933 concession was signed under duress, so in much the same way the deposed Qajar dynasty was blamed by Riza Shah for its ignorance and extravagance in submitting to the British government in May 1901 when the original oil concession was granted to William Knox D'Arcy. In both cases the oil company was charged with interference in the internal affairs of the country.

164

Contrary to the general understanding, the British government did not regard the newly formed company, named the Anglo-Persian Oil Company (APOC) in April 1909, as its chosen strategic instrument.[3] It was for financial reasons that the company prevailed upon the government of the day to take a 51 per cent shareholding in it. As a consequence of the first world war and the technological developments which it stimulated, consumption of oil rose and production in Iran increased from nearly 90,000 tons in 1913 to nearly 900,000 tons in 1918. Like the other major oil companies of the day it integrated its activities on a global basis. It was beginning to outgrow the operations envisaged in the concession. The market in Iran, or indeed in the immediate neighbourhood, was inadequate for the production potential. The major consumption areas in Europe were distant from Iran and in competition with nearer supplies from the United States and emerging production from South America, particularly Mexico and Venezuela. There were no facilities or amenities in Iran around the area of the oilfield and the refinery and loading points on Abadan island. Everything had to be imported and the operation made self-sufficient. Townships grew up, and utilities had to be provided, education promoted, communications and transportation established in an administratively neglected part of the country under the control of local chieftains, such as the Bakhtiyari Khans and the Shaykh of Muhammareh. These developments were viewed with misgiving in Tehran, which naturally resisted any encroachment on its authority.

Throughout the concessionary period this anomalous state of affairs was a constant source of irritation. The company was accused of interference in local affairs where central authority was lacking, but at the same time it was asked to undertake municipal responsibilities beyond its actual obligations. Services additional to normal operational requirements, such as housing, schooling and medical care, constituted a major ongoing cost. From the mid-twenties active steps were taken through education and training to increase the numbers of qualified Iranian staff, through the promotion of a policy of Iranianization to replace skilled Indian employees. This was never considered adequate and, despite agreements such as article 16 of the 1933 concession, constituted a further source of friction between the Iranian government and the company which persisted till nationalization. The Abadan Institute of Technology, constructed by the company in 1939, provided the only centre of technical training in Khuzistan at that time. More promising students were sent to England, especially to Birmingham University.

With the expansion of output during the first world war and the development of subsidiary marketing and refining companies, disputes arose over accounting procedures and the allocation of depreciation and expenses before the profit, on which the oil revenues of the Iranian government were based.[4] These were partially resolved in the Armitage–

Smith Agreement of December 1920, which concluded discussions initiated in 1919 by the Iranian Foreign minister of the day, Prince Firuz Mirza, Nusrat al-Dawleh. An eminent Scottish accountant, William McLintock, was retained by Prince Firuz for the Iranian government in November 1919 to act on its behalf in the examination of the company's accounts.

By the late 1920s however a revision of the concession had become desirable on economic and political grounds. Riza Shah was modernizing the country and reforming its institutions according to his standards. A new approach to concessionary relations was proposed by Sir John Cadman, distinguished scientist, professor and administrator, who became chairman of the company in 1927. In preliminary discussions, which began in 1926 and reached the first stage of negotiations in spring 1929 in Tehran, he offered a participating arrangement under which the Iranian government would receive a 20 per cent shareholding and a tonnage royalty. The principal Iranian negotiator, the minister of Court, Mirza Abdul Husayn Taymurtash pressed Cadman for more but in a deteriorating international financial situation of overproduction, and with the onset of the depression, Cadman was not disposed to go much further, the negotiations were adjourned and an opportunity for a radical change in concessionary principles was lost.

When Taymurtash returned seriously to the negotiating table at the end of 1931 the depression was worse and his own position less secure. Nevertheless, the Heads of Agreement for a new concession were agreed in London early in 1932, but then repudiated a few months later in Tehran on the grounds that a fall in royalty payments for the previous year precluded a settlement. In November 1932 the Shah, exasperated at the failure of his ministers to reach an agreement, cancelled the concession to wipe the slate clean. Taymurtash fell from favour, a victim of royal suspicion and internal intrigue, and lost his life in prison. Sayyid Hasan Taqizadeh, the minister of Finance, took over the negotiations. Cadman was in the United States at the time and the British government referred the dispute to the League of Nations in Geneva where Ali Akbar Davar represented the Iranian government.

As a result of private discussions at Geneva between Cadman, Davar and Husayn Ala (Iranian minister to France), the negotiations were transferred to Tehran in spring 1933 under the auspices of the League. Eventually, after unsuccessful discussions between Fraser and Taqizadeh, Cadman and the Shah reached a settlement approved by the League of Nations. It included a system of enhanced tonnage payments; a reduction of the concessionary area; a lengthening of the concessional duration; a guaranteed gold convertibility clause; a 20 per cent participation in the dividend payments of the company; and a definite commitment to the increasing Iranianization of staff. A massive programme of capital investment followed, the production of oil in Iran increased more rapidly than international production as a whole, and by 1938 Iranian exports were nearly ten million tons a year.[5]

In the circumstances, the 1933 concession was reasonable, but it later became an anathema to nationalist politicians. The Soviet government played on this sentiment in September 1944 when it sent Sergei Kavtaradze, vice-commissar for foreign affairs, to claim an oil concession in the north of Iran, and at the same time served notice to the United States of its own interest in the area.[6] This move was resisted by the prime minister, Muhammad Sa'id, with the assistance of Musaddiq, an old opponent of Riza Shah, in a speech to the Majlis, which contained a long denunciation of the AIOC. Finally on 2 December, through a bill tabled by Dr Musaddiq with the approval of the next prime minister, Murtaza Quli Bayat, the Majlis agreed not to authorize any government to conclude a new concession with a foreign power.

At the end of almost two years of confrontation with the Soviet Union over the withdrawal of troops, the liberation of the Soviet Union over the withdrawal of troops, the liberation of Azarbayjan and the northern oil concession, the Majlis approved a resolution submitted by the prime minister, Qavam al-Saltaneh, on 22 October 1947. It included, among other provisions, authorization for Iran to explore and develop its own oil resources and significantly,

> In all cases where the rights of the Iranian nation, in respect of the country's natural resources, whether underground or otherwise, have been impaired, particularly in regard to the Southern oil, the Government is required to enter into such negotiations and take such measures as are necessary to protect the national rights, and inform the Majlis of the result.

Qavam assured the British ambassador, Sir John Le Rougetel, that this did not imply any criticism of the company. There is no doubt, however, and Qavan referred to it in July 1952,[7] that he was taking a definite initiative over oil and serving notice that he was not just balancing a rebuff to the Russians with a gesture against the British, but that oil was on his parliamentary programme. Le Rougetel believed that it was Qavam's intention to try to arrange a better settlement with the AIOC, but not to make a great fuss about it. The peremptory ousting of Qavam shortly afterwards by the Shah and the appointment of the elderly Ibrahim Hakimi spoiled that opportunity and initiated a period of increasing political uncertainty.

The political repercussions of the attempts of the Soviet Union to obtain a concession had precipitated a more intense awareness of the importance of the oil issue in Iran. The side-effects of the entry of Allied troops into Iran on 25 August 1941, including the abdication of Riza Shah, contributed to that awareness. A new and lasting influence on the Iranian scene was the arrival of a substantial American presence that was not only concerned with the corridor of military supplies to the Soviet Union but also served in an advisory capacity in many aspects of Iranian life. A consequence of the disappearance of the strong hand of Riza Shah was the revival of political activities including those of the Tudeh Party, which had been sternly repressed in the mid-thirties.[8] Among its early actions was a strike organized against the AIOC in spring 1946 when occasion was taken to protest at congested conditions and inadequate accommodation in Abadan as a result of the shortages of materials and an influx of people caused by wartime demands.[9]

Negotiations surrounding the Supplemental Agreement, 1947–51

One of the priorities in the AIOC's post-war corporate policy was its emphasis on its concessional responsibilities in Iran, which had to be sustained by rising production, not less and preferably higher than the world average, in order to expand in international markets and produce more revenue for the Iranian government. Even during the war when production in Iran dropped as a result of the re-routing of tankers, Sir William Fraser, who had succeeded Cadman as chairman in 1941, agreed, in response to demands from Riza Shah, to guaranteed payments to the Iranian government at the previous average annual rates of return. This was initially opposed by the British government but accepted for two years after strong representations by Fraser.[10] During the post-war period, as planning for peacetime conditions was implemented, the maximization of oil production in Iran was an essential part of the AIOC's policy. There was also a recognition, confirmed by Fraser's visit to Iran in 1945, that the concession required updating; Sir Neville Gass, the director in charge of Iranian affairs who visited Tehran in late 1947 to assess the situation, thought that 'the concession was due for revision to bring it into line with modern thought and the progress of the industry.'

No longer just servants of the Shah, politicians were beginning to develop their own constituencies and form tactical alliances, factions, to promote their political ambitions. The Majlis, however, was a weak instrument for power as its procedural methods were more able to obstruct than advance firm administration. The provisions relating to a quorum were increasingly manipulated to delay legislation. As a result of the reforms and modernization of Riza Shah, political representation was more open to professional votes and wider urban representation from teachers, lawyers, army officers and government officials. At the same time some of the more traditional sectors of Iranian society, such as the merchants from the bazaars, the landowners and the clergy, felt themselves neglected. The interpretation and assessment of the influence of these emerging political forces was not easy because of the complicated personal rivalries which were involved. Political patterns were difficult to decipher. Ernest Bevin, for example, at one point perceived the Tudeh Party as a kind of social democratic influence, whereas Dean Acheson saw it as a carrier of Russian penetration.[11] Such movements in the political arena need to be appreciated in any judgement of AIOC's response to its position in Iran.

After the soundings made by Gass in November and December 1947 it was arranged that more substantive discussions should be held in May 1948, but these were postponed because of the internal political situation. Abdul Husayn Hazhir, minister of Court, succeeded Hakimi and his programme presented to the Majlis on 22 June 1948 included a reference to the law of 22 October 1947, and was the first occasion on which a specific statement of intent to negotiate with the company had been made. In a subsequent press interview Hazhir referred to 'increasing the Iranian share of the revenue'. His appointment was greeted with demonstrations against him organized by Ayatullah Kashani, who was making a strong political impact. By the end of August the authority of the prime minister, who was also the minister of Finance, was on the wane. No Iranian negotiating position had been prepared, but a press campaign was active over oil. No discussions took place till 27 September, when the purpose, according to Gass, was 'to see if there are in the light of present day conditions, any adjustments which should equitably be made . . . in mutual agreement'.[12] Hazhir stated that his government was not demanding a 'revision of the concession' and that 'if the necessary adjustments could be made within the framework of the Concession, this would be completely satisfactory to the Government.' The Iranian delegation presented a 25-point memorandum,[13] which had been drafted in the concessions department of the Ministry of Finance under the influence of the French jurist professor Gidel, whose knowledge of the oil industry was negligible.

During September and October there was much useful discussion on training, education and promotion, but no final agreement was reached on the 'annual and progressive' reduction of foreign employees because of differences over calculating it on a fixed arithmetical or percentage basis. There were disagreements over the definite obligation to be given by the company in respect of education in Khuzistan outside its areas of operations, which AIOC contended was not its responsibility but that of the government. Other main objects of attention included claims; the gold exchange rate; accountancy procedures; the supply agreement with the Admiralty; the consumption of oil products by the company; internal oil products within the country; customs exemptions; foreign exchange; the company's statutes and reserves and British government taxation. The Shah seemed satisfied, but suspected that the AIOC was bribing Kashani and Sayyid Zia to act against him. Gass at an audience with him on 17 October protested that it was not in the company's interest to do so. The AIOC suffered frequently from such allegations of interference from all political sides.

Most of the points concerned AIOC, but some were the responsibility of the British government. Indeed, some criticism had already been anticipated and the British government had been alerted to Iranian concern over the effect of British taxation on the company's profits, particularly over the imposition of dividend limitation. The British government's fiscal policy was framed to counter the increasingly dangerous post-war financial situation which the Labour administration had inherited.[14] The response of the Treasury was justifiable, but it seriously restricted AIOC's room to manoeuvre and greatly contributed to Iranian resentment and accusations that it acted as agent of the British government in depriving the Iranian government of the revenues to which it was entitled. On 1 June 1948 the company had complied with the government's direction not to increase the dividend payments for the previous year. On 21 May Fraser had requested a special dispensation in respect of dividend payments to the Iranian government, but the Chancellor of the Exchequer, Sir Stafford Cripps, was not prepared to make an exception.[15] Fraser regretted the decision 'notwithstanding the special position of the Company by reason of its concessionary obligations' and promised that 'if the Iranian Government considers that it will suffer hardship as a result of the decision, we will be willing to discuss with the Government any proposals which it may have to make in this connection.'[16] The Foreign Secretary, Ernest Bevin, also later intervened on behalf of the AIOC with the Chancellor, but unsuccessfully.[17] The Treasury would not make any exceptions.

In a revealing exchange with Sir Wilfred Eady, Joint Second Secretary, Treasury, on 9 August, Gass reported that he had told Eady of the Iranian government's complaint about the amount received by the British government in taxation in comparison with their receipts from royalty (see table 7.1). Between 1946 and 1951, a crucial period, a widening gap opened up as a result of increasing taxation. The AIOC considered that this was an intergovernmental issue but the Iranian government regarded it as a matter to be settled between the British government and the company. The AIOC, legally responsible for paying British taxation, not determining it, was caught in the middle.

Eady had made it clear that 'any attack on British taxation by the Iranian Government would be very ill received by the British Government.' He argued that 'the Iranian Government had benefited greatly from the victory of the Allies in that it has enabled us to develop the concession and bring progressively larger revenues to the Iranian Government from our expanding business.' He 'could not see that they were entitled to any larger share of profits than they were already obtaining, i.e. any higher rate

Table 7.1   *Benefits received by HMG, the Iranian government and other stockholders, 1932–50*

Stockholder	£
A **His Majesty's Government**	
Net dividends	22,500,000
Income tax, profit tax and Excess Profit tax	171,600,000
Total	194,100,000
B **The Iranian Government**	
Royalty, tax immunity payments and participation in distributions of profits	100,500,000
C **Other Stockholders**	
Net Dividends	17,400,000

Source: BP archives[18]

per ton of oil'. He held that 'the high price of oil was one of the great handicaps to world recovery today', and he was critical of the high Gulf of Mexico values. 'He felt sure that this state of affairs would not last.' Taking a more realistic approach, Gass stated, almost apologetically, 'we had not felt it was wise to exclude the possibility from our minds of giving the Iranian Government something more than they were now receiving for each ton of oil.' On the gold convertibility clause Eady said that the London gold price 'was pretty well on a parity with the New York price'.[19]

Thus, on two key issues affecting the Iranian government the company was at a disadvantage. It was a time when it was reconstructing its distribution installations after wartime losses, replacing tankers that had been sunk and renewing plant and equipment that was damaged. It was also a competitive period, a time to defend commercial interests. At the same time legal advice was that the concession itself should not be changed but only required modification in details, supplemental in kind. Legally, this may have been correct and perhaps politically expedient, but psychologically it was disastrous. It perpetuated a concession, which in the minds of some Iranians had become a symbol of British collusion with a dictator whose values and actions were being repudiated by increasingly articulate sections of Iranian society. In retrospect, it was a fundamental mistake because instead of looking to the future it seemed that the past was being preserved. The AIOC was hemmed in by the lack of flexibility in the government's fiscal policy and by the narrowness of legal advice.

A couple of weeks after the discussions were adjourned in Tehran, on 6 November the government of Hazhir resigned and was succeeded four days later by that of Muhammad Sa'id, who also pledged himself to pursue measures to ensure Iranian rights. Towards the end of January 1949,

Abbas Quli Gulsha'iyan, minister of Finance, a lawyer by training, indicated that he was fully empowered to act as the sole negotiator assisted by a committee. He had earlier stated on 21 December 1948 to Gass that he had

> personally no doubt that the government would be able to secure the
> necessary parliamentary approval. The Committee's arrangement with the
> company's representatives would of course have the Government's own
> backing and full approval. Therefore the Government would be in a position
> to submit these arrangements to the Majlis as a most satisfactory settlement.
> The Majlis would be very unlikely to reject the arrangements thus proposed,
> since the Government would make it clear that the only alternative to the
> acceptance of the arrangement would be the continuance of the concessional
> provisions as they stand now.'[20]

This seemed a confident assertion and a sign of the government's resolve to reach a settlement in the full knowledge of the attitude of the Majlis.

A few days later that stance was weakened when Taqizadeh was needled in the Majlis by Abbas Iskandari who accused him of treasonable action in signing the 1933 concession. In self-defence Taqizadeh complained wrongfully that the concession had been signed under duress, but correctly that it was the Shah who had taken the ultimate decision.[21] He disclaimed any responsibility for its prolongation. The controversy caused a tremendous stir and a stream of press abuse against the AIOC. Economically the position in Iran was deteriorating: budgets were voted *ad hoc* and the programme of the Seven Year Plan was reduced. The political scene was greatly disturbed by an attempted assassination of the Shah on 4 February 1949 and its aftermath of reprisals against clerical opposition and members of the Tudeh Party suspected of being involved.[22] It was not an auspicious time to begin oil negotiations. Moreover, they were protracted as the Iranian delegation consulted foreign experts, especially professor Gidel. Such consultations had also been a feature of earlier negotiations in the late 1920s and early 1930s with confusing rather than constructive results.

Twelve meetings were held between 13 February and 15 March. Gulsha'iyan confirmed that the validity of the concession was not disputed. No written memorandum was submitted to the representatives of the AIOC, but Iran objections and demands centred on internal oil sales to the government and others, a request for 20 per cent of the distributed profits of dividends, adherence to a fifty–fifty formula on the basis of the Venezuelan example and concessional revisions every 15 years. The negotiations stumbled on the problem of the fifty–fifty principle. Gass pointed out that in Venezuela (a delegation from which was visiting Iran at the time) output and profits were derived from the local production companies, not the parent companies. In Iran it was different because the

AIOC had never separated its different activities. Iran could not expect to participate in half of total group profits from the AIOC's world-wide operations, such as those in Iraq or Kuwait. Gass suggested to Gulsha'iyan that it was inconceivable that the ruler of Kuwait would allow the Iranian government to participate in royalties from the profits of Kuwait oil. This remained a crucial difference. It was also argued that in practice a fifty–fifty arrangement would not necessarily in all cases be an advantage to the Iranian government over what was being proposed in the Supplemental Agreement, especially if the profitability of the oil industry dropped.

Sa'id asked Gass – just as Taymurtash requested Cadman and Musaddiq later told Jackson – to look wider than just commercial considerations because of public expectations. He also stressed the poverty of the country, as did Musaddiq. Once again there was a temporary adjournment. The AIOC discussed its proposals with the Foreign Office and Treasury. Bevin informed the Iranian ambassador in London, Muhsin Ra'is, that 'the offer from the AIOC would represent the best either the Company or His Majesty's Government could do to assist the Persian Government.'[23] Bevin and his officials were 'satisfied that Sir W. Fraser fully grasps all the factors in the problem and had throughout been animated by a desire to reach an agreement which is fair to both sides'.[24]

Whatever the subsequent criticism of the Supplemental Agreement, there was no sign of disagreement between the AIOC and the British government on its final terms. The Iranian government was advised by Max Thornburg, formerly of the Texas Oil Company, wartime petroleum adviser to the State Department and then executive director of Overseas Consultants Inc. (planning advisers to the Seven Year Plan organization). His advice was hardly disinterested in view of his executive association with the plan and served principally to advance his own personal ambitions for the progress of the modernization programme.[25] Thornburg advocated that the Iranian government should hold out for greatly increased royalties, although he informed the AIOC that he was exerting a moderating influence.

In further negotiations in Tehran, which Fraser attended, the two sides moved close to an agreement on the figures for 1947 and 1948, for which the overall rate per ton of production worked out at 16 shillings, but the AIOC felt unable to guarantee payments indefinitely at this rate. Once more talks were adjourned and after further consideration Fraser agreed to guarantee a minimum £2.5 million payment in respect of dividends and allocation to general reserve, over and above the royalty tonnage payments that had been increased. The Iranian ambassador again approached Bevin. The Foreign Office was satisfied that the company's offer was 'a generous one', and the Iranian government was advised to accept it.[26] Gass returned to Tehran, authorized to offer up to £4 million instead of the £2.5 million which had been suggested if the other terms, which had been agreed, were formally accepted. Gulsha'iyan agreed on 3 July, but three days later after a confidential disclosure by Sa'id that agreement was close, the Finance minister reported that the Cabinet was divided and that the revised General Plan on employment was unacceptable. At this point Sir John Le Rougetel, the British ambassador, who had been kept informed, put forward a compromise for an exchange of letters about the General Plan which would lapse if the Supplemental Agreement was not ratified, but would be referred to arbitration if, the Supplemental Agreement having been ratified, no agreement was reached.[27] This was acceptable and the Supplemental Agreement was signed by Gulsha'iyan and Gass on 17 July.[28]

The protracted negotiations made ratification less likely because of the imminent end of the session of the Majlis. Deputies, understandably, resented being called upon to pass such important legislation in such a short time and were concerned about the forthcoming elections.[29] The political situation was tense with supporters of Qavam and Musaddiq challenging the Shah. The oil issue became a rallying point, a focus of national frustration. The economic importance of increased revenues was overtaken by political factors, which both the British government and the company undervalued. Because of the astute parliamentary tactics employed by Husayn Makki and the few other members of the National Front in the Majlis, the agreement was talked out and no vote was taken by the time of the last session on 28 July. This development coincided with increasing difficulties over the implementation of the Seven Year Plan. In conception the plan was to be a long-term development of education, communications, industrial infrastructure, improved administration, but in performance it was expected to bring about significant short-term financial gains.[30] It was regarded as an 'Open Sesame' formula, a cure-all solution, what Arthur Millspaugh, a former US financial adviser, referred to as a kind of 'Aladdin's lamp psychology', a national miracle of instant economic success. Something of this sentiment permeated Musaddiq's impression of the oil industry, the key to prosperity, progress and independence.[31]

Yet there was growing questioning by some of the values and attitudes implicit in industrial modernization. As professor T. Cuyler Young remarked,

the landed and mercantile classes are likely to perceive in the plan a threat to their present supremacy . . . and it is altogether probable that among these privileged classes there will be many who will strive to sabotage the whole effort. These supporters of the *status quo* will be abetted by the conservative clerics who fear that progress of industrialisation and modernisation is a threat to the Islamic religion, way of life and social structure.[32]

There was an intensification of the constitutional controversy over the role of the Shah and his reforms. His visit to the United States in late 1949 was an indication of the direction in which he was moving. All these political and economic developments and pressures inevitably affected relations between the Iranian government and the AIOC.

The devaluation of sterling on 18 September was an unwelcome reminder of the fragility of the British economy and reduced the respect for sterling as an international currency. In the autumn Sa'id visited London for medical reasons, called on Bevin on 26 October, saw Fraser and said that he would present the Supplemental Agreement to the next Majlis after the elections. Bevin assured him that the Supplemental Agreement was 'fair and reasonable . . . eminently reasonable to both parties'.[33] In response to Sa'id's claim that the Iranian government had received no American aid, Bevin was sympathetic, and promised to intercede, 'about the need for strengthening the Persian economy'. Sa'id raised the spectre of 'the pressure from the north'. A few weeks later, Hazhir, then minister of Court, was assassinated. In April 1950 Sa'id lost the support of the new Majlis and was replaced by Ali Mansur, whose appointment was unexpected and whose reputation for integrity was questionable.[34] Mansur soon asked the company for funds. He strove to give no offence, but lost the confidence of the Shah, the deputies and the US government. The Shah wanted him to present the Supplemental Agreement for ratification but Mansur prevaricated. The Shah decided at the end of May to replace him with Ali Razmara.[35]

In a last minute attempt to hold on to his position and with advice from Albert A. Lager, US petroleum attaché in the Middle East who told him that the Supplemental Agreement 'represented an extremely equitable arrangement', Mansur set up a special Oil Committee of the Majlis on 22 June 1950 ostensibly to speed the passage of the Supplemental Agreement.[36] However, two of his nominees for the Oil Committee, Tahiri and Shukra'i were induced to give up their seats to Allahyar Saleh and Ali Shayigan of the National Front. Thus, whereas Mansur had allocated three seats to the supporters of the National Front, they actually obtained five out of the 18 members. Instead of the committee being a means for early ratification of the Supplemental Agreement, it actually became a device for its obstruction.

On 26 June Mansur's government was dismissed. General Ali Razmara, whom the Shah once told Le Rougetel he would never appoint as prime minister, succeeded. On 2 July Henry Grady, the new American ambassador, arrived with ambitious plans for rescuing the Iranians from themselves and with promises of a generous provision of aid that were not fulfilled.[37] Grady had been successful in the post-war rehabilitation of Greece and much was expected of him, but it is questionable whether he was capable of matching those expectations. He was unsympathetic to the

British, his impressions of Iran were superficial and his relations with his colleagues temperamental. His performance was comparable with his naivety. In the disillusionment of the cold war Iran assumed a strategic importance for American defence planners, who regarded the country as a likely victim of a Soviet-inspired coup organized by the Tudeh Party. Rightly or wrongly, this coloured the State Department's appreciation of the Iranian political situation which it was convinced had to be stabilized by increasing the authority of the Shah and strengthening the economy. Thus in January 1948 the view of the State Department was: 'We continue to feel that US objectives in Iran can be best achieved by economic development to strengthen social structure and popular loyalty to central Government'; and on Soviet designs in mid-1950: 'it seems probable that the USSR will not attack Iran but will intensify its efforts to build up subversive forces within Iran and to weaken the country by means of propaganda, border activities and diplomatic pressure.'[38] A year later it was regarded as an 'impelling fact that Iran represents a tempting bait to Russia in its efforts to forge a chain of satellites around the soviet periphery'.[39]

At the same time the importance of oil in the Middle East was also stressed as increasing concessionary pressures were experienced not only in Iran, but also in Iraq and Saudi Arabia.[40] The Anglo-Iranian oil dispute was part of a wider assertion of national identity and national sovereignty over resources. The problem was the assessment of its strategic, political and economic implications in the context of the confrontation of American and Soviet interests, which the invasion of Korea came to symbolize. Indeed these issues came to exert a crucial effect on Anglo-American relations in respect to Iran from the moment Razmara became prime minister and Grady became ambassador.

The belief that Razmara would provide strong government for Iran and would prove to be the saviour of the nation was disappointed. He may have had a reputation as a decisive military leader and a moderate politician, but his uneasy relationship with the Shah, who both feared and admired him, his contempt for parliamentary procedures, his propensity to indecision, his deviousness, lost him the respect of potential supporters. Although Iran became a recipient of American Point IV aid, US financial assistance was insufficient for Razmara to make an impressive political début and he soon squandered what credit he was believed to possess.

He dithered over presenting the Supplemental Agreement and his half-hearted attempts in October to persuade the Oil Committee to co-operate with him showed little conviction.[41] He issued conflicting signals to the AIOC at his meetings with its chief representative in Tehran, E. G. D. Northcroft, alternatively expressing confidence and despair, and invariably asking for advances which he received but never acknowledged. He professed to have little time to spend on the oil problem and was content to leave it in the hands of the concessions department, which was not disposed to pull the prime minister's chestnuts out of the fire. When the Iranian ambassador, Muhsin Ra'is, left London at the beginning of August, he was informed by Fraser that if after the Supplemental Agreement had been signed the Iranian government still preferred payments to be made on a fifty–fifty basis, he was prepared to reach an accommodation 'which could perhaps help Razmara'. Nothing happened. In August Razmara wanted payment of what was due under the Supplemental Agreement even though it had not been ratified and he did not intend to present it to the Majlis for another six months. He estimated that government expenditure would amount to some £4–6 million a month and he required the money because not a single dollar's worth of American help had actually been received.

He made suggestions on Iranianization, disclosure of accounts, availability of gas and lower internal prices, which could have been met if he had displayed any urgency to present the Supplemental Agreement to the Majlis; but he preferred initially to enhance his image by provincial administrative reforms, which brought a hornets' nest about his ears. Bevin was disappointed that Razmara would not 'tell us exactly what was wanted in order to reach a settlement. It was the bazaar method of negotiation.'[42] He frittered away his early months in gestures which lacked substance.[43] Meanwhile, the Oil Committee with Dr Musaddiq as chairman and Husayn Makki as rapporteur grew more hostile to the Supplemental Agreement and members of the National Front thwarted much of the legislation of Razmara's government in the Majlis. It was a difficult début.

Grady became alarmist soon after his arrival in Tehran, telling Northcroft on 8 July that Razmara 'was the last effective chance for Iran'. The AIOC kept the British government informed of its discussions with Razmara on the Supplemental Agreement but the Foreign Office in August did 'not consider that to press the Company to make concessions now would increase the chances of its early ratification'.[44] The Treasury was reluctant to authorize any loan to Iran while there was nearly £50 million available under the Supplemental Agreement. In August, the US ambassador in London, William Douglas, was told by Bevin,

> We had made a good offer to Persia and I felt we should stick by it . . . The Persians must really make up their minds whether or not they are going to do business . . . there should be agreement between us and the Americans otherwise the Persian Government would try to play us off against each other.[45]

This shrewd opinion remained Bevin's attitude, but it was not reciprocated. There were warnings from the State Department about an impending crisis in Iran.

In mid-September ineffectual discussions were held in London between

British and American officials. Razmara's plight was recognized, but although the Foreign Office was sympathetic, it wanted assurances that 'Persia was doing everything she could to help herself'.[46] The Treasury was reluctant to contemplate a loan that did not justify normal financial standards.[47] Under strong American pressure Hugh Gaitskell, minister for Economic Affairs, felt that 'we should not be asked to supply dollars for loans for which the United States will get all the credit.'[48] George McGhee, Assistant Secretary of State, was disappointed, particularly after his early strategic briefing in Washington. 'They [Americans] think that we do not fully realise the extreme urgency and the political risks involved.'[49] Nevertheless, whatever further allusions were made to the state of concessionary conditions in the Middle East, later discussions between Acheson and Bevin did not change the policy of the British government.[50]

Max Thornburg claimed in November 1950 on a visit to the AIOC in London that he had been sent as an emissary by Razmara but the prime minister denied it, thereby weakening the credibility of both men. On 20 November Dr Musaddiq denounced the Supplemental Agreement. On 13 December Kashani publicly supported nationalization. On 25 December, as a parliamentary ploy, Razmara withdrew the Supplemental Agreement from the Majlis at short notice, infuriating many of the deputies. The Oil Committee was not to be treated so contemptuously and shortly afterwards rejected the Supplemental Agreement.

On 22 December Jackson confidentially wrote to Gus Long, chairman of Texaco, asking if the Aramco discussions 'will lead to increased payments; the answer was that negotiations are still continuing and no progress has been made'. This conflicted with the rumours circulating in Tehran but the British government was not better informed of the extent of possible terms, whatever earlier informal warnings there had been to new concessionary commitments. These were agreed at the State Department at meetings on 4 and 16 November, prior to negotiations between representatives of Aramco and Saudi Arabia. There was a British suggestion that Aramco might delay any announcement of what had been settled.[51] Once the terms were known its tax implications were early appreciated by officials in London 'because of the American provisions for the relief of taxation to companies paying income tax abroad'.[52]

When Aramco made its Fifty–fifty Agreement with Saudi Arabia, the first in the Middle East,[53] the details were not received by the AIOC till the public announcement at the end of December, despite frequent requests to the American oil companies involved. This was the *coup de grâce* for the Supplemental Agreement. Razmara too was shortly to expire on 7 March 1951, victim of a religious assassin's bullet. He kept to himself that he had received a second offer of a fifty–fifty arrangement in January from the AIOC as well as an advance of £25 million.

In itself the assassination of Razmara made little difference to the fate of the Supplemental Agreement. He had certainly rallied to its defence a few days before his death but not very effectively. On 22 February 1951 the Foreign Office and the AIOC had agreed that Razmara's latest proposals were no improvement on the Supplemental Agreement. On 9 March Kashani organized a massive demonstration in the Baharistan Square in favour of nationalization. On 15 March the Oil Committee recommended nationalization of the oil industry throughout the country, which was approved by the Majlis on 20 March. On 19 March Abdul Hamid Zanganeh, minister of Education in Razmara's government was assassinated. On 20 March the British government decided that the situation had become so dangerous that it would assume full responsibility for the oil negotiations with the Iranian government.[54] After this decision the AIOC itself took no direct initiatives over oil affairs with the Iranian government. It took measures to protect its appropriated assets, maintain its legal claims, and liaise with local and central authorities during the takeover of its installations in Khuzistan until its enforced withdrawal in early October 1951. Thereafter, it was a party to subsequent negotiations but did not propose any policy which came from the British and American governments.

The period of Dr Musaddiq

Husayn Ala succeeded Razmara as prime minister on 11 March. He told a representative of the AIOC on 19 March that he hoped to calm the situation and eventually bring about a settlement in accordance with nationalization, satisfying national prestige and continuing the British and AIOC partnership in Persia. In a note to Ala delivered on 14 March the Foreign Office, while continuing its support of the Supplemental Agreement, contemplated possible alternative corporate structures for an affiliated company operating in Iran on a fifty–fifty basis. In discussions on the problem in Washington, 9–17 April, the British government representatives maintained that whatever future arrangements were agreed they had to ensure that effective British control was retained. As the British ambassador to the United States, Sir Oliver Franks, said on 17 April, 'we were concerned above all with a vital strategic interest and we must therefore retain effective control'.[55] The strengths and weaknesses of Iran as they appeared to both governments were debated without any real agreement on the assessments. American officials requested that the British government make a gesture to nationalization but this appeared to conflict with the necessity of effective control over the oil operations.

At these meetings and a number of others the British and American governments differed in their strategic appreciation of events. The British were not prepared to consider the company as being expendable in order to satisfy American apprehensions over the vulnerability of Iran to Soviet infiltration or occupation.[56] For the Americans the strategic position of Iran transcended 'the desirability of supporting British oil interests in Iran'.[57] This is crucial to understanding Anglo-American differences. It is also important to note that much of the tone of frustration apparent in Morrison's comments after he took office as Foreign Secretary in March was due to his realization that any display of British weakness in the run up to the general election would be a serious handicap for the Labour government.

Both the American and British governments were convinced that they knew what would satisfy Iranian national ambitions, but they failed to understand the motivation that impelled Musaddiq to pursue with passion an oil policy involving total independence from foreign powers. He was not interested in a fifty–fifty solution which, for both the American government and American oil companies had become the benchmark for concessionary arrangements they did not want to go beyond. Musaddiq consistently pressed for better terms for Iran; he and his supporters were engaged in a political crusade, not economic salvation. He said to Grady on 28 June 1951, 'I assure you, Excellency, that we value independence more than economics.'[58] The Oil Committee on 26 April, after a series of secret meetings, proposed a Nine Point Plan for the implementation of nationalization. The oil bill was passed by the Majlis on 28 April, the day that Musaddiq was chosen to succeed Ala. He may not have been aware of the problems he would face. He may have imagined that the Anglo-Iranian Oil Company was so dependent on Iranian oil that it would accept his demands; indeed, that it would continue to function as before under new management. He may have assumed that the American government would always come to his rescue. He was absolutely certain of his mission for Iran and determined to defy all attempts to prevent its accomplishment.

It was axiomatic for Musaddiq, as Kazim Hasibi remarked on 16 October 1951, that 'Iran would never again sanction outside control in any form of its oil industry.'[59] With much of the limelight focused on Musaddiq and his close collaborators such as Hasibi and Makki, another important factor in Iranian nationalism must not be forgotten for its impact on the oil dispute and its effect on the fortunes of the National Front itself: the influence of Ayatullah Kashani, whose animosity against British interests was frequently very forcibly expressed and who regarded the Seven Year Plan as 'a godless enterprise'.[60] On 13 July 1951, addressing the Islamic Warriors Association, he proclaimed that 'The entire Iranian nation which is proud to live under the holy banner of Islam, expresses its hatred of any yielding or recourse to foreigners regardless of the bloc or group to which they belong.'[61] This religious fervour was a strong element in the situation, eventually causing a rift with the more secular-minded supporters of Musaddiq. Indeed, it has become an article of faith to which

Hasibi himself subscribes that the creator of oil nationalization was Kashani and not Musaddiq.[62] On the other hand the Imam of Tehran informed the Shah on 2 December 1951 that 'The National Front was a British creation.'[63]

Behind his urbanity and humour Musaddiq could not comprehend or, at any rate, refused to be deflected by, mundane matters of a commercial nature. The AIOC for him was a mode of imperialism, not an organization which disposed of 96 per cent of Iranian oil exports and which possessed technical expertise recognized throughout the world. Averell Harriman, with Walter Levy, his oil adviser, laboured in vain during his visit to Tehran in July to August 1951 to explain to Musaddiq and his advisers that 'Effective operations, particularly of a refinery of the size and complexity of that in Abadan require the employment of an integrated organisation rather than the employment of individual foreign specialists. Competent technicians would not themselves consent to employment except under conditions satisfactory to them.' As for customers: 'It is also true that only those who have developed markets for Iranian oil are in a position to commit themselves for its purchase in the large quantities produced.' Hector Prud'homme of the World Bank remarked in March 1952, 'It would be very difficult to reach any agreement in the atmosphere that prevails in Iran now. The oil problem is mainly a political problem . . . our difficulty was that we were dealing with political men and not businessmen.[64] This was particularly true of the refusal to permit any British technicians to return to Iran even if they were attached to operations managed by a different organization such as the World Bank.

In spite of a number of missions, no settlement emerged. The Jackson mission in June 1951, whose terms were drawn up by the British government in consultation with the AIOC, negotiated under the authority of the British ambassador in Tehran, Sir Francis Shepherd, who declared: 'we are seriously seeking a settlement with Musaddiq.'[65] At the first meeting of the two delegations on 14 June, Varasteh, the Iranian minister of Finance, requested of the AIOC that

1 Its board of directors and its Iranian management should deal with the provisional board of directors on all matters concerning Iran.
2 It should remit all proceeds from oil sales less deductible expenses to the Iranian government.
3 It should render a statement of all sales transactions to the provisional board.

Only when those demands had been fulfilled would the Iranian government listen to any proposals which might be submitted. Shepherd characterized the Iranian attitude as 'wholly unacceptable'. The State Department described it to the embassy in London as 'completely unreasonable, designed to remove all hope of negotiation except on terms of complete capitulation'.[66] In the midst of the negotiations Musaddiq summoned Mustafa Fateh, one of the assistant general managers of the AIOC, and informed him that if the company did not immediately recognize the nationalization laws he would enforce its dispossession. He instructed his officials to collect receipts from tanker captains loading oil at Abadan, and only offered to negotiate on compensation. The AIOC refused to issue receipts and the loading of the tankers ceased, bringing oil exports to an end.

Jackson offered to accept the principle of nationalization with its practical implementation, to advance £10,000,000 at once, followed by a further £3,000,000 monthly while negotiations and operations continued. All distribution activities, and the Iranian assets of the company were to be transferred to the National Iranian Oil Company (NIOC).[67] Within half an hour this outline settlement was rejected. At the time even Grady 'seemed pleased' with the offer and the American ambassador, Julius Holmes, described it as wise and 'generous'.[68] Morrison was disappointed at the rejection of a possible settlement, which 'all fair minded opinion would regard as eminently reasonable'. Acheson was worried. Musaddiq, realizing that the die was cast and, determined to press home his advantage, demanded that British staff take service with the NIOC. He proposed an anti-sabotage law that would have rendered the staff liable to trials in courts on treasonable charges. While this was a fair tactic, it was not reassuring and did little to promote an acceptable compromise. Gradually many of the non-productive staff and all dependants were evacuated. The production, refining and transportation of oil virtually ceased as the tanks filled up.

The passage of the nationalization laws was a political success; the rejection of the British proposals and the managerial takeover in Abadan was an obvious victory, even though it was achieved at the price of the stoppage of oil revenues and a deterioration in Anglo-Iranian relations. The oil dispute, which had become an international controversy, rang alarm bells in the State Department. Acheson was worried at the situation in which 'this atmosphere of threat and fear, which results from hasty efforts to force co-operation in the implementation of the nationalisation law, cannot but seriously affect the morale of the employees and, consequently, their willingness to remain in Iran.'[69] Inevitably, as oil revenues dried up, American concern about political stability in Iran increased. The British government appealed to the International Court for an interim ruling on 22 June to protect its rights in Iran. The Iranian government denied the Court's jurisdiction because 'the exercise of sovereignty is not subject to complaint' and, though it sent observers to the Hague, it refused to accept the terms of the decision of 5 July, which effectively meant the maintenance of the *status quo* until a final settlement was reached.[70]

Morrison not only as a Foreign Secretary but also as a Labour politician remarked on 22 June 1951 that

> the Prime Minister of Iran is not a Left-Wing Socialist or anything like that. He is a reactionary. He belongs to the well-to-do class which is being kept going by the working people in that country. That Government, out of the revenue from oil, were supposed to spend money on social development. They diverted the money.

Some may perceive this to be the prejudice of lunatic insularity, but it is not dissimilar to Acheson's judgement:

> Mossadeq's self-defeating quality was that he never paused to see that the passions he excited to support him restricted his freedom of choice and left only extreme solutions possible. We were, perhaps, slow in realising that he was essentially a rich, reactionary, feudal-minded Persian, inspired by a fanatical hatred of the British and a desire to expel them and all their works from the country, regardless of the cost . . . This unique character truly sowed the wind and reaped the whirlwind.[71]

Nevertheless, in spite of the Iranian view that the International Court's decision was 'unjust and contrary to Iran's independence and national sovereignty', President Truman wrote to Musaddiq on 9 July in an effort to break the stalemate. He commended 'the idea of a world controlled by law and justice' which had been enunciated in the Charter establishing the United Nations. He added that he wanted Averell Harriman to be received by Musaddiq 'as my personal representative to talk over with you this immediate and pressing situation'.[72] Musaddiq agreed on 11 July. It was the origin of Harriman's visit, which began on 15 July, and the associated mission led by Richard Stokes, Lord Privy Seal. It was greeted with demonstrations protesting at Anglo-American connivance, allegedly organized by the AIOC. Harriman, his oil adviser Walter Levy and his interpreter Vernon Walters established a relationship with Musaddiq as they attempted to instruct him in the facts of oil life, but Musaddiq was really not interested, and the discussions were 'completely unfruitful'.[73] Harriman believed that trusting in the good faith of Musaddiq and assuming that the principles of nationalization were respected, an acceptable arrangement in practice could be formulated to reconcile Iranian and British proposals, provided the provisions of the Nine Point Law of 2 May were set aside.

The British government was pessimistic but was persuaded by Harriman's patient appeal to negotiate at an intergovernmental level under his auspices. From the beginning, on 5 August, it was evident that Harriman had been misled or that Musaddiq had misunderstood the scope of the negotiations. For while Stokes was emphasizing the mutuality of interests in reaching a fair settlement, Musaddiq was declaring that it was impossible for him to go outside the nationalization laws. When the two delegations met on 6 August the Iranians had no formal proposals ready; their delegation disclaimed any plenary powers and was no more than a sounding board.

This style made negotiation difficult, for in the final stage Musaddiq was the ultimate authority, however much he seemed to play down his role. He could delay without offence and successfully used the ploy in later discussions with McGhee, the World Bank and Henderson. He never committed himself in writing except to take occasional notes: an expedient practice, perhaps, but one that sometimes led to a lack of consistency, even evasion. Stokes disclosed in the course of the fifth meeting of negotiations on 13 August the Eight Point proposals, which had been approved by Harriman. Overnight, Musaddiq informed Stokes that his proposals were unacceptable. Harriman kept aloof while they were being discussed with the Iranian delegation, provoking an Iranian assumption that further concessions might be made. At the last meeting on 19 August, however, he came off the fence to declare that the British proposals provided a good basis for the negotiation of a new settlement and conformed to the formula which had been submitted through him on the basis of which the British mission had come to negotiate.[74]

Harriman informed Musaddiq by letter that the seizure of foreign-owned properties without 'either paying prompt, adequate and effective compensation or working out new arrangements satisfactory to both parties, was not nationalisation but confiscation'.[75] Stating that the British proposals 'lacked due consideration to the economic and political independence of Iran', Musaddiq refused to sell at a discount, 'which is contrary to all the existing commercial practices'.[76]

In mid-September Harriman was pessimistic about reaching an agreement, as was the British government,[77] particularly when Musaddiq revoked the resident permits of the remaining AIOC staff in Iran on 25 September. The British government withdrew the last of the staff on 4 October and took the least offensive but least effective action in appealing urgently to the UN Security Council, whose response was essentially non-committal. After the ousting of the AIOC from Iran and British recourse to the International Court and the Security Council, and with the knowledge that Musaddiq would be coming to the United States, the US State Department adopted an even more active part. The British, it was argued, were far from the reality of the situation and immersed in elections, so the State Department would be the pace setter for new negotiations.[78] It was an unprecedented opportunity to persuade Musaddiq on his own to reach a settlement away from the pressures of Tehran and without the apparent obstructive presence of the British. The negotiations exhibited elements of success and failure, which characterized the oil dispute. The three governments were locked in a triangular hold from which they were unable to release themselves.

After the sessions of the Security Council, discussions began in Washington between Musaddiq and McGhee, with the occasional presence of Acheson and Paul Nitze. It was McGhee's contention, expressed in talks with a British delegation in April 1951, that although 'the availability of oil was very important . . . it was perhaps secondary to the general position of Persia in the pattern of world peace'.[79] The State Department was critical that 'the British had been tactically wrong again and again', but its view was not shared by all American diplomatic representatives, including William Gifford, the American ambassador in London. He cautioned that the British 'have on the whole conducted themselves responsibly in recent months and whatever their inclinations may otherwise have been, have deferred to our views at a number of crucial points'. He warned 'of a real Anglo American rift . . . if we are not careful'.[80] Moreover, the principal American oil companies with overseas concessions were convinced that a settlement 'which did not preserve proprietary and managerial rights for the foreign investors, would constitute a sacrifice of principle on the altar of expediency; a course which uniformally leads to much subsequent difficulty'.[81] Other members of the State Department, such as E. G. Miller concerned with South American affairs, detected 'a tendency to discuss our future course of action solely in terms of public relations rather than on the merits'. He was sceptical of 'any process of bailing out Iran for bankrupting itself' and worried about the 'sanctity of contracts'.[82]

Nevertheless, there were compelling reasons for the American government to encourage a settlement and the appearance of Musaddiq provided the catalyst for positive action. McGhee, who greatly sympathized with Musaddiq, spent some 80 hours in conversations from early October to mid-November and made a Herculean effort to persuade him to compromise on possible terms for an agreement. The State Department pressed the British government to accept the proposals. There is an assumption that, in support of British interests, it was American policy to put pressure on Musaddiq. Any impartial interpretation of the records would disprove this, but would also reveal the difficulties of the negotiations and how the main problems and issues hardly changed throughout the dispute. At an early stage McGhee stressed to Musaddiq that 'while we were anxious to see Iran get the best possible deal she could, we could not support an agreement which would destroy the whole fabric of the oil business throughout the world.'[83] Musaddiq was not impressed with sharing profits on the existing fifty–fifty basis, unable to understand 'why they should share with anyone'. Just before meeting Acheson on 24 October, Musaddiq had agreed 'in strictest confidence' that the Abadan refinery, provided it was not under British control, could remain in private ownership. Walter Levy was doubtful.[84] In discussions with Acheson present, Musaddiq denied accepting the return of any British technicians and refused to 'make any written agreements with anyone. It was an internal Iranian affair and could not be the subject of any written agreement with any foreign power.'[85]

Ultimately it was the question of price which dominated the discussions. Tactically, Musaddiq pressed for a quick settlement; then a partial agreement so that 'he would not go home empty-handed'; and finally a comprehensive solution, including housing and educational obligations, which McGhee believed 'would complicate the whole question'. McGhee was perplexed that Musaddiq persisted in his refusal to initial any agreement he would submit to the Majlis 'without publicly endorsing it'. Musaddiq was adamant that his price was $1.75 per barrel for crude oil and no explanation made him change his mind, remarking humorously that he was not running Iran for the entertainment of American public opinion'.[86] While some members of the State Department recognized that 'settlement is not possible until agreement on price is reached', Acheson thought 'things had gone very well and he did not expect Musaddiq to be difficult'. But Franks, the British ambassador, was unhappy that the Americans 'placed all the responsibilities for continuing or breaking-off negotiations on us'.[87] A 'basis for settlement of oil controversy', based on optimism rather than reality was prepared for immediate British acceptance. It accepted discrimination against British technicians, proposed compensation by the cancellation of claims and counter claims, and disposed the Abadan refinery to a Dutch company.

The British reaction was unwelcoming. Musaddiq's commitment was only 'vague promises to support it on his return to Tehran, but we have unfortunate experience of similar promises in the past'.[88] There were reservations about American objectives, for 'while they are prepared to sacrifice British interests and to ratify an act of expropriation at the expense of British interests, they do not seem to see that this will strike a blow at the security of foreign investments everywhere, theirs as well a ours.'[89] Sir Roger Makins, deputy Under-Secretary of State at the Foreign Office, said that without the Abadan refinery 'the whole plan would fall to the ground'.[90] Harriman and Linder failed to persuade the British government, and even further talks between Eden and Acheson in Paris did not reconcile their differences. The State Department was sure that Musaddiq 'had shown a greater realisation of practicalities than at any time before'. Eden declared that the Americans believed that the only alternative to Musaddiq is 'communism, and to save Persia from communism they are ready to sacrifice the interests of the Anglo-Iranian Oil Company and those of His Majesty's Government'. More bluntly he observed that 'without United States' encouragement he doubted whether Musaddiq would have survived so long'.[91] Acheson, admitting the problem of conflicting assessment from Tehran, was sure that 'the idea of waiting for the fall of Musaddiq would not work'. He could not help us 'in allowing AIOC to operate again in Persia' and 'would not let the Persian Government collapse'.[92]

Acheson was prepared to discard fifty–fifty arrangements, 'a shibboleth', and confident that the position of 'British staff working in Persia . . . was entirely negotiable'.[93] This was naive, for on his return to Tehran, Musaddiq asked Loy Henderson, who had replaced Grady, 'Don't you realise if we let in only two or three Britishers, Britain will in a short time again be running Iran?'[94] It was not long before the practical plug was pulled on the hypothetical proposals when Sir Frank Godber, chairman of Royal Dutch-Shell, stated that 'the refinery proposition would be quite impractical because it would not be possible to run a refinery of the size of Abadan without control over the operations in the Fields.'[95] Nonetheless, Acheson still urged a settlement, but Eden contended that it had to include the principles of (1) fair and full impartial compensation; (2) security for effective payment; (3) comparability of contractual terms; and (4) no discrimination.[96] Musaddiq was informed on 8 November 1951 that the basis for a settlement had not been agreed.

He had already complained to McGhee that 'the current unrest in Iran was the result of agitation by the former AIOC.'[97] He warned that 'Iran could become another Korea.' McGhee nevertheless continued his efforts to persuade Musaddiq to relax his opposition to British technicians and to take a more realistic attitude to price. Musaddiq replied that the British sometimes came to Iran 'as Mullahs preaching to the tribes' and that 'if he were to make an arrangement contrary to the popular will he would lose all his popularity in Iran'.[98] This was the heart of the matter and his political problem: 'he would be stronger if he went back without an agreement than if he had made one.' At the last meeting McGhee told Musaddiq: 'History would say that the Prime Minister had won a great victory but had been unwilling to harvest its fruits for his country.' Musaddiq did not dissent, claiming that 'his conscience would not allow him to do anything else'.[99] For all his patriotism, Musaddiq was a victim of his unfortunate past, a prisoner, excluded from office by Riza Shah, the scars of which he carried like the marks of a martyr. It was a personal and political tragedy.

It was a bitter disappointment to McGhee, but in spite of his warm personal rapport with and respect for Musaddiq, he recognized that the Iranian prime minister was 'warped by his extreme suspicion of everything British', and that his 'attitude probably doomed from the start our efforts to facilitate an agreement with the British'. Most importantly McGhee reported: 'Despite great efforts I was unable to get him to understand the facts of life about the international oil business.'[100]

American officials were pessimistic. Harold Linder of the State Department, who had been closely involved with the American initiative on discussions with Musaddiq, found that the Tehran Embassy officials were inadequately briefed about commercial matters and generally uninformed about the practicalities of the oil industry. It was recognized that in mid-December 1951, Iran was in 'an extremely fluid situation' and that 'Mossadegh changes his position with hours.'[101] Deputies and editors were taking sanctuary in the Majlis. There was apprehension that if no American assistance was available, 'the Tudeh party might well be in power within 6 months.' Nobody, including Ala, 'shared Mossadegh's confidence that he could keep the Tudeh out of the Majlis'. The Shah was indecisive. Linder's opinion of Musaddiq was not complimentary: 'a demagogue who had capitalised on the inadequacies or evils of the AIOC. He is not a reformer. He has ridden a wave of nationalism. He is also a Near Eastern trader who can only be convinced through the pressures which the government is beginning to feel.'

Linder characterized the situation as 'a poker game in which the stakes are enormous and both sides are bluffing – we that it is more important to preserve the oil structure than to have Iran go Communist; they, that it is far more important for us to keep Iran oriented our way politically, hence we are bound to render assistance'. It is not without interest at this time, that Mihdi Bazargan, a director of the NIOC, was addressing himself to its future which should be 'larger than a matter of compromise for the settlement of our personal and political prejudices'.[102] His perception was objective. He believed that

Like other international economic and social activities, the world oil industry could be compared to an electric network with which our own system must co-ordinate. Once we embark on the international scene and co-ordinate with this general system, we will keep pace with the world caravan and will not be left behind . . . this organisation, while preserving its Iranian nationality, will co-ordinate with other competent and well-experienced organisations . . . However, if we are negligent we will be left out of the caravan and will perish.

It was not the only time that Bazargan, who was later the first prime minister of the Islamic Republic, was wiser than many of his contemporaries.

Behind the scenes in Tehran there were arguments over oil policy, responsibility and authority, and some resignations.[103] Musaddiq's immediate reputation rested upon his exploitation of the oil issue and influence over the Oil Commission, the meetings of which he chaired before becoming prime minister. Hence he was obliged to consider its views and, as was revealed in his conversations with McGhee, had little room to manoeuvre; he was caught in a cul de sac. The opinion of Hasibi dominated the advice to the prime minister, sometimes in competition with that of Husayn Makki but, after Makki fell out with his colleagues, virtually on its own. It was Hasibi who asserted that Iran did not want money but its political independence at a meeting with McGhee in Washington, at which Musaddiq stated that 'he appreciated the economic discussions between oil experts but that for him and his country the problem was a political one'.[104]

Thus, the World Bank mission in spring 1952, which did not act on behalf of either the British or American governments failed to reach a settlement because of discrimination against British technicians, the lack of understanding on pricing, and the conflict over political and commercial interests. The rejection of the Joint Proposals of Truman and Churchill on 30 August 1952 was mainly due to the absence of an agreement on compensation. The frantic and unrealistic attempt of the outgoing Democratic administration to achieve a rapid settlement on 15 January 1953 failed primarily as a result of Musaddiq's indecision, and his refusal to accept impartial arbitration. When the Republican administration persuaded the British government to make more concessions on 20 February 1953 in order that it might obtain a diplomatic victory soon after taking office, it was rebuffed by Musaddiq, with unfortunate consequences. Musaddiq clutched at straws such as the settlement proposed by the American independent oilman Alton Jones in his misguided visit of August 1952 in much the same manner as Ali Razmara expected miracles from another former American oil executive Max Thornburg. Against the run of play on which he had been well advised, Musaddiq kept trying to set up secret deals with Italian middlemen, Japanese intermediaries and American brokers, whose promises were as empty as their purses.

Paradoxically the longer the dispute continued the more its worst effects were felt in Iran which was deprived of possible revenues of at least $200,000,000 a year; the AIOC had replaced its lost supplies, restored its fallen profits and was recovering its refinery capacity. Iranian oil was no longer essential in world markets, as the chart of crude oil production shows (see figure 7.1). Unfortunately, Musaddiq was still belabouring the past: he complained to the Majlis on his return to Tehran on 25 November 1951 of British policy in Iran; and on 20 March 1953 declared on Tehran Radio, nearly six months after breaking off diplomatic relations with the United Kingdom, that the operations of the AIOC in Iran 'was a form of plunder for which there is no precedent anywhere in the world'.[105] He spoke in apocalyptic terms of 'the sacred and courageous struggle' of the people of Iran; 'the greatest struggle in their history'; their triumph in the victory of nationalization. He invoked 'the protection of Almighty God' in

being authorised by the will of the nation to share in the movement launched to protect the independence of the country, to sever the grip of the foreigners and to re-establish the prestige, the glory and the honour of the Persia of

ancient times . . . the shattering of the chains of colonialism . . . toppling the
pillars of oppression.

It was the vindication of the 'Naft Nameh', the defeat of the latter day
Turanians, 'the British Government and its company horde'. It was not the
rhetoric but the anachronism which was at the heart of the matter. Yet,
historical judgement should be marked by humanity. As G. K. Chesterton
remarks in his life of Robert Browning, 'In studying the careers of great
men we tend constantly to forget that their youth was generally passed and
their characters practically formed in a period long previous to their
appearance in history'.[106] In conversation with Henderson during March
1953, Musaddiq repeated that the British objective in the area was 'to get
the Americans out of Iran and the whole Middle East . . . the British had
never wanted an oil settlement which would be reached with the assistance
of the United States.'[107]

Even the patient Henderson who knew Musaddiq well and who had
contributed greatly to the modified proposals of 15 January 1953 was
troubled by Musaddiq's attempt to handle – even when he did not fully
understand – all the details himself. Musaddiq's revival of fears about the
communist menace in February and March 1953 may have backfired,
making the Americans more anxious and less inclined to wait for a long-
delayed oil agreement before contemplating measures to forestall an
anticipated Tudeh-inspired uprising. Musaddiq told Henderson on 31 May
that 'it would be better to forget the oil problem' and concentrate on aid;
for without aid he foresaw 'the eventual fall from power of the
Government and its replacement by a Communist-dominated Government'.[108] Henderson held out no high hopes, but Musaddiq did not heed
the warning.

It was no doubt important and regretable that Henderson returned to
Washington in June 1953 certain that nothing whatever was to be hoped for
from Musaddiq. He had been enthusiastic that a settlement could have
been reached but he admitted to Makins, the British ambassador, his
mistake; Makins relates, 'He knew we had reached that conclusion a long
time ago, and now he had reached it himself. He thought that if it had been
possible to get the old man alone, something might have been done, but he
was now completely in the hands of his advisers.'[109] Henderson had
combined sympathy and understanding of Iranian, American and British
objectives with a personal appreciation of Musaddiq's appeal and his role
in nationalization. Musaddiq's failure to give him a sign of compromise,
like his treatment of McGhee, was perhaps the amber light for his eventual
displacement. A settlement would have been possible if Musaddiq had
shown a real inclination to compromise; intergovernmental agreement
would have left the AIOC no option but to agree to the terms if such a
settlement had been made.

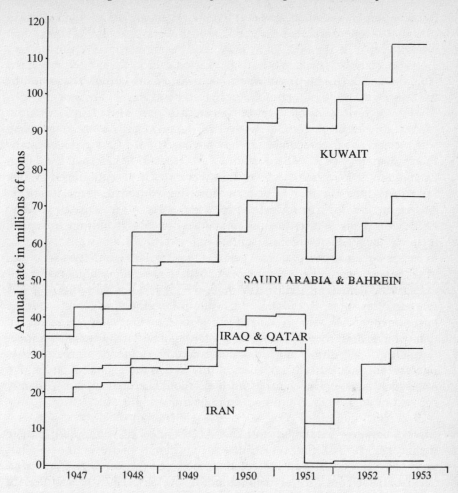

Figure 7.1 *Crude oil production in the Middle East, 1947–53*

The attitude of the United States, generally sympathetic, was growing weary. On 29 June 1953 President Eisenhower, in response to another appeal for more financial assistance, reminded Dr Musaddiq that

It would not be fair to the American taxpayers if the United States Government should extend any considerable amount of aid to Iran so long as Iran could have access to funds derived from the sale of oil and oil products . . . any American citizen would be deeply opposed to the purchase by the United States Government of Iranian oil in the absence of an oil settlement.[110]

In one of his comments from Tehran on the breaking off of Anglo-Iranian diplomatic relations George Middleton, British chargé d'affaires, had remarked that 'If the idea that the Americans are working against us and are supporting Dr Musaddiq and the National Front could be eradicated from the Persian mind, this would be the greatest single blow that could be dealt to Dr Musaddiq' – an opinion shared by Eden, and others.[111]

The Anglo-Iranian oil dispute was settled after Musaddiq's fall from office. In the event the AIOC received 40 per cent in the consortium which was formed of oil companies already having Middle East production, as Fraser had proposed. The testimony of Howard Page to the Church Committee in 1973 clearly shows that there was little enthusiasm among American oil companies to become involved. Moreover there was little alacrity by the department of Justice, which had anti-trust cases pending against the major American oil companies, to give them anti-trust protection. Once the issue of representation in the consortium was solved, the management and operating arrangements were mainly left to the executives of the major oil companies to negotiate with the assistance and encouragement of the American and British embassies. A reasonable settlement was reached after some six months, not without its difficulties for the Iranian government and in some respects over production and sales less attractive than could have been obtained by Musaddiq. The principal Iranian negotiator, Ali Amini, minister of Finance, had defended his country's interests ably, realistically and patriotically. It was unfortunate that he, like Taqizadeh and Gulsha'iyan before him, should have been subsequently accused of neglecting, if not disregarding Iranian interests.

It is short-sighted to consider the Anglo-Iranian oil dispute just as a contest between Musaddiq and the AIOC: it is of wider and greater significance. The dispute illustrates a transitional phase in the difficult process of the adjustment of relations between industrialized and less-developed societies for the exploitation of raw materials. Oil was already becoming a political and economic factor at the end of the Qajar period and became important during the reign of Riza Shah with his emphasis on a national programme of modernization. After more attention had been focused on it during the second world war it was inevitable that it would increase in influence. The issues of the oil dispute referred back to the concessional controversies of the late nineteenth century in tobacco, mining, communications, utilities, banking, even gambling, with their political and social implications; and they referred forward to the issues of the sovereignty of national resources, the transfer of technology and economic growth in relation to the standard of living. These are aspects of the North–South debate, which have yet to be satisfactorily resolved.

Notes

1 I.C.J. Pleadings, *Anglo-Iranian Oil Co. Case (United Kingdom v. Iran)* (Leyden, 1952) p. 439.
2 M. Mahmud, *Tarikh-i ravabit-i siyasi-yi Iran va Ingilis*, 5 vols (Tehran, 1949–53). On the oil issue see for example two Iranian authorities: Nasrollah Saifpour Fatemi, *Oil Diplomacy: Powderkeg in Iran* (New York, 1954) ('The Iranians have always considered the company as a branch of the British foreign office', p. xxiv, and 'In 1914 and 1941 the British invaded Iran in order to protect the interests of the company'); Homa Katouzian, *The Political Economy of Modern Iran 1926–79* (New York, 1981) ('the existence of the Anglo-Iranian Oil Company (AIOC) had provided a permanent vested interest for Britain in the Iranian political economy, exposing its domestic and foreign political relations to covert British interference and manipulation', p. 157).
3 See R. W. Ferrier, *The History of The British Petroleum Company*, vol. 1, *The Developing Years 1901–1932* (Cambridge, 1982), Ch. 5.
4 For accounts of these issues see Robert B. Stobaugh, 'The Evolution of Iranian Oil Policy', in *Iran under the Pahlavis*, ed. George Lenczowski (Stanford, 1978) pp. 201–52, and Mustafa Fateh, *Panjah sal naft-i Iran* (Tehran, 1954).
5 R. W. Ferrier, 'The development of the Iranian oil industry', in Hossein Amirsadeghi and R. W. Ferrier, *Twentieth-Century Iran* (London, 1977) pp. 93–127.
6 Bruce R. Kuniholm, *The Origins of the Cold War in the Near East Great Power Conflict and Diplomacy in Iran, Turkey, and Greece* (Princeton, 1980).
7 19 July 1952, State Department, 888 2553/1 2052.
8 Sepehr Zabih, *The Communist Movement in Iran* (Berkeley, 1966).
9 Ervand Abrahamian, 'The strengths and weaknesses of the labour movement in Iran in 1941–53', *Continuity and Change in Modern Iran*, ed. Michael E. Bonine and Nikki R. Keddie (New York, 1981) pp. 193–200.
10 Fraser was deputy chairman of the AIOC in 1929 and succeeded as chairman in 1941. He was also a chairman of the Iraq Petroleum Company and of the Kuwait Oil Company.
11 Bevin wrote, 'I cannot get it out of my mind that the Tudeh Party, though admittedly a revolutionary party, may be the party of the future in Persia which is going to look after the interests of the working man,' Bevin to Sargeant 5 July 1946, FO 371/52717 (Public Record Office, London); but Dean Acheson, *Present at the Creation* (London, 1969) p. 197, saw it as a Soviet and 'separatist movement'.
12 BP archives. See also the comments of Fraser at the Annual General Meeting of 20 December 1950:

> During the negotiations for the 1949 Supplemental Agreement the straight 50/50 profit-sharing scheme came up for discussion, but after lengthy examination it was discarded in favour of increased payments

under the existing methods of the 1933 Convention. In general the attitude of the Iranian Government representatives in these negotiations was that profit sharing should apply to the profits of the Company for all its activities, whether outside or inside Iran. No oil company could agree to operate on the 50/50 profit sharing principle unless the profits were confined to those arising from the country of operation . . .

In consequence, on hearing of the Saudi-Arabian Agreement and notwithstanding the conclusions reached during the negotiations for Supplemental Agreement, the Company lost no time in communicating to General Ali Razmara, the then Prime Minister, its willingness to examine with the Iranian Government suggestions for a new agreement on similar lines.

13   See L. P. Elwell-Sutton, *Persian Oil: a Study in Power Politics* (London, 1955) pp. 165–9.

14   Maynard Keynes described it as 'a financial Dunkirk'; see Alec Cairncross, *Years of Recovery British Economic Policy 1945–51* (London, 1985).

15   Cripps to Fraser 27 May 1948, FO 371/68731: 'your Company should conform to the policy of dividend stabilisation which His Majesty's Government regards as an essential factor in the effort to secure the economic position of this country.' Admittedly the financial situations of the two countries were completely different, but there was nevertheless an unmistakable contrast in the Treasury attitude to AIOC compared with that of the Bureau of Internal Revenue in the case of Aramco; see Irvine Anderson, *Aramco, the United States and Saudi Arabia: a Study of the Dynamics of Foreign Oil Policy* (Princeton, 1981).

16   See Fraser's statement to stockholders on 20 December 1951:

Stockholders will recall that the Company had taken the initiative in 1948 in opening discussions with the Iranian Government at the time when the policy of dividend limitation was introduced in this country, because of its effect on the Company's current royalty payments to the Iranian Government. Although in the long run the Government's position was fully protected by its interest in the General Reserve, this policy resulted in smaller current annual payments . . .

17   Bevin to Cripps, 18 February 1949, FO 371/75495, 'it is important both from the political point of view and for the future of the Company, that the Persians should be satisfied that they are receiving an equitable return from the exploitation of their oil resources'. Fraser was aware of the dilemma, he could not ask 'for any exemption from the laws of this country: I know that we should not get very far if we decide to approach the Government on this matter' (BP archives); 'the Inland Revenue were firm in their opinion that they would not break the United Kingdom taxation Law in order to make concessions to the Persians', Chadwick note, 'Anglo-Persian Oil Company', 2 April 1949, FO 371/75496.

18   (According to British government statistics.)

19   On the British government's figures for taxation and investment, see Noel-

Baker to Attlee, 29 September 1951, FO 371/91596, which includes statistics on p. 13.

20   BP archives.

21   See Rouhollah K. Ramazani, *Iran's Foreign Policy, 1941–1973: a Study of Foreign Policy in Modernizing Nations* (Charlottesville, Va, 1975) for part of the text, pp. 183–4.

22   On the implications, see for example Abrahamian, *Iran Between Two Revolutions*, pp. 249–50.

23   Bevin to Le Rougetel, 28 April 1949, FO 371/75496.

24   FO to Le Rougetel, 27 April 1949, FO 371/75499.

25   See *New York Times*, 9 January 1951, and BP archives.

26   Le Rougetel to FO, 23 May 1949, FO 248/1489.

27   Le Rougetel to FO, 15 July 1949, FO 248/1489.

28   For a different Iranian view see Husayn Pirnia, *Dah sal kushish dar rah-i hifz va bast-i huquq-i Iran dar naft* (Tehran, 1331/1952). Dr Pirnia, as the head of the concessions department within the Ministry of Finance, was a key person during the pre-Musaddiq negotiations with the AIOC and was opposed to the Supplemental Agreement.

29   Wheeler to Le Rougetel, 9 July 1949, FO 248/1489.

30   *Report on Seven Year Development Plan for the Plan Organisation of the Imperial Government of Iran*, 6 vols (Overseas Consultants, Inc., New York, 1949).

31   Arthur Millspaugh, 'Iran wants an "Aladdin's lamp" economy', *New York Journal of Commerce*, 10 December 1948.

32   In 'The race between Russia and reform in Iran', *Foreign Affairs* 28 (January 1950). Kashani referred to the plan as a 'godless enterprise', *Christian Science Monitor*, 12 January 1951.

33   Bevin to Le Rougetel, 26 October 1949, FO 371/75500.

34   He had been prosecuted in the mid-1930s for charges concerned with the Trans-Iranian railway when he was minister of Communications.

35   See Sepehr Zabih, *The Mossadegh Era* (Chicago, 1982), for the significance of this appointment.

36   Shepherd to FO, 15 June 1950, FO 371/82311.

37   There are many references to this subject in the volumes of the Foreign Relations of the United States. See Yonah Alexander and Allen Nanes eds, *The United States and Iran: a Documentary History* (Frederick, Md, 1980) p. 191, acting Secretary of State to the embassy in Iran, 3 January 1948: 'US objectives in Iran can be best achieved by economic development to strengthen social structure and popular loyalty to central Government.'

38   Ibid., p 195, memorandum for the president by the Central Intelligence Agency, 27 July 1950.

39   Committee on Foreign Affairs, House of Representatives, 20 July 1950, statement of George McGhee.

40   *Foreign Relations of the United States*, vol. 5, 1950, R. Funkhauser, 'Middle East oil (background paper for 11 September meeting)' pp. 76–96.

41   Husayn Makki, *Kitab-i siah* (Tehran, 1329/1954).

42   Bevin to Franks, 12 August 1950, FO 371/82375.

43   Shepherd to FO, 18 September 1950, FO 371/82342. It is only fair to state

that the American view expressed by McGhee was more complimentary: 'the best Government she [Iran] has had in years', PRO FO 371/82348, Ramsbotham note, 21 September 1950.

44 FO to Shepherd, 9 August 1950, FO 371.

45 Bevin to Franks, 12 August 1950, FO 371/82375.

46 Record Meeting at FO, 12 September 1950, FO 371/82342.

47 Furlonge to Strang, 14 September 1950, FO 371/82342.

48 Note, Financial assistance to Persia, Furlonge, 19 September 1950, FO 371/82342.

49 Ramsbotham note, 21 September 1950, FO 371/82342.

50 Bevin to Washington, 21 October 1950, FO 371/82342.

51 Shepherd to FO, 7 December 1950, FO 371/82377.

52 Brittain to Bamford, 22 March 1951, FO 371/91526; and see US Congress Senate Committee on Foreign Relations subcommittee on Multinational Corporations, *Multinational Report*, 93rd Cong., 2nd Session, Government Printing Office 1975, especially part 8.

53 Irvine H. Anderson, *Aramco, the United States and Saudi Arabia: a Study of the Dynamics of Foreign Oil Policy 1933–1950* (Princeton, 1981), and his contribution to this volume.

54 Minutes to Meeting held at FO, 20 March 1951, FO 371/91525.

55 Franks to FO, 19 April 1951, FO 371/91471.

56 Sir William Strang communicated his personal thoughts to Franks on 25 April after the Washington talks had ended and in reply to some observations of Franks: 'What is now happening in Persia is happening much more because the Persians are what they are than because of what the Company may have done or not done.' Like Middleton later, he summarized the British position,

whose hand would have been easier to play if the Americans had not already thrown away some of the cards. The main difference between us and the Americans in this affair seems to be that, to the Americans, in the fight against Communism in Persia, the Anglo-Iranian Oil Company is expendable. It is not possible for us to start from this premise. (Strang to Franks, 25 April 1951, FO 371/91529.)

57 Yonah Alexander and Allan Nanes eds, *The United States and Iran*, pp. 223–4. Joint Chiefs of Staff, Memorandum for the Secretary of Defense: the Anglo-Iranian Problem, 10 October 1951.

58 29 June 1951, State Department (S.D.) 788 00/6 2951.

59 16 October 1951, S.D. 888 255310/1651.

60 *Christian Science Monitor*, 12 January 1951, and Yann Richard, 'Ayatollah Kashani: Precursor of the Islamic Republic', in *Religion and Politics in Iran*, ed Nikki R. Keddie (New Haven, 1983) pp. 101–24.

61 30 July 1951, S.D. 788 00/6 2951. See also comment of professor A. K. S. Lambton that 'it was not until the movement was interpreted by the religious classes in terms of Islam that it received widespread support' ('The impact of the West on Persia', *International Affairs* (January, 1957) p. 24).

62 See also *Iran-i Ma*, 7 March 1952: 'All over the world people have realized

that it was Kashani who united the people of Iran in their attempt to eradicate the influence of AIOC opposition to Musaddiq.'

63 11 December 1951, S.D. 788 00/12 1051.

64 *The Times*, 24 March 1952. Even Dr Pirnia found it impossible to work with Dr Musaddiq and was dismissed; see Pirnia, *Dah sal kushish*.

65 Shepherd to FO, 15 June 1951, FO 371/91546.

66 Shepherd to FO, 16 June 1951, FO 371/91546.

67 Shepherd to FO, 19 June 1951, FO 371/91548.

68 Strang note, 20 June 1951, FO 371/91554; Strang note, 23 June 1951, FO 371/91556.

69 *The Times*, 28 June 1951.

70 All the proceedings before the International Court of Justice may be found in I.C.J. Pleadings, Anglo-Iranian Oil Co. Case (United Kingdom v. Iran) (Leyden, 1952).

71 Dean Acheson, *Present at the Creation* (London, 1971) p. 504.

72 Alexander and Nanes, *The United States and Iran*, pp. 218–19, letter from Truman to Musaddiq, 8 July 1951; Musaddiq's answer to Truman, 11 July, ibid., pp. 219–20.

73 An entertaining and penetrating account of these conversations is in Vernon A. Walters, *Silent Missions* (New York, 1978).

74 UK Government Publication, Cmd, 8425. See Shepherd to Attlee, 27 August 1951. FO 371/91582.

75 Alexander and Nanes, *The United States and Iran*, pp. 222, Harriman to Musaddiq, 15 September 1951.

76 FO to Tehran, 28 August 1951, FO 371/91581.

77 Cabinet memorandum by Foreign Secretary, 'The oil dispute with Persia', 23 September 1951, FO CAB 129/47.

78 This view permeated much State Department thinking, as for example, in brief resumé of Iranian situation, 6 October 1951, S.D. 888.2553/10–651.

79 Minutes of Meeting in State Department, 9 April 1951, FO 371/91471.

80 Gifford to Acheson, 5 October 1951, S.D. 888.2553/10–551.

81 Holman to McGhee, 29 October 1951, S.D. 888.2553/10–2951. In 1952 Standard Oil (NJ), Standard Oil (NY), the Gulf Oil Corporation and The Texas Company all resisted Acheson's attempts on 4 and 9 December 'to bolster the Iranian economy', in defence against communism, by exporting 'some 400,000 barrels daily of crude and products'. They wanted to know if 'the British had been consulted about such a plan', and required that

1 The principle of prompt compensation to Anglo-Iranians for its ceased assets and breech of this contract must be agreed and acted upon.

2 Iran must, of course, be put in no better position from the point of view of income received . . . the established principle of 50/50 profit sharing must not be impaired.

3 The US Government give the US companies full figures protection, should the scheme go through.

4 Any settlement arrived at with Iran would in no way undermine or impair US commercial interests in other foreign countries. (Ministry

of Fuel and power note, 'Iran', 12 December 1952, POWE 1937/82190, PRO.)

82　Miller to Matthews, 14 November 1951, S.D. 888.1553/11–1451.

83　Memorandum of conversation with Musaddiq, 9 October 1951, S.D. 888.2553/10–951.

84　Walter Levy's general comments to Linder and Funkhouser, 17 October 1951, S.D. 888.2553/10–1751.

85　Memorandum of conversation with Musaddiq, 24 October 1951, S.D. 888.2553/10–2451.

86　Memorandum of conversation with Musaddiq, 25 October 1951, S.D. 888.2553/10–2551; 28 October 1951, 888.2553/10.2751; 29 October 1951, 888.2553/10–2951.

87　McGhee to Acheson, 3 November 1951, S.D. 888.2553/11–351, and Franks to FO, 23 October 1951, FO 371/91606.

88　FO to Washington, 3 November 1951, FO 371/91607; Minutes of Meeting in British Treasury, 2 November 1951, S.D. 288.2553/11–251; and London to Secretary of State, 3 November 1951, S.D. 288.2553/11–351.

89　See for example, Ministry of Fuel and Power Memorandum, 'Persia', 29 October 1951, FO 371/91607; Meeting chaired by Eden at FO, 1 November 1951, FO 371/91608.

90　Meeting in Foreign Secretary's Rooms, 1 November 1951, FO 371/91608.

91　Eden to Franks, 4 November 1951, FO 371/91608.

92　Eden to FO, 5 November 1951, FO 371/91608. Eden was also not convinced that the right policy was simply to wait for Musaddiq to fall.

93　5 November 1951 (No. 457) FO 371/91608 Paris to FO. See also Paris to S.D., 5 November 1951, S.D. 888.2553/11–551.

94　Henderson to Secretary of State, S.D. 888.2553/12–2651.

95　Fergusson to Lloyd, 6 November 1951, FO 371/91610.

96　See Eden, *Full Circle*, pp. 198–203 and Acheson, *Present at the Creation*, pp. 510–11. There were American objections that 'we were too rigid and were insisting on "principles which were unrealistic in the sense that no Persian Government would accept them" ' (FO to Washington, 16 November 1951, FO 371/91616).

97　Memorandum of conversation with Musaddiq, 5 November 1951, S.D. 888.2553/11–551.

98　Memorandum of conversation with Musaddiq, evening 15 November 1951, S.D. 888.2553/11–1551.

99　Memorandum of conversation with Musaddiq, 17 November 1951, S.D. 888.2553/11–1751.

100　McGhee, *Envoy to the Middle World*, p. 390.

101　Notes on Linder's recent visit to Iran, 14 December 1951, S.D. 888.2553/12–1451.

102　*Bakhtar-i Imruz*, 3 December 1951 in S.D. enclosure in Tehran. Despatch No. 713, 13 December 1951.

103　Senators Abu'l Qasim Najm and Muhammad Sururi resigned from the Joint Oil Commission on 5 December 1951; see letter in *Journal de Tehran*, 6 December 1951, in S.D. 888.2553/12–751.

104 Memorandum of conversation with Musaddiq, 17 November 1951, S.D.
     888.2553/11–1951, and ibid., Nitze memorandum of conversation with
     Musaddiq and Hasibi, 17 November 1951. See also Fu'ad Ruhani, *Tarikh-i
     milli shudan-i san'at-i naft-i Iran* (Tehran 1352/1973) pp. 255–6, 335 in
     respect of the World Bank mission and the later Joint Proposal of Truman
     and Churchill.
105 See Cottam, *Nationalism in Iran* (Pittsburgh, 1979) p. 284, 'Mossadeq's
     atavistic view of British influence in Iran and the Middle East prevented him
     from understanding that the battle had been won when the British accepted
     the principle of nationalisation of oil'.
106 G. K. Chesterton, *Robert Browning* (London, 1903) p. 14.
107 Washington to FO, 11 March 1951, FO 371/104614.
108 Washington to FO, 8 June 1953, 2222 FO 371/104616.
109 Makins to Bowker, 26 June 1953, FO 371/104616,
110 Alexander and Nanes, *The United States and Iran*, pp. 234–5, Letter from
     President Eisenhower to Musaddiq, 29 June 1953.
111 Middleton, October 1952, FO 371/98605.

PART III

The British and American governments

8

Oil boycott and the political economy: Musaddiq and the strategy of non-oil economics

HOMA KATOUZIAN

The severe foreign exchange shortage caused by the loss of oil revenues forced Musaddiq's government to adopt the strategy of non-oil economics. This was not a coherent and comprehensive policy framework, but its different strands tended to complement and reinforce each other. Hence, by August 1953 the balance of payments was on a steady course, and the domestic economy was under control.

The background[1]

When, in March 1951, Persian oil was nationalized, few Iranian politicians would have believed that the Anglo-Iranian oil dispute would drag on for as long as it did. Indeed, many of the leading members of the National Front thought that the resulting energy shortage in Britain would lead to an early settlement. On the other hand, they argued that even if the conflict was not settled quickly, the resulting manpower shortage in the oil industry could be met by exporting crude, rather than refined, petroleum. This point was made in a parliamentary debate, three months before the nationalization act, by Dr Muzaffar Baqa'i who went much further and declared that it would be better for the Iranian oil industry to be destroyed by an atom bomb than to remain in the hands of the Anglo-Iranian Oil Company.[2] Baqa'i may not have been entirely convinced by his own atom-bomb rhetoric, but the circumstances reveal three important assumptions behind the oil nationalization. First, that the matter would be settled fairly quickly. Secondly, that there would not be an oil blockade and boycott, so that crude oil would be able to be exported. Thirdly, that as long as a foreign concessionaire controlled the Iranian oil industry, the attainment of full independence, and the extension and strengthening of democratic government would not be possible.

Regarding the question of independence and democracy, the same attitude had been behind Musaddiq's policy of 'passive balance' (otherwise termed 'negative equilibrium') in the 14th Majlis (1944–6). Musaddiq, it will be recalled, had opposed the grant of the north-Iranian oil concession to the Soviet Union. And when the Tudeh Party argued that such a concession would result in a balance between Soviet and British interests in Iran, he retorted (in the Majlis meeting of 2 December 1944) that this would be tantamount to a person without an arm having his other arm amputated in order to attain physical balance. He was not opposed to the sale of Iranian oil to Russia, or any other oil deal with them without the grant of an oil concession. What he strongly opposed was the grant of an oil concession to *any* foreign power. And in order to forestall such a possibility without a wide public discussion, he moved quickly and introduced a private-members bill to the Majlis which forbade the grant of an oil concession to non-Iranians without Majlis approval.[3] That was the reason why the Tudeh Party press turned their guns against him at the time, opposed his oil nationalization bill later in the 16th Majlis, and described him as an agent of American imperialism.[4]

Musaddiq himself missed no opportunity to emphasize the primacy of politics in the oil dispute. For example, in a long parliamentary speech when he was still leader of the opposition, he said that 'the National Front proposes the policy of nationalizing the oil industry throughout Iran so that the [Anglo-Iranian] oil company will stop interfering, and using influence, in the political affairs [of this country]. The formation of the Irano-Soviet Oil Company in northern Iran would have resulted in the Soviet Union treating us in the same way as the British Oil Company [sic].'[5] Early in his premiership, in a press conference with American journalists, he described the nationalization of the Iranian oil industry as 'the one and only way of stopping the illegal and illegitimate interferences of the former oil company in the internal affairs of Iran.'[6] After the failure of the Stokes mission to settle the oil dispute, he said, in a long address to the 16th Majlis (on 10 December 1951), that the government had no choice but to accept any amount of hardship for the country's hard-won independence, and that 'surrender' would mean 'deprivation from the advantages of democratic government'.[7] In short, oil nationalization was intended primarily to remove political interference by the AIOC in internal Iranian politics, and to acquire full independence as a necessary condition for the establishment of democratic government in Iran.

The oil dispute: the search for a solution

The failure of the Stokes mission which went to Tehran to negotiate a settlement of the oil dispute was due to British government insistence on the formation of another company along the lines of the consortium which was later created. This went against the political premises on which the nationalization policy was based. Musaddiq had emphasized that the National Iranian Oil Company would sell any amount of oil to Britain and to other traditional buyers of Iranian oil; that the AIOC would be compensated on the basis of the pre-nationalization value of the company's shares (as this had been done in Britain and elsewhere in the case of nationalized industries); that NIOC would be ready to re-employ British technicians in the oil industry; that it would be prepared to employ European, but non-British, managers if this proved to be technically necessary. Stokes, however, did not agree to any of these proposals, and kept insisting on the formation of a new company.[8] The negotiations were suspended, but as Stokes himself emphasized, both then and later, they were not broken off. Following the takeover of the Abadan oil installations by the Iranian government in September 1951, Britain took the matter to the United Nations Security Council. Their complaint was about Iran's refusal to accept the International Court's injunction against the repossession operations in Abadan, because they argued that the Court had no jurisdiction in the case. Musaddiq personally led a delegation to the council and won the argument. The visit to America also provided an opportunity for Musaddiq to talk to top American officials about the oil dispute. Ambassador McGhee has recalled his negotiations with Musaddiq both in his memoirs and in a chapter in this volume. Perhaps the most important result of these negotiations was Musaddiq's agreement to sell Persian oil to AIOC at $1.10 a barrel, which was about 65 cents less than the (lower) Persian Gulf price. This, according to McGhee, would have implied a fifty–fifty profit-sharing arrangement, and should have been acceptable to Britain. Musaddiq was asked to delay his return while Dean Acheson, the Secretary of State, took the package to Paris to obtain Sir Anthony Eden's agreement, Eden refused, and advised the Americans not to be anxious to reach an agreement with Musaddiq.[9]

The World Bank's attempt at mediation in January–February 1952, expressly did not offer a solution for a permanent settlement: it offered to restart the production and sale of Iranian oil at $1.75 for a period of two years, paying 58 cents to Britain, 50 cents to Iran, 30 cents towards production costs; and retaining the balance (37 cents) pending the final settlement of the dispute.[10] Musaddiq was at first persuaded, but later he changed his mind on the insistence of a couple of his close advisers. Queries about the price and the employment of British technicians have been mentioned as part of the stumbling block, but the real reason was the bank's refusal to take on the task 'on behalf of the Iranian government'. The government's legal worry was that, otherwise, the agreement may imply a retreat from the Repossession Act (*Khal-i yad*), but their (more important) political consideration was that the opposition (and especially the Tudeh Party) would accuse them of a complete sell-out if the bank did not formally act on their behalf.[11]

As the conflict dragged on, the Labour government left office, and the Conservative government which replaced it was in no mood to continue direct negotiations with Iran. However, after the International Court's decision in favour of Iran (22 July 1952, one day after the public uprising which put Musaddiq firmly back in power), Britain took the initiative, and made a major diplomatic move by obtaining President Truman's support of what has since been known as the Truman–Churchill proposal. The proposal's main point was that Iran should voluntarily consent to the International Court's arbitration over the compensation issue. Iran responded by putting forward a counter-proposal of its own, the main point of which was that Iran would agree to the Hague's arbitration on the condition that compensation to the AIOC would be determined on the basis of the market value of its property at the time of nationalization. This was rejected by Britain on the argument that compensation should include AIOC's loss of profit until 1990.[12] It was at this time that, in a long letter to *The Times*, Stokes took a publicly sympathetic view of Iran's case, and wondered why direct negotiations had been broken off by the Conservative government.[13]

The final opportunity for a settlement came up in February 1953. Once again the main bone of contention was that Britain was insisting on the International Court's arbitration for compensation to include the AIOC's loss of profits until 1990. Iran retreated from its previous position: this time, they did not mention the market value of the AIOC's property as the only basis for compensation, but merely asked Britain to state its maximum claim for compensation from the outset, as this is normally the case in any legal dispute over business and financial matters. This was now Iran's only proviso for going to arbitration, but it was rejected by Britain.[14] In July 1953, Musaddiq made two further attempts to resolve the issue, but they did not succeed because, by then, the Anglo-American powers were determined to talk only to a successor government.[15]

The reasons for the lack of a settlement were perceived differently in London and Tehran. From the beginning, a strong (and, later, dominant) trend of opinion in Britain maintained that Musaddiq was too intransigent – perhaps too anti-British – to be able to come to an acceptable solution.[16] The problem, however, hinges less on Musaddiq's personal and emotional atributes as on the meaning of the term 'acceptable' in this connection.

Musaddiq was ready to compensate the AIOC, and said so many times. The terms of compensation were open to negotiation, but they excluded the possibility of AIOC's return to Iran in one form or another. In his counter-proposals to the various proposals mentioned above (except that of the World Bank) Musaddiq was concerned not to concede, *either* the creation of a new operating company similar to the consortium that came into being in consequence of the 1954 Amini–Page agreement; *or* compensation to the AIOC that would *include the loss of future profits in consequence of its closure by the nationalization act*. The Iranian perception of these proposals was that they would either have had to give up the spirit of oil nationalization, or to compensate the AIOC not just for its investment but for all the oil which they would have produced in the next 40 years. That was why they kept insisting on the compensation to be based either on the value of the AIOC's property, or on a maximum claim made by Britain at the outset.

The question of the legality or illegality of the 1933 Agreement was also related to this matter. Any sovereign state can legitimately nationalize and compensate an industry operating on its soil (e.g. the British coal and rail industries after the war) even though – as is usually the case – its existence and operations are legally impeccable. In other words, whether or not the 1933 Agreement had a legal or moral basis, the Iranian government was well within its rights to nationalize it and compensate the AIOC for its losses. The 'illegality' issue was often invoked in response to the British argument that the AIOC should be compensated for the cancellation of the concession, which meant compensation for all the oil in the ground which would have been produced for another 40 years. This would have been analogous to the owners of British coal-mines having been compensated not for the market value of their property but for the value of the coal remaining under the ground. That is why Musaddiq's offer to compensate the AIOC on the terms paid to any nationalized company in Europe, including Britain, was also ignored.

If Musaddiq was inflexible, he seems therefore to have been so by insisting on basic principles which would have been observed if the dispute had been between two equal nations. On the other hand, the fact of the matter was that Iran was not powerful enough to maintain its position. The two sides thus dug in for a war of attrition from which Iran finally emerged as the loser.

Britain's principal weapon was the boycott of Iranian oil. It was then that the Iranian government realized that the main problem they faced was not the technical difficulties of refining oil, but the politico-economic question of exporting crude oil. The AIOC's argument was that Iranian oil was its property, and its sale (not authorized by the AIOC) was illegal. Other (mainly American) major oil companies joined the boycott by refusing to handle Iranian oil. This was in part to help a sister company; but the principal reason was to prevent other oil-exporting countries (in whose territories they operated) from learning a 'bad' lesson from Iran's example.

At the same time, oil production elsewhere (notably in Kuwait) was stepped up to compensate for the loss of Iranian oil to the international market. The British naval presence in the region was an effective deterrent against other buyers of Iranian oil, and the efforts of Italian and Japanese companies to import oil from Iran – although bold and daring – did not get far. Thus oil revenues ceased to flow to the Iranian economy in any significant amount until the fall of Musaddiq's government.

The strategy of non-oil economics

Not only Musaddiq and his government, but also his opponents – for a short time providing a semblance of unanimity in the Majlis – had hoped and believed that the British government would come to an early settlement, and that in the meantime the United States would provide economic aid to Iran. But, even before the arrival of the World Bank mission, it was clear that, prior to a settlement of the oil dispute, American aid would not be forthcoming. As early as 24 November 1951, Musaddiq himself indicated (in a report to the Majlis of his recent visit to the United States) the difficulty of obtaining US aid. Jamal Imami, the *de facto* leader of the Majlis opposition, retorted that the whole campaign had been in the hope of receiving higher revenues from oil, as well as American aid. Musaddiq replied that he would not compromise Iranian sovereignty and independence merely to obtain American support.[17]

There was great fear of economic hardship in the country, not least among the upper classes who – from the very beginning – had been unhappy about the turn of events. The Shah had never quite approved of Musaddiq who had been imposed on him by the Majlis when he had wished to appoint Sayyid Zia to premiership.[18] Furthermore, Musaddiq, being a staunch constitutionalist, had from the outset stopped the Shah from intefering in the appointment of provincial governors and ambassadors and in foreign affairs.[19] He was soon to clash with the Shah over the appointment of the Defence minister. It is therefore not surprising that the Shah and the upper classes in general anticipated disaster in consequence of the strategy of non-oil economics.[20] Much upper class complaint rested on the fact that luxury imports had become very expensive or unobtainable. Yet, to some extent it reflects the fact and fiction of the situation as they were perceived by the political public. There is much direct and indirect evidence that the government was itself very conscious of the country's economic difficulties. But there is also evidence that it was determined to overcome these difficulties and free the economy – as the evidence shows they eventually succeeded in doing – from its dependency upon the oil revenues. Although Musaddiq was not charged with any economic offence, the matter came up now and again in the course of his military trial. For example, towards the end of his trial he said that one of the reasons why his government had been brought down was because his opponents realized that 'gradually, the Iranian economic situation would improve such that it could sustain itself without oil revenues.'[21]

The issue of the 'printing of notes' continued throughout Musaddiq's premiership, and it was frequently used by his opponents to predict disaster. As we shall see, there were definite limits imposed on the volume of notes in circulation: first by law; then by convention. The logic behind this convention may be put down to old school economic policy, but the opposition to Musaddiq's expansion of the volume of the domestic currency was also due to fears of inflationary consequences. We cannot enter a debate on monetarism *versus* Keynesianism in this paper. But, apart from the fact that the country was underdeveloped and the urban monetary economy was still a limited sector, there was a considerable amount of slack capacity due to the suspension of oil-related expenditures, which could be brought into production by increases in aggregate monetary demand.

Prior to oil nationalization, under Razmara's premiership a Seven-Year Plan had been drafted for economic development. The plan consisted of a number of macro-economic expenditure projects with emphasis on rural development and the socio-economic infrastructure.[22] Oil revenues were to contribute 37.1 per cent of the plan's financial requirements, and another 31.9 per cent was expected to be financed through borrowing from the World Bank. The virtual standstill in oil operations and exports, the British blockade, AIOC's refusal to pay the royalties it owed Iran up to the nationalization act, and the freezing of Iran's considerable sterling facilities by the Bank of England was therefore a sudden and substantial shock to the economy. Besides being a source of substantial exports and foreign exchange earnings, oil revenues could be used to supplement domestic consumption and investment. The loss of the revenues, therefore, presented the government with a balance-of-payments, a fiscal, and a monetary crisis.

Traditionally, the domestic currency had been 'covered' by gold and foreign exchange reserves. An act of 1942 had set up a 'Currency Supervisory Board' (or Issue Department) with the sole authority for the fiduciary issue. The same act had specified that 60 per cent of the currency in circulation should be 'backed' by gold, and the remaining 40 per cent by convertible foreign exchange reserves. This law was repealed early in 1947, but it was not replaced by another, and continued to be enforced in practice. In August 1951, while the Stokes mission was still in Tehran, the Majlis authorized the government to issue new notes against £14 million from the foreign exchange reserves. This naturally reduced the foreign reserve 'backing' of the currency in circulation.[23]

The loss of substantial oil revenues in foreign exchange was bound to have important external and internal repercussions for the economy. A series of decisions had to be taken in order to meet the difficulties which this would cause both for the balance of payments and for the financing of domestic (current and development) expenditures.

International trade: policy and performance

The balance of payments was a more immediate cause for concern. The government took steps to contain the foreign payments deficit due to the loss of the oil revenues. Under Riza Shah, foreign trade – that is, both exports and imports – had been brought under government control by the successive Trade Monopoly Acts of 1931 and 1932. At the same time, the government was authorized to issue import licences to the private sector for the items which it did not wish to import directly. A system of import quotas was introduced which imposed a ceiling on the total value of imports, as well as sub-ceilings for individual items. In addition, there was a complete prohibition on the import of certain items: exportables, foreign products for which there were adequate supplies of domestic substitutes, and luxury goods.

The abdication of Riza Shah in 1941 had important economic repercussions, one of which was a much greater participation of the private sector in foreign trade. By 1947, the only major import commodity of which the government still held the monopoly was tea. The import quota system remained intact, but both its operation and the ceiling import values varied considerably according to the country's economic circumstances. More specifically, as the country's foreign exchange reserves improved, there was a tendency for the government both to relax the ceiling figure and to allow substantially higher imports to enter the country. For example, in 1950–1, the official ceiling value for total imports was R3,695 million, whereas the actual figure was R6,049 million. Even in 1951–2, the first year of the oil crisis, actual imports were as high as R5,434 million compared with the total quota figure of R3,208 million.[24] Yet, given that the oil dispute began at the beginning of this period, the discrepancy for this year would appear to be licentious. This was partly because of the country's comfortable foreign reserve position at the time, and partly because of the earlier hopes that the oil dispute would be settled fairly quickly, and/or significant amounts of US foreign aid and credit would be forthcoming. There was a more important reason, however: by overstating their import bills, the importers of authorized items could build up reserves for the importation of restricted goods; likewise, by understating their export receipts, export merchants could accumulate exchange in foreign countries for financing restricted imports. This was the main reason why total imports were still considerably higher than the ceiling quota for 1952–3: R3,776 million worth of actual imports as compared with the quota value of R2,600 million. Still, there had been a substantial drop in the value of total imports compared to the previous year. This result would have been unlikely without a quota system. But the more important reason behind the decline in total imports was the effective devaluation of the Iranian rial, of which more below.

The year 1952–3 (and the following months up to the *coup d'état* of 19 August 1953) was the real period of economic crisis. The government was by then seriously concerned about the problems facing the economy, both because no settlement of the oil dispute was in sight, and because the proportion of the country's foreign exchange reserves which could be used for foreign trade payments was being depleted. As we have seen, Iranian money had to be 'backed' by gold and foreign currency, and so the country's total reserves were never wholly available for foreign transactions. This was an unnecessary restriction, both on the use of foreign reserves and on the issues of new money, which had survived from the old school economics of 30 years before. And if it had not been largely adhered to over the period, the problem of external and internal adjustment would have been considerably easier. However, given the situation, the government launched its strategy of 'non-oil economics' (*iqtisad-i bidun-i naft*).

Musaddiq and his colleagues declared that, with a tolerable degree of sacrifice, the economy could survive the loss of the oil revenues for as long as it was necessary. Although this was consistent with their priority of political over economic matters in the oil dispute, the evidence suggests that they were now aware that the economic difficulties may spoil the political objective itself, and that the strategy of non-oil economics was at least partly intended to show to the other side that economic problems would not shake their resolve. That was the reason why Musaddiq never ceased to look for an acceptable solution to the oil dispute.

To deal with the foreign exchange shortage, imports were divided into necessary and luxury goods, and exports were divided into more and less marketable goods. Necessary goods could be imported against more marketable exports, while luxury goods could be allowed in against export of products which were less competitive in the international market. In addition, a large number of import items, ranging from meat and poultry to military weapons and rubber and its products, were put on the prohibited imports list.[25] At the same time, efforts were stepped up to promote the country's non-oil exports. A number of barter deals were concluded with Germany, France, Italy, Hungary, Poland and Czechoslovakia. At the same time, measures were taken to encourage and facilitate greater exports through the open market.[26] By a stroke of good fortune this was a boom period in the international market for commodities, and hence there was no shortage of demand for Iranian non-oil exports which the depreciation of the rial had made more competitive.

Currency depreciation probably played a greater role in containing imports, and promoting exports, than the other steps taken by the government. Although there was an official exchange rate of 32.5 rials to the dollar, the exchange rate was managed according to a complex procedure, and the effective market rate was appreciably less than the official rate of exchange. A system of exchange certificates (*gavahinameh-i arz*) which could be bought and sold on the market was in operation. Therefore, a decline in the supply of foreign exchange would result in a rise in the market price of the certificates, which would mean a depreciation of the local currency. Key products, for example necessary food and medicine, were imported at the lower official exchange rates, while other products were imported at the higher market rates of exchange certificates depending on their relative priority. Market exchange rates varied a good deal over the 1950–3 period. The government held a considerable quantity of exchange certificates, and when necessary it bought or sold certificates in order to reduce or raise the market exchange rate.[27] On a number of occasions the government helped increase the exchange value of the rial in this way. But, in general, there was a steady trend for the depreciation of the rial throughout the period: from 40 rials to the dollar in mid-1950 to 100 rials to the dollar in the summer of 1953, a decline of 250 per cent. The depreciation of the rial caused domestic import prices to rise, and external export prices to fall, and this helped improve the balance of payments.

Table 8.1 shows the Iranian balance of payments for the period 1949–55. In row 4 of this table, we observe that, in 1950–1, the current account balance for the oil sector was R3,524 million; it was R965 million in 1951–2, and fell to R−136 million in 1953–4. In 1952–3, which was the crucial year of adjustment to a non-oil economy, there were no significant exports and imports of oil. Altogether, from the year 1951–2 oil ceases to help improve the current account of the balance of payments. The non-oil sector's balance can be seen in row 8 of the table. Here we observe a steady decline in this sector's deficit from R−5,506 million in 1949–50 to R−1,122 million in 1952–3. The deficit rises to R−2,333 million in the following year, but much of this must be due to a rise in imports after the fall of Musaddiq's government in August 1953, in part as a result of American aid paid to the post-*coup d'état* government.

Rows 4 and 8 put together present the current account balance (see row A). The deficit of R−1,982 million in 1949–50 falls to R−584 million in the following year, but it rises to R−2,125 million in 1951–2, the year in which there were still hopes of a quick settlement of the oil dispute, and/or receipt of American aid. In 1952–3, however, the current account deficit drastically falls to R−1,122 million, rising to R−2,472 million in the following year, for reasons already mentioned. Figures in row B include a number of items: long-term and short-term capital movements, private and official grants, as well as errors and omissions. Perhaps the only important fact revealed by these figures is that Iran did not receive a significant amount of foreign aid during the nationalization period. Consequently, the overall balance (row C), had a deficit of R−1,980 million in 1951–2, but this fell to R−530 million in the following year, and rose to R960 million in 1953–4 when American aid had begun to flow in. Note that the current account deficit for 1954–5 is quite high, in spite of substantial oil exports during that year.

Table 8.1 *Balance of payments of Iran, 1949–55, in millions of rials*

		1949–50	1950–1	1951–2	1952–3	1953–4	1954–5
Oil sector							
1	Exports	15389	22184	6829	—	90	2798
2	Imports	−2979	−914	−256	—	−226	−270
3	Profits and other payments abroad	−886	−17590	−5708	—	—	1414
4	Balance (1+2+3)	3524	3680	965	—	−136	1114
Non-oil sector							
5	Exports	1244	2110	2710	2807	2958	3912
6	Imports	−6287	−6049	−5434	−3776	−5390	−7425
7	Services (net)	−463	−325	−366	−153	99	−235
8	Balance	−5506	−4264	−3090	−1122	−2333	−3748
A	Current account balance (4+8)	−1982	−584	−2125	−1122	−2472	−2634
B	Capital account balance*	992	874	145	592	3442	2723
C	Overall balance (A & B)	−990	290	−1980	−530	960	89

* Includes errors and omissions as well as private and official grants.

Source: based on IMF, international financial statistics, October and December 1955

The government's main success was in managing to contain, and then reduce, the current account deficit over the period 1951–3 when the net contribution of the oil sector to the country's export earnings had all but disappeared. The key to this success was the steady increase in non-oil exports (row 5) and the rapid decline in imports. The fall in imports was dramatic (see row 6) and it was a consequence of the imposition of import quotas, the increase in customs duties, and – especially – the depreciation of the rial. The question as to whether there was a trade surplus or deficit during this period has attracted a good deal of attention. The problem arises from the fact that export and import values could be converted into rials at various – official and unofficial – rates. Hence, there would be trade surpluses or deficits depending on the rate of exchange used for the conversion of the values. Here I have used the IMF figures which in fact show considerable deficits rather than surpluses.[28]

Throughout the period, Iran's foreign exchange reserves were adequate to meet the country's exchange requirements even if the government had not taken the steps described above to increase exports and reduce imports. Most of the reserves, however, were frozen in accordance with the note cover law. There was little economic justification for the requirements of this law, but the abandonment of note coverage in the apparently difficult economic circumstances of the time would have resulted in a state of panic, and the opposition would have made capital out of a reasonable economic decision. However, given the political impracticability of a drastic change in the practice of note coverage, the adjustment measures for reducing the balance of payments deficit ensured that the foreign exchange reserves available for use in international payments were quite adequate. At the beginning of the Iranian calendar year 1332 (1953–4), the amount of usable foreign exchange reserves other than the frozen reserves (for note coverage) stood at R1.1 billion.[29]

Fiscal and monetary policy

Apart from its impact on foreign exchange reserves and payments – and hence on the foreign trade sector of the economy – the virtual shut-down of oil production and refining was a sudden shock to the domestic sector.

However, by contrast to the foreign trade sector where the impact of the boycott was confined to the loss of the direct oil revenues received in foreign exchange, there was, in the domestic sector of the economy, a *revenue effect* as well as a *cost effect*. *The revenue effect* was the sum of the *direct* revenues foregone and all the *indirect* revenues – for example taxes on the income of AIOC's foreign employees, and customs revenues from its non-exempt imports – arising from the company's operations, which could be as high as 30 per cent of the direct revenues. *The cost effect*, on the other hand, comprised the cost of the wages and salaries of AIOC's former Iranian employees, in addition to all the other overhead costs of the National Iranian Oil Company. The *total* revenue effect was about R1.5 billion, and the cost effect amounted to R2.0 billion.[30] Therefore, other things remaining equal, the government was faced with an annual deficit of about R3.5 billion on the oil account, a sum which was about 38 per cent of the budgeted expenditures for the year 1951–2 (1330).

In order to take the measures that were necessary to increase revenues and reduce expenditure, the government asked the parliament for 'delegated powers' (*ikhtiyarat*) for a period of six months, which was later extended for a further period. A few members of parliament had doubts about the wisdom of this measure and these turned into outright opposition when the government asked for its extension. The government nevertheless obtained the powers which it had asked for. In times of war and other crises, democratic governments are granted special powers. In this case, all the government asked for – as Musaddiq himself explained to the Majlis – was the power to put parliamentary bills immediately into effect before they were debated in parliament.[31]

Fiscal measures to increase public revenues took several forms. Steps were taken to increase income tax receipts, but they were unlikely to have much success because of the inadequacy of the administrative machinery for their collection. However, the government managed to increase its revenues from indirect taxes, and especially customs duties. Between 1949–50 and 1953–4, government receipts from customs revenues increased from 43 per cent to 71 per cent of dutiable imports, in spite of the fact that imports were declining, and the import quotas discriminated against luxury imports which carried higher tariff rates. Another source of increase in public revenues was the rise in the price of goods, especially tobacco, tea, sugar and opium, produced by state monopolies. This was in the nature of an implicit excise tax, and it enabled the monopolies to gain considerably higher profits.

The sale of foreign exchange for raising public revenues was – generally – not a policy option because of the note coverage convention. In this respect, the government had to make do with a transfer of the £14 million from the reserves, which had been authorized by the Majlis in August 1951. At the official rate of 90 rials to the pound sterling, this would have enabled the government to raise slightly less than R1.3 billion. However, the sale of these reserves was spread over a long period, and the government managed to raise substantially higher sums when the value of the pound appreciated considerably in the open market. It was also a useful instrument for stabilizing the unofficial exchange rate whenever it appeared to be falling too low.

As early as September 1951, the Majlis authorized the government to issue public bonds up to the value of R2 billion, or $50 million at the official exchange rate. The bonds, described as 'popular [or national] debt', carried a 6 per cent 'prize' (i.e. interest), and were redeemable after two years.[32] They were to be issued at R500 each, and sold in four lots of R500 million. In practice, only the first lot, one-quarter of the total value, was issued. The country was poor, and becoming poorer because of the loss of oil revenues; the rich were not particularly concerned to help the government;[33] and the nominal rate of interest which the bonds carried was considerably less than the formal and informal market rates. Government bonds are a regular feature of modern market economies, but were unprecedented in Iran. That is probably why Musaddiq's 'popular debt' bills have sometimes been regarded as an extraordinary event.[34]

Theoretically, foreign borrowing would have been a useful option. However, apart from its routine aid and technical assistance through Point IV, America was not prepared to provide financial support to Musaddiq's government.[35] On the other hand, the Soviet Union did not provide any help either: they even refused to repay to Musaddiq's government the war debt they owed Iran. In the early days of oil nationalization hopes were raised for a loan of $25 million, at a 3.5 per cent rate of interest, from the Export–Import Bank of America. For this, as for many other routine executive decisions in that period, parliamentary approval was necessary. Accordingly, in July 1951, a bill was submitted to both houses of parliament to authorize the borrowing.[36] Shortly afterwards, the Anglo-Iranian negotiations failed to produce a solution to the oil dispute, and in September the oil installations were taken over. From that time the Americans placed as a condition to the granting of aid that the oil dispute was resolved with terms acceptable to both parties, and contrary to common belief the $25 million loan from the Export–Import Bank did not materialize.[37] The American refusal to provide financial assistance for Musaddiq's government had a significant share in strengthening the position of his conservative opposition, and his gradual loss of support from the right wing of the National Front.

The government was left with little choice but to balance its budget deficits by means of various domestic fiscal and monetary policies, including an increase in the fiduciary note issue. In September 1952, Musaddiq invited Dr Schacht, the German financial expert, to Iran for consultation. It is not known whether or not Schacht ultimately presented a formal report on monetary policy in Iran, but the indirect remarks which he made to the Iranian press give the impression that he did not attach much importance to the traditional note coverage policy.[38] Dr Schacht had been a practitioner of 'Keynesian' policies before Keynes's *General Theory*, and it would not come as a surprise from him to recommend an active monetary policy when effective demand had been considerably reduced due to the loss of oil revenues.

In 1950–1 (1329) (i.e. the year before oil nationalization came into effect) the projected budget bill had not been formally passed by the Majlis *in toto* as an act of parliament. It had, however, been generally enforced, and in September 1951 (1330), it was eventually approved by the Majlis *ex post facto*. At the same time the Majlis decided to allow the same budget to be applied in the year 1951–2 (1330), on the basis of an average expenditure per month of one-twelfth of the previous year's total expenditures, and without, once again, a formal budget act for that year.

Given the flexibility thus afforded to the government, it was able to try to reduce expenditures as much as possible, as part of the effort to cut down the potential budget deficit. Consequently, in 1951–2 (1330), total expenditures were cut from the R11.2 billion *budgeted* for the previous year, to R9.7 billion – a drastic expenditure cut of R1.5 billion. But this is bound to be an overestimate because the *actual* expenditures in 1950–1 (1329) were less than the *budgeted* R11.2 billion for that year. Ruhani has mentioned the figure of R9.5 billion for the *actual* expenditures in 1950–1,

Table 8.2 *Summary of the budget, 1951–4 (1330–2) in billions of rials*

	1 *1951–2 (1330)*	2 *1952–3 (1331)*	3 *1953–4 (1332)*
1 Revenues	7.8	7.8	9.5
2 Expenditures	9.7	10.3	10.0
3 Deficit	−1.9	−2.5	−0.5

Sources: Bank Melli Iran, *Bulletin*, various issues and dates; Bank Markazi Iran, *Bulletin*, and *Annual Report and Balance Sheet*, various issues and dates up to 1969; Plan Organization, *Review of the Second Seven-Year Plan Programme of Iran* (Tehran, 1960). *Ruznameh-i Rasmi-yi Kishvar*, several issues, 1951–5

but this is certain to be an *underestimate*, because he has assumed that the decision to keep the same budget for 1951–2 as well would necessarily mean that the actual expenditures in 1950–1 had been the same as 1951–2.

The same procedure was repeated in 1952–3; that is, the Majlis authorized the government to base its monthly expenditures on the practice of the two previous years, without passing a formal budget act, together with details of revenues and expenditure.[39]

For 1953–4, however, this informal and pragmatic procedure was abandoned, and a formal budget bill was presented to the parliament. This in itself indicates a feeling on the part of the government that the moment of economic crisis had passed, and that the economy had adjusted to a normal course.

Table 8.2 shows the budget summaries for the years 1951–2 to 1953–4 (1330–2). In both 1951–2 (1330) and 1952–3 (1331), government revenues were R7.8 billion. However, the figure for 1951–2 includes about R0.8 billion (R800 million) from direct and indirect oil revenues in that year, so that the domestic, non-oil, revenues were about R7.0 billion. In the next year (1331), there were virtually no oil revenues at all, but the efforts to increase non-oil revenues had compensated for the loss of the R0.8 billion oil revenues of the previous year – hence the equality between the revenue figures for 1951–2 (1330) and 1952–3 (1331). In the formal budget bill of 1953–4 (1332), the revenue *estimate* was significantly increased to R9.5 billion. This would indicate the government's confidence in the next year's economic and financial prospects, although the estimate would still appear to have been on the optimistic side.

On the other hand, the figures in row 2 of table 8.2 show no substantial variations in the annual expenditures for the three years. They increased from R9.7 billion in 1951–2 (1330) to R10.3 billion in 1952–3 (1331), and fell slightly to R10.0 billion rials for 1953–4 (1332). Yet, the expenditures now included substantial payments towards the upkeep of the oil industry which were no part of the ordinary budget.

However, the most interesting aspect of the table is the size of, and variations in, the budget deficit. We noted above that, in 1951–2 (1330), the deficit could have been as high as R3.4 billion, but the cut in projected expenditures down to R9.7 billion reduced the actual deficit to R1.9 billion in that year. As mentioned before, 1952–3 (1331) was the central year of the crisis when the actual budget deficit rose to R2.5 billion (see table 8.2, row 3, column 2). On the other hand, the whole of column 3, which shows a small deficit of R0.5 billion (500 million), must be interpreted in a different light. First, the figures in this column refer to government *estimates* of revenues and expenditures for 1953–4. In other words, they were the government target figures for that year, which, in any case, were not realized in practice, since the government fell in August 1953 (Murdad 1332). Consequently – and with the immediate American grant received by the Zahidi government *as well as* the prospects of more aid, and oil revenues, in 1954–5 – the actual revenues, expenditures and deficits turned out to be substantially higher in that year. Secondly, the column 3 estimates show the government's eagerness to close the deficit, mainly by increasing revenues, and partly by reducing expenditures. Thirdly, Musaddiq's government did not have to finance the small deficit of R0.5 billion for that year since it fell long before the financial year ended. The upshot of these observations is that, as Dr Ali Amini, Zahidi's finance minister, pointed out in the 18th Majlis, the government had to finance a total budget deficit of (R1.9 + R2.5 =) R4.4 billion in its 27 months of office.[40]

The problem of financing this deficit created much economic and political difficulty for the government. Having reduced the potential deficit of 1951–2 (1330) to R1.9 billion, it managed to meet the deficit from the authorized sale of £14 million (R1.3 billion) plus the $8.75 million (R0.6 billion) loan from the World Bank (see table 8.3). In the next year, however, the deficit rose to R2.5 billion for which there was no deficit finance available. The hopes of raising R2 billion from the sale of public bonds having been largely dashed, the government then issued a provisional bill under the Delegated Powers Act, and increased the fiduciary note issue by R3.1 billion. But this did not necessarily reduce the foreign exchange 'backing' of the local currency, because the depreciation of the rial had substantially increased the value of the foreign exchange reserves in local currency items.[41]

A moment's reflection on the figures in table 8.3 would show that the R1.9 billion deficit in 1951–2 (1330) was financed by the sum of R1.3 billion from the sale of foreign exchange, plus R0.6 billion from the World Bank loan. For the rest of the period, the government financed its R2.5 billion budget deficit from the sum of R3.6 billion raised through the note issue and the sale of public bonds. This left a balance of R1.1 billion in the Treasury for 1953–4 which would have been more than adequate to finance

Table 8.3   *Budget deficit and deficit finance, 1951–3 (April 1330–August 1332) in billions of rials*

	Budget deficit	Deficit finance	Balance
1 (April 1951–April 1952)	−1.9	1.9	0.0
(i) Sale of £14 million	—	(1.3)	—
(ii) World Bank loan	—	(0.6)	—
2 (April 1952–August 1953)	−2.5	3.6	1.1
(i) Note issue	—	(3.1)	—
(ii) Public bonds	—	(0.5)	—
3 Total: 1 + 2	−4.4	5.5	1.1

Source: table 2 and the sources therein; Dr Muhammad Musaddiq, *Khatirat va taʻallumat-i Musaddiq*, book 2 (Tehran, 1986); J. Buzurgmihr, *Dr Muhammad Musaddiq dar dadgah-i tajdid-i nazar-i nizami* (Tehran, 1986)

the projected deficit of R0.5 billion for that year (cf. table 8.2, row 3, column 3). The R1.1 billion balance was made up of R0.8 billion cash in the Treasury tills, plus R0.3 billion liquid assets. In addition, the government had R0.9 billion worth of saleable goods in its possession, which brought the total value of cash and (liquid as well as illiquid) assets held by the Treasury up to R2 billion. Therefore, Dr Amini's claim in the 18th Majlis that, at the time of the overthrow of Musaddiq's government, 'there was not a farthing in the government's hands'[42] was a gross exaggeration.

So much for the government's fiscal policy, and the ways and means, first of cutting down, then of financing the budget deficit. I deliberately use the old-fashioned term 'budget deficit' in preference to the modern 'public-sector borrowing requirement', if only because hardly any borrowing was involved in the financing of the budget deficits (save, that is, for the total sum of R1.1 billion borrowed from the World Bank and the Iranian public). This brings us to a consideration of the monetary situation, and the government's monetary policy.

It has been observed by the writers in the field that, between 1951 and 1953, government debt to Bank Milli increased by R1.8 billion or, in other words, the government borrowed this sum of money from the bank over the period. This observation is technically correct, but it needs to be qualified in some important ways. First, the borrowing was done by the National Iranian Oil Company for the payment of R1.2 billion of its annual R2.0 billion deficit. Therefore, it had no part in financing the government's budget deficits. On the contrary, it was the government that made up the remaining R0.8 billion from the ordinary budget. Secondly, it was borrowed, *on a monthly basis*, from April 1952 to May 1953. Thirdly, R0.3

billion of the loan were repaid on a regular monthly basis, so that the *net* NIOC borrowing from Bank Milli over the 15-month period (April to July 1953), was R1.5 billion; that is, a monthly average sum of R0.1 billion.[43]

It has also been correctly noted from published statistics that the money supply increased from R14.1 billion in 1950–1 (1329) to R22.3 billion in 1953–4 (1332). But, once again, this simple observation requires some important qualifications. The money supply statistics refer to the sum of notes in circulation plus sight deposits, or current accounts: M_1. The money supply thus measured increased from R14.1 billion in 1950–1 (1329) to R14.4 billion in 1951–2 (1330). This small increase of R0.3 billion was due to a combined rise in notes in circulation (to be distinguished from *new* note issue) and sight deposits. In the following year, however, the money supply increased by R3.6 billion to R18.0 billion. This was due to the issue of R3.1 billion worth of new notes, mentioned above, plus an R0.5 billion increase in sight deposits. Thus, by August 1953, when the government fell, the money supply was R18.0 billion; and the total increase in the money supply over its period of office had been R3.9 billion. The money supply figure of R22.3 billion for 1953–4, mentioned above, refers to April 1954 when Zahidi's government had been in power for seven months. Therefore, Dr Amini's subsequent reference to Musaddiq's 'inflationary policy' was in fact much more true of his own: during the whole of Musaddiq's 27 months in office, the money supply increased by R3.9 billion; whereas in the first seven months of Zahidi's government it rose by R4.3 billion.

The expansion of the money supply and the depreciation of the rial (which inevitably led to higher import costs) had the greatest influence in raising the general price level. But the evidence suggests that later (vague and non-quantitative) criticisms of the government's 'inflationary policy' have been exaggerated. Table 8.4 shows changes in various price indices from 1951 to 1955. In 1951–2 (1330) the wholesale price index rose by 12.7 per cent; it fell to 4.5 per cent in the following year. The average annual change for the two years taken together is 8.6 per cent. The price index for home-produced goods rose by 6.0 per cent in 1951–2, and 7.9 per cent in 1952–3, with an average annual increase of 7.0 per cent. However, the most appropriate index for judging the impact of inflation on the ordinary consumers' budget is the cost of living index which increased at an average annual rate of 6.5 per cent. By comparison, prices had been falling sharply in 1950–1 (not shown in the table). But, to a large extent, this was a consequence of the fall in the import costs brought about by the 1949 devaluation of sterling. However, in 1953–4, when the post-*coup d'état* government was no longer in financial difficulty, the first two indices rose much more sharply than in any of the two previous years, while the rise in the cost of living index was still higher than in 1951–2.

There is some disagreement on the rate of inflation in different sources,

Table 8.4   *Changes in various price indices 1951–2 (percentages)*

	Wholesale	Home-produced goods	Cost of living*	
1951–52	12.7	6.0	4.5	(6.3)
1952–53	4.5	7.9	8.6	(7.1)
1953–54	20.4	13.7	5.9	(9.2)
Average **1951–53**	**8.6**	**7.0**	**6.5**	**(6.2)**
1954–5	18.7	23.1	16.8	(14.4)

* Figures in brackets are based on Bank Markazai Iran, *The Revised Cost of Living Index* (Tehran, 1962).
Source: based on International Monetary Fund, *International Financial Statistics*, various issues

which is at least partly due to the differences in the base year chosen for calculating the original indices. For example, changes in the cost of living index based on Bank Markazi's figures (shown in brackets in table 8.4, column 3) are all different from the corresponding IMF-based figures in the table. Yet, the most significant difference is that the bank-based figure of 9.2 per cent for 1953–4 is 3.3 per cent higher than the IMF-based figure of 5.9 per cent, and this is the year in which most of the inflation was due to the expansionary policies of the government of Zahidi, *not* Musaddiq. At any rate, the two average figures – 6.5 per cent and 6.2 per cent – for 1951–3 are quite close to each other. Finally, the price index changes for 1954–5 have also been quoted in table 8.4, so that a comparison of these and the figures for 1953–4 with those of the 1951–3 period would reveal that the post-coup inflation rates, when Dr Amini was minister of Finance, were much higher than in the previous period. In a word, the evidence shows that, especially for the circumstances, the rates of inflation were moderate and manageable.

The absence of reliable GNP figures makes it difficult to comment on the overall production and growth performance of the economy with a reasonable degree of confidence. According to one estimate, from 1950–1 to 1953–4, the average annual money growth rate of GNP was 11.0 per cent.[44] Compared to the average annual increase in the cost of living index, this would mean an annual *real* growth rate of 3.7 per cent which, in the circumstances, would be a significant – and in fact unlikely – achievement. What can be said about this issue with confidence is that the economy had not been declining in consequence of the loss of oil revenues and the resulting economic problems.

The strategy of non-oil economics was controversial among different political groupings. Not only did the conservative press sharply disagree with it but even the Tudeh Party's satirical publication, *Chilingar*, told Musaddiq to 'take a bucket and sell the oil'.[45] Doubts about the possible success of this strategy also existed within government circles, and among their supporters, although they were not expressed publicly. In a sense, the strategy of non-oil economics could be said to have been 'forced' on the government by the circumstances. But it was not inevitable, and a settlement of the oil dispute outside the basic Iranian terms would have been the obvious alternative. Musaddiq, therefore, consciously opted for running the economy without the oil revenues, and in doing so he had the support of most of his ministers and National Front colleagues.

From the above discussion of specific policies designed to make the economic strategy work it might appear that they were based on a coherent and comprehensive policy framework. There is no evidence that such a policy framework existed, and in fact it is likely that policies were a good deal less systematic than would seem from this brief analysis. Yet, all the various measures were taken with a view to meeting the (external and internal) effects of the loss of the oil revenues. In this sense credit must be given to the government for the fact that the different policies tended to complement and reinforce each other.

Economic reform and development

While the government was in difficulty in meeting its external payments and current domestic expenditures it was not in a position to follow an ambitious strategy of economic development. Therefore, the activities of the plan organization which was set up in 1949 to implement the Seven-Year Plan were bound to slow down. Yet, the slowdown of the plan's operations was not confined to the period of Musaddiq's premiership alone, and it continued well into 1954, despite the immediate $60 million American aid to the post-*coup d'état* government. Between 1949 and September 1954 – that is, in the first five-and-a-half years of the period of the plan – actual expenditures were less than 50 per cent of planned expenditures. In the first 18 months of Musaddiq's premiership, that is between April 1951 and September 1952, R548 million were spent on development projects by the plan organization. This was 38 per cent short of planned expenditures for the period in question. In addition R272 million were spent on transport, R125 million on industry, and the remaining R151 million on agriculture, the oil company and social services. The plan organization allocated R63 to its share of the Development Bank, and a few other firms of which it was a shareholder. A further R60 million were spent to cover the current expenditure deficits of some public enterprises.[46]

For the period September 1952 to September 1954 (i.e. a year after the overthrow of Musaddiq's government) detailed expenditure figures are not available. It appears that the plan organization spent over R2,300 million during this period, but it is not clear how much of this was spent up to August 1953. Development expenditures were not limited to the activities of the plan organization, however. A notable example is the construction of an extensive water distribution network in Tehran which was virtually completed during Musaddiq's government.

But perhaps more than the implementation of the Seven-Year Plan, the government was under pressure from it own supporters, and especially from the left wing of the Popular Movement, to carry out redistributive reforms. It is doubtful if, in the circumstances of the oil boycott period, the government would have been able to effect major social and economic reforms. As we have seen, tax reform legislation was passed by parliament, but it is uncertain how effectively they were applied by the existing administrative machinery. Similarly, detailed and extensive labour laws were enacted for the protection of industrial and service workers.[47] However, the most sensitive reform issue was the question of a land reform which was openly and emphatically advocated by some Popular Movement parties, and the Third Force party in particular. The ideal of the abolition of the traditional land tenure system was clearly consistent with the spirit of the movement led by Musaddiq. On the other hand, it is doubtful if the government was in a position to open an entirely new front while it was already busy fighting on several external and internal battlefields. Fundamental changes of this kind require a government firmly in control, with few external worries, and with adequate political, economic and law-enforcement means to carry out its decision. As it was, the government had to abandon the Majlis elections in several constituencies because the interferences of the army, the gendarmerie, the local magnates, the Tudeh Party, and the Popular Movement forces had resulted in bloodshed and upheaval. At the same time, the government felt obliged to take some steps towards the reform of landlord–peasant relations. In December 1952, a parliamentary bill obliged the landlords to pay 10 per cent of their annual share of the agricultural produce back to the peasantry, and a further 10 per cent into a fund for rural development. In addition, the act abolished all peasant obligations to landlords other than the payment of their share of the crop. The terms of reference of the legislation were fairly wide, and included the setting up of development councils at the village level, with peasant participation. The other major piece of legislation affecting landownership was intended to combat speculation in urban land.[48] These measures came fairly late during Musaddiq's government, and they were not implemented by his successors. Indeed, the act that had allocated 20 per cent of the landlords' crop share to the peasantry and rural development was abolished by post-*coup d'état* governments.

Concluding notes

The Popular Movement and its government had set themselves the interrelated tasks of nationalizing Iranian oil, attaining full political independence for the country, and extending and strengthening the system of parliamentary democracy. Although as the movement gathered momentum, and Musaddiq formed a government, the economic significance of the oil issue became increasingly evident, the oil dispute was until the bitter end dominated by political considerations. This was the most important single reason why the two parties in the dispute failed to arrive at a mutually acceptable solution until the overthrow of Musaddiq.

Having been surprised by the difficulty of reaching a quick solution, the government decided to follow a strategy of 'non-oil economics', in the hope that the long-term survival of the Iranian political economy without oil revenues would persuade the British government to come to a settlement which would be consistent with the spirit as well as the letter of oil nationalization.

The evidence suggests that the government measures in adjusting the economy to the sudden shock of the loss of oil revenues were efficient as well as responsible. The foreign trade policy – that is, the effective depreciation of the rial, the revision of the import quota system, various measures for promoting non-oil exports, and the increase in customs duties – enabled the government to contain, then reduce, the balance of payments deficit, and ensure an adequate supply of foreign reserves. In the circumstances, and especially in view of the fact that a considerable proportion of gold and foreign reserves were conventionally required for the note coverage, the foreign trade policy was successful, and it could have been sustained in the longer term.

Similarly, efforts to maintain internal equilibrium succeeded in increasing non-oil revenues, as well as reducing current and development expenditures. The revenue-increasing policies consisted of the sale of a limited amount of foreign exchange, tax and tariff reforms, increasing the price of public enterprise goods, borrowing from the public, and obtaining credit from the domestic banking system. The expenditure-reducing measures were directed towards the abolition of state subsidies on consumer goods, making considerable savings on the cost of civil and military administration, and cutting down on certain development expenditures. Therefore, and in spite of its popular image, the government followed a tough austerity programme which, without popular consent, it would be difficult to see through in similar conditions. Yet, the rate of inflation was not high, and there is no evidence of a decline in the general standard of living.

If it were possible to distinguish sharply between the economic and political factors that influence major historical events, it could be safely concluded that, on purely economic grounds, the fall of Musaddiq's government was by no means inevitable. On the other hand, and in spite of the economic reality described in this paper, there was a growing concern that the government might not be able to win the economic battle. In this respect, political propaganda emanating from within as well as without the country was effective.

Had the government been able to reach a solution to the oil dispute, it would have been in a much stronger position to survive in the longer term, and to lay the foundations of the country's economic and political development. It ultimately lost because it was far too weak to struggle for long against the combined strength of domestic forces and concerted international power.

Notes

1 This paper was written when the author was visiting professor of economics at the University of California, Los Angeles, to which the author is grateful for intellectual and material support. The author is also grateful to James Bill, Habib Ladjevardi and Roger Louis for their useful comments on a draft of this paper, although they are not implicated in the views expressed or the errors that remain.

2 See Ja'far Mihdiniya, *Zindigi-yi siyasi-yi Razmara* (Tehran, 1984) pp. 154–5.

3 See Homa Katouzian, *The Political Economy of Modern Iran* (London and New York, 1981) ch. 8. See further H. Kay-Ustuvan, *Siyasat-i muvazineh-i manfi* (Tehran, 1948–50) esp. vol. I.

4 See for example *Behsu-yi Ayandeh*, 26 November 1950; see further, ibid. 17 July 1951, and 5 August 1951; and *Mardum*, 8 July 1951.

5 *Nutqha-yi Duktur Musaddiq*, vol. IV (Paris, 1969)

6 See *Nutqha va maktubat-i Duktur Musaddiq*, vol. VIII (Paris, 1972) pp. 59–62.

7 *Nutqha va maktubat* V pp. 121, 173.

8 Ibid., pp. 51–71. Note, however, Stokes's personal belief in Iran's case against the AIOC in his letter of 10 September 1951 to the British prime minister. See, Francis Williams, *A Prime Minister Remembers* (Attlee's memoirs) (London, 1961).

9 See further Ambassador George C. McGhee, *Envoy to the Middle World* (New York, 1983), ch. 31; Sir Anthony Eden, *Full Circle* (London, 1961), ch. 9.

10 See F. Ruhani, *Tarikh-i milli shudan-i san'at-i naft-i Iran* (Tehran, 1971), ch. 17; M. Fateh, *Panjah sal naft-i Iran* (Tehran, 1956).

11 See further, Dr Muhammad Musaddiq, *Musaddiq's Memoirs* (forthcoming) (the text as well as this author's Introduction); Musaddiq, *Nutqha va maktubat*, vol. VI, Paris, 1970, pp. 172–179; Katouzian, *Political Economy*.

12 See Musaddiq, *Nutqha va maktubat*, various vols; Ruhani, *Tarikh*; H. Katouzian, Introduction, in *Musaddiq's Memoirs*; Hamid Enayat, 'British

Public Opinion and the Persian Oil Crisis from 1951 to 1954', M.Sc. degree, University of London, 1958.

13 *The Times*, 6 September 1952.

14 See Musaddiq, *Nutqha va maktubat*, various vols; *Musaddiq's Memoirs*; Ruhani, *Tarikh*, ch. 23; Eden, *Full Circle*.

15 See further, *Musaddiq's Memoirs*; Ruhani, *Tarikh*, ch. 25.

16 For accounts of the British perception of the problem see Eden, *Full Circle*; Wm Roger Louis, 'Musaddiq, oil and the dilemmas of British imperialism', and R. W. Ferrier, 'The Anglo-Iranian oil dispute: a triangular relationship' in this volume.

17 Musaddiq. *Nutqha va maktubat*, vol. V, pp. 101–5.

18 See for example *Musaddiq's Memoirs*; Jalil Buzurgmihr, *Taqrirat-i Musaddiq dar zindan* (Tehran, 1980).

19 See for example Cyrus Ghani ed., *Yaddashtha-yi Duktur Qasim Ghani*, vol. 9 (London, 1982), letter by Sadr al-Ashraf to Dr Ghani, pp. 551–3.

20 See further letters by H. Qizil-Ayagh and A. Fayyaz, in *Yaddashtha-yi Duktur Qasim Ghani*, vol. 10, pp. 532–536.

21 See Jalil Buzurgmihr ed., *Musaddiq dar mahkameh-i nizami*, vol. 2 (Tehran, 1984) p. 777.

22 See H. Motamen, 'Development planning in Iran', *Middle East Economic Papers* (1956); see further, N. S. Roberts, *Iran: Economic and Commercial Conditions* (Overseas Economic Surveys, Board of Trade, London, 1948); G. B. Baldwin, *Planning and Development in Iran* (Baltimore, 1967); B. Olsen and P. N. Rasmussen, 'An attempt at planning in a traditional state: Iran', in E. E. Hagen ed., *Planning Economic Development* (Homewood, Ill., 1963).

23 See J. Bharier, *Economic Development in Iran, 1900–1970* (London, 1971).

24 See H. Motamen, 'Iran's experience with import quotas', *Middle East Economic Papers, 1955*; and the International Monetary Fund, *International Financial Statistics*, various issues.

25 See H. Tavanayan-Fard, *Duktur Musaddiq va iqtisad* (Tehran, 1983).

26 See Ruhani, *Tarikh*, ch. 27.

27 See ibid.; Tavanayan-Fard, *Duktur Musaddiq*; and P. L. Clawson and C. Sassanpour, 'Adjustment to a foreign exchange shock, Iran, 1951–54' (mimeograph, 1985).

28 See Ruhani, *Tarikh*; Fateh, *Panjah sal*; Clawson and Sassanpour, 'Adjustment'.

29 See Bank Melli Iran, *Annual Report*, 1951–5.

30 See *Ittila'at*, 22 July 1952; Ruhani, *Tarikh*; and Clawson and Sassanpour, 'Adjustment'.

31 See *Ittila'at*, 23 July 1952.

32 For the Act, see Tavanayan-Fard, *Duktur Musaddiq*, ch. 7, pp. 192–3.

33 As Khalil Maliki pointed out at the time, the poorer sections of the urban community were keener to buy popular debt bills. Musaddiq himself expressed the same view in a Majlis speech in April 1952. See H. Katouzian, *Khatirat-i siyasi-yi Khalil Maliki* (Tehran, 1981).

34 The fact that no less than an act of parliament was required for their issue reinforces this view, although this was part of a pattern, and it shows an

unreasonable degree of parliamentary control over executive decisions. That was one of the main reasons why Musaddiq had to ask for 'delegated powers'.

35 For details of Point IV assistance, see Motamen, 'Development planning in Iran'.

36 That is possibly why it is sometimes thought that the loan was received, whereas it in fact was not. See, for example, Tavanayan-Fard, *Duktur Musaddiq*, and Clawson and Sassanpour, 'Adjustment'.

37 This is documented in various places, for example, in Musaddiq's letter to President Eisenhower (in May 1953). See, Musaddiq, *Nutqha va maktubat*, vol. VIII, pp. 159–61.

38 See *Ittila'at*, September 1951.

39 See, *Ittila'at*, 23 May 1953 for the report of the Standing Budget Committee of the Majlis on budgetary procedure between 1950 and 1954 (1329–32).

40 This came in his speech on 10 October 1954, in which he quoted the figure of R4 billion (instead of the true figure of R3.2 billion) for the value of Musaddiq's fiduciary note issue. He added that the total deficit of R4.4 billion had been financed by the (alleged) R4 billion note issue as well as the sale of foreign exchange and public bonds, borrowings from Bank Milli, unauthorized use of foreign exchange reserves, etc. The minister seems to have overlooked the fact that, according to his own figures, the government should have been able to finance its total deficit of R4.4 billion by the use of the alleged R4 billion note issue, and the R0.5 billion public debt sales alone. See *Ruznameh-i Rasmi-yi Kishvar* 2820 (16 October 1954).

41 See among countless references *Musaddiq's Memoirs*; J. Buzurgmihr, *Duktur Musaddiq dar dadgah-i tajdid-i nazar-i nizami* (Tehran, 1986); and Buzurgmihr ed., *Musaddiq dar mahkameh-i nizami*.

42 See Amini's speech in *Ruznameh-i Rasmi-yi Kishvar*. As we have seen, the figure of R1.1 billion is the difference between the government's total deficit of R4.4 billion (confirmed by Amini himself), and the R5.5 billion raised by various means for deficit financing. If we were to believe Amini's implicitly higher figure for the deficit finance available to the government, it would mean that an even higher cash balance than R1.1 billion should have been left in the Treasury for use by Zahidi's Finance minister (see *n*.40 above). However, apart from the fact that the R1.1 billion has been thrown up by the figures themselves, Musaddiq has independently confirmed the existence of R0.8 billion cash, plus R1.2 billion worth of liquid and illiquid assets in the Treasury in August 1953. See *Musaddiq's Memoirs*.

43 See, J. Buzurgmihr, *Duktur Muhammad Musaddiq dar dadgah*, for the exact details of NIOC's monthly borrowings from, and repayments to, Bank Milli from April 1952 to May 1953.

44 Based on the econometric estimates of GNP in K. Afshar, *Monetary Estimates of Iran's GNP 1900–1975*, unpublished Ph.D. thesis, The Florida State University, 1977.

45 See *Chilingar*, 10 March 1952.

46 Motamen, 'Development planning'.

47 This included extensive legislation covering social insurance, etc. For the full text, see Tavanayan-Fard, *Duktur Musaddiq*, pp. 263–96.

48 See ibid., pp. 203–23.

9

Musaddiq and the dilemmas of British imperialism

WM. ROGER LOUIS

'When the events of 1951 come to be recorded in later years in the wider context of Persian history,' reflected the British chargé d'affaires in Tehran, 'I think it will be found that the murder [in March] of General Razmara marked a turning-point.'[1] Razmara was Musaddiq's predecessor as prime minister; had he lived, Musaddiq might not have come to power in April 1951. A solution to the oil controversy might have been found along the lines of a fifty–fifty division of the profits, and the oil industry of Iran might not have been nationalized. For those who like to muse about turning points and the part played by individuals and nations in the breakup of the British Empire, the Persian oil crisis of 1951–4 provides much food for thought, not least in the larger context of the Middle East. 'If Persia was allowed to get away with it,' stated the Minister for Defence in the Labour government, Emmanuel Shinwell, in July 1951, 'Egypt and other Middle Eastern countries would be encouraged to think they could try things on: the next thing might be an attempt to nationalise the Suez Canal.'[2] Had the British and the Americans failed, rather than succeeded, in ousting Musaddiq by covert methods in the summer of 1953, then perhaps – a large perhaps – the entire history of the Middle East in the 1950s would have been different. Certainly the successful toppling of Musaddiq indicated, to the British at least, that individuals and political parties could still be manipulated to advantage. If diplomacy and secret operations failed to maintain British commercial concessions, or to secure military installations, then force might be necessary. 'How different would the position have been if the late [Labour] Government had not flinched from doing this at Abadan', wrote the prime minister, Winston Churchill, in 1952.[3]

It could be that, had Churchill been in office and faced the actual decision whether or not to dispatch an expeditionary force with, in his own phrase, 'a splutter of musketry', he might have responded in the same way as Attlee and judged that the risks of intervention were too great. 'I wish some of the Tories had been with me', complained Richard Stokes, the Labour minister who travelled to Tehran in August 1951 in an abortive attempt to reach a settlement; 'If they had seen that great refinery with its 37,000 Persian workers, they would have realised that you can't run it by force.'[4] Even so, it could be argued that the restraint of the Labour government was an aberration, and that the return of the Tories in October 1951 signalled a return to business as usual, meaning, in this case, intervention whenever necessary.

The British public overwhelmingly believed that the Iranians should be held accountable, if not actually punished, for expropriating a British company.[5] The Anglo-Iranian Oil Company was a source of national pride. Abadan was not merely the largest refinery in the world, it was also Britain's single largest overseas asset. After the second world war the Ministry of Fuel and Power had estimated the value of the physical plant alone to be £120 million: 'not much less than the estimated cost of retooling and modernising the coal industry in this country'.[6] It would be almost impossible to calculate the effect on Britain's post-war recovery if the Iranian oil revenue were lost. The feckless Iranians, in the stalwart British view, had committed no less than an act of piracy. Within the government the permanent under-secretary at the Ministry of Fuel and Power, Sir Donald Fergusson, perhaps best expressed the sense of indignation:

> It was British enterprise, skill and effort which discovered oil under the soil of Persia, which has got the oil out, which has built the refinery, which has developed markets for Persian oil in 30 or 40 countries, with wharves, storage tanks and pumps, road and rail tanks and other distribution facilities, and also an immense fleet of tankers. This was done at a time when there was no easy outlet for Persian oil in competition with the vastly greater American oil industry.
>
> None of these things would or could have been done by the Persian government or the Persian people . . .[7]

Many years later, after his death, *The Times* emphasized Fergusson's 'great sense of humour' and 'his reputation for . . . human understanding.'[8] In his judgement, at the time of the oil crisis the Iranians failed to recognize the benefits brought to them by a magnificent British industry; they were ungrateful.

The refinery at Abadan represented not only wealth but also that intangible in Britain's presence in the Middle East, 'prestige'. In the words of the British Resident in Kuwait, Francis Pelly, Abadan stood 'for something . . . huge, a symbol which not even the most sceptical Arab could deny of British energy, British wealth, British efficiency and British industrial might'. After the British evacuation from Abadan in October 1951, oil from Kuwait, as will be seen, increasingly compensated for the loss in Iran. A minor gulf state now assumed major importance at a time when Britain's regional position had been shaken. The annual report from the Residency in Kuwait in 1952 provides a picturesque description of this transformation from an unusual British angle:

> In the Persian Gulf, 1951 is likely to be remembered as the year of Abadan. On the Arab littoral this was particularly true of Kuwait. The town is only half an hour's flight from Abadan and the Kuwait Oil Company is half-owned by Anglo-Iranian Oil Company. There was constant inter-communication between the two places. The Anglo-Iranian Oil Company took sand for their building operations from Kuwait and supplied bitumen for the Kuwait roads. Their tugs with the Persian colours on the smoke stacks were a common sight in Kuwait harbour . . .
>
> Where age is a merit it was remembered that it [the British concession in Iran] had its origins in days when the Kuwait greybeards of 1951 were young men. In the Gulf not even the rising stars of the United States could outshine it. Singapore might fall and India be relinquished but these were in every sense far away places to the concrete Arab mind. The Abadan refinery was almost within smelling range of Kuwait.[9]

Another British Resident, Sir Rupert Hay in Bahrain, concurred in Pelly's judgement about the decline of Britain's 'prestige'. 'I have little doubt', Hay wrote, that the 'catastrophe' at Abadan 'underminded our whole position in the Gulf'.[10]

In British eyes there was one man who was responsible for this deplorable state of affairs: Muhammed Musaddiq. Sir Francis Shepherd, who served as ambassador in Iran from March 1950 through the crisis of 1951, regarded him as little more than a 'lunatic' (a recurrent word in his dispatches) or at best a buffoon. In view of the ambassador's low opinion of 'Oriental character', and of Iran itself as a country of 'Oriental decadence', it is hardly surprising that he and Musaddiq found conversation difficult. One point that he did impress upon Musaddiq and, it seems, all other Iranians he met, was that Iran had not been allowed to develop 'at the hands of a virile and civilised nation'. The Iranians lacked the benefits of a nationalist movement which British imperialism might have inspired. There were at least two major, underlying assumptions in Shepherd's quintessentially British outlook: Iranian politics was irrational; and the nationalist movement was not authentic but merely a 'preliminary flicker' of genuine nationalism.[11]

Both in Tehran and London the old Middle East hands of British officialdom developed more sophisticated interpretations of Musaddiq and Iranian nationalism. Shepherd's ideas 'may well have been sound at the time of Musaddiq's rise to power', wrote R. F. G. Sarell of the Eastern department of the Foreign Office, but some nine months after Musaddiq's advent they no longer held true. Shepherd had believed that Iranian nationalism was a 'spurious' movement concocted by Musaddiq and a few other anti-British extremists in order to divert attention from the corruption of the ruling propertied classes. It had no roots and commanded no genuine popular support. Sarell took issue with that superficial analysis. Probably reflecting the consensus of his colleagues, he penned the most searching estimate of Iranian naionalism in the 'post-Shepherd' era (in fact he wrote in the same month that Shepherd left Iran to become ambassador in Poland, January 1952). Sarell argued that Shepherd was correct in holding that only a minority of the population had originally supported the nationalist movement. But the explanation of Musaddiq's subsequent popular appeal lay in the genuine sentiment that existed against the Anglo-Iranian Oil Company. Musaddiq wished to expel the parasite of western capitalism, and he exploited the xenophobia and latent nationalism into a coherent national movement only because the general sense of dissatisfaction in Iranian society was also being expressed in Islamic terms by the religious leaders, especially the Ayatullah Kashani. Musaddiq and Kashani thus roused nationalist sentiment and transformed the situation: 'by claiming to represent the real spirit of the nation against alleged foreign exploitation he [Musaddiq] and the other leaders of the movement, notably Kashani, were able to produce a state of emotional excitement in which criticism could be stifled.'[12] This was a remarkable British interpretation for the early 1950s. It bore the scholarly influence of both H. A. R. Gibb and Ann K. S. Lambton.[13]

Sarell's critique of Iranian nationalism may be taken as the collective estimate of the Eastern department of the Foreign Office, or, perhaps, as representative of the 'official mind'. It included a historical analysis of the forces in Iranian society that had produced Musaddiq and the tensions between the 'classes' that might, or might not, sustain him:

> In the early period of the Nationalist movement as now many of its leaders in fact belonged to the religious classes. The other class from which the Nationalist leaders were drawn in the past was the middle-class bazaar merchants, to whom the exclusion of the West and restriction of competition offered the promise of financial gain; between this group and the religious classes there has been a traditional connection, and the support of leaders such as Kashani is still drawn largely from the bazaar.

Calculations about the response of the bazaar, as will be seen, played a critical part in British plans to topple Musaddiq. Sarell next discussed the 'classes' from which Musaddiq drew his support:

The main support for the nationalist movement . . . comes from the military, professional, and bureaucratic classes, to whom nationalism opens the way to political power. In so far as nationalism is accepted by the masses it is probably because of their intuitive clinging to the Shia'. Nationalism appears to them as a reaction against the West, that is the non-Islamic world, but in so far as it penetrates to the masses it is transformed by their social traditions, and differs from the nationalism of the intellectuals . . . Any alliance between the intellectuals and the masses is likely to prove unstable, because the former are out of touch with the latter, and the intellectuals, failing to understand the masses, despise them.[14]

Such was the drift of British official thought in January 1952.

This chapter will focus on the years 1952–4. In *The British Empire in the Middle East* I examined the crisis of 1951 in detail, mainly from the perspective of the Cabinet and the Foreign Office. Here I shall attempt to move the story forward on the British side by examining the 1952–4 records to see what they reveal about the end of the Musaddiq regime and the resolution of the oil controversy. Some key questions, rephrasing ones that recur in the official files, are: Is it possible to do business with Musaddiq? If so, how; and in any event, can British policy be aligned with that of the United States and, just as important, the policy of the Anglo-Iranian Oil Company? If not, how might Musaddiq be unseated? And, to recast the question posed by Richard Stokes over the BBC at the height of the 1951 crisis, What might be saved?

The British and Musaddiq 1951–3

Almost from the beginning of the crisis in 1951 a strong current of thought in the Foreign Office held that Musaddiq's 'pathological' but shrewd anti-British attitude would make any discussion futile. This view was consistently put forward in minutes written by Eric Berthoud, the assistant under-secretary supervising economic affairs. He did not however take a day-to-day part in Iranian questions. Indeed by a sort of gentleman's agreement he remained one step removed because early in his career he had been an employee of the Anglo-Iranian Oil Company. But whenever the occasion arose he freely ventured his opinion, which usually reinforced the judgement of a close friend, Ann K. S. Lambton. In the early 1950s Miss Lambton was Reader in Persian at the School of Oriental and African Studies at the University of London. Previously she had served in an official capacity during the second world war as Press Attaché at the embassy in Tehran. She was respected not only as a scholar but also as an authority on contemporary Iranian affairs. Her views, even though usually expressed indirectly through Berthoud's minutes, carried weight. In effect she urged the Foreign Office to boycott Musaddiq as far as possible and to deal with him only when necessary to preserve public order. This was an attitude she maintained consistently. 'Miss Lambton spent last weekend with us', Berthoud wrote a year and a half after Musaddiq entered office. She still held, as she had when he came to power, that it was impossible to negotiate with him because his entire position was based on anti-British sentiment: if he began making concessions he would destroy his own basis of power. Thus, in Miss Lambton's judgement, 'It is still useless to accept any settlement with Dr Musaddiq' because he would immediately renege.[15]

Lambton believed that it would be possible to undermine Musaddiq's position 'by *covert* means'. One way in which this could be done would be to give heart to the substantial body of Iranians who feared the risk of being denounced as traitors but whose idea of the Iranian national interest coincided with the British conception. She thought it might be possible through the public relations officer at the British Embassy in Tehran gradually to change the public mood and thus give an opportunity to intelligent Iranians who were well disposed to the British to speak out against Musaddiq. According to one of Berthoud's minutes in June 1951: 'Miss Lambton feels that without a campaign on the above lines it is not possible to create the sort of climate in Tehran which is necessary to change the regime.' With discreet efforts on the part of the British, it would be possible to co-operate with Iranians who were certain that Musaddiq's programme of nationalization would only lead to economic suicide on a national scale. For this delicate and difficult task Lambton recommended Robin Zaehner, lecturer in Persian (and later professor of Eastern religions) at Oxford. She regarded him as the 'ideal man' to conduct the covert pro-British campaign. Again according to Berthoud in June 1951:

> Dr Zaehner was apparently extremely successful in covert propaganda in 1944 at the time that there was a serious threat that the Russians would take over Azerbaijan. He knows almost everyone who matters in Tehran and is a man of great subtlety. The line then was, of course, to mobilise public opinion from the bazaars upwards about the dangers of Russian penetration.[16]

Those words were written only a month and a half after Musaddiq came to power. Such were the British origins of the covert operations that culminated in his overthrow in 1953.

Zaehner's views about Iranian politics can be summed up in one of his favourite words, 'intrigue'. He regarded Iranian politicians and political parties as part of a fascinating game, a constant jostling for supremacy in which the British, though in the background, played an almost natural part. As he saw it, the British and their allies in the internal political struggle could win out if they had the will power and the skill to prevail in the perpetually shifting set of alliances and personalities. For example Zaehner was contemptuous of the Shah, whom he viewed as vacillating, indecisive and opportunistic; he was in short an unreliable ally. Zaehner was well informed of palace politics through the Shah's *eminence grise*, a Swiss named Ernst Perron. Perron, like Zaehner himself, was a gossip, but Zaehner held firm political convictions beneath a loquacious style. Like Lambton, Zaehner believed that the British Embassy in Tehran had to align itself decisively with influential Iranians who perceived their own self-interest to be identical with the British. Zaehner's extensive minutes (now accessible at the Public Record Office) reveal that he regarded the wealthy Rashidian family – the brothers Sayfullah, Qudratullah and Asadullah – as allies of that kind. They held the same view about Musaddiq as did Zaehner. Sayfullah Rashidian told Zaehner in January 1952: 'even if Musaddiq were offered everything he wanted plus £100,000 he would still say "no".'[17] That comment reinforced Zaehner's own judgement. From the outset Zaehner, again like Lambton, believed that it was impossible to do business with Musaddiq.

One of the more expedient yet suitable alternatives to Musaddiq, in Zaehner's judgement, was Qavam al-Saltaneh. In a famous chapter in his long political career, Qavam had been premier at the time of the Azerbayjan crisis in 1946. He had managed to secure the withdrawal of Soviet troops by promising Stalin an oil concession in northern Iran. The Majlis later cancelled the concession. Whatever lessons the British might derive from that episode, it nevertheless seemed obvious that Qavam was far preferable to Musaddiq. Qavam, in the British view, was just as much a nationalist as Musaddiq, but more anti-Soviet and less anti-British. The following minute by Zaehner records a conversation with one of Qavam's supporters, Abbas Iskandari, and gives a clear indication of the British intention to get rid of Musaddiq in late 1951:

After concluding our discussion on the ways and means of overthrowing Musaddiq, Iskandari went on to assure me (in Persian) that it was Qavam's desire to work in closely with the British and to preserve their legitimate interests in Persia without jeopardising Persia's political and economic independence.

Zaehner's own views about the nature of economic imperialism also become clear:

I said that the independence of Persia had always been the corner-stone of our policy, but we were prepared to admit that economically Persia had been largely dependent on the A.I.O.C. just as we and Europe in general were dependent on American aid. In the modern world no such thing as economic independence existed any more: and Persia must face this fact.

Iskandari said that this was understood and that Qavam-us-Saltaneh greatly preferred that British influence should be exercised in Persia, rather than that of the Americans (who were foolish and without experience), or of the Russians who were Persia's enemies.

There was to be a firm, if implicit, alliance between Qavam and the British. Qavam would have a free hand and, with patience, the legitimate commercial interests of the British would be restored:

> If we were prepared to accept Qavam-us-Saltaneh's assurance that he would come to an agreement satisfactory to both sides [i.e. the Iranians and the British], we must give him a free hand in the use of methods. Public opinion had been worked up to such an intensity of anti-British feeling that it would need a month or two to change it. Qavam-us-Saltaneh did not wish to disclose in advance exactly what his methods would be, but we knew by experience that with him everything came out right in the end, however curious the beginning might be.[18]

All of this, according to Zaehner, seemed to be 'very much on the cards'.

Here a general observation should be made about the British, Qavam, and Musaddiq. Zaehner's estimate of Musaddiq was accurate: economic dependence was precisely the point Musaddiq was not prepared to admit, at least to the British. In Qavam the British hoped they had found a collaborator, perhaps a devious one, in the traditional mould.

A word should also be said at this stage about the British Embassy in Tehran and Zaehner's influence within it. The embassy itself occupied 15 acres in the heart of the city. The staff included political officers, 'oriental counsellors', consuls, economic and commercial officers, administrators, information officers, military attachés, intelligence officers, cypher clerks, stenographers, and typists. The British compound was a world within itself, as much of a state within a state, in miniature, as the Anglo-Iranian Oil Company. The British diplomatic enclave symbolized foreign dominance. Its members in 1952 could still joke that the Iranians believed its water supply contained miraculous life-invigorating qualities. Musaddiq denounced the embassy as a 'nest of spies'. Yet the British in Tehran were acutely aware of the limitations of their influence, which in some ways was anachronistic. If Zaehner could be regarded as a 'spy' he was an eccentric one. He held his brief directly from the Foreign Secretary of the Labour government in 1951, Herbert Morrison. The assignment was to try, if possible, to manipulate internal politics in order to bring about the political demise of Musaddiq. It was no secret that this was Zaehner's job. An Oxford don, bon vivant, erudite philosopher and linguist, he relished the lighter side of his duties. He drank heavily. To those who wished to learn

about Iranian politics, he recommended *Alice Through the Looking glass*.
He introduced other members of the embassy to the pleasures of opium.
He had no stomach for the more sinister side of intelligence operations.
Nor had he the discipline for rigorous secrecy. He was responsible to the
Foreign Office, not the secret service. The MI6 officer in the embassy, C.
M. Woodhouse, was therefore not entirely sorry to see him relinquish his
duties in the autumn of 1952. Yet Zaehner's racy and deft way of doing
business (for example with the Rashidians), and his inside track to the
palace (through Perron) were political assets. Not least Zaehner developed
firm friendships with younger members of the embassy. He assisted the rise
of Samuel Falle, at that time a junior 'Oriental Counsellor', who played a
critical part in the events of 1953–4.

As an 'Oriental Counsellor' Falle was fluent in Persian. His specific
assignment was to cultivate the younger anti-Musaddiqists. He sympathized with their nationalist aspirations. He believed that the British were
acting in the best interests of the Iranians (as well as in legitimate self-
interest) by promoting Qavam. He wrote in April 1952: 'If Qavam comes
to power he will try to act as a dictator – dissolve the Majlis and arrest
dissident elements, among them probably Musaddiq and Kashani. On oil
he is keen to reach an agreement with us . . .'[19] Through Falle's minutes
may be traced the mounting excitement during the spring and summer of
1952 when it seemed to be a question not *if* Musaddiq would fall but *when*.
Having brought the country to the brink of economic ruin, Musaddiq, it
now appeared, would be replaced by Qavam. The problem was the Shah.
He feared, rightly in the judgement of Zaehner and Falle, that he could not
dominate Qavam. The British were indeed uncertain whether the Shah
would support him. According to Falle:

> Even if Musaddiq falls the immediate future leaves plenty of room for
> anxiety. The Shah wants Musaddiq to go quietly without any fuss and seems
> to be determined that the new Prime Minister be a weak man. . . Such an
> appointment would in all probability be catastrophic and could not lead to
> the order and security which are vital if the country's problems are to be
> solved. Hence we come back to our problem which is that Qavam is the only
> man who can deal with the present situation, but that the Shah will not have
> him . . . The Shah's irresolution is extremely dangerous in these critical
> times. . .[20]

As the critical time of July 1952 approached, when it looked as if Musaddiq
might collapse mainly because of Qavam's own initiative, Falle judged
that, whatever the Shah might do, the British should throw their weight
behind Qavam: otherwise 'there is chance that the whole work of the
country might be paralysed for a time and render an oil solution more
difficult. . . My conclusion is that at the moment Qavam is the only man

who can work effectively. . .'[21] Though only a junior officer, Falle with his full-blooded and decisive views carried influence. It is not surprising that in the next year he was brought into the discussions with the CIA.

One person who usually agreed with Falle was the head of mission, George Middleton, who served as chargé d'affaires from January 1952 until the rupture of relations between Iran and Britain in October. Middleton had a broad outlook. He could see the question of Iran's future in relation to the United States and the Soviet Union as well as the Anglo-Iranian Oil Company. While his colleagues often became caught up in Zaehnerian 'intrigue' of Iranian politics, usually with the anti-Musaddiqists, he remained uncommitted to the view that Musaddiq essentially was a 'lunatic'. Indeed Middleton stood out conspicuously among the British as recognizing in Musaddiq the qualities of a highly cultivated and intelligent human being. Certainly among the British in Tehran Middleton was almost alone in regarding Musaddiq not merely as an anti-British nationalist but as a nationalist figure attempting to bring about an Iranian renaissance. Musaddiq in his view had an almost mystical feeling about nationalization. Both Musaddiq and Middleton had been educated in France. They conversed easily in French. Middleton was then 42; Musaddiq was 70. The older man was cordial to the younger, even though they usually disagreed on almost everything. 'He was a highly civilised person', Middleton recalled much later, in 1985.[22]

Musaddiq had an inveterate mistrust of the British. No Englishman who listened to his animated conversation could doubt that he actually believed the British to be somehow responsible for the poverty and general *malaise* of Iran.[23] Some remarks recorded in a confidential letter by Middleton in February 1952 well convey the flavour of Musaddiq's sentiments. As Musaddiq 'bounded up and down excitedly', he dwelt on the corruption of previous governments, the danger of Iran falling to the communists, and the interference of the Anglo-Iranian Oil Company in the country's internal affairs. Corruption could be combated. Even the disaffected intellectuals, whom he denounced with contempt, could be prevented from turning communist by providing them with a 'dole'. But the secret 'agents' exploiting the divisions of Iranian society seemed genuinely to worry Musaddiq. He held, according to Middleton, that:

> the Iranian people could be divided into three classes: communists, agents of the ex-Anglo-Iranian Oil Company and patriots. He would eliminate the first two and the nation would then be united and strong as never before. I remarked that the A.I.O.C. had already left. Musaddiq replied that their agents were still everywhere and because they were all self-interested they were perhaps an even greater danger than the communists.[24]

Did Musaddiq actually believe his own conspiratorial rhetoric? If not,

some sort of accommodation with the British might still be possible. Or
was the anti-British obsession so integrated into his political personality (as
Zaehner held) that Musaddiq could never come to terms with the British
oil company? If so then further discussion was virtually useless. Middleton,
who probably knew him as well as any Englishman, had to admit that he
saw no clear-cut answers. But he was willing to give Musaddiq the benefit
of the doubt. The anti-British rhetoric was part of Musaddiq's political
armoury. The real question was whether or not Musaddiq intended to
come to terms on the oil question.

Musaddiq to the British may have been irrational about certain things,
but at least he was consistent. He saw in the Anglo-Iranian Oil Company
the personification of the evils of economic imperialism, and he never
deviated from that view. The British for their part were also consistent.
From the outset of the crisis in 1951 they had been prepared to admit the
principle of nationalization. With a Labour government dedicated to
nationalization, they could hardly do otherwise. But they insisted that the
Anglo-Iranian Oil Company was entitled to fair compensation. Musaddiq
himself agreed that the company should be compensated, but he flatly
disagreed on a more fundamental point: he held that the foundation of the
British position in Iran, the concession agreement of 1933, was both illegal
and immoral. In this respect Musaddiq stands as the forerunner of a later
generation of Asian and African nationalists who believed that the western
powers had no right in the first place to impose economic and political
conditions to 'development'. Here, to be fair to the British, it is important
to bear in mind the *Zeitgeist* of post-war Britain. The most influential
sentiment, perhaps, was expressed by Sir Donald Fergusson, who believed
that the Iranians had no real right to their own oil because its discovery and
exploitation was entirely due to British enterprise. For the British, at least,
the Iranian oil dispute was the first major crisis to demonstrate the
unbridgeable gulf between the two outlooks as represented by Musaddiq
and Fergusson. The controversy raised a basic issue for the British, one
they could not afford to concede: if Musaddiq's view prevailed, especially
on the validity of the 1933 concession, then nationalists throughout the
world could abrogate British concessions with impunity.

To George Middleton the significance of the oil dispute was the sanctity
of treaties. He was never in any doubt that the British had to hold firm on
that point in all respects, legally, politically and morally. But he did not
think that the British could simply maintain a negative attitude, if only
because the United States, while agreeing on the need to uphold the
sanctity of treaties, would expect some kind of compromise. 'We cannot
indefinitely maintain a basically negative attitude,' Middleton wrote in
early 1952, 'nor do I suppose the Americans will easily acquiesce in a policy
of passive resistance to Musaddiq.'[25] As if those things were not difficult
enough, Middleton judged that there was a further, insidious, psycho-

logical stumbling block. The British recognized the principle of national-ization but continued to protest the way it was carried out. They would accept nationalization as an accomplished fact if the Iranians agreed to provide acceptable compensation. But they also insisted that the oil industry be run 'efficiently'. Virtually no British experts believed that the Iranians could manage a refinery so complex as the one at Abadan. Therein lay Middleton's point about national psychology. The Iranians knew that the British regarded them as inefficient if not incompetent; even more, that the British thought of them as inferior human beings. This was a psychological reality that bore as much on the actual negotiations as the abstract debate about the validity of the 1933 agreement and the practical amount of compensation to be paid to the company.

According to British calculations, the Iranian economy would take a serious turn for the worse in the spring of 1952. Within a year of Musaddiq's rise to power, British economic sanctions – the boycott of Iranian oil and the success in blocking its access to almost all foreign markets – would demonstrate the futility of the Musaddiq regime. Or so it was hoped. According to Middleton's reports the economy was sagging but not collapsing. If Musaddiq did not respond soon to economic pressure, there would be the danger that he might be replaced by something worse, either by a communist regime or by the fundamentalist religious faction led by Kashani, whom Middleton described as 'a sly, corrupt and anti-Western demagogue'.[26] The spring and early summer of 1952 was also the time when the British awaited the result of Musaddiq's case against the Anglo-Iranian Oil Company before the International Court of Justice at the Hague.[27] When the court decided in July 1952 that the dispute lay beyond its jurisdiction, the ruling increased rather than alleviated the tension. The international legal action coincided with rapidly developing events within Iran. After much hesitation the Shah decided to accept Qavam as prime minister. Here was the test of the Zaehnerian interlude in Iranian politics.

The political crisis of July 1952 proved that British policy had been based on a radical miscalculation. Qavam had neither the military nor the public support to sustain himself in office. He was ousted by pro-Musaddiq forces within a week in office, on 21 July. Musaddiq himself returned to power buoyed up by mass demonstrations and determined to consolidate his position against both the Shah and the British.

Middleton immediately described the events of 21 July as 'a turning point of Persian history'. Musaddiq had been returned by mob riots, which to Middleton signified close co-ordination of forces within Iranian society that previously had regarded each other with hostility. Middleton wrote the day after:

It seems clear to me that the bloody riot of the 21st July was a highly organized affair . . . The National Front demagogues, notably Kashani, gave an outward appearance of a spontaneous popular surge of feeling to these riots. But in fact I believe these were almost certainly organised by the Tudeh. Reports reaching me are that the demonstrations were as much anti-monarchial as anti-'imperialist' . . . Moreover there was a cold determination and ruthlessness behind the manifestations which is typically communist . . .

Mob rule now prevailed. The constitutional position of the Shah had been weakened. Middleton believed that the Shah himself bore large responsibility.

The mob successfully defied the security forces and from now on the consent of the mob will be the decisive factor in judging the acceptability of any future government . . . In all this it seems to me that the influence and prestige of the Court has been fatally weakened. The Shah has I suppose been anxious to avoid bloodshed and to act in every respect as a constitutional sovereign who must bow to the majority of public opinion. In fact by his vacillations and weaknesses and in the absence of an informed and educated public he has allowed the initiative to pass to the Tudeh and to the mob which the Tudeh controls.

This was a decisive week, in Middleton's judgement, for the future of western influence in Iran. The Shah, and 'a small section of educated Persians', would probably continue to look to the United States and Britain for help but, Middleton warned, 'I fear that their influence and consequently ours will be a declining one and that it may be beyond our power to stop the drift towards communism.'

Middleton had always been sceptical of Musaddiq. Scepticism now hardened into disillusionment. 'His strength lies in his powers of demagogy,' Middleton wrote in his report to the Foreign Office, 'and he has so flattered the mob as the source of his power that he has, I fear, made it impossible for a successor to oust him by normal constitutional methods.' Middleton believed that the sense of power deriving from the mob had gone to his head. Musaddiq thought he could control the Tudeh as well as Kashani. He was now more than ever incapable of 'reasonable' discourse:

[H]e is surrounded by a gang as little amenable to reason as himself and there does not appear to be a single person in his entourage with whom one can discuss matters in a rational way . . . I think that his principal motivation just now is spite against the Americans and ourselves and he will stop at nothing to vent his dislike even though in effect it means alliance with the communists.

Middleton wrote those lines in the July crisis in the immediate aftermath of Musaddiq's return to power. The chronology is significant because it marks, in the testimony of the British official least unwilling to co-operate with him, Musaddiq's point of no return: 'Musaddiq appears to be beyond reasonable thought and to be swayed entirely by emotion.' In other words, he had crossed the rubicon into irrationality: 'his megalomania is now verging on mental instability.'[28]

Musaddiq of course must have been well aware of the British attempt to dislodge him by aiding Qavam. Their days were now numbered. The opportunity for expelling them came in September with the presentation of a joint offer made by Britain and the United States to settle the oil controversy. As will be explained in the next section, Musaddiq found the offer unacceptable. The British explanation was quite simple: whatever they held out, he demanded more; as the economy of the country deteriorated, he played on the emotions of the mob to retain power. The British in Tehran believed they were witnessing the virtual collapse of the Iranian state, a debacle that could be fatal because Musaddiq was playing the game of the communists:

> Dr Musaddiq by his own action has largely implemented the known programme of the communist Tudeh Party; the Shah has been reduced to a cypher, the Army fatally weakened, the British 'imperialists' dispossessed, the central authority of the Government weakened and the economic and financial structure of the nation reduced almost to chaos.
>
> Without having had to commit their forces in strength, the communists are in the fortunate position of seeing Persia reduced to the point where the advent of a communist régime seems almost to be part of the logic of history.

Musaddiq now demanded £50 million in unpaid royalties from the Anglo-Iranian Oil Company. He argued more dramatically than ever that the concession of 1933 was invalid. 'The popular belief has been carefully fostered,' Middleton reported, 'that the A.I.O.C. is responsible for the existing ills of Persia and indeed for the miseries which the country has suffered during the past 50 years.' Thus Britain owed Iran reparations for past wrongs rather than Iran an indemnity for nationalizing a British company. *Alice Through the Looking Glass* now seemed to be an entirely accurate way of viewing the situation in Iran.

In October 1952, one year to the month after the eviction of the Anglo-Iranian Oil Company, Musaddiq 'kicked out', in Middleton's explicit phrase, the official British delegation. Musaddiq had become the victim of 'his own brand of jingoistic nationalism'. Polite yet melodramatic to the end, he explained to Middleton that 'he was a fatalist' and things would now have to take their own course. He had 'tears in his eyes' as he wished Middleton success in his future career. Middleton himself on the eve of his departure reflected that it might have been a false assumption all along to believe that rationality could prevail and that Musaddiq might come to terms. Lambton and Zaehner, it may be inferred, had proved to be right: 'Perhaps it was a mistake,' Middleton wrote, 'to fall in at all with the American view that Musaddiq is "negotiable".' Lambton expressed the point even more emphatically: 'the United Kingdom policy of not making unjustifiable concessions to Dr Musaddiq was right and would have been successful had it not been for American vacillations.'[29]

The American connection, the Anglo-Iranian Oil Company, and the coup of August 1953

Until the political crisis of July 1952 there had been a basic difference in outlook between the British and the American governments. From the outset the Americans feared the economic collapse of the Musaddiq regime which might bring about communist rule. Economic assistance was necessary to counter Tudeh exploitation of chaos, poverty and despair. The British were sceptical. They did not minimize the danger of a Tudeh coup, but they did not believe that Musaddiq could be appeased. Nor would economic assistance have any tangible effect on the political situation. If anything it would merely delay the fall of Musaddiq. Sarell had written in early 1952:

> The State Department's repeated reference to impending economic collapse in Persia seems to us to betray a misreading of the Persian situation and a diagnosis too much in terms of a Western industrial state. Their theories on this subject have no doubt been sedulously fed by Dr Musaddiq's own propaganda . . . forecasting 'collapse in about 30 days'.
>
> It is our view that such terms are meaningless in Persia. A primitive agricultural community such as Persia, where some 80% of the population are estimated to live off the land at bare subsistence level does not 'collapse' economically. It sags, and no doubt more of the population will die of starvation than usual. We do not believe in the imminence of the catastrophic phenomenon forecast by the State Department.

The crisis of July 1952 brought the British closer to the American assessment. To reiterate George Middleton's basic point, in his own words, Musaddiq had now 'worked himself up to a pitch of excitement at which he was no longer capable of rational thought'. He might well play into the hands of the communists. The British thus now believed, again in Middleton's words, that something was necessary 'to check Communist activity in Persia'.

Nevertheless the British and the Americans remained poles apart in their assessment of Musaddiq. The British continued to hold that the end of the Musaddiq regime would not necessarily lead to communism while the Americans believed that Musaddiq for all his faults was the only person who might prevent a communist revolution. In the immediate aftermath of the July crisis Bernard Burrows (a former head of the Eastern department of the Foreign Office now serving in Washington) reported a conversation with Charles Bohlen, a State Department official for whom the British had high respect. Bohlen had delivered an 'emotional tirade about Persia . . . his view seemed to be that Musaddiq and Co. were the only people left who could conceivably save Persia from Communism and we ought, therefore, to make up our minds that we must make a deal with them.'

The British thought the Americans were responding excessively. Whatever might be happening in Iran could be explained more plausibly within the framework of Iranian politics rather than by the paramount American preoccupation at that time, the 'loss' of China. Nor did the British believe that the fate of Musaddiq would set off a chain reaction. Yet, according to Bohlen, 'if Persia went Communist Iraq and probably the rest of the Middle East would also, and our position would be lost anyway. We ought therefore to concentrate on saving Persia from Communism at all costs.' This 'domino' theme also appeared in the American press, notably in articles written by Joseph and Stewart Alsop (a pair of reporters the British followed closely because their writing often revealed underlying assumptions of high American officials). The Alsops wrote after Musaddiq's return to power:

> This country [the United States] may be faced with the choice of allowing Iran to go the way of China, or intervening forcefully to support any anti-Communist forces in Iran, however reactionary and blindly nationalist. It is believed in Washington that a Communist take-over in Iran must be averted at whatever cost, even the cost of a break with Britain on Middle East politics.

The Americans seemed to believe that the British would rather see Iran go Communist than to make an 'unsatisfactory' oil agreement with Musaddiq. This was the explicit challenge: 'whether we were now more interested in stopping Communism than in an oil settlement'.[30]

If there were to be an oil agreement, it would probably have to be based on the premise that the return of the Anglo-Iranian Oil Company was impossible. This was an American assumption as well as an Iranian one. But it was not necessarily a British one. As long as there seemed to be the prospect that Musaddiq might fall for reasons of his own making (because for example the Iranians themselves might see that he was leading the country to economic ruin), then there was hope that the AIOC might be reinstated under the façade of a new management company. In the first half of 1952 British policy pursued the hallowed course of 'masterly inactivity' – keeping the Americans in play (for example through joint discussions with the World Bank as an intermediary with Musaddiq) and putting forward no constructive solution. There were good reasons for this negative approach. Any alternative to the company would mean a breaking of the British monopoly. Thus the Americans were justified in their standard criticism that the British were merely 'standing pat'. Even before the July crisis, however, certain officials in the Foreign Office began to recognize that something had to be done, if only to counter the American suspicion that the British would allow Iran to drift into communist revolution before giving up the concession. The driving force behind the effort to arrive at some solution, however unpalatable it might be to the company and the champions of privileged position, was the Deputy Under-Secretary, Sir Roger Makins. It came as a revelation to him that both the Treasury and the Ministry of Fuel and Power seemed to be just as hostile to compromise as the AIOC. 'We are indeed faced with a solid wall of Bourbonism and Micawberism in dealing with this question,' Makins wrote in June 1952, 'of which the failure to deal with the re-organisation of the A.I.O.C. in the last six months is a symptom.'

The actual architect of the reorganization of the Iranian oil industry, on the British side, was Peter Ramsbotham, then at the 'oil desk' of the Foreign Office. Through his minutes may be traced the steps that eventually led to the consortium agreement of 1954. Ramsbotham approached these problems with an eye toward a realistic settlement and with a sense of humour: 'A concession is probably neither definable in law nor as a term of art', he once wrote. Whatever a 'concession' might once have amounted to in Iran, it now had to be replaced. He had in mind a 'contractual arrangement' whereby a new company would negotiate a fifty–fifty principle of profit sharing with the Iranian government. The Anglo-Iranian Oil Company would receive compensation for losses (possibly through arbitration). Ramsbotham's language made explicit the nature of the proposed arrangement: the new managing company would be a 'façade' that would enable the Iranians to save face, and the new agreement would include a guarantee that would prevent them from interfering 'in the company's day to day operations'. He was well aware of the danger of attempting to make this fabrication a purely British façade: 'a reconstructed British company would not be able to operate as the sole company inside Persia as this would be too transparent a restoration of British monopoly.' Therefore American and perhaps other foreign oil companies would have to be allowed into the new arrangement. This proposal drew a protest from the Foreign Secretary himself. 'I do not like the idea of bringing American companies in', Anthony Eden wrote in May 1952.[31]

Eden's past experiences help to explain his attitude toward Iran in 1952. At Oxford he had studied Persian, which he continued to refer to as 'the Italian of the East'. He had served as parliamentary under-secretary at the

Foreign Office at the time of the Iranian oil crisis of 1933. He had been to Iran and had seen the oilfields. In 1951 he had denounced the Iranians for stealing British property. Upon becoming Foreign Secretary again after the fall of the Labour government, one of his first major anxieties became 'Old Mossy'. Behind the caricature of Musaddiq as a buffoon in pajamas negotiating from behind an iron bedstead, Eden saw a shifty operator who was impervious to reason because of his antipathy to the British. He occasionally referred to him as a megalomaniac (a word he usually reserved for Nasser). He certainly regarded him as one of the shrewdest and most devious 'Orientals' he had ever encountered. Eden wrote in his memoirs: 'Interviews with Musaddiq, whether in bed or out of it, affable or corrosive, did not advance us one jot.' The problem of Iran was of course only one of many that Eden faced, but in retrospect he regarded it as the most difficult to resolve. He wrote at the end of the critical year 1954:

> It is a strange thing about this year that though many people have written about the problems which we have, we hope, solved, Western European Union, Egypt, Indo-China, Iran, Arabia (Buraimi), very few have given much credit to Iran, which was, I believe, the toughest of all.[32]

His success in dealing with the Iranian crisis in fact derived in large part from delegating responsibility and listening to the advice of his permanent officials. In 1952 it was Sir Roger Makins, probably more than anyone else, who convinced him that he was wrong in his initial response to the question of the American oil companies. Makins held that the Americans would have to be allowed into the Iranian oil industry or there would be no hope of a settlement.

The principal opponent to radical reorganization was Sir Donald Fergusson. From his position of permanent under-secretary at the Ministry of Fuel and Power, he was in a position effectively to block any proposal the Foreign Office might put forward or, conversely, to shape an outcome that would, in his view, correspond to the British national interest. Fergusson had been a member of the Stokes mission to Iran in 1951, when the British had made certain proposals to Musaddiq. The British would recognize the principle of nationalization and would relinquish the concession in favour of a contractual arrangement. In return for compensation, they would help to establish a new management company that would efficiently run the Iranian oil industry on the basis of a fifty–fifty division of profits. This compromise represented the limit of Fergusson's generosity, which scarcely included the Americans. He was almost as distrustful of them as of 'the Persians'. After Makins wrote to him of the possibility of reopening discussion with both the Iranians and the Americans in the spring of 1952, Fergusson responded:

I fear that we are in some danger of finding ourselves in a position where, having talked vaguely about resuming negotiations and making concessions, we shall be accused by the Americans of bad faith because we are unable to agree to specific concessions which their backroom boys will produce at short notice and in large quantities.

The fact of the matter is that there is very little that we can do by way of making concessions . . .[33]

Only with extreme reluctance did Fergusson concur that somehow the Americans had to be accommodated, but not at the expense of the legitimate interests of the Anglo-Iranian Oil Company. He held that the British and American governments were not the appropriate parties to negotiate a settlement. The AIOC itself, he thought, was the only competent body to reach an agreement with the Iranians. Fergusson's attitude well represented what Makins referred to as 'Bourbonism'.

'I suppose one can never be certain of anything in Persia', Makins wrote, but waiting like Mr Micawber for something to turn up would surely not yield results favourable to the British. Makins and Fergusson could both agree that there was no room for false optimism. Yet they were pulling in quite opposite directions: Makins towards collaborating with the Americans; Fergusson towards aligning the government's policy with the company's, or at least remaining true to sound British business principles. This was a first-class bureaucratic row. Makins eventually prevailed. He did so because of Eden's influence within the Cabinet and because of the transcendent importance of the political issue at stake. In Eden's own words: 'It is our national interest to obtain a settlement, not on account of the oil but because Persia's independence is very much our concern.' Eden thus demonstrated the qualities of a statesman. And he exerted pressure on his colleagues. He spoke to the Chancellor of the Exchequer, R. A. Butler, and to the Secretary of State for Co-ordination of Transport, Fuel and Power, Lord Leathers, who was Fergusson's minister. Fergusson was a loyal, efficient and extremely tenacious civil servant. From about mid-1952 onwards he began to redirect his energies toward bringing the AIOC into line with government policy, the Eden policy. He was exceedingly sceptical whether the chairman of the company, Sir William Fraser, was capable of seeing beyond the strictly commercial limits of the problem. Fergusson minced words with no one. He told Fraser himself that he was 'a damn bad negotiator'. After reading a report of one of Fergusson's conversations with Fraser, Eden made a memorable comment which will probably always be associated with the Iranian oil controversy: 'Fraser', noted the Foreign Secretary, 'is in cloud cuckoo land.'[34]

Sir William Fraser (Lord Strathalmond) holds a unique place in the history of British overseas expansion not only because he dominated the Anglo-Iranian Oil Company but also because of his autocratic personality.

A particularly rugged Scottish individualist, he had been born and bred in the British oil industry (his father had been founder and managing director of the Pumpherston Oil Company, the leading Scottish shale-oil company). He personified the sense of adventure and enterprise that the British public associated with 'Anglo-Persian', as the company used to be called. He had been chairman since 1941. According to a notice in *The Times* after his death, he was 'a Scotsman to his fingertips . . . He had a razor-keen business brain combined with a sense of caution such that few, in an industry where tough bargaining is an accepted way of life, were likely to get the better of him.'[35] In business affairs as with his acquaintances, he was accustomed to having his way. It must therefore have been galling to confront Musaddiq's brand of Iranian nationalism that aimed to repudiate everything he represented – even though Fraser maintained that nothing other than ingratitude should ever be expected from 'the Persians'. In fact Musaddiq's estimation of him was probably not much different from that of Fergusson, who believed that Fraser intended to exact the last possible pound from Iran whatever the consequences. Fergusson believed that Fraser should be removed from the chairmanship of the company. So did most other officials including the governor of the Bank of England. Even the National Provincial Bank, the AIOC's bankers, believed that he had outserved his time.[36] Fraser however had great staying power: 'The retirement of Sir W. Fraser has been under consideration at various times in the past 2 years', wrote Christopher Gandy of the Eastern Department in 1954; 'He is still there.'[37] He did not retire until 1956, and did not die until 1970 – long enough for his friends to maintain that he had understood Iranian nationalism better than his critics and should be given credit for reorganizing the Iranian oil industry in the form of the consortium arrangement of 1954.[38]

In fact Fraser resisted down the line. Part of the problem was his open contempt for civil servants. He was generally scornful of those who chose to earn their living by working for the state, and he was specifically disdainful of their knowledge of the oil industry. 'We had a pretty sticky meeting with Sir William Fraser last night', Makins wrote on 19 July 1952.[39] The date is significant because this was the time of Qavam's brief advent to power. Fraser argued that Qavam would come to a reasonable agreement. The company did not wish to rush; indeed, as Fraser explained, there was no particular need for AIOC to return to Iran. The losses at Abadan had already been more than recovered by the Kuwait fields. By the early 1950s Kuwait reserves were estimated at 16 per cent of the world's total; Saudi Arabia reserves were about 10 per cent.[40] Thus the Foreign Office did not have a strong hand to play against the company. Fraser was not unresponsive to appeals to patriotism, but it was probable that his business instinct would prevail.[41] Nevertheless there was progress. By July 1952 Fraser had agreed in principle to a management company in

which the major American oil companies might participate. The more he
thought about it, the more Fraser thought it would be best for AIOC to
retain the initiative in this new arrangement. He himself would go to Iran
to discuss the matter with Qavam. The following Foreign Office minute
indicates Eden's response to Fraser's proposal: 'The Secretary of State had
been horrified at the suggestion that Sir William Fraser should go out to
Persia to conduct negotiations.'

Speculation about Fraser bartering with 'the Persians' was short lived.
After Musaddiq's return to power in late July 1952 the calculations
changed. This was the period when American and British outlooks began
to converge. The longer Musaddiq remained in power, the greater would
be the danger of an eventual communist takeover. There remained serious
differences, however, in the American and British points of view.
According to the British ambassador in Washington, Sir Oliver Franks, the
Americans distrusted the Anglo-Iranian Oil Company to the extent that
they doubted whether any solution would be possible if Fraser were a part
of it. The Americans and the British also continued to disagree in assessing
the stability of the Musaddiq regime. In the British view economic
assistance would sustain the Musaddiqists while in the American view
economic aid was necessary to prevent a communist takeover. 'We must go
on trying to restrain them', Makins wrote of the Americans in August;
'They are agog for action', reported Franks. The result was the
'Truman–Churchill proposal' of September 1952 whereby the amount of
compensation would be arbitrated; the AIOC wold negotiate with the
Iranian government for the resumption of oil production; and the United
States would grant $10 million in budgetary aid. 'It is very important that
we should not lose momentum', wrote R. J. Bowker, the assistant under-
secretary supervising the Eastern department; 'At any minute Musaddiq or
the State Department may have another bright idea.'[42] The offer was
presented. Musaddiq responded with a demand for £50 million as an
advance against oil. This was another turning point. The Americans now
moved still closer to the British assumption that it was impossible to do
business with Dr Musaddiq.

The autumn and winter of 1952 was the critical period when the British
and Americans began together to plan covert operations against
Musaddiq. Here a word must be said about the nature of the archival
evidence. In late 1952 and early 1953 there occurs something like a sea-
change in the British documentation. It is not merely a coincidence that
this was the beginning of the Eisenhower Administration and the advent of
Allen Dulles as head of the CIA. Until this time British intelligence
operations, if impinging on foreign policy, were discussed fully and
candidly within the secret counsels of the Foreign Office. One can read
minutes, for example, about the possibility of assassinating the Mufti of
Jerusalem during the second world war. During the Musaddiq period the

records were suppressed. This is not only because of those grim guardians of state secrets whose function in life is to cause frustration among historians by 'weeding out' sensitive documents. With the Eisenhower presidency the cold war was stepped up several pitches. Even within the Foreign Office officials stopped writing about matters they previously had debated in the ordinary course of minutes and private correspondence. The nature of historical analysis is thus affected. British policy remained constant; but it now had a deeper subterranean stream that is much more difficult to fish for historical detail.

The British detected a change in mood as well as a shift in policy in Washington. The Truman Administration, in this view, had been exceedingly cautious in dealing with Musaddiq. Indeed, Dean Acheson, the Secretary of State, and George McGhee, his stalwart lieutenant who dealt with the Iranian question, seemed to them to err in judgement by treating Musaddiq as a sort of charming oriental gentleman (rather than as a demented and extraordinarily devious and dangerous anti-British extremist). 'The difficulty with the previous Administration', wrote Sir Pierson Dixon (the deputy under-secretary who succeeded Makins when he became ambassador in Washington in January 1953), 'was that we were continuously being pushed to make new concessions whenever Musaddiq shifted his ground. The new Administration seem to realise that we have now reached the limit of concession.' This was a decided improvement over the 'vacillation' described by Lambton and Zaehner. 'Much more robust' were Dixon's words to sum up the change.[43]

It would suit one's taste for historical symmetry if a similar contrast could be made between the Tory government and its Labour predecessor. Unfortunately it was a Labour Foreign Secretary, Herbert Morrison, who had instructed Robin Zaehner to work for Musaddiq's overthrow by covert means, and it was Churchill himself, as will be seen, who sustained that course of action to its logical conclusion. On the other hand Eden proved to be just as cautious and capable in his handling of the Iranian issue (as distinct from the Egyptian) as any Labour Foreign Secretary might have been. There are no generalities that can be drawn other than that personalities and the quirks of fortune played a large part in the outcome of the Iranian issue in 1953. So much has been made of the conspiracy to overthrow Musaddiq that it is well to bear in mind that things might have turned out quite differently with only a slight variation of circumstance. Indeed, as C. M. Woodhouse points out in his autobiography, *Something Ventured*, Musaddiq might well have fallen without any assistance from the British and Americans.

'Monty' Woodhouse could be described at once as a guerrilla fighter, undercover agent, politician, and man of letters. He had fought with the Greek resistance during the second world war. He was a colonel at the age of 27. He later became Conservative MP for Oxford, chief editor of

Penguin Books, director of Chatham House, and a distinguished historian of Greece. In 1951–2 he headed MI6 in Iran. It seemed to him at the time that joint action by Britain and the United States would be the only way to prevent the Red Army from marching southwards and forging a satellite state in Iran on the model of eastern Europe. Stalin may not actually have had that in mind, Woodhouse reflected later, but in the early 1950s it had certainly seemed possible. With the Shah and Kashani playing the respective parts of Hamlet and Thomas à Becket, Musaddiq appeared to Woodhouse as 'a wily theatrical, tragi-comic figure . . . [whose] abiding enemy . . . was Britain'. The principal danger was not Musaddiq's crusade against the Anglo-Iranian Oil company, which was serious enough from the British point of view but was not Woodhouse's main concern; from his background of the Greek civil war the overarching menace was that of a communist takeover: 'the longer he [Musaddiq] held office the more probable it became that Iran would pass under Soviet control.' This of course was close to the American view, specifically the one held by Loy Henderson, the American ambassador in Tehran. Henderson had long experience with the Russians and played a critical part in aligning the American and British positions: 'Loy Henderson changed the atmosphere in the US Embassy towards sympathy with the British case.'[44]

When Woodhouse arrived in Tehran in August 1951, Robin Zaehner had already re-established the alliance with the Rashidian brothers. He had worked with them secretly during the war against the Nazis. Their network was still intact. They had influence not only in the Majlis but also in the bazaars. They knew how to manipulate mobs. Woodhouse recognized Zaehner's brilliance in enlisting the Rashidians, but he regarded him as a dangerous amateur so far as serious undercover work was concerned. Zaehner himself did not possess the stamina or the ruthless determination to see his anti-Musaddiq plans through to completion. Perhaps, since he had a philosophical temperament, he was plagued with self-doubt.[45] In any case he began to question the wisdom of intervention. He yielded control of contact with the Rashidians to Woodhouse. After Musaddiq evicted the official British delegation in October 1952, Zaehner played his last hand, nearly upsetting Woodhouse's carefully laid plans. Woodhouse made the mistake of inviting Zaehner to meet with him and Eden, and other high officials, to discuss future operations. Zaehner gave a gloomy account. He had been disillusioned with Qavam and now mistrusted the capacity of the Rashidians to dislodge Musaddiq. A late convert to the principle of non-intervention, Zaehner now emphatically believed that the British should let Iranian affairs take their own course. Woodhouse was appalled at Zaehner's defeatism. He grasped at a straw held out to him by Eden, who said that nothing could be done anyway without the help of the Americans. A less enterprising person than Woodhouse might have let things go at that. If Woodhouse himself had not seized the initiative at this point there might never have been a coup against Musaddiq, at least not one partly sponsored by the British.

Woodhouse interpreted Eden's comment to mean that he should explore possibilities with the Americans. He went to Washington in mid-November 1952. Bedell Smith (Allen Dulles's predecessor) told him, 'You may be able to throw out Musaddiq, but you will never get your own man to stick in his place.' The question of Musaddiq's successor was by no means the only problem. The Rashidians were anti-American. Woodhouse did not know whether they would play until events actually unfolded. The Americans for their part generally did not rule out the possibility of a combined move against Musaddiq, nor did they quail at the price, which Woodhouse described as perhaps half a million pounds plus the £10,000 a month already being paid to the Rashidians. Not all of the American bureaucracy, however, fell in so wholeheartedly with these ideas. Woodhouse found the CIA ready to carry the discussions forward but the State Department hesitant to become involved. There was a lingering 'silliness' among some Americans, he wrote later, 'that Musaddiq could be retained and manipulated, and who dreaded the consequences of his downfall'.[46] This was at the end of 1952. Woodhouse had made progress at the undercover level. At the other level, the one of high policy, the British were content to let things drift: 'We are in no hurry', wrote Sir Pierson Dixon in December; 'Our Policy is to play the hand along until we can sound out the attitude of General Eisenhower's Administration to the Persian Oil problem.'

In one of Eden's first conversations with Eisenhower in late 1952, the president-elect kept repeating, 'Then you don't think there is anything that can be done in the next sixty days?' Eden said he feared not, then nor thereafter. In his judgement the risks of intervention were too great. Yet the Americans insisted on some sort of action. 'The President kept repeating that we could not do nothing', Eden reported to Churchill several months later in March 1953. This was thus a ringing and persistent theme. 'The difficulty of this situation', Eden went on, 'remains that the Americans are perpetually eager to do something. The President repeated this several times.'[47] The British again acquiesced in another 'package deal' (as Eden described it to the Cabinet), whereby they once more adjusted their terms but maintained their position that the company would have to receive 'fair compensation'.[48] The sticking point was now Musaddiq's reluctance to guarantee the AIOC compensation for future losses. Musaddiq himself seemed genuinely anxious to restore Iran's business reputation, and by all accounts, including his own, he desperately needed the cash. But the Foreign Office believed that his anti-British antipathy would preclude his acceptance of any joint Anglo-American offer. This was probably an accurate judgement. As for Eisenhower, Eden concluded that he was 'obsessed' with the danger of a communist Iran, and far too solicitous of Musaddiq. When the final stalemate approached in the spring of 1953, Sir Pierson Dixon wrote, 'The plain fact is that we don't care how violent and unreasonable Musaddiq may be in announcing a breakdown. In fact the more unrestrained he is the more clearly our proposals will stand out as reasonable in the eyes of Persia & the world.' On 10 March Musaddiq rejected the final offer. The 'high policy' of concerting American and British action in order to give Musaddiq a last chance had now come to an end, much to British relief.

With such a concern for the reputation of Britain in 'the eyes of Persia' and the world at large, it is not surprising that Dixon and his Foreign Office colleagues were exceedingly wary of the other level of British policy, that of covert operations. In February 1953 Woodhouse's plans were called to a halt. The principal influence in this decision was Dixon's. As deputy under-secretary he was proving himself to be just as 'robust' (one of his favourite words) as his predecessor, Makins, and just as influential with Eden. Dixon believed that if the British and Americans sat tight then the Musaddiq regime would fall of its own accord and they could then devise a solution to the oil problem with its successor. He was clear about priorities: 'The continuing tension in Persia', he once wrote, 'is probably doing more harm in the M.E. than a "bad" settlement would cause.' Unfortunately the Ministry of Fuel and Power and the Treasury did not agree. Here too he saw a strong argument for biding one's time. The other departments would eventually concur in a settlement because the oil embargo could not be indefinitely sustained. Dixon held steady course, 'always', in his own words, 'on the basic assumption that there must be a fair basis for compensation'.[49] He was a man of principle. He demanded respect for the British position. He wished above all to avoid the compromise of Britain's good name by underhand actions of uncertain effectiveness and doubtful morality. Those were some of the reasons why, on 21 February, he curtailed the anti-Musaddiq conspiracy.[50] Yet his decision was shortly reversed. One cannot but pause to wonder how events would have transpired had he not been overruled. He was not challenged by Eden, who saw eye to eye with him. Eden at the time was hos-pitalized by a gall bladder operation and did not return to the Foreign Office until after Musaddiq's fall. What then was the reason for deciding to resume covert operations? The answer can be summed up in one word: Churchill.

Churchill had been involved in the high politics of Persian oil since the days before the first world war. It was he who had championed the conversion of the Royal Navy from coal to oil and who had played a major part in the purchase by the British government of a majority of shares in the Anglo-Persian Oil Company. He had calculated at the time that the saving on the price paid for oil alone would amount to about £40 million. And he had stated:

On this basis it may be that the aggregate profits, realised and potential, of this investment may be estimated at a sum not merely sufficient to pay all the programme of ships, great and small of that year and for the whole pre-war oil fuel installation, but are such that we may not unreasonably expect that one day we shall be entitled also to claim that the mighty fleets laid down in 1912, 1913, and 1914, the greatest ever built by any power in an equal period, were added to the British Navy without costing a single penny to the taxpayer.[51]

Churchill therefore had every reason to take a renewed interest in the fate of Iranian oil in the early 1950s. After Eden became ill, Churchill took on responsibility for foreign affairs and, as Woodhouse points out, reversed the course: 'Churchill enjoyed dramatic operations and had no high regard for timid diplomatists. It was he who gave the authority for Operation Boot to proceed.'[52]

'Operation Boot' was the British name, 'Operation Ajax' the American name for the anti-Musaddiq plan. It is certain that Eisenhower was fully aware of 'Operation Ajax' and gave it his endorsement.[53] Like Churchill, Eisenhower worked from documents and mastered details. He knew his own mind and, contrary to the political mythology of the period, was by no means the captive of either of the Dulles brothers, John Foster or Allen, though Allen certainly had his ear on this question. This is not the place for a discussion of the American side of the problem, but one point should be stressed. There was still an air of old-fashioned espionage about operations Boot and Ajax. Musaddiq was to be toppled. But neither Churchill nor Eisenhower were in the business of assassinating a fellow head of state.

The candidate to replace Musaddiq was General Fazlullah Zahidi. He had figured prominently in British and American discussions in Tehran after the collapse of the Qavam regime in July 1952 as the only alternative to Musaddiq. During the second world war Zahidi had been seized by the British at gunpoint and interned as a pro-Nazi, which now turned out to be an advantage since he was not tainted with a pro-British reputation. Sam Falle had written these statements about Zahidi: 'In this country of weak men he is comparatively strong'; 'He is strongly anti-communist'; 'He was imprisoned by the British during the war and is not considered to be a British stooge'; 'He is on good terms with some members of the National Front – among these is Kashani . . .'; 'He should be able to count on the support of a section of the Army'. Falle's analysis continued with a shrewd assessment of the Shah and the part he might, or might not, play in any future confrontation: 'The Shah still has some symbolic standing with the public throughout the country and the Army although the latter are angry with him because they think he has let them down. If he does not show some signs of decisiveness and manliness in the near future he will lose what little is left of his prestige.'[54] Whether or not the Shah would steel himself for the eventual showdown with Musaddiq, no one could predict. 'There still remained the problem of persuading the nervous Shah to play his role,' Woodhouse wrote of the actual crisis in the summer of 1953, 'which would consist simply of signing two decrees (*firmans*), one dismissing Musaddiq and the other appointing Zahedi in his place.'[55]

It is important to bear in mind that after October 1952 the British themselves operated in Iran only indirectly. 'It's always unfortunate and makes things more difficult', Sir Samuel Falle recalled with understatement in 1985, 'if you don't have diplomatic relations . . . We couldn't negotiate on the spot, nor could we continue our contingency plan from an Iran base.'[56] Anti-Musaddiq activities were now monitored from Cyprus, where the Rashidians were kept in touch by radio. The Rashidian organization now embraced deputies and senators of the Majlis, ranking officers in the army and police, mullas, merchants, newspapermen and, not least, mob-leaders. And there was another dimension to the British plan. In southern Iran some of the tribal leaders were in the pay of MI6. Both the urban and the rural components would be activated simultaneously in order to counter Tudeh support of Musaddiq. Here a major stroke of luck played to British advantage. The prelude to the Iranian crisis coincided with Stalin's death on 25 March. In the subsequent period of indecision the Russians failed to succour the communists in Iran. The Tudeh organization was cast adrift, leaving among other things a packing case of postage stamps overprinted with the words 'Republic of Iran' as a reminder of what might have happened had the Soviet Union intervened.

Probably nothing would have come of the elaborate British preparation had it not been for the parallel set of plans devised by the principal agent of the CIA in the Middle East, Kermit Roosevelt.[57] Shortly after 25 April (the date the two governments agreed upon Zahidi as a successor to Musaddiq) Roosevelt was given a green light to co-ordinate fully the details of the conspiracy. Operation 'Ajax', like operation 'Boot', was based on a group of Iranians with close family ties. Both organizations were rooted principally in the bazaar or business community, with the British having stronger contacts with the Shah, the Americans with the military and clergy. The two networks now meshed. It might appear in retrospect that the underground Iranian and Anglo-American combinations were unbeatable, but at the time they appeared, at least to the British, to be a ramshackle affair with little chance of success.

Roosevelt himself secretly crossed the border into Iran on 6 July. He knew virtually nothing of the Persian language. To the British he was an amateur. Nevertheless he won their respect. The success of the operation was due to his organizational brilliance and decisiveness. At first everything seemed to go wrong. The Shah finally decided to issue the *firmans* in part because of Roosevelt's persuasiveness, but Musaddiq arrested the emissary handing him the decrees, thus preventing Zahidi from receiving the royal designation. The Shah fled the country. Zahidi went into hiding. The story has of course been told many times.[58] Yet it is important to remember the public mood. One contemporary account is especially revealing of how Roosevelt, by circulating press copies of the Shah's decrees and mobilizing the mob, managed to reverse the tide on 19 August:

> With the army standing close guard around the uneasy capital, a grotesque procession made its way along the street leading to the heart of Tehran. There were tumblers turning handsprings, weight-lifters twirling iron bars and wrestlers flexing their biceps. As spectators grew in number, the bizarre assortment of performers began shouting pro-Shah slogans in unison. The crowd took up the chant and there, after one precarious moment, the balance of public psychology swung against Musaddiq.[59]

With those events the British were only indirectly involved, which is not to say that they should be exonerated. For the post-August 1953 course of Iranian history, the British, like the Americans, bear heavy responsibility.

Over 300 were killed in heavy street fighting. Musaddiq, true to style, was captured in his pyjamas. At his trial he eloquently stated that he was being judged by the agents of foreigners for having struggled against the enemies of Iran. As the narrative of this paper has made clear, his accusation was not without an element of truth, though, as Woodhouse states, British and American involvement in the coup was only one element in Iranian politics and did not determine the subsequent set of events over the long run. Few could have anticipated the Shah's later tyranny or the extent of American illusion. But what of the British decision at the time? Does the intervention of August 1953 stand in history as a wise and proper action, or the reverse? It is of course an unanswerable question, but, according to Woodhouse, the principal participant and witness who has studied seriously the post-war period, the British involvement in the coup was justified because of the international situation. Otherwise, in his view, Iran would have been subjected to communism and perhaps Soviet domination. One might take serious issue with that assessment, but it represents the convictions of the British government of the time.

In another chapter in this book, James Bill emphasizes the lasting and negative effect of the 1953 intervention on the relations between the Iranian and American peoples. For the British the result is more difficult to assess. Anthony Eden at the beginning of the crisis still listened to the advice of his permanent officials, who on the whole warned him of the perils of intervention. Nations, like individuals, cannot be manipulated without a sense on the part of the aggrieved that old scores must eventually be settled. As the crisis progressed, however, Eden and certain others became convinced that Musaddiq could be removed, and the outcome seemed to demonstrate that, in one way or another, the countries of the Middle East could still be coerced. In the short term, the intervention of 1953 appeared to be effective. Over the longer term, the older advice not to interfere would seem to be the better part of political wisdom.

Here

Notes

1 George Middleton to Eden, 'Confidential', 24 March 1952, FO 371/98593 (all references to British official documents refer to records at the Public Record Office, London). In the introductory section to this paper I have drawn on the chapter on 'The Persian oil crisis' in Wm Roger Louis, *The British Empire in the Middle East 1945–1951* (Oxford, 1984). In the historical literature of the subject one book is especially relevant because of its contemporary and critical examination of the policies of the British government and the Anglo-Iranian Oil Company: L. P. Elwell-Sutton, *Persian Oil: a Study in Power Politics* (London, 1955). In the 1975 edition Elwell-Sutton stated that he was content that the book 'should reappear in its original form as a record of the struggle of a small Asian country for independence and international recognition'. For the company itself, as well as for background to this chapter, see especially R. W. Ferrier, *The History of The British Petroleum Company*, vol. 1, *The Developing Years 1901–1932* (Cambridge, 1982). I wish to thank Brian Lapping for making available to me the transcripts of Granada Television's *End of Empire: Iran*.

2 Confidential Annex to Chiefs of Staff (51) 86, 23 May 1951, DEFE 4/43.

3 Minute by Churchill, 17 August 1952, PREM 11/392.

4 Speech made by Stokes over the BBC, 15 October 1951, Stokes Papers Box 3 (Bodleian Library, Oxford).

5 For public reaction to the crisis see Hamid Enayat, 'British public opinion and the Iranian oil crisis from 1951 to 1954' (MA thesis, University of London, 1958).

6 Memorandum by K. L. Stock (Ministry of Fuel and Power), 17 September 1946, FO 371/52343.

7 Fergusson to Richard Stokes, 'Top Secret Private & Personal', 3 October 1951, FO 371/91599.

8 Obituary in *The Times*, 6 March 1963.

9 Kuwait Administration Report for 1951, 'Confidential', FO 371/98378.

10 Hay to Eden, 'Confidential', 31 October 1952, FO 371/98378.

11 See especially Shepherd to Furlonge, 'Confidential', 6 May 1951, FO 371/91459. For a sympathetic British portrait of Musaddiq see Ellwell Sutton, *Persian Oil*, pp. 7–8 and 193–4:

> To most people in the west he was a puzzling figure of fun – funny because of his tears, his fainting fits, his propensity for conducting public business in grey woollen pyjamas and a plain iron bed; puzzling because of his extraordinary success in getting away with the most outrageous

and impossible demands . . . The Persians, it seemed, had suddenly gone mad; following the lead of a crazy old man, they had thrown out a sound and honest commercial concern, destroyed their oil industry, and dealt a crippling blow to their country's economy. They had ignored the generous and disinterested advice given them not only by Britain, but by America and the rest of the world . . . The bald-headed, hawk-nosed old doctor's antics were even troubling the serene waters of British politics . . .

His power over people was further reinforced by his charm of manner, his emotional and (to the westerner) incomprehensible flow of oratory, and withal his sparkling sense of humour, often expressing itself in theatrical behaviour and apparently hysterical outbursts. For many years a sick man, he never allowed this to deflect him from his tenacity of purpose. Perhaps this was never more vividly revealed than in his deliberate flouting, with Persia's insignificant resources, of the combined might of Britain and America. In this he displayed a moral strength and rectitude that has no counterpart in any western country of today.

12 R. F. G. Sarell, 'Nationalism in Persia', 13 February 1952, FO 371/98596. Sarell's estimate was a rejoinder to Shepherd's 'A comparison between Persian and Asian nationalism in general', for which see Louis, *British Empire in the Middle East*, pp. 639–40. Shepherd had previously served in Indonesia (one of the bases of the 'comparison') where the nationalist movement appeared to him to be much more fully developed.

13 Sarell actually quoted Gibb on religious leaders restating 'the basis of the Islamic community in terms of nationalism' in the course of the memorandum. For Lambton's published views see especially her essay, 'The impact of the West on Persia', *International Affairs* 33.1 (January 1957). Her private opinions, as will be seen, were influential in the Foreign Office.

14 Sarell, 'Nationalism in Persia'.

15 See minute by Berthoud, 13 October 1952, FO 371/98701.

16 Minute by Berthoud, 15 June 1951, FO 371/91548.

17 Minute by Zaehner, 5 January 1952, FO 248/1531 (embassy archives).

18 Minute by Zaehner, 10 November 1951 FO 248/1514. For British calculations about alternatives to Musaddiq other than Qavam, notably Sayyid Zia, and other important details about the origins of the conspiracy against Musaddiq, I am indebted to an unpublished essay by Mark J. Gasiorowski, 'The 1953 coup d'état in Iran'.

19 Minute by Falle, 28 April 1951, FO 248/1531.

20 Minute by Falle, 30 June 1952, FO 248/1531.

21 Minute by Falle, 2 July 1952, FO 248/1531.

22 Transcript, Granada, *End of Empire: Iran*.

23 See e.g. Kingsley Martin, 'Conversation with Dr Mossadeq', *New Statesman*, 11 January 1952:

Dr Mossadeq received me in bed – a plain iron bed in which he bounced rather than lay . . . I saw no signs of the over-excitement or hysteria that some journalists have written about; he did not weep, though he laughed shrilly, stretching out his hand in a claw-like gesture that made him look at times like a benevolent pterodactyl. Here was a man of much force and capacity . . . He believed that it was not enough to get rid of a Company which had exploited his country, but that it was right to make sure that no other body or foreign Power would be in a position to exercise the influence in Iran that the Anglo-Iranian Company had possessed.

Martin was sympathetic, His experience was hardly compatible with *Alice Through the Looking Glass*, which had, to his irritation, been recommended to him by Zaehner.

24 Middleton to A. D. M. Ross, 'Confidential', 11 February 1952, FO 371/98618.
25 Middleton to R. J. Bowker, 'Strictly Personal & Confidential', 4 January 1952 FO 371/98618.
26 Middleton to Bowker, 'Secret & Personal', 28 July 1952, FO 371/98602.
27 See Alan W. Ford, *The Anglo-Iranian Oil Dispute of 1951–1952* (Berkley, 1954), part 2, section 6.
28 Minute by Middleton, 22 July 1952, FO 248/1531; ibid; Middleton to Eden, 'Confidential', 28 July 1952, FO 371/98602; Middleton to Bowker, 'Personal & Secret', 28 July 1952, FO 371/96802; ibid.
29 Middleton to Eden, 'Confidential', 23 September 1952, FO 371/98604; ibid; Middleton to Eden, 5 October 1952, FO 371/98700; Middleton to Ross, 'Personal & Confidential', 20 October 1952, FO 371/98605; see minute by Berthoud, 13 October 1952, FO 371/98701.
30 Minute by Sarell, 22 January 1952, FO 371/98608; Middleton to Bowker, 'Personal and Secret', 1 September 1952, FO 371/98697; Burrows to Bowker, 'Secret', 30 July 1952, FO 371/98603; ibid; article of 30 July 1952 enclosed in ibid; Burrows to Bowker, 30 July 1952, ibid.
31 Minute by Makins, 7 June 1952, FO 371/98690; minute by Ramsbotham recording a F.O. meeting, 26 April 1952, FO 371/98690; ibid., see also his minute of 26 April 1952, FO 371/98689; minute by Eden, 4 May 1952, FO 371/98689.
32 *The Memoirs of Anthony Eden: Full Circle* (Boston, 1960) p. 227; ibid., p. 242.
33 Fergusson to Makins, 27 May 1952, FO 371/98689.
34 Quoted in a minute by Ramsbotham, 19 June 1952, FO 371/98690; as quoted in a minute by Bowker, 20 August 1952, FO 371/98694; minute by Eden, 18[?] July 1952, FO 371/98690.
35 Sir Eric Drake in *The Times*, 3 April 1970.
36 George McGhee, *Envoy to the Middle World* (New York, 1983) p. 341.
37 Minute by Gandy, 25 January 1954, FO 371/100078.
38 Obituary in *The Times*, 2 April 1970: '[In] 1954 . . . a new international consortium was established in which the company held 40 per cent and was compensated for what it had relinquished. This scheme was devised by him and it was largely by his efforts that it was brought to a successful conclusion.'
39 Minute by Makins, 19 July 1952, FO 371/98691.
40 Benjamin Shwadran, *The Middle East, Oil and the Great Powers* (New York, 1959) p. 390.

41 'I have little doubt', wrote A. D. M. Ross of the Eastern department, 'that both from motives of proper pride and from patriotism the Company would, in fact, bestir themselves to get into the Persian business again if they were asked to do so by Her Majesty's Government' (minute of 1 July 1953, FO 371/104616). Others were more sceptical.

42 See minute of 23 July 1953, FO 371/98691; minute by Makins, 9 August 1952, FO 371/98692; Franks to Eden, 'Secret', 24 August 1952, FO 371/98694; minute by Bowker, 23 August 1952, FO 371/98694.

43 Minute by Dixon, 19 February 1953, FO 371/104613.

44 C. M. Woodhouse, *Something Ventured* (London, 1982) pp. 106, 110, 114 and *passim*. Some of the information in the following passages is based on conversation with Mr Woodhouse as well as various other sources of private information.

45 This would confirm my own recollections of him over breakfasts in Oxford.

46 Woodhouse, *Something Ventured*, p. 118; ibid., p. 121.

47 Minute by Dixon, 5 December 1952, FO 371/98703; see Eden to Sir C. Steel, 'Top Secret', 4 December 1952, FO 371/98703; as reported in Makins to F.O., 'Top Secret', 7 March 1953, FO 371/104614.

48 For this round of the abortive talks see CAB 129/58 *et seq*; and Eden, *Memoirs*, pp. 232–5.

49 Minute by Dixon, 22 February 1953, FO 371/104613; minute by Dixon, 30 November 1952, FO 371/98703; minute by Dixon, 19 March 1953, FO 371/104614.

50 See Woodhouse, *Something Ventured*, p. 123, who does not however identify any of those involved in the decision except Eden.

51 Winston S. Churchill, *The World Crisis*, vol. I (New York, 1923), p. 134.

52 Woodhouse, *Something Ventured*, p. 125. See Christopher Andrew, *Secret Service: the Making of the British Intelligence Community* (London, 1985) p. 494.

53 See Stephen Ambrose, *Eisenhower: the President* (New York, 1984) p. 111.

54 Minute by Falle, 'Confidential', 2 August 1952, FO 248/1531; ibid.

55 Woodhouse, *Something Ventured*, p. 126.

56 Granada transcripts, *End of Empire: Iran*.

57 See Kermit Roosevelt, *Countercoup: the Struggle for the Control of Iran* (New York, 1979).

58 And the unpublished British documents add precious little to it. See for example the 'Tehran Situation Report Evening August 22 Secret' written by the official in charge of the 'Persian desk', Christopher Gandy (FO 371/104570). Gandy knew of MI6 involvement. But he and his Foreign Office colleagues were careful to write all documents as if the change of government had been an entirely Iranian development. Thus, according to the account prepared by the Eastern department:

> Musaddiq rose to power on a platform of nationalism and opposition to dictatorship. His collapse was due to his abandonment of the second of these principles and his increasingly dictatorial methods; and also to his failure as a nationalist, both by his inability to create a working oil industry of Persia's own and by his increasing reliance on a foreign-

inspired organisation, the Tudeh (Communist) party. (Memorandum of
24 August 1953, FO 371/104570)

This became the standard line within the government as well as the
interpretation given to the public. The British were much more discreet than
the Americans. Until the publication of Woodhouse's book, hints of MI6
involvement came mainly from American circles. Roosevelt, in the first edition
of his book which he was forced to withdraw, attempted to obscure the
complicity of the British government by alleging, erroneously, that the
conspiracy originated with the Anglo-Iranian Oil Company. See Thomas
Powers, 'A book held hostage', *Nation*, 12 April 1980.

59 *Saturday Evening Post*, 6 November 1954, quoted in Woodhouse, *Something
Ventured*, p. 129.

10

America, Iran, and the politics of intervention, 1951–1953

JAMES A. BILL

In 1950, the United States stumbled into the thick of a sticky and explosive confrontation between Britain and Iran concerning the political and economic role of the Anglo-Iranian Oil Company (AIOC). Although questions of production, pricing and labour conditions had always been the sources of tension between Britain and Iran, the major issue was one of national sovereignty. The existence of a concession allowing a large and powerful foreign corporation to exert complete control over the exploration and exploitation of the country's major resource was thoroughly condemned by nationalist forces in Iran. By the late 1940s nationalism had become a major political force in Iran and throughout the third world.

The AIOC reacted with a lack of sensitivity to the demands of the developing political forces. In response to the mounting Iranian domestic pressures pushing for a new relationship with the AIOC, in 1948 and 1949 the company sent Neville Gass on negotiating trips to Iran. The result was the Gass–Gulsha'iyan Agreement (also known as the Supplemental Agreement) which was signed by the government of Iran on 17 July 1949. The major thrust of this agreement was to increase the revenues to Iran by raising the royalty from 22 cents to 33 cents per barrel. Although the chairman of the AIOC argued strongly that this arrangement was the best offered to any Middle Eastern country by any oil company at the time, it was not viewed as such in Iran. Nor elsewhere. In 1949, for example, the devaluation of sterling had a negative effect upon the revenue Iran received from the company. This and numerous other factors, including the failure to provide adequately for the improvement of the conditions of Iranian workers, were not seriously addressed by the agreement.

In the frank words of the official historian of the AIOC:

The official failure to mitigate their impact, in spite of requests, at the least, showed an insensitivity to Iranian susceptibilities and a lack of appreciation of the exposed position of the AIOC. It contrasted with the American Treasury which facilitated the adoption of the 50:50 Agreements in the Middle East in 1950.

The AIOC historian goes on to state:

The Company, more concerned with the efficiency and cost of its operations in Iran, was over cautious in admitting the suitability of a growing number of Iranians to a widening range of posts. This was doubtless an error of judgement similar to the assessment by the Suez Canal Company of the competency of Egyptian pilots.[1]

Sir William Fraser, and a number of his associates in the company, did not understand the social and political forces in Iran. They seemed genuinely astonished when the agreement was widely condemned by a wide cross-section of Iranian society. In both the 15th and 16th Majlis the agreement was the subject of much fiery and emotional criticism. While a number of Iranian political polemicists castigated the agreement without even bothering to read it, many responsible and eminent political leaders, some with sensitivity to the British position, also opposed it. That the oil commission members voted unanimously to reject the Supplemental Agreement is an important indicator of the degree of its unpopularity in Iran.

In an important memo written on 10 September 1950, the leading petroleum analyst for the US Department of State summarized the situation in Iran. After discussing the provisions of the Supplemental Agreement, he went on to write:

The Iranian Majlis, however, refused the agreement in a 1949 session marked by emotional excesses and have since shown no disposition to sign. AIOC and the British are genuinely hated in Iran; approval of AIOC is treated as political suicide.[2]

In 1951 Allahyar Saleh told the United Nations Security Council that in 1950 the Anglo-Iranian Oil Company had earned a profit approaching £200 million from its oil enterprises in Iran. Of this, Iran had received only £16 million as royalties, share of profits and taxes. The company's profits that year alone, after deducting the share paid to Iran, amounted to more than the sum of £114 million paid to Iran during the entire past half century.[3] The Iranians often quoted the fact that Iran received considerably less in royalties than the sums paid in taxes to the British government. In 1948, for example, Iran received £9 million in royalties compared to the £28 million paid in taxes to the British government. In 1949 and 1950 the figures were

£13.5 and £16 million in royalties and £23 and £50.5 million in taxes respectively.[4] British Foreign Secretary Anthony Eden later revealed his understanding of the Iranian position when he wrote: 'I understood their feelings, for it must seem to them ingenuous that His Majesty's Government, as a large shareholder, should take increasing sums in taxation, and refuse the increased dividends from which the Iranian Government would have benefited.'[5]

Far more intolerable to Iran than the financial considerations was the question of national sovereignty. The AIOC refused to allow Iranian officials to examine their accounts and would announce unilaterally what the payments were to be. They did not always live up to contractual obligations to employ increasing percentages of local employees at all levels. About 70 per cent of the unskilled and semi-skilled labour force was Iranian, while the increase in the proportion of salaried Iranian personnel rose only slightly between 1935 and 1948. The AIOC's operation in Iran 'remained a classic example of an enclave organization – a foreign-oriented industry superimposed on an entirely different economy, without any real economic linkages between it and the rest of the economy'.[6]

The size of the expanding chasm that opened between Iran and Britain can be seen in the distorted perceptions that dominated the thinking of each side. The British felt that their influence in Iran was benign and that without English technological support Iran would have remained a backward desert land. Their many interventions in the past had served to protect Iran from its aggressive Russian neighbour to the north. Therefore, even some of the most learned of 'old Persian hands' in Britain professed horror at the ingratitude displayed by Musaddiq and the Iranian nationalists.

After praising AIOC's 'genuine benevolence' which 'far exceeded any contractual or legal obligations', Brigadier Stephen Longrigg writes:

> The whole of this effort, the whole of a half-century of generous and enlightened treatment of its own workers and the public was, in the final destiny of the Company in Persia, not only treated as of no account, but attacked in terms suggesting not mere neglect but the crudest exploitation.[7]

Even talented Iranologist Peter Avery, after critically describing the nationalization of AIOC, approvingly quotes a correspondent's observation about the 'innate national yearning' of Iranians for 'self-immolation'. Avery then explains the facts of power politics in Iran: 'The heyday of national self-assertion, however, was to have its price; the squeeze, administered by the more powerful to the weaker, had inevitably to begin.'[8]

The Iranian viewed the British as a nation of satanically clever and shrewd manipulators whose actions always brought power and prosperity to the British Isles while smilingly and secretly planting seeds of decay and impotence elsewhere. For a century, the Iranians tended to blame any negative occurrence on 'the hidden hand of the English'. Musaddiq described the British to special envoy Averell Harriman in Tehran in 1951 in the following terms: 'You do not know how crafty they are. You do not know how evil they are. You do not know how they sully everything they touch.' When Harriman responded that the British were pretty much like most other people, some good, some bad, and most in between, Musaddiq responded: 'You do not know them. You do not know them.'[9]

In Iranian politics, everyone's political opponent was automatically considered to be a tool of the British. The charge traditionally emanated loudest from the weaker party in any competitive relationship. Generations of Iranian political leaders carry the reputation of being British agents. Despite the fact that the relationship between Musaddiq and the British was one of mutual distrust and intense dislike (already in the 1930s the British had tagged Musaddiq as a 'demigogue and a windbag'),[10] even he was accused of being pro-British by the Shah. In this kind of environment, it would have been impossible for the AIOC to convince the Iranians that it was seriously engaged in a programme designed to protect the interests of Iran as much as those of England – even had it been true.

In mid-1950, political events in Iran began to move very rapidly. An 18-member oil commission was established in the Majlis, and after meeting through the summer and fall of 1950, on 25 November 1950 it voted to reject the Supplemental Agreement. The chairman of this commission was Muhammad Musaddiq. He and other nationalist political leaders of the time increasingly began to demand the nationalization of the oil company. One month later, the Saudis publicly announced their Fifty–fifty Agreement. Although the AIOC now hinted that it might also be willing to consider a fifty–fifty agreement, the company insisted that it would not negotiate as long as Iran was considering the option of nationalization. But, by now, 'the 50–50 sharing of profits from oil had come too late – several years too late to stem the tide of nationalization.'[11] In the words of an American journalist in Tehran at the time: 'Now, as previously, Anglo-Iranian seems to suffer from the time lag which has caused it to miss not only one bus but a whole series of busses.'[12]

On 3 March 1951, Prime Minister Razmara spoke before the Majlis, supporting the Supplemental Agreement and opposing the idea of nationalization. His assassination four days later only hardened the respective positions. On 15 March 1951, the Iranian Majlis passed a bill to nationalize the oil industry. The Senate ratified this action five days later. After a two-month transitional premiership by Husayn Ala, Muhammad Musaddiq became prime minister of Iran on 29 April 1951. The nationalization of the AIOC was described by one observer as 'the most traumatic experience to afflict the international oil industry in the past forty-five years.'[13]

Dr Muhammad Musaddiq: a brief profile

The opposition to British policy in Iran crystallized with the influence of the personality of Muhammad Musaddiq. Born in Tehran on 19 May 1882 into what was the most prominent Iranian political family in the last century, Musaddiq began his political career before the turn of the century when he was still in his teens.[14] Educated in Tehran and Europe, he held a number of provincial positions and was elected as deputy to the 5th and 6th Majlis. It was as deputy to the 5th Majlis in 1925 that Musaddiq spoke and voted against Riza Khan's accession to power as the first Pahlavi Shah. Riza Shah saw to it that Musaddiq was not elected to the 7th Majlis. During the Riza Shah period (1926–41), Muhammad Musaddiq was frozen out of politics, spending most of his time at his estate in Ahmadabad near Tehran. He also spent short periods of time abroad for medical reasons, in exile in Birjand, and in gaol for political reasons.

In 1944 Musaddiq was elected to the 14th Majlis when he immediately gained national recognition by cleverly deflecting Russian and American drives to gain oil concessions in Iran. In October of 1949 at the age of 67, Musaddiq was the moving force behind the establishment of the National Front. This loose coalition of political groups professed liberal, democratic goals and strongly opposed all forms of foreign intervention into the internal affairs of Iran. It was Musaddiq and the Front who mounted a major challenge to the traditional style of politics in Iran and to the forces that supported this system.

Muhammad Musaddiq has been one of the least understood political figures of the century. Both diplomats and learned scholarly observers have seriously misinterpreted him over the years. Much of the literature has mistakenly focused on his physical characteristics – his age, his dress, his health, his walk, his manner of speech, his etiquette, his hearing. Writer Gérard de Villiers describes Musaddiq as 'a pint-sized trouble-maker' with 'the agility of a goat' as he 'pranced before a group of journalists'.[15] Both de Villiers and Leonard Moseley describe Musaddiq as having a 'yellow' face and a running nose that he did not bother to wipe.[16] Western observers were fascinated by Musaddiq's pyjamas and proclivity to weep.

The American mass media provided particularly emotional and misleading portrayals of Musaddiq. Besides the continuous distorted exaggerations of his personal characteristics, the US press labelled him a dictator, even going so far at times as to consider him the Iranian equivalent of Mussolini, Hitler and Stalin. The *New York Times*, for example, routinely described him as a 'dictator' – a term the paper never once used to describe the Shah during the 25 years he ruled Iran after Musaddiq's political demise.[17] Such images seriously hindered communication and understanding and contributed to the political confrontation that took place in the early 1950s. A closer examination of Musaddiq's background and politics would indicate that he was a shrewd statesman, a man of principle, an old-fashioned liberal democrat, and an individual who contained within himself the hopes and aspirations of the bulk of the Iranian people at the time. He was a statesman who achieved great success and enormous failure.

From an early age, Muhammad Musaddiq never seemed to tire of tilting at political windmills in Iran. As a young and relatively inexperienced finance official in the early years of this century, he attempted to implement massive reform measures. In their secret profile of Musaddiq the British claimed, undoubtedly with considerable accuracy and some satisfaction, that the young administrator 'destroyed indiscriminately the good with the bad, and at the end the organization was worse off than before, as he proved himself entirely incapable of making reforms'.[18] Within his own extended family, Musaddiq had a reputation of inflexibility and unwillingness to extend favours to kinsfolk; he consciously attempted *not* to extend any special assistance to relatives. A grandson points out that relatives simply did not count when Musaddiq made political and economic decisions: 'When the person with whom he was dealing was a relative, that person was considered last.'[19] His conviction and courage were especially noted in his public opposition to Riza Shah in the fall of 1925.

Muhammad Musaddiq was a beloved, charismatic figure to Iranians of all social classes. His wry and outrageous sense of humour was infectious although not understood in the West. His very emotionalism and physical frailty were characteristics that endeared him to his people who saw in him the embodiment of a weak and embattled Iran. In the words of one keen scholar of Iran who was not sympathetic to Musaddiq: 'In thus behaving, Mossadeq was, perhaps very consciously, presenting the antithesis of the stern, authoritarian figure common to traditional Iran. Instead, he substituted the figure of tragedy, the man of sorrow who took upon himself burdens and obligations to be resolved by self-sacrifice.'[20]

Musaddiq was an old-fashioned liberal who believed neither in ideological dogma nor in the use of coercion in government. On several occasions, he stressed to the people that democracy was the best form of government. If not, he liked to ask, then why had the most powerful western countries adopted such a system? In his own words in 1944:

> If the ship captain is one individual only, whenever that individual becomes incapacitated or whenever he dies, the ship is doomed to sink. But if there are many captains, the illness or death of one particular man has no effect on the safety of the ship . . . No nation goes anyplace under the shadow of dictatorship.[21]

When forced to resort to extraordinary means to maintain his premiership as Iran entered a crisis in 1952–3, he was visibly uncomfortable and unhappy. In the end, he was overthrown because he would not risk wide-scale bloodshed in his land; he refused to compromise with Iran's external opponents while at the same time he refused to annihilate his enemies at home. As his followers insisted for years afterwards, Musaddiq lacked the killer instinct. Or, in the words of a perceptive Iranian feminist and physician: 'Politically, Dr Musaddiq had a slipped disc.'[22] Twenty-five years later, Iranian revolutionaries swore that they would never repeat 'the Musaddiq mistake'.

Throughout his political career, Musaddiq had one pre-eminent political preoccupation: he was utterly opposed to foreign intervention and interference in Iran. In his own words as a deputy to the 14th Majlis: 'The Iranian himself must administer his own house.'[23] In the words of a French newspaper:

> The opposition called him an Anglophile. The Russians entitled him the servant of American imperialism. The British labelled him a Communist. But, in the end, it was clear that Musaddiq was a national champion who without any foreign support whatsoever fought for the independence and freedom of his homeland.[24]

Since the major means through which external influence was exerted in Iran was through oil, the ultimate confrontation between Musaddiq and the foreign-controlled petroleum industry was inevitable. After successfully derailing an American–Russian drive for oil concessions in 1944, Musaddiq next prepared himself to take on the powerful Anglo-Iranian Oil Company which had been active in Iran for four decades. Musaddiq entered this fray with considerable support at the core of which was the new consciousness of a deeply nationalistic middle class. Articulate, well informed and angry, the members of this class rallied around Musaddiq as they sought to take control of their most valuable natural resource – petroleum.

The United States and the Musaddiq movement

By the late 1940s, the United States had become deeply concerned about events in Iran and especially about the position that the Anglo-Iranian Oil Company had taken with respect to Iranian requests and demands. State Department officials argued that the Iranian position was not without merit and that unless a compromise was reached, nationalization could easily become a reality. In the words of the petroleum adviser to Assistant Secretary of State George McGhee in 1951:

A year before nationalization, in May 1950, the State Department sent out a cable saying that we took the threat of nationalization seriously and recommended that others do the same. In September George McGhee was asked by the British Foreign Office to discuss the problem with the board of directors of the Anglo-Iranian Oil Company. He walked into the room, told them how seriously we took the threat of nationalization, also told them that the American companies who had been apprized of the situation in Iran felt Sir William Fraser could give in on the terms Razmara was asking. There were four terms, nonfinancial terms. The American companies, when we presented these terms to them, were amazed that no more money was involved, at least in the short run. The terms were that Iran should get prices as low as AIOC sold anyone else; they should have a program of 'Iranization,' which is constantly a source of friction – more Iranians in the higher jobs; they also wanted a check on the books because they got 20 percent of the general reserves and the profits.

Sir William Fraser, in a masterful statement, said, 'One penny more and the company goes broke.' We felt that was unrealistic . . .[25]

Early American disagreement with the British was easily seen in the crackling tension that existed between George McGhee and British officials. McGhee was a brilliant young man who was born in Waco, Texas and was educated at the University of Oklahoma before he attended Oxford as a Rhodes scholar. A self-declared Anglophile, McGhee had over the years developed many close friendships with influential British personalities. In June 1949, McGhee was appointed Assistant Secretary of State to Dean Acheson with whom he had very strong personal and professional relations. Despite his respect for Britain, George McGhee had serious reservations about British policy in Iran. He felt strongly that the British were forcing nationalization upon themselves and on more than one occasion he bluntly told them so. In return, the British referred to him as 'that infant prodigy' who was recommending a policy of 'appeasement' in the face of Iranian pressure.[26]

McGhee was a key official in a Democratic Administration that was relatively sensitive to the tides of nationalism then beginning to assert themselves in Asia and the Middle East. His views were shared in large part by Henry Grady whom he recommended to be America's ambassador to Iran in replacement of John Wiley. Grady, who served in Iran from July 1950 until September 1951, was an official with great personal experience in administering American aid programmes in the region, having competently directed the huge US aid programme in Greece after the war. As an Irish-American with an innate sympathy for the principle of self-determination of nations, Grady had little respect for British foreign policy. Like McGhee, Grady was not popular in England. In the words of a leading scholar of British imperialism: 'He had developed a substantial reputation in British circles for meddling in the affairs of the British Empire. He sympathized with nationalist aspirations.'[27] Grady was a hardheaded, short, baked-potato-like figure who is still sardonically criticized in the hallways of British Petroleum. He did, however, understand the strength of the nationalist urge in Iran and correctly foresaw the explosive consequences of AIOC policy at the time.

According to Grady's associates at the American Embassy at the time, the ambassador sensed trouble, and in a trip to London six months before nationalization he attempted to explain this to high-ranking officials at AIOC. Grady's pleas were ignored and, upon his return to Tehran, he held a country team meeting in which with emotion he critically recounted the response his arguments had received in London. Another important American diplomat stationed in Tehran at the time described the attitude of the AIOC as 'high-handed'. AIOC had a 'piggy-wiggy' attitude towards their profits and 'they didn't seem to realize that the world had changed.'[28]

In Britain, the inflexible hardline approach was best exemplified by the attitude of Sir William Fraser who, unlike his predecessor Sir John Cadman, was relatively insensitive to the changing times. Although Fraser had been a protégé of Cadman, he failed to understand the intricacies of the social and political relationships of the Middle East. Fraser and his colleagues seemed to American officials to be quite unaware of the situation of Iran. In the words of a State Department official at the time:

In December [1951], we had a meeting of the chiefs of mission from all of our Near East posts, and as a final problem in the oil picture, they discussed what we should do in the case of nationalization of AIOC property. Unfortunately AIOC didn't take the hint; they felt they didn't have to give in. Harriman in his comments following his Tehran trip said he never in his entire experience had known of a company where absentee management was so malignant. Walter Levy says Harriman spent more time in Tehran than the total combined time of the board of directors of AIOC. They didn't know what was going on or the needs and demands of the Iranian people.[29]

In Britain, there were several key officials who generally supported the Fraser school of thought. These included Geoffrey Furlonge, the head of the Eastern department of the Foreign Office, Emmanuel Shinwell, the Minister of Defence, and especially Labour Party Foreign Secretary Herbert Morrison, all of whom favoured an active, even interventionist approach. These views were shared by the British ambassadors in Iran at the time, Sir John Le Rougetel and especially Sir Francis Shepherd. Shepherd was clearly contemptuous of Iranians and his diplomacy was not subtle. It is not surprising, therefore, that he reported that US Ambassador Grady was 'by temperament quite unsuited to dealing with Persian deviousness and intrigue . . .' Morrison and Shepherd may not have disagreed too much with the opinion of a writer in the *Daily Telegraph* who assessed the British capacity in the following words: 'We have only for one moment to stretch out a terrible right arm and we should hear no more from Persia but the scampering of timid feet.'[30]

Labour Party leaders such as Prime Minister Clement Attlee and Foreign Secretary Ernest Bevin, on the other hand, were opposed to any direct intervention in Iran and favoured a prudent, more conciliatory approach. British government officials did in private strongly criticize the AIOC and its ownership. In a memorandum to Morrison, for example, the minister Kenneth Younger wrote in October 1951:

> The principal reason why our advance information was inadequate was the short-sightedness and the lack of political awareness shown by the Anglo-Iranian Oil Company. They were far better placed than anybody to make a proper estimate of the situation but, as far as I am aware, they never even seriously tried to do so.[31]

Even within the AIOC, there was not unanimity. Sir Frederick Leggett, AIOC's experienced labour adviser in Iran criticized his own company which in his opinion 'still seemed to be thinking in terms of offering a little money here and another sop there, but all this . . . was entirely beside the point. What was required was a fresh start, on the basis of equal partnership.'[32]

In the early years of the crisis, the American leadership agreed with the Attlees, Bevins, Youngers and Leggetts. In March 1951, Secretary of State Acheson stated that: 'We recognize the right of sovereign states to nationalize provided there is just compensation . . .'[33] Also, in a meeting between British and American officials in Washington in April of 1951, the Americans made it clear that they recognized the Iranian right to nationalize. In these early days of the crisis, the British seriously considered a military response. They were finally dissuaded from doing so because of the unsettled political situation in newly independent India, the conflict between India and Pakistan over Kashmir, and ongoing political crises in Egypt where British interests were being severely challenged. An even more important reason for the British decision not to intervene militarily was the strong US opposition to any such move.

The policy of the Truman Administration as developed by Secretary of State Acheson was to attempt to placate the British while at the same time trying to convince Musaddiq to agree to a compromise solution. United States leaders were convinced that any British military attack was not only unwarranted but also might serve as a pretext for Soviet intervention. As Acheson put it in mid-May 1951: 'Only on invitation of the Iranian Government, or Soviet military intervention, or a Communist *coup d'etat* in Tehran, or to evacuate British nationals in danger of attack could we support the use of military force.'[34] Anthony Eden, who had replaced Morrison as Foreign Secretary later admitted that 'the temptation to intervene to reclaim this stolen property must have been strong, but pressure from the United States was vigorous against any such action.'[35]

While holding off the British military urge, President Truman sent trouble-shooter and special envoy Averell Harriman to Iran in July of 1951. Harriman, and his team, which included oil expert Walter Levy and diplomat-linguist Vernon Walters, were greeted upon arrival in Tehran by rioting crowds reportedly organized by the Tudeh Party but in part provoked by British agents. Harriman and Levy made a major effort to instruct Musaddiq in the realities of international oil economics and politics. They managed to convince him to receive another British negotiating mission which arrived in Tehran on 4 August 1951 under the leadership of Richard Stokes. Stokes, a wealthy businessman but a somewhat clumsy negotiator, also failed in his mission even though he felt that a business deal could be arranged.

Harriman, Levy and Walters all established excellent personal rapport with Musaddiq but were unable to break the impasse. At one point when Levy was attempting to convince the prime minister that it would be in Iran's interest to accept a negotiated settlement, Musaddiq responded by asking Levy about the Boston Tea Party when America was struggling desperately against British colonial control. What, he asked Levy, would American independence leaders have responded if some Persian mediators had come aboard the ships anchored in Boston harbour and asked the colonists not to throw that tea overboard?[36]

During the time that the American negotiating team was in Iran, Husayn Makki took its members on a tour of the oilfields and facilities in the south-west. There, they were shown the separate facilities and the superior quarters enjoyed by the British staff. Much was made of drinking fountains that were marked 'Not for Iranians'. In the discussions, the Harriman team pointed out that the Iranian employees of the AIOC were immeasurably better off than their compatriots who worked for local industrialists. The response was that the comparison must be made with British counterparts who enjoyed superior salaries and living conditions. At one point, the Americans went so far as to ask Musaddiq about the working and living conditions of the peasants who lived on his estates. Despite this, the Harriman team recognized the Iranian labour grievances and considered them legitimate.

Musaddiq visited the United States between 8 October and 18 November 1951. During this visit, he presented Iran's case before the UN Security Council and engaged in intensive discussions with high-level American diplomats, including President Truman and Secretary of State Acheson. Most of the negotiations were carried out between Musaddiq and George McGhee who estimates that he spent over 75 hours in discussions with Musaddiq. Painstakingly, McGhee and Musaddiq worked out a proposal to solve the impasse, and then Musaddiq delayed his return to Iran while the British elections took place on 25 October 1951.

The main points of the McGhee–Musaddiq proposal included the following:

1 A national Iranian oil company would be established and would be responsible for the exploration, production and transportation of crude oil.
2 The Abadan refinery would be sold to a non-British firm which would select its own technicians.
3 The AIOC would establish a purchasing organization to buy, ship and market Iranian oil.
4 The contract would be in effect for 15 years and would provide for a minimum of 30 million tons of oil a year.
5 The price of petroleum would be determined through negotiations between Iran and Britain and would not exceed $1.10 per barrel.

The final result of this pricing scheme would in fact have closely approximated the fifty–fifty profit-sharing arrangement then in effect in Saudi Arabia. American officials were very hopeful that these terms would be an acceptable foundation for negotiation to the new British government.[37]

Immediately after the elections, the new Conservative government in Britain, with Anthony Eden as Foreign Secretary, met on five separate occasions with American officials to discuss the proposal. In the end, the British refused to accept the compromise. Eden found the nationalization principle unacceptable. The exclusion of British technicians from Iran was another requirement that upset the British government. Acheson telephoned the Department of State from Paris after his final meeting with Eden and asked the department to inform the waiting Musaddiq that the British had rejected the proposal. George McGhee, who had worked so hard to hammer out the details of the proposal, was shaken and deeply disappointed by the news. In his words: 'There was silence as we grasped the fact that we had failed. To me it was almost the end of the world – I attached so much importance to an agreement and honestly thought we had provided the British a basis for one.'

McGhee then went to see Musaddiq who was staying at the Shoreham Hotel. The prime minister 'merely said, "You've come to send me home." "Yes," McGhee responded, "I'm sorry to have to tell you that we can't bridge the gap between you and the British. It's a great disappointment to us as it must be to you." ' McGhee concludes: 'It was a moment I will never forget. He accepted the result quietly with no recriminations.'

Musaddiq had made the best offer in his power during those fall days in

Washington in 1951. Walter Levy has indicated that given the political situation in Iran at the time, Musaddiq had very little room for manoeuvre. He not only did not trust the British, he did not trust many Iranians. He did not know who he could count on. In the words of US diplomats stationed in Iran at the time, Musaddiq and his government were prisoners of the politics of the 'street'. And this was already before his coalition had begun to fall apart and many of his supporters, cutting their own deals, deserted him.

The United States, meanwhile, had taken important actions to placate the British. On 10 May 1951, the Department of State issued a press release that stated: 'Those United States oil companies which would be best able to conduct operations such as the large-scale and complex industry in Iran have indicated to this Government that they would not in the face of unilateral action by Iran against the British company be willing to undertake operations in that country.' This effectively helped the British impose a collective boycott upon Iranian oil operations and exportation. George McGhee himself played an important role in this policy and has written: '. . . I am not sure that my British friends ever quite understood the strong efforts I had made to keep American oil companies from taking advantage of AIOC's difficulties . . .'[38] Special attention was given to independent American companies who had every incentive to attempt to penetrate the rich Iranian market at this time. But they too ultimately agreed to stay away from the Iranian scene. For this, they would claim their reward in 1955.

The Truman Administration was also concerned about the possible contagion of the nationalization in Iran. If Iran could nationalize the powerful British oil company, then why couldn't the other oil-producing countries do the same thing to American companies? On 24 May 1951, only days after the release of the important State Department memorandum quoted in the paragraph above, Arthur Krock reported the following revealing conversation with President Truman:

> But these foreign oil countries have a good case against some groups of foreign capital. The President said he thought Mexico's nationalization of oil was 'right,' even thought so at the time; but it was regarded as 'treason' to say so. If, however, the Iranians carry out their plans as stated, Venezuela and other countries on whose supply we depend will follow suit. That is the great danger in the Iranian controversy with the British.[39]

The Iranians were quite aware of this American position. The deputy minister of Court, for example, bluntly told the Second Secretary of the US Embassy in Tehran that America's position in Iran 'was primarily motivated by commercial interest'. He said that the US would not permit any oil agreement that would totally benefit Iran because if this occurred 'the Saudi Arabs would ask for a similar deal'.[40]

Despite this American position, the British were very suspicious of American intentions. Their own Iran specialists in the field hinted that there seemed to be evidence that Musaddiq and Kashani were receiving significant financial support from an external source and that it 'was not impossible' that the United States was that source.[41] Also, the British suspected that the United States was attempting to use Musaddiq as a wedge to help drive American oil interests into their Iranian preserve. The position taken by American oilman George McGhee when he recommended that AIOC come to an accommodation with Iran added to British suspicion. They became even more deeply concerned when Harriman and Levy openly suggested that the AIOC's former dominant position in the country would almost certainly have to be changed. The fact that the United States provided Iran with both economic and military aid in 1951 and early in 1952 did nothing to allay the British suspicions.

As the oil crisis dragged on, as political events in Iran became increasingly stormy, and as the British applied diplomatic pressure, the United States began to shift its position. As time went on, US decision-makers came around to the British idea that the best way to confront the situation was to actively seek the overthrow of the Musaddiq government and to assure its replacement with a regime more amenable to compromise and negotiation. Before Eisenhower took office in early 1953, there had been some discussion in Washington (especially in the CIA) of covert political measures to intervene in Iran. In general, however, this policy was not discussed at the higher levels until 1953.[42]

There were four major interrelated reasons why the United States changed its policy from one of diplomacy and conciliation to one of intervention and confrontation. Two of the reasons can be classified as major immediate causes and two as contributing causes. The two general political causes were (1) US preoccupation with the communist challenge in Iran; and (2) US concern about the accessibility of the rich Iranian oil reserves to the western world. Of the two tactical contributing causes, one was positive and the other negative in character: the first was the effective British campaign to bring the United States to accept their approach to the crisis; the second was Musaddiq's own political methodology which ultimately proved to be counter-productive and self-defeating.

As the early 1950s unfolded, the United States government became increasingly obsessed with the challenge of communism. China had recently adopted a communist government; the Korean war was in progress; the Chinese had invaded and occupied Tibet; and Ho Chi Minh and the Vietminh were striving for control in Vietnam. At home, ideologues such as Senator Joseph McCarthy, who had built their political careers upon the foundations of hysterical threats of communist infiltration, were in the ascendancy. American policy makers had great difficulty throughout this entire period distinguishing nationalist movements from communist movements in the third world. This distinction was especially difficult to see in Iran where there was in fact a strong and well-organized national communist movement represented by the Tudeh Party. Also, ignorance of things Iranian did not enable American leaders to draw such critical distinctions. The mass media only reinforced the confusion by portraying Musaddiq himself as a communist and his movement as communist inspired or communist controlled.[43] *Time* magazine went so far as to refer to the Musaddiq national movement as 'one of the worst calamities to the anti-Communist world since the Red conquest of China'.[44] This massive national preoccupation with communism as a direct and immediate threat to the United States was a powerful force behind the American decision to support a move against Musaddiq and his government.

The second major reason for the dramatic change in American policy relates to the politics of oil. Many knowledgeable analysts believe that Musaddiq was used as an American wedge to break the AIOC's monopolistic grip on Iran's oil resources. According to Mustafa Fateh, the best informed Iranian oil economist long employed by the AIOC, there is no doubt that American and British oil interests reached an entente on this issue. In exchange for American support in overthrowing the Musaddiq government, the British grudgingly permitted US companies a 40 per cent interest in Iranian oil. Fatih pointed out that American companies had made several attempts to penetrate the Iranian fields but had failed before the appearance of Musaddiq.

A decade earlier, in October 1943, James Byrnes, then director of the Office of War Mobilization, wrote a letter to President Roosevelt decrying the fact that Britain controlled all of Iran's oil. According to Byrnes, the government should request the British to assign the United States one-third of their interest in Iranian oil as compensation for American contributions to the war effort.[45] Although the president took no action on this recommendation, it was clear that the United States had an eye on Iranian oil. While Roosevelt denied to Winston Churchill early in 1944 that the United States was looking with 'sheep's eyes', it is probably true that they did have at least one eagle's eye on these reserves. The British certainly thought so in the early 1950s. Not only did they believe that the Americans wanted access to Iranian oil, they also thought that the United States was attempting to push an agreement in order to weaken the AIOC *vis-à-vis* the large multinational American companies. In August 1950, for example, the British Foreign Office reported that 'the State Department may have been over much influenced by the American oil companies, who wish to see our companies driven into an uncompetitive position by constant pressure to raise their royalties and labor conditions.'[46]

There is little doubt that petroleum considerations were involved in the American decision to assist in the overthrow of the Musaddiq government.

In an extraordinary meeting on 10 October 1951 between Secretary of State Dean Acheson and Assistant Secretary George McGhee with the heads of the five major American oil companies, Mr McGhee stated that the US government had 'at all times sought to keep in mind both the importance of maintaining the continued independence of Iran and the impact of any action we might take on the U.S. oil interests in the Middle East which were represented by the group present, as well as on oil and business interests elsewhere'. The oil companies' response was somewhat blunt and self-serving:

> Representatives of the [oil] group emphasized the very grave consequences of giving the Iranians terms more favorable than those received by other countries. They expressed the opinion that if this were done the entire international oil industry would be seriously threatened. The opinion was offered that even the loss of Iran would be preferable to the instability which would be created by making too favorable an agreement with Iran. Other representatives pointed out that not just the oil industry was involved but indeed all American investment overseas and the concept of the sanctity of contractual relations.[47]

One important plan seriously considered by the United States government involved the formation of an American oil consortium to be formed of various American companies. This all-American consortium would purchase oil from Iran and would then sell it to other international companies, including AIOC. This plan was favoured by Secretary of Defense Robert Lovett and General Omar Bradley; it also caught the interest of Secretary of State Acheson. The Justice Department, however, strongly opposed it on the grounds that it ran counter to the anti-trust litigation then underway against the American oil companies. Another plan considered at somewhat lower levels was proposed by Charles Rayner of the Department of Interior. This proposal recommended that the British government immediately withdraw from its position in AIOC and that the company be placed 'preferably under Dutch of American leadership'.[48] Such proposals indicate that the United States had definite interest in gaining entry to the Iranian oil business.

Thus, both the politics of oil and the preoccupation with the communist threat were major reasons for the American policy change. Furthermore, both factors were interrelated and mutually reinforcing. The irony is that at the time when one branch of the US government (the Department of State) was in close and constant contact with the oil companies concerning the Iranian crisis, another branch of the government (the Department of Justice) was vigorously pursuing an anti-trust campaign against the companies.

On 23 January 1952, President Truman sent a memorandum to the secretaries of State, Defense, Interior, Commerce, and to the Federal Trade Commission which stated: 'I have requested the Attorney General to institute appropriate legal proceedings with respect to the operations of the International Oil Cartel. I should like for you to cooperate with him in gathering the evidence required for these proceedings.'[49] Throughout 1952, the Department of Justice pursued this investigation charging among other things that the oil cartel used the mechanism of joint companies to eliminate competition both in price and in production. Early in the proceedings, a US District Court ruled that the AIOC was an instrumentality of the British government and was therefore immune from investigation. Also, in early 1953, President Truman moved the investigation from a grand jury format to a civil action proceeding. In the process, the Department of Justice found itself confronted politically by the Department of State, the Department of Defense, and the Joint Chiefs of Staff. In the last days of the Truman Administration, a major debate took place in Washington concerning whether or not this anti-trust campaign should be pursued. It is important to recall that at this time the US government had enlisted the co-operative support of the various oil companies in the struggle with Musaddiq.

Given the difficulties in Iran and the growing concern about the spread of communism, the Department of Justice saw its anti-cartel case neutralized by arguments stressing national security. Both Acheson and then Dulles used the national security argument to encourage co-operative relations between US foreign policy makers and the leaders of the oil companies. In the words of a Department of Justice official of the time: 'The pressures were continuous from month to month, sometimes from week to week, to downgrade the importance of prosecution of the cartel case.' The White House issued a statement to John Foster Dulles summarizing the American position on this important issue: 'It will be assumed that the enforcement of the antitrust laws of the United States against the Western oil companies operating in the Near East may be deemed secondary to the national security interest . . .'[50] There was, in the end, little doubt among decision makers in the executive branch of government in Washington 'that the global battle against Communism must take precedence against any complication about anti-trust'.[51] These major concerns about communism and the availability of petroleum were thus interlocked. Together, they drove America to a policy of direct intervention.

Within this general political context, Dr Musaddiq himself unwittingly adopted a political tactic that only reinforced the decisions referred to above. In order to encourage desperately needed financial and moral assistance from the United States, he began to raise the spectre of a communist threat to his country. He argued that American assistance was essential if Iran were to stay out of the communist camp. In a letter to

President Eisenhower of 28 May 1953 requesting badly needed American financial assistance, for example, Musaddiq warned: 'there can be serious consequences, from an international viewpoint as well, if this situation is permitted to continue. If prompt and effective aid is not given this country now, any steps that might be taken tomorrow to compensate for the negligence of today might well be too late.'[52] This approach had exactly the opposite effect to the one desired by the prime minister. Rather than attracting aid, it provided further justification for those US policy makers who agreed with the British that intervention and overthrow were the only realistic alternatives.

The American drift to the British position was also hastened by the enigmatic nature of Musaddiq himself whose negotiating techniques were enormously frustrating to the very best diplomats in the United States. George McGhee, Averell Harriman, and Vernon Walters all failed despite weeks of intensive discussions with the Iranian prime minister.[53] Dr Musaddiq zigged and zagged, advanced and retreated, hurried and stalled until the American negotiators were hopelessly confused. In the words of Walters who enjoyed excellent personal relations with Musaddiq:

> It seemed to me that he reversed Lenin's adage that one must take a step backward in order to take two forward. Dr Mossadegh had learned to take one step forward in order to take two backward. After a day's discussions, Mr Harriman would bring Mossadegh to a certain position. The next day when we returned to renew the discussion, not only was Mossadegh not at the position where he was at the end of the previous day, he wasn't even at the position where he had been at the beginning of the day before that. He was somewhere back around the middle of the day before yesterday.[54]

According to Secretary of State Acheson: 'It was like walking in a maze and every so often finding oneself at the beginning again.'[55] Although Musaddiq was no more stubborn than the British, he repeatedly insisted that the days of British exploitation in Iran were over, that nationalization would stand, and that Iran would determine the compensation to be paid by the AIOC.

Not only dictated by his own personal convictions, Musaddiq's unyielding position was essential within the context of the social forces at work in Iran at the time. Fierce pressure was exerted continually from the communist left, the growing nationalist middle, and the xenophobic religious right. Economic rationality models and cool financial reasoning made little sense in this climate of political upheaval and nationalist fervour. Also, Musaddiq was a magnificent negativist in that he had the courage to challenge but lacked the capacity to construct. In a secret meeting of the Majlis Oil Commission in 1951 he argued that, in order to defeat communism, reforms had to be made. In order to implement reforms, money was essential. In order to obtain money, nationalization was necessary. When questioned how he proposed to convert oil into money by a nationalization that made it impossible to sell and market that oil, he responded: 'I have no intention of coming to terms with anyone. Rather than come to terms with the British, I will seal the oil wells with mud.'[56] In this situation, the United States ultimately found Britain to be a more congenial and predictable party to deal with. The British understood this and applied diplomatic pressure on the United States throughout the period.

American foreign-policy makers were somewhat in awe of the British experience and expertise concerning Iran. Eden, for example, had read oriental languages at Oxford and had emphasized Persian as his first language of study and Arabic his second. He was extremely knowledgeable about Iranian history and culture, and his diplomatic experience with Iran dated back to 1933 when he was under-secretary in the Foreign Office at the time of the tense negotiations with Iran over the oil agreement. With very few exceptions – primarily, American citizens from missionary backgrounds who had lived in Iran – the United States was still largely illiterate in Iranian matters. The personal connections that American and British officials maintained with one another in conjunction with the aura of Britain's special knowledge of Iran combined to pull America to the British position. Anthony Eden himself has stated that he knew 'that the United States Ambassador took the view that the United States ought not to intrude its views too much in a matter where large British interests were at stake'.[57]

While Acheson and the Truman Democratic Administration were becoming increasingly exasperated and impatient with the situation in Iran, it was with Dulles and the Eisenhower Republican Administration that the United States decided to intervene. Kermit Roosevelt, the field commander of the American intervention, has stated that the plan was deliberately withheld from the Democrats since they were considered too sympathetic to Musaddiq. According to Roosevelt:

> Acheson was absolutely fascinated by Dr Mossadegh. He was in fact sympathetic to him. I didn't feel like raising the matter with him. Neither did Allen Dulles, because we knew that Foster Dulles was going to be taking Acheson's place. We saw no point in getting the outgoing administration involved in something we thought they might be less enthusiastic about than the Republicans . . . Allen Dulles said, 'Let's not get this thing evolved until the Republicans and my brother Foster take over.'[58]

The change in administration in Washington in January of 1953 occurred 14 months after the Conservative government of Winston Churchill and Anthony Eden came to power in Britain. In the words of David Bruce, US ambassador to France who had been meeting with the British in Paris about the oil crisis, the new British government was quite different from its predecessor; it had a new attitude 'which starts from Churchill with the roar of a wounded lion, becomes more articulate with Eden, as he remembers twitting the Laborites for weakness during the campaign, and is fully rationalized by the civil servants . . .'[59]

The new governments in Britain and the United States were more susceptible to the arguments of the oil industry and were considerably more paranoid about the communist threat. Furthermore, they both had little patience or sympathy for nationalist movements in areas of the world where they had vested economic and political interests. Thus, both new governments were more willing than their predecessors to conduct an operation of direct intervention into Iran.

The intersection of interventionary ideas occurred in November of 1952 when the British approached the United States both in Washington and London concerning a covert operation. In Washington, the major British operative, C. M. 'Monty' Woodhouse, met with American officials at the State Department and the Central Intelligence Agency and made his proposal for what the British termed 'Operation Boot'. Meanwhile in London, Kermit Roosevelt, the head of CIA operations in the Middle East, was approached with the same plan by Woodhouse's colleagues. In his discussions with American officials in Washington, Woodhouse chose to use the threat of communism as his basic argument. In his own words;

> Not wishing to be accused of trying to use the Americans to pull British chestnuts out of the fire, I decided to emphasize the Communist threat to Iran rather than the need to recover control of the oil industry. I argued that even if a settlement of the oil dispute could be negotiated with Musaddiq, which was doubtful, he was still incapable of resisting a *coup* by the Tudeh Party, if it were backed by Soviet support. Therefore he must be removed.[60]

Richard Cottam, who was a minor participant in the events in Iran in the early 1950s has stated the following: '. . . it remains my feeling that the British understood the extent of paranoia in this country concerning communism . . . This was the heyday of Joe McCarthy . . . and that the British community played on that fear in order to help pressure us to involve ourselves in the coup.'[61] Given the mentality of the American Administration at the time, this tactic proved highly successful.

The methodology of the American intervention

The American intervention of August 1953 was a momentous event in the history of Iranian–American relations, which were damaged for the next 25 years; following the revolution of 1978–9, America's troubled relations with the Islamic Republic of Iran turned into open hostility. From the Iranian perspective, the manner in which the United States chose to intervene in their internal affairs was at least as reprehensible as the decision to intervene itself. The fact that the CIA joined hands with interventionist England in co-ordinating the activities of royalist Iranians and distributing money to hired demonstrators was a matter discussed and condemned by Iranian citizens for years afterwards. This was recalled in the anti-American chants and speeches heard during the revolution in the late 1970s.

Over the years following the fall of Musaddiq, the word CIA became the most pejorative political term in the vocabulary of Iranian nationalists. The term came to imply a particularly evil and vulgar type of imperialism which over time became closely associated with United States policy. The sullen buildup of resentment towards America was due to great disillusionment because a former ally and respected friend had deserted to join the enemy. Given these feelings, it is essential to take a brief look at the intervention itself.

American intelligence organizations had been active in Iran since the late 1940s when they had numerous operatives stationed there. These agents focused their attention upon Soviet activities in Iran and worked especially hard to neutralize the appeal of the local communist organization, the Tudeh Party. Among the methodologies utilized were the forging of letters and books ostensibly written by leading Tudeh personalities; the use of the Iranian press to discredit Tudeh political programmes; and direct payments to Iranian politicians who opposed the local communist movement. In its zealousness, American intelligence also directed activities against the National Front and, among other things, planted articles in the press depicting Musaddiq as a crypto-communist.[62]

The CIA intervention in Iran in 1953 was well known to Iranians but was not widely publicized in the United States until the revolution in the late 1970s. Except for scattered magazine articles and occasional books specializing in the history of the CIA itself, this intervention was ignored in most of the major scholarly accounts of the period.[63] With the publication of books by the two other major intelligence agents who oversaw the operation, it is now possible to understand the extent of American involvement.[64]

With a new administration in control in Washington and with a new ambassador in Tehran, the United States prepared a dramatic covert operation whose goal was to overthrow the Musaddiq government in Iran. The key actors in Washington were Secretary of State John Foster Dulles, his brother Allen Dulles who headed the CIA, General Walter Bedell Smith who had preceded Allen Dulles as head of the CIA and then became Under-Secretary of State, and Frank Wisner who was then deputy director for Plans in the CIA. Wisner's assistant at the time was Richard Helms, who actually played no important role in the 1953 intervention. The key linkage figure in the operation and the man who connected Washington and the field was Kermit 'Kim' Roosevelt who headed CIA operations in the Middle East.

In the middle levels of the Washington bureaucracy, there were individuals who were less than enthusiastic about the project. Within the CIA itself, the two Iran intelligence analysts in Washington were not informed of the operation until it was under way. When finally made aware of the plans, they predicted imminent failure.[65] Despite these kinds of doubts, the CIA and State Department, with Foster Dulles's special encouragement, committed themselves to the operation.

Allen Dulles, Frank Wisner and Richard Helms had all worked together in the Office of Strategic Services and when operating out of Germany had shared a house together. Having been directly involved in struggling against communist infiltration in Eastern Europe following the second world war, they were deeply preoccupied with the communist threat whenever and wherever it should appear. Dulles, Wisner and Roosevelt were intelligence activists who believed strongly in the efficacy of covert operations. Their personalities are well summarized in the following passage:

> All were gregarious, intrigued by possibilities, liked to do things, had three bright ideas a day, shared the optimism of stock market plungers, and were convinced that the CIA could find a way to reach it. They also tended to be white, Anglo-Saxon patricians from old families with old money, at least in the beginning, and they somehow inherited traditional British attitudes toward the colored races of the world – not the pukka sahib arrogance of the Indian Raj, but the mixed fascination and condescension of men like T. E. Lawrence, who were enthusiastic partisans of the alien cultures into which they dipped for a time and rarely doubted their ability to help, until it was too late.[66]

In Iran, the key personality was that of Ambassador Loy Henderson who had replaced Henry Grady in September of 1951. Born in Arkansas in 1892, Henderson earned a degree in law from Northwestern University. He had a long career as a foreign service officer and had worked on Soviet and East European affairs through the 1920s and 1930s. He served as American ambassador to Iraq from 1943–5, preceded George McGhee as Assistant Secretary of State for Near Eastern and African affairs from 1945–8, and served as ambassador to India and Nepal before moving to Iran. Henderson was a smooth, distinguished diplomat who was viewed by his associates as a thorough professional. One of Henderson's colleagues has compared Henderson and Grady in the following terms:

Henderson was a diplomat's diplomat, extremely popular and admired by his staff. He was able to establish the personal relationships with Iranians which Grady found difficult to do. Henderson and Mossadeq had really a very good personal relationship until the crisis which unseated him. Henderson's emphasis was more political than economic, perhaps because the times demanded it. Henderson was a team player inside the bureaucracy. He gracefully accepted Kim Roosevelt's role and cooperated completely, although his instincts and style may have been quite different and he may have had doubts about the wisdom of this course of action.

On balance, I feel that Henderson is the better pro – versatile and charming, hard-boiled and good leader. But Grady must be given credit for taking on the British when he realized they (and we with them) were heading for disaster.[67]

Despite his diplomatic polish, Henderson's own political views were deeply coloured by what he considered the omnipresent threat of Soviet communism. He subordinated any possible personal sensitivity to local social forces to this overriding consideration. According to his friend, Kermit Roosevelt, Henderson played a very prominent role in the meeting of 25 June 1953 at the Department of State where US leaders made the final decision to go with 'Operation Ajax', as the intervention into Iran was called in the United States. Henderson, who had flown in from Tehran to attend this crucial meeting, weighed in with the following words: 'Mr Secretary, I don't like this kind of business at all. You know that. But we are confronted by a desperate, a dangerous situation and a madman who would ally himself with the Russians. We have no choice but to proceed with this undertaking. May God grant us success.'[68]

As the British and Americans prepared the final plans for the intervention, an ironic situation developed because of the reluctance of Foreign Secretary Eden to approve such a direct, blatant, and risky operation. Eden may have been outraged by the Iranian act of nationalization, but he was clearly not willing to approve this kind of intelligence adventure. Ultimately, he did not have to. In April, he underwent the first of three operations related to a serious gall bladder problem and did not return to the Foreign Office until October. By that time, the meddlesome Musaddiq problem had been disposed of; Winston Churchill had had no reservations whatsoever about the joint American–British intervention and enthusiastically approved it. According to C. M. Woodhouse, Churchill enjoyed covert operations and it was he who gave the order for Operation Boot to proceed.[69] Eden heard the news of the final result when on a cruise of convalescence between the Greek islands. In his words, 'I slept better that night.'[70]

Using the pseudonym, James F. Lochridge, Kermit Roosevelt slipped across the Iraqi border and into Iran on 7 July 1953. In hiding in Tehran, he orchestrated the plot that overthrew Musaddiq and replaced him with the Shah. Although Ambassador Loy Henderson remained outside Iran during most of the clandestine operation, he co-ordinated affairs closely with Roosevelt. In Iran, Roosevelt had two highly competent CIA country heads, both of whom were attached to the embassy with diplomatic cover. The one who played an important planning role left the country soon after Roosevelt arrived and was replaced by the second. The key British agent who had done so much to plan the operation and to convince the Americans to co-operate, Monty Woodhouse, also left the country long before the actual operation began. Attached to the embassy were other CIA employees who lived in Iran and provided important continuity and intelligence.

Also involved in the overall operation were General Norman Schwarzkopf (the former US adviser to the Iranian gendarmerie) who flew into Iran in full public view on 1 August 1953, and the Shah's omnipresent twin sister Princess Ashraf who had arrived in Iran on 25 July. Although the visits of Princess Ashraf and Schwarzkopf were brief, they were important. Both met the Shah and worked hard to reinforce his flagging self-confidence. Ashraf had earlier been contacted in France by Colonel Stephen Meade and British intelligence agent Norman Derbyshire who convinced her to use her special influence with the Shah to make certain he co-operated with plans for the operation. Meade was a regular army officer who had on several occasions been on loan to the CIA. Meanwhile, in Beirut and Cyprus other American officials and Iran experts were monitoring events and proferring advice.

Roosevelt and his team boosted the confidence of the Shah, made important contacts with the military and General Fazlullah Zahidi, and developed ties with the lower-middle-class rent-a-crowd leaders of south Tehran. This was done through the medium of two clusters of Iranian brothers who in fact provided the key links between Roosevelt and Iran. One set of brothers was America's own and provided contact with the military. The other brothers were British contacts introduced and loaned to the United States for the purpose of implementing the operation. These brothers were especially noteworthy because their role in linking Iran and America through the influence of Kermit Roosevelt continued long after the Musaddiq period.

These important linkage figures were the Rashidian brothers, Sayfullah, Asadullah and Qudratullah. Like their father before them, they had very strong ties with the British and had worked with the British in Iran in the 1940s. Sayfullah, the eldest, was a musician and philosopher who was the brains of the triumvirate and a superb conversationalist and host. He was a student of political history and liked to quote verbatim from Machiavelli. Asadullah was the organizer, political activist, and confidant of the Shah, while Qudratullah was the businessman and entrepreneur. It was Sayfullah and Asadullah who helped coach Kermit Roosevelt through the escapade in 1953 and who in fact represented the active link that bound Britain and the United States in the adventure.[71]

The first act of Operation Ajax failed when Musaddiq got word that he was to be ousted, Colonel Nimatullah Nasiri, the officer who tried to serve him with political eviction orders signed by the Shah, was arrested on the spot and the Shah made a hasty flight out of the country on 16 August 1953. Rather than cancel the operation at this point, Roosevelt took it upon himself to move forward with plans to call into the streets his paid mobs from south Tehran along with the royalist military officers led by General Fazlullah Zahidi. In the actual implementation of these plans, the Iranian brother teams played a crucial role. After much confusion and street fighting, the royalists won the day, and on 19 August 1953, Muhammad Musaddiq was forced to flee his residence and was quickly arrested. On 22 August the Shah flew back to Iran in triumph.

The actual outcome of the plot was in serious doubt until the very end as the Tudeh-directed mobs controlled the streets for a time on 16–17 August but were attacked on 18 August by the Iranian army on Musaddiq's orders. The following day when the paid royalist 'counter-mobs' appeared, Tudeh supporters stayed off the streets. Not only was there internal division and vacillation within the ranks of the communists, the Soviet Union provided them little support. In their assessment of the period, Joseph and Stewart Alsop discuss the 'extreme prudence' of Soviet Middle East policy of the day.[72] Stalin's death on 5 March 1953 led to hesitancy and indecision in Soviet policy. Moscow was unable to clearly judge the nature and strength of the Musaddiq movement: if the Soviets had chosen to get involved, the outcome might have been different.

Although the operation ultimately succeeded, American credibility in Iran was crippled for years afterwards. At least 300 Iranians died in the street fighting and many more were wounded. When Ambassador Henderson flew back to Tehran from Beirut after the first part of Operation Ajax had failed, he immediately met Kermit Roosevelt, with whom he discussed what Henderson should say to Musaddiq when asked about American support for the Shah. Roosevelt recommended that Henderson lie. Henderson agreed, stating: 'I will make it quite plain that we have no intention of interfering in the internal affairs of a friendly country.' To which Roosevelt responded: 'To this noble sentiment I made no comment. Diplomats are expected, if not required, to say such things.'[73]

The duplicity of the venture extended to other Americans who were in Iran at the time and who did indeed know the language and culture intimately. The most noteworthy example is 'professor Roger Black', a thinly-disguised eminent American scholar who is alleged to have unwittingly assisted Roosevelt by introducing him to several of his Iranian contacts.[74] This distinguished gentleman who knew Iran intimately was of the opinion that it was in America's national interest to work with the moderate middle-class nationalist groups. His sympathetic interpretations of Musaddiq and the National Front upset Roosevelt who later mistakenly explained it in terms of the professor's 'sense of guilt' for having been used so crudely – even though Roosevelt admits that 'Black' had nothing to do with the operation.[75]

A summary analysis of the American intervention into Iran known as Operation Ajax reveals the following 16 conclusions:

1 The Democratic Administration of President Harry Truman and Secretary of State Dean Acheson were reluctant to adopt the threatening tactics contemplated by key British officials to counter the nationalization in Iran.

2 The Eisenhower Administration, with the encouragement and support of Secretary of State John Foster Dulles, CIA Director Allen Dulles, and Under Secretary of State Walter Bedell Smith, decided to intervene directly to overthrow the government of Dr Musaddiq.

3 There were deep differences of opinion concerning the wisdom of such a course of action both in Britain and in the United States. These differences became less after the changes in administration that took place in both countries.

4 The idea of the intervention originated with the British (SIS/MI6) who used the threat of a possible communist takeover as their major tactic in attracting American involvement. The British and the Americans co-operated fully in the venture. In the words of one American expert who helped devise the plan: 'It was a joint effort.'[76]

5 The coup could not have succeeded without substantial Iranian participation. Yet, the Iranians would not or could not have acted without American/British direction and the psychological support that this involvement carried with it. In the informed view of Monty Woodhouse: 'There may be reasons for not being dogmatic in claiming that the revolution of August 1953 in Tehran was planned and executed by our Anglo-American team. Still, I think it was. We may have done no more than mobilize forces which were already there, but that was precisely what needed to be done, and it was enough.'[77]

6 The intervention succeeded despite the enormous lack of expertise concerning Iran on the part of field commander Kermit Roosevelt and his superiors in Washington. It also succeeded in the face of the pseudo-professional nature of the implementation of the plan.[78]

7 The action succeeded because of the deep fragmentation of the social and political forces in Iran at the time; the tenuous nature of the economy; the organizational skills of the handful of leading Iranian

actors involved; the liberal and idealistic nature both of Dr Musaddiq and of his followers in the National Front; the reluctance of the Soviet union to intervene; and the element of good luck.

8   The communist Tudeh Party in Iran was relatively small and did not enjoy the support of either the nationalist middle classes or the masses of Iranian people. In the words of a State Department intelligence report prepared in January of 1953, Musaddiq himself was neither a communist nor a communist sympathizer; he was in fact hated by the Iranian communist leadership. The report indicated that Musaddiq's nationalization had 'almost universal Iranian support' and that the Tudeh Party deemed Musaddiq's overthrow 'a high priority'. It carefully listed 13 ways in which Tudeh objectives differed from those of the National Front.[79] In the end, the Tudeh Party's strategy proved weak, indecisive and self-defeating during the political showdown in August 1953.

9   The intervention bought 25 more years for the Pahlavi dynasty and enabled the international oil industry to export with favourable terms 24 billion barrels of oil during this period. Western consumers paid very modest prices for this precious resource during these years: the average posted price of Iranian crude was about $1.85 between 1954 and 1960 and $1.80 between 1960 and 1971.[80]

10   The American action in Iran in 1953 was followed by a general purge of the remaining elements of the Tudeh Party whose influence was almost completely annihilated in the country. One US Congressman summarized a view shared by a number of key decision makers in Washington at the time when he, in somewhat exaggerated terms, stated: 'We saved Iran for the free world when the rest of that area had gone over to the Communists.'[81]

11   By crushing the Musaddiq move to nationalize, the United States and Britain discouraged further movements towards unilateral nationalization of the oil industry in the third world. Although the Suez Canal was nationalized in 1956, it was to be almost two decades before there were to be any more major oil nationalizations.

12   The operation in Iran was considered for years in Washington to be one of the major success stories of direct covert intervention. As such, it acted as a catalyst for other CIA interventions, beginning with that in Guatemala in 1954.

13   Operation Ajax locked the United States into a special relationship with the Shah and brought a high level of American intelligence and military activity into Iran.

14   The US intervention alienated generations of Iranians from America and was the first fundamental step towards the eventual rupture of Iranian–American relations which were finally severed as a result of the revolution of 1978-9.

15   The events of 1953 in Iran damaged the image of the United States
     among the burgeoning forces of nationalism that came to prominence
     in the Middle East during the 1960s and 1970s. In the words of William
     O. Douglas: 'When Mossadegh in Persia started basic reforms, we
     became alarmed. That man, whom I am proud to call my friend, was a
     democrat in the LaFollette-Norris sense of the term. We united with
     the British to destroy him; we succeeded; and ever since our name has
     not been an honored one in the Middle East.'[82]
16   The 1953 intervention aborted the birth of revolutionary nationalism
     in Iran which would burst forth 25 years later in an especially virulent
     form at the time of the Iranian revolution.

The United States and Muhammad Musaddiq: the political legacy

American policy in Iran during the early 1950s succeeded in ensuring that
there would be no communist takeover in the country at the time and that
Iranian oil reserves would be available to the western world at advantageous terms for two decades afterwards. It also deeply alienated Iranian
patriots of all social classes and weakened the moderate, liberal nationalists represented by organizations such as the National Front. This paved
the way for the incubation of extremism both of the left and of the right.
This extremism became unalterably anti-American and could already be
seen in its embryonic stages during these years.

Both the Tudeh Party on the left and Ayatullah Kashani and others on
the right condemned American intervention along with that of Britain and
the Soviet Union. Kashani consistently criticized American links with
Britain. In November 1951, for example, he stated, 'we don't want any
outside government interfering in our internal affairs . . . The United
States should cease following British policy otherwise it will gain nothing
but hatred and the loss of prestige in the world in general and in Iran in
particular.'[83] Although he maintained close and constant contact with US
Embassy personnel in Iran at the time, Kashani never hesitated to castigate
United States policy in front of them. On one occasion, he told embassy
counsellor A. R. Richards that the US aid programme was useless because
it emphasized military priorities rather than attempting to really improve
the living conditions of the deprived masses. And, he asked Richards,
'What good could a well-equipped and well-trained army of even 250,000
do against 18 million hungry people in Iran?'[84] By its actions in Iran in
1953, the United States guaranteed the implacable opposition of an
important faction of the religious right while at the same time effectively
undercutting the strength and credibility of the liberal, nationalist centre.

This distrust was deepened in the years following the fall of Musaddiq
since America bound itself increasingly tightly to the Shah and his policies,

which in turn only increased the doubt and distrust of the Iranian middle and lower classes. The key part of the American intelligence team that carried out the intervention was a major factor in the tightening relationship between Pahlavi and the United States. The key connection here was a Roosevelt–Rashidian economic and political alliance that acted to support Muhammad Riza Shah Pahlavi. The Rashidians became wealthy entrepreneurs and financiers whose business ventures were international.[85] Roosevelt's public relations firm represented the Shah's interests in the United States. The Rashidians spoke often of their friend 'Kim' who stayed with them during his many subsequent trips to Iran, which in the 1960s averaged five or six a year. During this time, Roosevelt maintained his own parallel path to the Shah with whom he had closer relations than any American diplomat or ambassador posted to Tehran. Although this angered and annoyed leading members of the US diplomatic mission in Tehran, they were unable to do anything about it. Roosevelt's line to the Shah was through the Rashidians to the commander of the Imperial Guards, General Muhsin Hashimi-Nijad, to the monarch himself. Back in Washington, Roosevelt had his own personal connections that led directly to the White House.

In this way, certain American agents involved in the coup continued to exert influence on America's Iran policy long after 1953. The elegant Rashidian home in north Tehran and their bank near Firdawsi Square became the centres for continued Roosevelt–Rashidian collaboration. This was only one important personal-political connection that bound the US tightly with the British and the Shah until the revolution. However significant, this particular linkage existed as a constant and grating reminder to the growing body of informed Iranian nationalists that the Shah remained in power through American and British intervention.

The fall of Musaddiq marked the end of a century of friendship between the two countries and began a new era of US intervention and growing hostility against the United States among the awakened forces of Iranian nationalism. A sense of the spirit of the American establishment during this period is captured in an article that appeared in *The Reporter* in November 1953. In this long discussion of the Musaddiq movement, the American author warns new Iranian Prime Minister Zahidi in the following words: 'Like other leaders with empty treasuries, he [Zahidi] will learn that the sun rises and sets according to the schedule laid down by our Constitution for the sitting of the United States Congress.' And the writer ends his analysis and advice by predicting that the new government in Iran 'won't be with us long unless it can prove that being nice to the West is more profitable for Iran than being as consistently nasty as Old Mossy was'.[86] This crude message was translated in the leading Iranian weekly news magazine shortly after it appeared in *The Reporter*.

Many aspects of the Musaddiq movement of 1951–3 were reflected in the Khomeini-led revolution that shook the world 25 years later. Fiercely nationalistic, the movement of the 1950s was anti-western in tone with special antipathy reserved for the British. But even in 1953 there were signs of strident anti-Americanism. Slogans such as one labelling the US Embassy a 'nest of spies' were already shouted in the streets of Tehran in early 1953. Musaddiq, like Ayatullah Khomeini after him, was designated as *Time* magazine's Man of the Year and was presented throughout as enigmatic, irascible, and quite mad. In its cover story on Musaddiq in January 1952, *Time* presented the old man as fanatical and chided the West for lacking the 'moral muscle' to deal with him. Although he engaged in continual discussions and debates with American representatives, Musaddiq ultimately refused to compromise and became a political casualty as a result.

The revolution of 1978–9 was also influenced by the experiences of 1951–3. Khomeini and the other leaders of the revolution vowed not to allow a repetition of what they termed 'the Musaddiq debacle'.[87] Convinced that the United States through the auspices of the CIA would attempt to replay the Kermit Roosevelt record, they took every precaution to keep this from happening. Anti-American rhetoric was kept at a fever pitch; every word, act or signal from Washington was thoroughly scrutinized; Khomeini himself remained aloof from any American emissaries or diplomats; Iranian civil and military officials with close ties to the United States were executed, imprisoned or retired; and, finally, when the danger of a Pahlavi restoration attempt was seen as imminent, American diplomats were taken hostage.

The American intervention of 1951–3 influenced but did not determine the revolutionary events of 1978–9. Although the American image was severely tarnished by the actions taken against Dr Musaddiq, the United States had numerous opportunities to rethink and revise its policy towards the Shah's Iran in the quarter century before the revolution. As time passed, however, America slowly tightened its relationships with the Pahlavi regime, a regime it had helped rescue in the early 1950s. In the process, American policy alienated increasing numbers of Iranian citizens who came to view American actions as policy extensions of the 1953 intervention. In the streets of Tehran in 1978, a major slogan constantly repeated was 'Death to the American Shah!' In short, American policy between 1953 and 1978 emphasized a special relationship with the Shah and his political elite while largely ignoring the needs and demands of the Iranian masses.

In the years between 1953 and 1978, much happened in Iran to prevent history from repeating itself. Apart from the internal social dynamics which included the explosive growth of an alienated professional middle class; the clumsy political miscues of the Shah and his inner circle; the widening gap between the haves and the have-nots; and the adamant opposition of the popular Shii religious leaders – apart from these, the external ingredient was a major factor that contributed to the developing revolutionary equation. An increasing American presence and an interventionary American policy became integral parts of the Iranian political process after 1953.

Here

Notes

(Sections of this chapter are also presented in James A. Bill, *The Eagle and the Lion*, New Haven and London, 1988.)

1 Ronald W. Ferrier, 'The development of the Iranian oil industry', in Hossein Amirsadeghi ed., *Twentieth-Century Iran* (London, 1977) p. 106.
2 Richard Funkhauser, 'September 10, 1950 background paper', US Congress, Senate, Committee on Foreign Relations, Subcommittee on Multinational Corporations, *Multinational Corporations and United States Foreign Policy Hearings*, part 7 (20–1 February, 27–8 March, 1974), 93rd Cong., 2nd sess. on multinational petroleum companies and foreign policy (Washington, DC: Government Printing Office, 1974), p. 126.
3 Saleh in *U.N. Security Council Official Record*, 6th year, 563rd Meeting, 15 (S/PV 563, 1951) as quoted in Jerrold L. Walden, 'The international petroleum cartel in Iran: private power and the public interest', *Journal of Public Law* 11 (Spring, 1962) 70. Another source indicates that the Anglo-Iranian Oil Company stated its total royalty payments to Iran at the end of 1950 to be about £150 million. See Benjamin Shwadran, *The Middle East, Oil, and the Great Powers 1959*, 2nd rev. edn (New York, 1959) p. 159.
4 Ibid. Both Musaddiq and later the Shah made this point often. See *The Speech of H. E. Dr. Mossadegh Concerning the Nationalization of the Petroleum Industry in Iran* (Tehran, 1951) p. 31. According to the Shah: 'The company knew of our irritation due to the high percentage paid in corporation taxes to the British Government; these taxes in fact greatly exceeded the royalties to Iran' (Mohammed Reza Shah Pahlavi, *Mission for My Country* (New York, 1960) p. 90).
5 Anthony Eden, *Full Circle* (Boston, 1960) pp. 214–15.
6 Julian Bharier, *Economic Development in Iran 1900–1970* (London, 1971) p. 160. The figures on the work-force are drawn from p. 162.
7 S. H. Longrigg, *Oil in the Middle East: its Discovery and Development*, 3rd edn (London, 1968) p. 157.
8 Peter Avery, *Modern Iran* (New York, 1965) p. 423.
9 Vernon A. Walters, *Silent Missions* (Garden City, NY, 1978) pp. 247–8. This is a fascinating account of the Harriman–Musaddiq negotiations.
10 Seymour to Eden, 12 April 1937, FO 371/20837. (References to British official documents refer to documents at the Public Records Office, London.)
11 Charles W. Hamilton, *America and Oil in the Middle East* (Houston, 1962) p. 47.
12 The words of Edmund Stevens reporting for *The Christian Science Monitor*, 16 April 1951.

13 Christopher T. Rand, *Making Democracy Safe for Oil* (Boston, 1975) p. 133.

14 There is considerable disagreement in the Persian and English sources concerning Musaddiq's date of birth. The years given range from 1879 to 1885 with at least one source presenting each of the seven years in this span. Many Persian sources indicate 1879 (1258 by the Iranian calendar) while the other extreme of 'about 1885' is the date given in the Brtish Foreign Office biography. Based on a survey of the sources, and discussions with members of Musaddiq's family, I believe the date to be 1882, or 29 Urdibihisht 1261. See Ali Janzadeh, *Musaddiq* (n.p., 1979) p. 5. This book, which contains Musaddiq's autobiographical notes in his own handwriting, is the most reliable source I have located with respect to Musaddiq's life.

15 Gérard de Villiers, *The Imperial Shah: an Informal Biography*, trans. June P. Wilson and Walter B. Michaels (Boston, 1976) pp. 156, 170.

16 Compare de Villiers, *Imperial Shah*, p. 168 and Leonard Mosley, *Power Play: Oil in the Middle East* (Baltimore, Md, 1973) p. 199.

17 William A. Dorman and Mansour Farhang, manuscript on the American mass media and Iran. See their book *The U.S. Press and Iran: Foreign Policy and the Journalism of Deference* (Berkeley, Calif., 1987).

18 Seymour to Eden, 12 April 1937, FO 371/20837, p. 32.

19 Personal interview with Hidayatullah Matin-Daftari, Tehran, 26 June 1974.

20 Donald N. Wilber, *Contemporary Iran* (New York, 1963) p. 89.

21 Musaddiq, Majlis speech of 7 March 1944, in Husayn Kay-Ustuvan, *Siyasat-i muvazineh-i manfi dar Majlis-i Chahardahum*, vol. I (Tehran, 1949) p. 34.

22 Personal interview, Austin, Texas, 18 April 1976. National Front leader Shapur Bakhtiar later stated that Musaddiq's reluctance to use force during those August days was something for which he would never forgive the old prime minister. 'Musaddiq should have reacted immediately, and by martial law killed all the people who were involved in this story' (from film transcripts of Granada Television, *End of Empire: Iran*).

23 Cited in Janzadeh, *Musaddiq*, p. 230.

24 Ibid., p. 241.

25 Richard Funkhauser, 'The problem of near Eastern Oil', Lecture to National War College, 4 December 1951, in *Multinational Corporations, Hearings*, part 7, p. 170.

26 Wm Roger Louis, *The British Empire in the Middle East 1945–1951* (Oxford, 1984) pp. 596, 656.

27 Ibid., p. 653.

28 Personal interview with American diplomat, Washington, DC, 11 November 1981.

29 Funkhauser, 'The problem of Near Eastern oil', in *Multinational Corporations, Hearings*, part 7, p. 170.

30 Shepherd to Furlonge, 'Confidential', 14 May 1951, FO 371/92535/EP 1531/356, quoted in Louis, *The British Empire*, p. 654; Louis, *The British Empire*, p. 739, *n*.5.

31 Cited in Anthony Sampson, *The Seven Sisters: the Great Oil Companies and the World They Made* (New York, 1975) p. 120. This extraordinary memorandum is worth reading in its entirety.

32 Cited in Louis, *The British Empire*, p. 650.

33 David S. McLellan, *Dean Acheson: the State Department Years* (New York, 1976) p. 387.

34 Dean Acheson, *Present at the Creation* (New York, 1969) p. 506.

35 Eden, *Full Circle*, pp. 216–17.

36 Personal interview with Walter Levy, New York, 3 January 1985. Some of the material in the following paragraphs is drawn from this interview.

37 The summary of the content of this working proposal is taken from George McGhee, *Envoy to the Middle World: Adventures in Diplomacy* (New York, 1983) pp. 400–2.

38 Ibid., pp. 403, 403, 337, 322.

39 Arthur Krock, *Memoirs* (New York, 1968) p. 262.

40 Memorandum of conversation, Ahmad Human (deputy minister of Court) and John H. Stutesman (Second Secretary, US Embassy), 6 November 1951, Record Group 84, Box 29 (1950–2), National Archives, Washington, D.C.

41 Louis, *The British Empire*, p. 685, *n*.26.

42 For an informed discussion of American intelligence operations in Iran following the second world war, see Mark J. Gasiorowski, 'The 1953 *coup d'état* in Iran', *International Journal of Middle East Studies* 19 (August 1987) pp. 216–86.

43 An example of the level of the reporting can be seen by listing a few of the titles of the articles that appeared on Iran at the time. 'Portrait of a man dreaming up a coup: great ham act goes to waste', *Life* 35 (23 November 1953) 37–9; 'Crackdown in the Middle East: red-inspired Iranians retreat', *Newsweek* 42 (23 November 1953) 40–2; 'Iran: in the red', *Newsweek* 42 (21 September 1953) 49; and 'Iran: mooo', *Time* 62 (30 November 1953) 40.

44 'Iran: whose ox is nationalized?', *Time* 57 (26 March 1951) 31.

45 Byrnes to Roosevelt, memorandum of 15 October 1943, repr. in US Congress, Senate, Special Committee Investigating the National Defense Program, Hearings, part 41, 1948, Petroleum arrangements with Saudi Arabia, 80th Cong., 1st Sess. Mustafa Fateh also refers to the Byrnes letter on p. 500 of his important book, *Panjah sal naft-i Iran* (Tehran, 1956). See also Michael B. Stoff, *Oil, War, and American Security* (New Haven, Conn., 1980) p. 131.

46 McGhee, *Envoy to the Middle World*, p. 322.

47 Department of State, Memorandum of conversation, 'Iranian oil problem', 10 October 1951, Papers of Dean Acheson, Harry S. Truman Library, Independence, Missouri.

48 For details of these proposals, see Department of State, 'Memorandum of Conversation', 8 October 1952, Papers of Dean Acheson, Harry S. Truman Library, Independence, Missouri; and Department of the Interior, confidential memorandum, Charles Rayner to C. S. Snodgrass, 'Iranian Oil Problem', 22 October 1951, Papers of Dean Acheson, Harry S. Truman Library.

49 US Congress, *Multinational Corporations, Hearings*, part 7, p. 99.

50 The testimony of Leonard J. Emmerglick who was special assistant to the Attorney General in 1952, ibid., p. 109; ibid.

51 Sampson, *The Seven Sisters*, p. 126.

52 The Musaddiq letter as well as Eisenhower's response are reprinted in Y. Alexander and A. Nanes eds, *The United States and Iran: Documentary History* (Frederick, Md, 1980) pp. 232–5.

53 Both Harriman and Walters explicitly expressed deep disappointment in their ineffectiveness in dealing with Musaddiq and each indicated that he was not used to diplomatic failure. See Walters, *Silent Missions*, pp. 258–9, 263. George McGhee found the British as intransigent as Musaddiq and was extremely disappointed by his inability to effect an agreement. In his words: 'My real regret in leaving the department when I did in December 1951 was that I had not been able to solve the Iranian crisis' (McGhee, *Envoy to the Middle World*, p. 17).

54 Walters, *Silent Missions*, p. 250.

55 Acheson, *Present at the Creation*, p. 510.

56 Personal interview with Dr Hasan Alavi, member of the Majlis Oil Commission, Tehran, 1 February 1966.

57 Eden, *Full Circle*, p. 224.

58 Kermit Roosevelt, quoted by Robert Scheer in *Los Angeles Times*, 29 March 1979, p. 1.

59 Department of State, incoming telegram, from David Bruce (Paris) to Secretary of State (Washington), 10 November 1951, Papers of Dean Acheson, Harry S. Truman Library.

60 C. M. Woodhouse, *Something Ventured* (London, 1982) p. 117. Woodhouse stresses this strategy, writing in an earlier place: 'I was convinced from the first that any effort to forestall a Soviet *coup* in Iran would require a joint Anglo-American effort. The Americans would be more likely to work with us if they saw the problem as one of containing Communism rather than restoring the position of the AIOC' (see p. 110).

61 From film transcripts of Granada Television, *End of Empire: Iran*.

62 For details, see Gasiorowski, 'The 1953 coup d'etat'.

63 The exception often quoted is Richard and Gladys Harkness, 'The mysterious doings of CIA', *The Saturday Evening Post*, 6 November 1954, pp. 66–8.

64 See Woodhouse, *Something Ventured* and Kermit Roosevelt, *Countercoup: the Struggle for the Control of Iran* (New York, 1979). Although accurate in its general thrust, Roosevelt's *Countercoup* is very careless in its detail and must be used with extreme care.

65 Personal communication with one of the two analysts.

66 Thomas Powers, *The Man who kept the Secrets: Richard Helms and the CIA* (New York, 1979) pp. 43–4. Helms was at the time known to be critical of the use of covert operations.

67 Personal letter, American diplomat who served with Henderson in Iran, 4 January 1985.

68 Roosevelt, *Countercoup*, p. 18.

69 Woodhouse, *Something Ventured*, p. 125.

70 Eden, *Full Circle*, p. 237.

71 Asadullah and Sayfullah Rashidian are identifiable in the Roosevelt book as Nossey and Cafron – 'Laughing boy' and 'the mad musician'. Sayfullah Rashidian was indeed a pianist and musician; but he was anything but mad. (The 'Boscoe brothers' mentioned in the book refer to another set of brothers.)

72 Joseph and Stewart Alsop, *The Reporter's Trade* (New York, 1958).

73 Roosevelt, *Countercoup*, pp. 183–4.

74 Ibid., pp. 41, 78–9, 127.
75 Personal interview with Kermit Roosevelt, Washington, DC, 12 November 1981. The Roosevelt–'Black' relationship was the first major case where the United States government used knowledgeable American Iranologists to achieve its policy goals which were developed without at the same time heeding the advice and recommendations of these experts. Journalists were used even more blatantly.
76 Personal interview, 13 January 1981. Just as American operatives (e.g. Kermit Roosevelt) like to magnify their role in the venture, so too do British officials overstate theirs. British intelligence has alleged, for example, that 'Roosevelt really did little more than show up in Iran with CIA funds to encourage agents the British had organized and then released to American control' (see Christopher Andrew, *Her Majesty's Secret Service: the Making of the British Intelligence Community* (New York, 1985) p. 494).
77 Woodhouse, *Something Ventured*, p. 130.
78 In the words of Charles Maechling, Jr: 'The reconstructed dialogues of the internal deliberations of the U.S. government reveal not a shred of serious evaluation of either the Iranian situation or the long-term interests of the United States, and often border on the frivolous' (see Maechling, 'Coup or counter coup in Iran', *Foreign Service Journal*, December 1979, p. 38).
79 US Department of State, Office of Intelligence Research (OIR), *Iran's Political and Economic Prospects through 1953*, Intelligence Report Number 6121, esp. p. 10.
80 These statistics have been calculated and provided for me by Dr Fereidun Fesharaki in a personal communication of 13 February 1981.
81 Statement by Congressman B. Carroll Reece. See US Congress, House of Representatives, Committee on Government Operations, *Hearings Before a Subcommittee on United States Aid Operations in Iran*, 84th Cong., 2nd Sess., 2 & 31 May, 1, 5, 8, 11–13, 18–19, 25–7 & 29 June, and 16 July 1956, p. 796.
82 Douglas, 'The U.S. and Revolution', in K. E. Boulding et al., *The U.S. and Revolution* (Santa Barbara, Calif., 1961) p. 10.
83 Kashani, cited in *Shahid* 535 (3 Azar 1330/24 November 1951).
84 Telegram, Ambassador Loy Henderson to Secretary of State, 12 November 1951, Record Group 84, Box 29 (1950–2), National Archives, Washington, DC.
85 The Rashidian name appeared in the US Senate Hearings on the Grumman sale of F-14s to Iran where the Lavi brothers, agents for Grumman, admitted that of $3.1 million in Grumman commissions, $2,480,000 was paid over to International Services, an organization in which the Rashidians were the principal party. US Congress, Senate, Committee on Foreign Relations, Subcommittee on Multinational Corporations, *Multinational Corporations and United States Foreign Policy: Grumman Sale of F-14's to Iran*, 94th Cong., 2nd Sess., 9 August Executive Session, and 10, 13, 15 & 27 September 1976, pp. 133–4.
86 Harlan Cleveland, 'Oil, blood and politics: our next move in Iran', *The Reporter* 9 (10 November 1953) 19.
87 Personal interviews with Khomeini representatives, Tehran, 26 November–1 December 1978.

11

Recollections of
Dr Muhammad Musaddiq

GEORGE C. McGHEE

My association with the oil crisis in Iran began in June 1949, when I became Assistant Secretary of State for Near Eastern, South Asian and African Affairs. My meetings with Prime Minister Musaddiq took place between 8 October and 18 November 1951; during this period I had approximately 80 hours of conversation with him. My official relationship with Iranian affairs was terminated in December 1951.

My own background included two aspects which were relevant to my approach to the Iranian oil problem. I was trained as a geologist and geophysicist and had, before joining the Department of State, direct experience as an independent oil producer and as an appraisal engineer for oil reserves and values. I had not, however, been employed by any of the international oil companies. Also, during three years of graduate studies at Oxford, I acquired great respect for the British as a people, and for their government in its handling of its international relations and obligations, including the period of the liquidation of their once extensive empire, as detailed in my memoir, *Envoy to the Middle World*.[1] I later served for four years as chairman of the board of the English Speaking Union of the United States.

I engaged in talks with Musaddiq, pursuant to my duties in the department, when he came to New York to make his appeal to the Security Council of the United Nations in defense of the Iranian government's nationalization of the Anglo-Iranian Oil Company.[2] The Council had taken this matter up at the request of the British government, following British failure to get action on this issue by the International Court.

As I indicated in my book, we suspected that the US government may have unwittingly encouraged Musaddiq to come to New York personally, despite his age, by a mistake (too complicated to explain easily) in delivering to him a personal message from President Harry Truman intended for the British prime minister. Had the president wished to communicate with the government of Iran he would at that time normally have addressed the Shah. Since we had up to that point not had close relations with Musaddiq, sharing British scepticism of him, this message may have encouraged him to decide to represent his country at the international level.[3]

Since Musaddiq would be in New York, the president and Secretary Acheson agreed that we should take advantage of his presence to continue efforts we had been making to assist the British and Iranians to reach agreement on oil. This I strongly supported and the British, who had initially requested our assistance in helping resolve the oil crisis, did not object. Our most conspicuous effort up to that time had been made in Ambassador Averell Harriman's mission to Tehran, starting 15 July 1951 and lasting two months. Harriman had succeeded in bringing about direct negotiations between the two countries, through the mission of Richard Stokes. These negotiations were, however, not productive.[4]

There was almost a unanimous view on the part of the British government and Anglo-Iranian Oil Company officials who had been involved in negotiations with Musaddiq, which was shared by Ambassador Harriman as a result of his experience, that it would not be possible to negotiate any reasonable agreement with Musaddiq. I did not contest this view, which history may have shown to be correct; however, I was so concerned that the free world might lose Iran if the issue between the AIOC and Iran was not resolved, that I believed we had to make every effort to help achieve a successful result.

My recollections of Musaddiq come from liking him as a man; having enjoyed the many hours of discussions I had with him; admiring his patriotism and courage in standing up for what he believed best for his country; combined with a sadness that his efforts were, probably as a result of his own deficiencies, so futile. Almost all of our discussions, starting from my first visit to his room in the Cornell Medical Center on the evening of the day he arrived in New York, were conducted as he lay in his bed and I sat on one side at the foot of the bed, with Colonel (later General) Vernon Walters, the able linguist and negotiator who had been assigned to translate for me, sitting on the other side. Frequently Musaddiq, occasionally both of us, would make a humorous sally and he (more than I) would be convulsed with laughter, his eyes beaming.

Many have spoken of Musaddiq's curious appearance, as well as his unconventional personal habits. It was his tendency to weep during public speeches (though he never did with me, probably considering it not worth the effort), to do business in bed wearing pyjamas, and to laugh convulsively. He was tall, gaunt, balding, with a long thin face and an oversized beak nose. His face was highly mobile, the variety of poses giving him an almost comical aspect. And yet, underneath his lugubrious exterior there was evidence of a deep firmness, determination, and clarity of purpose.

I attempted, of course, to gain Musaddiq's confidence, as any negotiator would. I made it clear, however, that I did not share his deep distrust of the British. He saw in the British influence in Iran the source of all the country's problems. He was absolutely obdurate in this view. I pointed out the high regard in which the British were generally held, their reputation for standing by their word, and their good record for granting independence to their former colonies such as India and Pakistan.[5]

Over the hours of our conversation Musaddiq displayed a startling naivety about economics and business generally, not just the oil business. Paul Nitze, head of Policy Planning and with considerable business experience, joined me in many of my discussions with Musaddiq. Paul and I took turns trying to educate him in business realities. But in the end he invariably appeared not to believe, or to disregard, what we said. 'You don't understand', he would reply to our arguments; 'That's not the problem. It's a political problem.'[6] Under the surface there was always the impression that he was sure Iran was of such importance to Britain, the United States, and the West, that we would pay any price to prevent it from collapse or falling to the Soviets. Both I, and later Acheson, tried to make it very clear to him that we would never agree to an oil deal with Iran that would establish a precedent that might destroy the international base of the world oil industry.

Musaddiq also gave the impression that he was very much alone, that he distrusted those who had accompanied him to the United States, and even those who advised him in Iran and governed for him. Many of his supporters represented extremist religious and nationalist views. He seemed always to feel he might be assassinated like his predecessor, General Razmara, who was shot by a religious extremist because he was negotiating on oil with the British. Musaddiq was painfully aware of the virtual impossibility of an Iranian head of government reaching agreement with a foreign company, particularly one owned by a powerful country like Britain, over the development of its natural resources. No terms agreed could ever be good enough. There was a suspicion on the part of the public that he might yield to bribery or pressure.

As a consequence, Musaddiq would never let me or anyone else negotiating with him on our side meet separately with his aides. After we had pressed him to let us explain our point of view to other members of the gorup, he finally acceded, but only with himself present. Paul Nitze and I prepared elaborate charts showng oil prices and world market demand, and we each gave carefully prepared explanatory remarks. When we had finished, we turned to the group and asked if there were any questions. Quick as a flash Musaddiq, before they had a chance to reply, said to us, 'You see, you can't convince them.'[7] The meeting was over.

Musaddiq never, during our discussions, retreated in any way from the principle that Iranian oil had been nationalized. This he considered a *fait accompli*. He was negotiating how to get nationalization accepted and working. After all, nationalization was universally recognized as a right of every sovereign government, even though the qualification of prompt and adequate compensation was always raised. No developing country, however, was ever in a position to pay full compensation in cash based on future expected profits. It was generally known that the United States had in 1938 acquiesced, after a long and bitter negotiation, to Mexican nationalization of US oil interests there, for a paltry $14,000,000. Recently the Arabian-American Oil Company (Aramco), gave up the richest oil concession in the world for a negligible payment and the right to operate the Saudi Arabian oil fields and purchase the oil.

Musaddiq only retreated, and this to my great surprise, late one evening in his New York hotel suite, as regards the Abadan refinery, the largest in the world. He volunteered that the refinery had not, as had been generally assumed, been included in the nationalization decree. I assumed that this meant it still belonged to the AIOC, and that although the company would have to dispose of it, the terms of sale would be negotiable. Later, he not only confirmed this both to Acheson and myself, but agreed that Shell Oil (Anglo-Dutch) would be an acceptable purchaser. Perhaps it was because he had less confidence in Iran's ability to run the refinery than he had in its ability to produce oil in its oilfields. When I expressed my surprise that Abadan had not been nationalized, he agreed to my suggestion that we both write this out in our own handwriting – he in French and I in English, and exchange.[8] When I read in the press the next day that he would never give back the refinery, I was confident that he had leaked this only as life insurance, and that he would try to carry out what he had promised me.

On two occasions I arranged a change of scene for Musaddiq from the hospital and his hotel suite. One day Paul Nitze and I took him out to my farm near Middleburg, Virginia, an hour west of Washington. He inspected the farm and Walters translated a discussion between Musaddiq and my farmer, a dignified older man whom everyone respectfully called Mr Lloyd. They got along famously together, Musaddiq explaining the difference between farming in arid Iran and in northern Virginia. But Paul and I didn't get any closer to a solution to the oil problem.

On another occasion my wife and I gave a small reception for Musaddiq in our Washington residence. In deference to his presumed debilities it was kept very low key. Ambassador Harriman was there as well as several Cabinet and sub-Cabinet members. There was, however, almost no give and take in discussions with any of the Iranian party. They all seemed afraid of each other, reluctant to express themselves. Musaddiq made friends with our five-year-old son Michael, who had crashed the party in pyjamas.

As a gesture of good will, President Truman offered Musaddiq the facilities of the Walter Reed Hospital (US Army), so he moved there for several days from his modest apartment in the Shoreham Hotel. After a thorough investigation, the staff doctors at the hospital reported that they could find nothing wrong with him, apart from the effects of his age.

Vernon Walters, after the Washington discussions, reached the conclusion that Musaddiq did not really want an oil agreement at the time. In their final meeting Musaddiq had said to him, 'Don't you realize that, returning to Iran empty-handed, I return in a much better position than if I returned with an agreement which I would have to sell to my fanatics?'[9]

The Shah, following the failure of the former ambassador to the United States, Husayn Ala, to form a government after the assassination of General Razmara, wrote later that he originally welcomed Musaddiq assuming the prime ministership. 'How could anyone be against Mosadeq? He would enrich everybody, he would fight the foreigner, he would secure our rights. No wonder students, intellectuals, people from all walks of life, flocked to his banner.'[10]

Musaddiq was selected prime minister by an overwhelming vote, and the Shah wrote, 'His success had exceeded his own fondest dreams, as well as those of his followers. He was to enjoy my full support for a year and my toleration – agonizing though it was for me – during many months thereafter.' The uneasy alliance between the Shah and Musaddiq was, probably predictably, not to last long. In February 1953 Musaddiq made his first attempt to get the Shah to leave Iran.

It will, perhaps, be of interest to follow the course of my negotiations with Musaddiq for a proposal that could be put to the British government as a basis for a settlement.[11] In July 1949, the AIOC and Iran had agreed the terms of the Supplemental Agreement, which Iran then rejected, that would have doubled Iran's oil income – at that time about $30 million per annum. According to the British government AIOC contributed in 1951 about £100 million to the British balance of payments. Lord Stokes had made an offer on behalf of the AIOC following the Harriman mission; however this was rejected. A few days before General Razmara's assassination, the AIOC had made him a verbal offer on a fifty–fifty profit-sharing basis, which we had recommended since it was in accordance with the Aramco–Saudi agreement, but which Razmara did not make public.

Musaddiq's first thought when I met him in New York was to win US and British approval for Iranian nationalization of AIOC interests in Iran, and work out a *modus vivendi* for their management by the government National Iranian Oil Company (NIOC). He was willing to accept a suitable executive arrangement to manage the oil operations, which had been the principal problem during the Harriman and Stokes negotiations. He was also willing to accept an arrangement for the acquisition of outside technology (from a non-British oil company). He would pay compensation to AIOC on the basis of the aggregate value of the company's shares before nationalization, which he understood was $27 million. Alternatively, he would accept the terms of the most favourable nationalization law then in existence, or any that arose from direct negotiation. He did not want to rely on the findings of a suitable international commission, which I had suggested to him.

These terms, although probably not acceptable to the AIOC which was thinking in terms of compensation based on expected future revenues, was a logical start. Corporate takeovers have in many cases been accomplished by purchase of a majority of stock in the market. This was a better offer than the US companies got in Mexico. Musaddiq went on to assure me that he would agree to former purchasers being given the right to buy the same amount of oil they had been taking for a fixed number of years. The AIOC would get their required amount and could represent third parties. In essence this was the principal feature of the nationalization of Aramco by Saudi Arabia, where the cash consideration was nominal.

The principal issues remaining, both very important, were prices and the nationality of the foreign executives and technicians who would produce Iranian oil. Former AIOC employees and British technicians generally could occupy any position except that of the top technical director. The board of the NIOC could consist of three Iranians and four neutrals (non-British). This should not have been too damaging to British sensibilities. However, in his later meeting with Truman and Acheson, Musaddiq made a sharp about-face: there could be no British technicians at all. This alone, we later discovered, was enough to give the British a basis for rejecting Musaddiq's offer.

The question of price took an interesting turn. Musaddiq agreed to a small (perhaps 10 per cent) reduction in the sales price for Iranian oil, which was then approximately $1.75 a barrel Persian Gulf Posted Price. He balked at the $1.10 a barrel price Acheson and I proposed, which we calculated would give AIOC the approximate advantage of fifty–fifty profit sharing. We explained that it was the difference between selling retail and wholesale. He was finally persuaded by Acheson's explanation of the difference between the price he got for beef on the hoof at his Maryland farm and the price in the butcher shop in Baltimore. Musaddiq agreed not to ask more than $1.10 a barrel.

There were other conditions and problems remaining, but we considered the whole package, including his continued willingness to sell the now denationalized Abadan refinery to Shell (actually an Anglo-Dutch company), added up to something the British could at least use as a basis for negotiations. Musaddiq had shown understanding of the issues involved and a willingness to negotiate on every issue except one – the one that could be expected to doom his offer – the exclusion of British technicians.

We waited until the new Conservative government, which had just been elected in England, assumed office.

Acheson presented our proposal to Eden at a luncheon meeting in Paris. Eden, having campaigned on criticism of the Labour government handling of the Iranian oil issue, was not in a mood to make concessions to Musaddiq. He preferred to wait for his expected fall. Eden was unhappy about the compensation arrangements; however, it was obvious that the Iranians could pay only out of profits from oil. The right to 50 per cent of profits (which was called Nationalization without Compensation) was the best possible method of payment. But the exclusion of British personnel entirely from a company the British had created and were proud of, was too much for a Britisher such as Eden. Eden thanked Acheson for our efforts but said in essence, referring to Musaddiq, send him home.

When I called on Musaddiq he took it gracefully. 'I know what you have come to tell me,' he said. There were no recriminations. He knew that he, and we, had failed. I explained that we were sorry that we had not been able to bridge the gap between him and the British. And it was in essence his stubborn anti-British attitude that had led to this failure. But was it, in the end, a failure? I offer a few conclusions regarding the personality and works of Muhammed Musaddiq, including the questions of who he was and whether the great struggle he engaged in, in an effort to free his country, was a success or failure.

1   Dr Musaddiq's background influenced him, on both political and economic grounds, to be a conservative; he had no reason to be attracted to socialism or communism. He was basically, I believe, a patriotic Iranian nationalist, whose lifelong aim was to free Iran from what he perceived to be foreign domination. Although he was undoubtedly more suspicious of the Soviets, the most immediate problem he considered to be the British government and the AIOC, which were operating the Iranian oil industry. He could not separate the two, particularly in light of the British government's majority ownership of the company and the close ties between the British Embassy ih Tehran and company officials in their protection of the AIOC's concessionary interests.

2   Musaddiq was in 1951 approaching 70 and exhibited personal peculiarities that might lead to the conclusion that he was suffering from senility, or partial irrationality. My own observations did not necessarily confirm this. I did, however, perceive several factors that undoubtedly affected his judgement. First was his well-known, almost psychotic anti-British bias, as he blamed the British for all of Iran's difficulties. I also observed devious modes of thinking and wily manoeuvres to achieve his goals, which reflected, I believe, his lifetime of experience in coping with great power interests in Iran, not just those of the British and the Soviets but those of

the United States. He must also have been affected by what he perceived to be a constant threat against his life, posed by the Shii extremists led by Abu'l Qasim, and by the extreme nationalists led by Husayn Makki. This, I believe, led him to take actions to protect himself. Within these limitations, however, I found his mental processes and reactions to be reasonably normal. He continued to govern as prime minister until his arrest and removal from office in August 1953.

3   In the end it must be concluded that Musaddiq failed, insofar as he was not able to take advantage of the opportunities he had created through the nationalization of the AIOC for the benefit of his country. If one assumes, however, that the British government was fundamentally opposed to dealing with Musaddiq on the question of nationalization – recognized as valid in international law – one can conclude that he never had a chance. Although his problem was complicated by his lack of experience, it is not clear he could ever have negotiated an agreement with the British acceptable to Iran. It is also clear that he did not have any real chance of success in producing and marketing Iran's nationalized oil.

4   In his efforts to free Iran from foreign influence or domination (depending on who uses the word), however, Musaddiq must be recognized as having been successful. He forced the AIOC to withdraw from Iran greatly reducing British influence. He prevented any other foreign government from filling the vacuum. No other foreign power has, since the demise of the British, succeeded in establishing comparable influence in Iran. Although a client of the United States the Shah remained quite independent of us, not hesitating to force OPEC to quadruple the oil price, which we opposed. The new situation that Musaddiq created was readily accepted, and was made full use of by the Shah, in his later furtherance of Iranian interests. Although Musaddiq was a political leader, in contrast to the religious leaders of the present regime, he is generally accorded in Iran today, at least by the educated classes, a very high position among his country's great men.

5   Although Iran paid a heavy price in lost revenues from 1949 until 1953, its mistakes and shortcomings were at least its own. With the fourfold OPEC oil price rise of 1973, and later increases, its oil revenues were to reach heights the Iranians had not thought possible. The AIOC and the British would, however, have been better off if they had been able to negotiate an agreement during the 1951–3 period on something like the fifty–fifty formula, which Acheson and I considered possible at the time. It was not just a question of saving the revenues lost before the 1953 concession agreement negotiated with Iran with the help of Herbert Hoover, Jr, by a consortium of oil companies. Although the financial aspects agreed to were essentially the same as fifty–fifty profit sharing, the

AIOC was forced to cede over 50 per cent of its interest to US and other oil companies. They thereby, because of the diminution of their interest, lost anyway over half of the revenues they would have received from 1953 to the final Iranian expropriation of foreign oil interests in 1978.

6 On the face of it, the overthrow of Musaddiq in 1953 provided the consortium 26 years of additional oil revenues, before the final overthrow of the Shah in 1979. But was this victory good for Iran and longer term western interests? Much of the oil revenue of this period would have accrued in any event to the government of Iran. The fact was that Britain and the United States colluded to overthrow by force the constitutionally elected prime minister of Iran, and restore the Shah. This was not only publicly proclaimed to the world but exulted in as a great victory. Undoubtedly it contributed substantially to the ultimate rise to power of the Khomeini regime, and to the development of a schizophrenic, Islamic-based, deeply anti-western attitude among the Iranian people, which will last a very long time. The rejoining of Iran with the western world will be indefinitely postponed.

Neither Truman nor Acheson nor I would in the early 1950s have accepted the policy of overthrowing Musaddiq made by Eisenhower and Dulles in 1953. Apart from the political risks involved, which have now been clearly revealed, it would have been rejected on the grounds of international morality. The undue reliance of the Eisenhower era on subversive methods, which Kennedy attempted to curtail, took a heavy toll on the prestige of our country abroad. It resulted, I believe, in a great loss of confidence in us by other nations, particularly the new nations of the developing world struggling for survival and self-respect after the demise of the colonial era.

Notes

1 George McGhee, *Envoy to the Middle World* (New York, 1983) p. xvii.
2 Ibid., p. 393.
3 Ibid., p. 389.
4 Ibid., p. 392.
5 Ibid., p. 390.
6 Ibid., p. 391.
7 Ibid., p. 401.
8 Ibid., p. 395.
9 Vernon Walters, *Silent Missions* (New York, 1978) pp. 246–63.
10 Mohammed Reza Shah Pahlavi, *Mission for My Country* (London, 1961) p. 91.
11 McGhee, *Envoy*, ch. 31.

PART IV

Intellectual and historical perspectives

12

Intellectual trends in the politics and history of the Musaddiq era

R. K. RAMAZANI

Ever since the fall of the government of Dr Muhammad Musaddiq, a plethora of ideas has been advanced to explain his failure. Although few analysts disagree that the Anglo-American intervention was the immediate cause of his fall, most scholars differ about the distant causes of his failure. In economic terms, he is blamed for making the country bankrupt, for losing the financial support of the bazaar, and for peddling the notion of an 'oil-less' economy. In ideological terms, he is accused of being conservative, or too liberal, or even communist. And in political terms, he is criticized for losing the vital support of the army, for lacking constructive programmes, and for hurting the cause of liberal, democratic nationalism by falling prey to irrationality.

Yet, these and similar ideas have so far failed to relate Musaddiq's tenure to the larger context of Iranian history, society and culture in a search for the deeper meaning of his failure. Iranian society was not a *tabula rasa* before the Musaddiq era; nor has it been since. Musaddiq's experience has been part and parcel of the longer, larger and continuing encounter between Iranian society and the modern world.

The ultimate argument of this essay is that Musaddiq's failure reflects the still unresolved normative problem of Iranian society as to how to come to terms with the challenges posed by the values and realities of 'world culture'. In reaching this final argument, I advance three interrelated propositions. First, the Musaddiq failure was a defeat of an essentially anti-imperialistic, rather than liberal and democratic, nationalism. Second, nation-wide factionalism – rather than simply factional defections from the National Front – invited the Anglo-American intervention in which the royalist faction fully participated. Third, and finally, factionalism does not simply stem from socio-political or socio-cultural malaise in Iranian history, as some leading Iranian intellectuals contend; rather, it is an aspect

307

of the larger unresolved normative problem of the relation of Iran's culture to 'world culture'. In other words, as long as the Iranian intellectual and political elites disagree about the core values, guiding principles, and basic institutions of the polity and as long as the people of Iran have not reached a level of political development that will permit them to freely debate and accept their governance, the problem of factionalism will continue, resulting in cycles of socio-political convulsion and authoritarian rule in the future, as in the historical past.

Explaining the failure of Dr Musaddiq

Let us begin with a rapid survey of the principal explanations about the failure of the Musaddiq government. The literature on the subject is considerable and no interest will be served by cataloguing the wide variety of viewpoints. Major explanatory ideas, however, fall into several categories, each characterized by the overall emphasis of several analysts. Thus, the opinions about the failure of the Musaddiq government are discussed below in terms of analytical stress on economic, ideological and political factors, granted, of course, that some analyses cut across two or more categories.

Economically, Musaddiq's failure to solve the oil nationalization crisis – which threatened to bring the economic collapse of the country as a result of near financial bankruptcy – incited opposition to him.[1] Other explanations appear to blame Musaddiq's failure on the dissatisfaction of the bazaar merchants from whom he had enjoyed considerable support. But some analysts seem to link the decline of support in the bazaar to 'threatened religious tenets', probably attributable to the perceived threat of communism.[2] One analyst goes so far as to link the deteriorating economic conditions to the loss of Iran to the Soviet Union. He says:

> Nationalization of the Anglo-Iranian Oil Company brought the economy of the country to a standstill, emptied the treasury, deprived the country of the opportunity to secure foreign credits, and unleashed many destructive forces that might have produced not only the overthrow of the monarchy but also subjection of Iran to the Soviet Union, making it a satellite state.[3]

Other economic explanations emphatically distinguish the two problems of oil revenues and the Tudeh Party, but only to speculate that continued oil revenues and foreign aid would have reduced the appeal of the communists to certain groups in the society. The government, according to this explanation, would have been able to push economic development programmes along the lines of the Seven-Year Plan, reducing somewhat the 'grievances of urban workers, the bureaucracy, students, the peasants, and perhaps ultimately the tribesmen.'[4] This same explanation suggests that the notion of an 'oil-less' economy is not all that absurd. Without oil revenues the economy could have worked for a short while. Even then it would have required, however, lots of 'national determination' and no 'Tudeh agitation'. Realistically, under the circumstances, no such blissful state could possibly have existed and hence this statement amounts to mere speculation.

Ideologically, the failure of Musaddiq is most often attributed to his 'conservatism', and most leftists blame him for not having been revolutionary enough. One observer states categorically: 'Mossadegh mistakenly aimed his appeal mainly at the country's urban middle classes and intellectuals, neglecting the mass of the Iranian population, 75 percent of whom are peasants . . .'[5] The Fida'iyan-i Khalq group is highly critical of Musaddiq. Their leader, Bizhan Jazani, asserts that the National Front played no role in mobilizing and leading the masses and that Musaddiq's relations with his associates were 'paternalistic'. He avers that Musaddiq's 'understanding of the American imperialists and their role was deeply erroneous'.[6] Like many leftists, Jazani sees Musaddiq's rise to power as being the result of 'contradiction' between the United States and Britain. His return to power in July 1952 was, Jazani says, as a result of the support of the Tudeh Party and the Soviet Union, 'and above all as a result of the spontaneous uprising by the whole people . . .' It is interesting to note that anti-Tudeh communists belonging to the Sazman-i Vahdat-i Kumunisti (Organization of Communist Unity) beat the Tudeh Party with the Musaddiq stick for its reluctance to co-operate with the National Front.[7]

The Mujahidin-i Khalq, on the other hand, blamed the downfall of Musaddiq on a coup that was engineered by the United States and the sister of the Shah, Ashraf Pahlavi, a coup that was funded (to the tune of ten million dollars) by the United States and implemented by General Zahidi and such hoodlums as Sha'ban the brainless. They praised Musaddiq for having the support of 'the whole people'. He accomplished 'the most highly valued services in the history [of Iran] in spite of the severest imperialist pressures'.[8] These words were declaimed by Sa'id Mihsan, a founder of the organization, during his trial before the Shah's military tribunal in 1974.

Musaddiq's failure has also been attributed to his mistaken foreign policy of 'negative equilibrium'. One variation on this explanation faults him for not adhering strictly to the tenets of that doctrine in practice.[9] Musaddiq is criticized for having befriended and antagonized both superpowers by pursuing contradictory policies; he is said to have underestimated the strength of Anglo-American co-operation, which was highly motivated by the imperatives of the cold war between the eastern and western blocs; and it is said that he overestimated his own ability, first by trying to use the American card against the British, and then by playing the Russian card against the Americans. The basic question that such a critique does not address is how the analyst's own proposed policy of 'absolute non-alignment' (*bitarafi-yi mutlaq*) could have possibly worked, considering that Musaddiq's foreign policy partly reflected such endemic ills as factionalism, personal rivalry, threat of political violence and other difficulties bedevilling his domestic politics.

This brings us to the political explanation of the failure of Musaddiq. This category ranges over a whole variety of factors, including the breakup of the National Front coalition because of the defection of Baqa'i and Kashani; Musaddiq's increasing involvement with the Tudeh Party after July 1952; the struggle over the control of the military; the agitation over Musaddiq's 'dictatorial powers' and referendum. But it is the quality of his own leadership and temperament which seems to engage the attention of most political observers. Four major examples of the assessment of his leadership will follow.

First, Musaddiq's failure to resolve the oil dispute is blamed on a combination of the ill advice of his close associates and his own 'unjustifiable fear of unpopularity'. The proponent of this view states that Musaddiq made 'the greatest mistake of his career – a mistake, moreover, that condemned the Iranian Popular Movement to ultimate failure . . .' by rejecting the World Bank proposal. Presumably, his colleagues advised him against this solution, for the Tudeh Party would charge 'treason', and he would lose popularity.[10]

Second, Musaddiq failed not only because his moves were 'poorly planned', but also because of a more endemic factor in the Iranian body politic. As one observer puts it,

> He underestimated the strength of the opposition, and did not have sufficient support within the armed forces. The crucial issue was confirmation of the traditional adage that an Iranian ruler survives as long as he is successful. So long as Mossadegh was on top the Shah could command little support; but as Mossadegh's position weakened, the Iranians once again began to hedge their bets.[11]

Third, Musaddiq was, above all, the victim of his own policies rather than 'economic hardship'. These policies lacked 'any positive content'. This proposition is advanced as follows:

> Once he had, as Mossadeq and his supporters saw it, liberated Iran from the clutches of British imperialism, he had no ideas about the path on which he wanted Iran to tread and, after the expulsion of the A.I.O.C., his policy consisted of a number of uncoordinated expedients designed to keep himself in power and to delay the onset of the economic embarrassments which he himself had created. In order to obtain power, and in order to sustain himself

in power, he had called to his aid various disparate forces and enthusiasms – which, being neither loyal to himself nor congruent with each other, he was unable to use, either as an instrument of national regeneration or as a means of consolidating his own authority . . .[12]

Fourth, and finally, one of the most sympathetic students of Iranian nationalism attributes Musaddiq's failure and that of 'liberal, democratic' nationalism to his 'irrationality':

In essence, Iranian Nationalism foundered on the shoals of its own irrationality. It had won a victory of immense proportions in March 1951, but failing to understand how near victory it was, Nationalism consumed itself in a negative struggle with forces which it had virtually defeated. Although a mass movement of the size and intensity of the National Movement will inevitably be to a large degree based on an irrational appeal, rationality can prevail if the leadership rises above the emotionalism of the mass and gives sensible direction. The conclusion is inescapable in this case that Mossadeq was as much a prisoner of irrationality as were many of his least literate supporters.[13]

More nationalism than liberalism

Being based on a serious study of Iranian nationalism, the explanation that Musaddiq's failure was the defeat of 'liberal, democratic' nationalism deserves close scrutiny, for three reasons.

First, while it is safe to suggest that Musaddiq and a few of his close associates – such as Allahyar Saleh, Abdullah Mu'azzami and Ali Shayigan – were inspired by democratic ideals, it is questionable whether any systematic ideological formulation based on liberal values by the Musaddiqists existed at the time. As early as 1944, Musaddiq himself had said, 'Whatever I have said during my lifetime is my programme.'[14] And even ten years later he still had no clear ideological position. According to his close associate Mihdi Bazargan, when he established the National Resistance Movement after the coup of 28 *Murdad* (19 August 1953), Musaddiq sent him a personal message of thanks and support. The message said that Bazargan had accomplished 'what we did not have the opportunity to give attention to, that is, you have provided ideological and organizational foundation for the national struggle'.[15] We have no way of checking this important testimony, but considering Bazargan's evidently more religious predisposition, compared with Musaddiq's more secular orientation, one would suppose that he would not have found Bazargan's formulation all that palatable. As a matter of fact, because of this ideological uncertainty the search for some kind of formulation has continued as evidenced, for example, by the claim of the so-called Third National Frontists who have tried to expound what they call 'Musaddiq ideology' (*maktab-i Musaddiq*), insisting that his 'negative equilibrium' was philosophically rooted in the 'principle of rediscovery of the self' (*asl-i khud bazyaftan*).[16]

Second, the great heterogeneity of the elite support of the National Front itself casts doubt on the characterization of the nationalist movement as liberal and democratic. Except for a handful at the centre – who may be said to have cherished liberal values, at least in theory – the vast majority of factions on the right and the left of the Front's spectrum represented all sorts of undemocratic orientations. If one were to characterize the members of the old Iran Party in the middle as largely liberal in their outlook, then the Toilers Party of Muzaffar Baqa'i on the left could hardly be regarded as liberal; nor could the irredentist Pan-Iran Party of Daryush Furuhar on the right; and nor could the fascist National Socialist Party of the Iranian Workers – a group best known by its Persian acronym, Sumka, by the black uniform of its members and by its leader Munshizadeh.

Even more important, the problem of the narrow base of elite support for the liberalism of the Musaddiqists was compounded by the association of Ayatullah Abu'l Qasim Kashani's Mujahidin-i Islam and possibly Navvab Safavi's Fida'iyan-i Islam with the National Front. With their generally religious orientation, they contradicted the Musaddiqists' essentially secular thrust as well as their liberalism. For this important reason, the analyst who has most forcefully equated the Iranian nationalism of the Musaddiq era with liberalism reveals his difficulty in reconciling this contradiction in saying that the Fida'iyan 'almost by definition could not have been intimately associated with the National Front'. Because the supporters of this organization were 'the most bitter opponents of the secular trend, the Fida'iyan was the natural enemy of the Nationalist movement'.[17] But this is perhaps an expression of the analyst's own wish rather than an empirical fact.

Two pieces of evidence make it difficult to wish away the Fida'iyan's association with the National Front. One – as yet unrefuted – is a Fida'iyan claim that during the Musaddiq period they were in 'advance contact' with the National Front before various political demonstrations.[18] The other is that although at times Kashani seemed to be trying to distance himself from the Fida'iyan – particularly on the issue of terrorism[19] – he was associated with them and the basic premise of his ideology was fully compatible with theirs. Both firmly believed that Islam and politics were inseparable, a conviction that clearly contradicted the essentially secularist commitment of the Musaddiqists at the centre of the National Front. Furthermore, the Fida'iyan leaders insist that they consulted Kashani before participating in any 'demonstration'.[20]

The point needs to be emphasized, however, that the anti-liberal and religious orientation of the Kashani group and the Fida'iyan does not change the fact that the nationalist movement as a whole was primarily secular in nature. This phenomenon stemmed from the ascendancy of the influence of the modernized intellectuals in Iranian politics at the time. This ascendancy in turn reflected several major developments. The modern middle and lower classes had expanded considerably by the time of the rise of Musaddiq to power. By then about 10 per cent of the population (about 16 million) consisted of the modern middle classes and even before then both white and blue collar workers had grown large enough for the Tudeh Party to be able to count on the support of about half a million members and sympathizers.[21] Moreover, contrary to conventional wisdom, many modernized intellectuals who joined or formed various political groups and parties after the fall of Riza Shah had participated in the processes of modernization during his rule. According to Mihdi Bazargan, in doing so they had been motivated by 'belief in and concern for, reforms, social and cultural change and economic development, all aimed at realizing (national) renewal and evolution'.[22] The younger intellectuals, he says, were 'more radical' and had, more or less, leftist and socialist ideas. They were even more critical of Riza Shah's dictatorial regime than older moderate intellectuals, but they, too, were optimistic about the prospects for change. Finally, the Shii clerics, as contrasted with the intelligentsia, had little influence in politics at the time. Unlike the modernized intellectuals, they had suffered grievously during the rule of Riza Shah. Those religious leaders like Mudarris who had opposed the Shah either kept quiet or were suppressed. Others, like Ayatullah Burujirdi, did not rock the boat and, by and large, the ulama were generally on the defensive rather than simply 'quietist' as is so often said. The best evidence in support of this point is Ayatullah Ruhullah Khomeini's 334-page defensive treatise, *Kashf-i asrar* (Discovery of secrets) published in 1943 in response to a blistering 38-page critique of Shiism by a follower of Ahmad Kasravi, called Hakamizadeh.[23] At the end of his *Asrar-i hizar-saleh* (Secrets of a thousand years), Hakamizadeh posed 13 critical questions.[24] Without ever mentioning his opponent by name, Khomeini addressed these questions in his treatise, first attacking 'enlightened intellectuals', and then linking their ideas to the 'ignorant thoughts' of Ibn Taymiyya whose efforts to free Islam from religious 'imitation' (*taqlid*) he denounced.[25]

The third difficulty in characterizing the nationalism of the Musaddiq era as simply liberal and democratic is the undeniable primacy of the anti-imperialism in the nationalist movement. The Musaddiqists claimed that their struggle against Britain and the Anglo-Iranian Oil Company (AIOC) was aimed at Iran's complete national independence and that their ultimate goal was 'liberty and democracy' for Iran. But a detailed study of Iran's foreign policy during the Musaddiq era has shown that the immediate objective of national independence, in practice, became the absolute and overriding goal of the nationalist movement.[26] I should add here that the achievement of that goal was sought almost at any price, including the destruction of the cherished institutional symbols of liberal, democratic politics, that is, free parliamentary elections and a genuinely representative Majlis. Given this anti-imperialist thrust of the nationalist movement, it is reasonable to say that *it was more nationalistic than democratic* in nature.

In 1917, E. G. Brown characterized the nationalism of the Constitutional period as more nationalistic than democratic. More than 20 years ago a similar conclusion was reached independently.[27] It would appear, therefore, that in practice both the constitutional government and the Musaddiq government accorded the goal of national independence, as opposed to individual liberty, the highest priority. Moreover, during both periods the end of national self-determination enjoyed varying degrees of popular support. Although it may be said that the general goal of national independence continued during the authoritarian rule of Riza Shah and his son, their integral nationalism aimed at serving the interests of the Pahlavi dynasty and did not have the kind of popular support enjoyed by Constitutional nationalism and nationalism under Musaddiq.[28]

More factionalism than nationalism

Implicit in the above discussion has been the proposition that the Musaddiq government was destroyed more by factionalism than by any of the economic, ideological and political factors emphasized by other scholars. In this section, I attempt to make this proposition more explicit by showing that, contrary to conventional wisdom, it was not simply factional defection from the National Front that undermined the Musaddiq government. Rather, it was a more nation-wide political fragmentation that first weakened the base of popular support for the nationalist government and eventually played into the hands of Britain and the United States which dealt the *coup de grâce*. Let us examine this proposition from the perspectives of the principal factions of the critical 1941–51 decade.

From the perspective of his supporters, Musaddiq's rise to power marked the dawn of the period of 'constitutional revival' after a long and hard national struggle. Musaddiq had not only effectively opposed the Soviet demand for an oil concession in 1944, but had also persuaded the 14th Majlis to pass a law prohibiting the granting of oil concessions to any foreign actor, in keeping with his doctrine of 'negative equilibrium'.[29] The 15th Majlis latched on to this law in 1947 and declared the Qavam–Sadchikov oil agreement 'null and void'. In 1950–1, Musaddiq and eight of his supporters in the 16th Majlis managed to persuade the parliament to nationalize the oil industry throughout the country. At this time, they also recommended his premiership to the Shah.

To the Tudeh Party it appeared that the rise of Musaddiq to power could be used to revive the communist movement.[30] They sorely needed a boost, as their membership had been nearly decimated. Those suspected of being communist had been outlawed in 1931. They had lost their leader, Taqi Arani, in 1937, when he died in gaol under Riza Shah. Some eight members of the original group of 53 communists formed the Tudeh Party in 1941, after having been released from gaol. At the time everything seemed to favour their renaissance. Besides a clear ideological stance, they had a well-organized party, and enjoyed the full protection of the Soviet's military presence in Iran from 1941 to 1946. they also had some very powerful propaganda machinery which at one time included 50 pro-Tudeh newspapers in Tehran and the provinces.[31]

Nevertheless, they suffered one defeat after another. In the 14th Majlis, the nationalist deputies stole the show from them in the crusade against the American Millspaugh mission. The Musaddiqists also took the spotlight in their successful fight against Soviet demands for an oil concession, demands which the Tudeh deputies supported. When Qavam appointed three Tudeh leaders to his Cabinet, their party appeared to be riding the crest of its political power. As it turned out, however, the Tudeh Party was in fact being used as a tool in the destruction of the Soviet-supported communist rebel regime in Azarbayjan. After the attempt against the Shah's life in 1949, all Tudeh activities were banned, and it remained an outlawed party.

The Shii fundamentalist faction saw the nationalization of the oil industry and the accession of Musaddiq to premiership as compatible with their ultimate objective of establishing the rule of Islamic law in Iran. Towards that end, Sayyid Mujtaba Navvab Safavi, with the help of Sayyid Husayn Imami, and the two brothers Sayyid Abdul Husayn and Sayyid Muhammad Vahidi, established the Fida'iyan-i Islam in 1946. Modelled after the Muslim Brotherhood, it boasted of having 'ideological, political and military dimensions'. Terrorism was their preferred means. In 1946, they killed Ahmad Kasravi, the leading Iranian historian.[32] In 1978, the same organization proudly claimed that he had been killed because he had wanted to 'purify Islam' in Iran, that is, to separate religion from politics. In 1949, they assassinated the Court minister – formerly prime minister – Abdul Husayn Hazhir, claiming that he was a 'British agent'. In 1951, they assassinated Prime Minister Ali Razmara and Dr Abdul Hamid Zanganeh, charging that they had 'opposed the nationalization' of the oil industry.[33]

The pro-Shah faction saw the rise of Musaddiq as promising trouble for it.[34] The Shah himself knew Musaddiq well as an opponent. Musaddiq had been an opponent of Riza Shah and had demanded that the Shah reign as a constitutional monarch rather than rule like his dictatorial father. He had doggedly opposed foreign influence in Iran. The young Shah, however, had his own ideas. He wanted to consolidate his political control, and he knew that the army could be a decisive instrument of power, as it had been for his father. But it had been discredited, for it had collapsed ignominiously before the Anglo-Russian invasion forces. The young Shah saw an alliance with the United States as one way of acquiring money to modernize the military and the economy, thus strengthening his rule against rival political factions. Such an alliance would, furthermore, protect his regime from the Soviet Union which had also been the *bête noire* of his father. He was rebuffed by the United States, however, in 1949, and so turned to the AIOC in his search for increased revenues. But Musaddiq spoiled his game by leading the movement to nationalize the oil industry, insisting that what was at stake in the struggle against the AIOC was Iran's moral and political rights, not financial gain.[35]

Factionalism during both the Constitutional period and the Musaddiq era made it possible for royalists to take part in foreign intervention to overthrow rival nationalists. In 1908 Muhammad Ali Shah participated in the Russian intervention against the nationalist government, and in 1911 the pro-Shah Cabinet engineered a *coup d'état* against the Majlis.[36] In the first instance the participation of the Shah and his lackeys such as Salar al-Dawleh, Shuja al-Dawleh and Shapshal Khan in the predatory Russian intervention resulted in the strangling of Malik al-Mutakallimin, the popular nationalist orator, and Mirza Jahangir Khan, the editor of the well-known newspaper *Sur-i Israfil*.

Without belabouring a point which has been made in detail elsewhere,[37] ever since his accession to the throne, the Shah had single-mindedly cultivated Anglo-American friendship and told the American minister as early as 1941 that he wished to ally his government with the US government. He strengthened the army with the aid of the United States, played up his anti-Soviet and anti-communist stance, and eventually participated in the Anglo-American intervention to overthrow the nationalist government of Dr Musaddiq. Just as Muhammad Ali Shah had been supported in his anti-nationalist activities by the notorious Shapshal Khan, Muhammad Riza Shah was aided in his action by such goons as 'Sha'ban the brainless'.

The causes of factionalism

If indeed factionalism undermined nationalist governments during both the Constitutional period and the Musaddiq years, how does one explain the problem of socio-political fragmentation in Iranian history? I turn to modernized intellectuals for answers. They had been more influential than religious thinkers during the Musaddiq era. Furthermore, they believed that factionalism (*tafraqeh*) was a major obstacle in developing national consciousness and creating a modern political community. Shortly after the second world war, in particular, a growing number of Iranian intellectuals perceived national salvation as attainable through discarding the old ways of life.

This trend in Iranian thought was best evidenced by the historic first meeting of Iranian writers in 1946. Some 70 men of letters gathered together to celebrate the occasion in Tehran. The gathering included such older generation literary leaders as Dihkhuda and Bahar and such younger generation figures as Jalal Al-i Ahmad and Chubak. In reviewing the historically important interrelationship between Iranian literature and social and political life, Bahar saw Iran at the crossroads of history: one path, he said, led to 'oldness' and the other to 'newness'. Sounding the same theme in greater detail, Parviz Khanlari called for 'progress and advancement, for eradication of corruption, and for reformation of social and political malaise'. Given these general concerns of the intellectuals, I discuss below their specific concern with the endemic problem of factionalism through the works of three leading modernized Iranian thinkers. My choice has been guided by several considerations. First, although only one of the three lived through the Musaddiq era the other two had died shortly before and hence all were close to the spirit of the time. Second, these three writers represent different kinds of thinkers, a social critic, a historian, and a novelist. Third, the influence of their works on other intellectuals as well as on Iranian society has been universally acknowledged. Fourth, they all address, in one way or another, the 'malaise' of factionalism. Two of them explicitly prescribe remedies.

One of the thinkers is Jalal Al-i Ahmad (1923–1969). Among other things, he is a well-known social critic and was a political activist. He first joined the Tudeh Party and then Khalil Maliki's Third Force. He is also believed to have influenced the thought of Ali Shari'ati, the so-called ideologue of the Iranian revolution. Al-i Ahmad is certainly concerned with the problem of factionalism in Iranian social and political life. To him, however, the factional conflict that matters most in Iranian history is the one between the intellectuals and the clerics. During the tobacco protest (1891–2), he writes, the ulama acted independently and 'apparently' won the 'Social Struggle' at first, but then because of conflict between the modernized intelligentsia and the clerics the country suffered a setback.[38] In the Constitutional Revolution, he says, the two groups co-operated, but their gain was brief because the right-wing clerics split; not all the clerics were committed to the cause of constitutionalism.

Although he cites two other instances from Iran's historical experience to show the evil consequences of factional strife between the clerics and the intellectuals, it is his account of the Musaddiq period that is most relevant here. He says that despite all the obstacles that the Tudeh Party placed in the way of the National Front, as long as the clerics and the 'liberal intellectuals' co-operated against imperialism, the nationalist movement was successful, indeed so successful that foreign powers – the United States and Britain – had to resort to 'direct intervention' to destroy the National Front. Nevertheless, Al-i Ahmad blames the failure of the nationalist movement on the factional quarrel between Kashani and Baqa'i on the one hand and Kashani and Musaddiq on the other.

Al-i Ahmad tries to explain the roots of the conflict between the clerics and the intellectuals. He actually ends up blaming the intellectuals. He accuses them of harbouring a negative attitude toward the clerics, an attitude that has been influenced, he argues, by two historical developments: the French Revolution and the Russian Revolution. The intellectuals, he says, are too impressed by the *Encyclopedie* and the *philosophes* (of the Age of Enlightenment) such as Voltaire, Rousseau, and Diderot, and by the 'social democracy in Germany and England, which founded scientific socialism, and eventually led to Marx, Engels, Lenin and the October Revolution'.[39]

In other words, the main cause of the clash between the intellectual and the religious leaders throughout the modern history of Iran has been the alleged fact that Iranian intellectuals have blindly imitated western intellectuals. Just as western intellectuals quarrelled with the Christian clergy in the historical past, the Iranian modernized intellectuals have fought the Muslim clerics. This is an absurd imitation, he believes: the 'situation' in eighteenth-century Europe vastly differed from that of thirteenth-century Islamic Iran. Although the general theme of *Gharbzadigi* (Westoxication) – for which Al-i Ahmad is best known – surfaces in his *Dar khidmat va khiyanat-i rawshanfikran* (Concerning the service and treason of the intellectuals), it is the latter work that is most useful for elucidating his views on Iranian factionalism. Although he defines factionalism in the narrow sense of conflict between the intellectuals and the clerics, he nevertheless seems to postulate a general socio-political law in these terms:

Whenever clericalism and intellectualism go hand in hand or one follows the other [in Iranian politics] there is in the Social Struggle a gain, progress and a step toward perfection and evolution. And whenever these two have clashed with, or ignored, each other or have singly participated in the struggle, there has been, from a social perspective, a loss, a setback, and a step backward.[40]

Ahmad Kasravi, our second leading writer, acknowledges the pervasiveness of factionalism in Iranian culture, society and politics. To be sure, Al-i Ahmad exaggerates, when in praising Kasravi's scholarly works, he says, 'Only one of his books on constitutionalism is worth more than all the literary, historical and research products of the twenty years [of Riza Shah's rule].' He also vastly overestimates when he says of every 100 Iranians 70 to 80 read Kasravi's books. Nevertheless, the influence of the historian Kasravi on modern social and political thought in Iran has been widely acknowledged.

Kasravi's views on factionalism in Iranian politics are much broader than Al-i Ahmad's. To him, perhaps the single most serious of all 'maladies' (*aludehgiha*) in Iranian culture and society is factionalism, a malady that he believes is the by-product of both indigenous socio-cultural ills and ideological malaise imported from abroad. He seems to single out dialectical materialism as probably the greatest of all the *imported* evils, although he does search for the roots of factionalism in Iran's indigenous soil. Kasravi divides the factors that he believes underpin lack of socio-cultural cohesion, and political fragmentation, in Iran into nine categories. These include such factors as 'diverse religious traditions' (*kishha-yi gunagun*), a great variety of languages, a multitude of tribal groups, and mass illiteracy.[41]

Of all these categories, however, it is the category of religious traditions that stands out in Kasravi's attack on Iranian societal maladies. The followers of these religions or sects include Shias, Shaykhis, Karimkhanis, Baha'is, Christians, Zoroastrians, Jews, Isma'ilis and others. Although Kasravi emphasizes the value of 'virtue', it is not a religious virtue that he seeks, but a civic virtue. As a vigorous advocate of a secular approach to life, he criticizes all religious traditions, which he holds partly responsible for factionalism. But the great weight of his criticism falls squarely on Shiism or what he seems to call pejoratively *shi'agari*.

Kasravi questions the very concept of divine rule which Muslim fundamentalist clerics advocate. On the contrary, he insists on the notion of the sovereignty of the nation. He denounces those ulama, whom he derogatorily calls *mullaha*, for nine other reasons, besides their claim to temporal and spiritual authority. He rejects, for example, the Shii concepts of *ghaybah* (occultation of the Twelfth Imam) and *qiyamah* (resurrection). He also denounces such religious practices as the pilgrimage to Shii holy shrines in Qum, Mashhad, Karbala, Najaf, and other sites, charging that these amount to 'idol worship'.[42] In attacking the clerics, he taunts: 'If sovereignty is yours, why don't you work at it?'; 'If leadership is yours and you can exercise it, why don't you want to take it?'[43]

Unlike Al-i Ahmad, Kasravi sees the Shii clerics as a cause of Iranian backwardness. The reason he views them in such a negative light is his belief that the root cause of all social ills, and factionalism in particular, is 'the obfuscation of the mind'; the Shii clerics he argues play the leading role in perpetuating ignorance, particularly among the masses of the people.[44] Given this diagnosis, he prescribes national rejuvenation by 'enlightening the mind'. Through education, he wants to change the outmoded belief system, backward attitudes, and anachronistic habits of the people. Such transformations are necessary for eradicating factionalism and developing in its place national consciousness and national unity.

Kasravi's secular nationalism, however, seems to decry chauvinism and xenophobia. His 'three pillars of politics' (*seh payeh-i siyasat*) shows that he is an advocate of both enlightened nationalism and internationalism. The virtue of the individual person is the first prerequisite to freeing the collectivity of the nation from ignorance and socio-cultural malaise. 'A man who is not virtuous', he writes, 'can not partake of the world's virtues'[45] and this is the 'world law' (*ayin-i sipihr*). Although his second pillar calls for the nation's control of Iran's foreign policy, he sees no reason why Iran should not pursue a conciliatory policy towards the Soviet Union and Britain, the great powers of concern to the Iranians at the time he was writing. Furthermore, Iran should be concerned with the 'welfare of the world' (*niki-yi jahan*) and should 'fight' all international ills through co-operation with other well-meaning peoples of the world.[46]

In a discussion of the problem of factionalism as viewed by Iranian intellectuals, it would be remiss not to mention Sadiq Hidayat, our third writer. First, although he is neither a social critic like Al-i Ahmad, nor a historian, like Kasravi, he is a superb critic of social classes. Second, there is some resemblance between the ideas of Kasravi and Sadiq Hidayat in their views regarding the clerics. To both men, the clerics are responsible for the obfuscation of the minds of the masses of the people. Third, as the star literary artist of Iran, Sadiq Hidayat has been widely read by Iranians. His story of *Hajji Agha* is as relevant to an understanding of the Iranian society today as it was in 1945 when it was first published.[47]

A businessman by profession, Hajji Agha's wheelings and dealings extend to politics and religion as well as commerce. He hires a cleric, another major character in the story, who is satirically called Hujjat al-Shari'at (Living proof of God's law). A third principal character in the story is Monadi al-Haqq (Proclaimer of the truth). While the first two characters represent the reactionary classes, the third character – an enlightened poet who is said to express the ideas of Hidayat himself – presumably represents the Iranian modernized intelligentsia. While Hajji Agha and his hired cleric oppose every social change, the poet condemns the *status quo*, which protects the vested interests of such selfish, corrupt and hypocritical characters as Hajji Agha and his servile cleric.

Let me sample a few lines from Hidayat's story on each of these characters. Their discourse portrays the diametrically opposite views of the traditional and the modern classes as a major source of factionalism in the Iranian society and culture. Hajji Agha instructs the cleric as follows:

what we [the traditional entrepreneurial and clerical classes] want – though in the name of religion – is to give currency once more to the old customs and practices. We need fanatics, breast-beaters, Passion play zealots, credulous people of all kinds – not pious Muslims, for God's sake! We must arrange matters so that the peasant not only thinks he needs you and me, but is grateful for it . . . .[48]

After listening to Hajji Agha's harangue on the ideas of the modernized poet, whom he calls 'a Bolshevik', the cleric says: 'There's a highly regarded Tradition of the Prophet to the effect that when the Holy One is due to come again, musicians and poets and mountebanks will be present in greater numbers. Poetry and painting and music and sculpture are all works of Satan.'[49]

The poet says:

What mankind is seeking is not the thief or the bandit or the sponger: man needs a meaning for his own life. One Ferdowsi [Iran's leading epic poet] is enough to justify the existence of millions like you [Hajji Agha], and you – whether you like it or not – derive a meaning for your life from him and take a pride in him. But now that science and art and culture have departed from this land, it is obvious that only theft and spying and villainy can give life meaning and worth . . . If the nation had any sense of honor, it would long since have got rid of the lot of you. A nation whose fate is in the hands of scroundrels.[50]

The unresolved normative questions

So far I have argued that Musaddiq's nationalism was more anti-imperialistic than liberal and democratic, and it failed more because of factionalism than the kind of economic, ideological and political reasons that other scholars have generally advanced. I have also examined the works of three quite different thinkers to show that the problem of factionalism has long been a significant source of concern in Iranian social and political thought. Moreover, we have seen how these thinkers tried to explain the problem of factionalism and what they seemed to prescribe for it. In the final section of this chapter, I attempt to introduce my own explanation of factionalism and hence explain the wider causes of Musaddiq's failure. In doing so, I would like to emphasize in advance that the problem of political fragmentation in Iranian society has continued since the Musaddiq era, and factionalism is not a uniquely Iranian problem. Let me expand briefly on these two points.

Factional politics prevailed during the Constitutional period and the Musaddiq years, that is, during the two major phases of Iranian nationalism before the Iranian revolution. Despite the revolution, however, factionalism has continued. To be sure, the supporters of Khomeini claim that the revolution has been uniformly Islamic, but the evidence suggests otherwise. Although Ayatullah Khomeini did eventually capture the leadership of the revolution, there is no doubt that a whole variety of other groups, including the National Front, participated in the revolutionary process from the beginning. In accepting Khomeini's overall leadership, Karim Sanjabi, the leader of the Front, believed that he was joining the national movement to the Islamic movement in a coalition against the Shah's regime.[51] Moreover, the revolutionary regime has over the years behaved quite nationalistically, despite its strident Islamic rhetoric.[52]

I would suggest that factionalism in Iranian society and politics has not only continued since the Musaddiq era, but has actually intensified in tandem with the spread of national consciousness among an ever larger number of people in the twentieth century. Just as the percentage of politically aware participants in the nationalist movement of the Musaddiq years exceeded those of the Constitutional period, the percentage of those who participated actively in the Iranian revolution greatly surpassed the percentages of those active in the two previous periods. Most students of Iran believe that large masses of the people participated in the revolutionary process and few observers would deny that populist tendencies partly characterize revolutionary politics in Iran today.

Yet, paradoxically, an increased sense of national identity among a growing number of people has been accompanied by a greater degree of factionalism, at least in the short term. Those scholars who had theorized that the processes of modernization in such forms as expanding industrialization, spreading education and improving communication would transform communalism, tribalism and factionalism into modern nationalism were surprised by the religious aspect of the Iranian revolution and the outburst of a myriad of religious as well as secular groups upon the political scene. In sheer exasperation over an intense factional struggle for power and ideology among various groups, Mihdi Bazargan complained, during his premiership, that the country was in practice being run by 'a thousand chiefs'. Today, Iran may have one chief, but it still has many political factions. There are a few which exist surreptitiously within the country, while there are many anti-Khomeini dissident groups in exile.

Factionalism is not a uniquely Iranian problem. From the western shores of the Persian Gulf to the eastern coasts of the Mediterranean, there is not a single country in which political fragmentation does not prevail. Lebanon is only the most extreme example: All Middle Eastern countries face the problem of factionalism. It is prevalent among many third world nations, despite the great cultural, societal and political differences that distinguish them from one another. For this reason, I hope my propositions about the root causes of factionalism in Iran will be suggestive with respect to the study of factional conflict in other third world societies.

Given the continuation and intensification of political fragmentation in

Iran since the Musaddiq period and its general pervasiveness, we must again ask, how does one explain factionalism? With reference to Iranian society, the three intellectuals discussed above provide different explanations. Al-i Ahmad finds the roots of factionalism in the anticlerical attitudes of the modernized intellectuals who allegedly imitate the conflict between western intellectuals and the Christian clergy. Had he lived to see the Iranian revolution, he would have noted that the two groups failed once again to co-operate in the political process and would have added a seventh instance to his six instances of setbacks in Iran's 'Social Struggle' – that of the conflict between the clerics and the intellectuals since the Constitutional Revolution. Kasravi believes that ethnic, linguistic and, above all, religious divisions contribute to factional antagonism. But he holds the Shia mullas especially responsible for the obfuscation of the minds of the masses of the people and hence for factionalism. While Al-i Ahmad prescribes clerical–intellectual co-operation as the solution to the problem, Kasravi advocates 'enlightening the mind' of individuals and groups as the road to salvation. Had Kasravi lived to see the Iranian revolution he would have been astounded by the rule of the mullas.

Finally, Hidayat seems to imply that factional divisions spring from the clashing values and attitudes of the traditional and modern classes, the 'two cultures'. He would wish to see the eventual triumph of his modernized poet over the traditional businessman and his hired hypocritical mulla. Had Hidayat lived to see the Iranian revolution, like Kasravi, he would have been astonished by the rule of the clerics. No less than Kasravi, he would have resented the fact that the mullas and their allied capitalists of the bazaar have managed to preserve their vested interests, despite the revolutionary regime's avowed ideological support for the poorer masses of the people, the *mustaza'fin*.

Regardless of how these thinkers explain the roots of factionalism in Iranian society and politics, they seem to share one basic assumption: as long as there are political factions there is factionalism. It is partly because of such an assumption that their prescriptions for remedying factional conflict sound so simple: stop imitating the western intellectuals and co-operate with the clerics, says Al-i Ahmad to the Iranian intelligentsia; free the minds of the masses of the people from the shackles of Shii superstitions, says Kasravi; and eliminate corrupt capitalists and hypocritical clerics, says Hidayat.

Yet, there is no society to my knowledge that is without factions. All kinds of political systems, including western industrial democracies, are battered by conflicting opinions, interests and ambitions of diverse social groups, professional associations and political parties. In other words, factionalism in Iran is neither simply a socio-political malaise reflecting, as Al-i Ahmad sees it, the intellectual–clerical conflict, nor a purely socio-cultural phenomenon reflecting, as Kasravi perceives it, the great diversity of ethnic, linguistic and especially religious traditions and belief systems. Rather, I submit, it is a by-product of a basic unresolved normative problem in Iranian socio-political thought and action. This problem in turn stems from a deeper, larger and older encounter between Iranian civilization and 'world culture', a culture that is premised, according to Lucian W. Pye, on 'advanced technology, and the spirit of science, on a rational view of life, a secular approach to social relations, a feeling for justice in public affairs, and, above all, on the acceptance of the belief that the prime unit of the polity should be the nation-state'.[53]

More important, it is a culture that poses the most fundamental question to which Iranian society has not yet found any widely acceptable answer: by what guiding principles and with what basic institutions do Iranians propose to govern themselves in the face of the challenge of the values and realities of the modern world? Should the overriding precepts and primary procedures in society and politics be sacred or secular in nature? Should the highest end of the political system be individual liberty or the welfare of the community? If the welfare of the community, should it be the national Iranian community or the transnational Islamic community, the *umma*?

To assume that these fundamental normative questions have been already answered is empirically indefensible. If anything, the corpus of Iranian thought ever since the late nineteenth century shows that although the intellectual and political elites have tried to grapple with these questions, they have failed to provide widely acceptable answers. They have split along religious and secular lines. Within these two main schools of thought, they have further split along numerous religious and secular lines, ranging from Islamic Marxism and Islamic liberalism to Islamic fundamentalism, and from secular liberalism and conservatism to fascism and communism. Long before the Musaddiq era, the advocates of the 'religious' school of thought included such well-known figures as Sayyid Jamal al-Din Asadabadi, Sayyid Muhammad Tabataba'i, Sayyid Abdullah Bihbihani and Shaykh Fazlullah Nuri, and those of the 'secular' school of thought included such equally well-known personalities as Mirza Taqi Khan Amir Kabir, Hajji Mirza Husayn Khan Sipahsalar and Hasan Taqizadeh. During the Musaddiq era, on the religious side there were Kashani, Navvab Safavi, and at that time the less-known Khomeini; while on the secular side, besides Musaddiq, there were such intellectuals as Baqa'i, Khalil Maliki, Bazargan and Kiyanuri.

The followers of Musaddiq and the disciples of Khomeini, of course, each would contend that their respective leaders have indeed shown what the Iranian response to the challenge of world culture should be and by what political precepts and procedures the Iranian society should govern itself. But such contentions fail to meet the test of ideological and practical realities. To date, neither *Rah-i Musaddiq* (Musaddiq's path), nor *Khatt-i Khumayni* (Khomeini's line) – let alone a myriad of other less competitive schools of thought such as Marxism – has acquired a modicum of acceptance among the nation's intellectual and political elites. Nor have the ideologies associated with either Musaddiq or Khomeini become acceptable within the public at large as effective responses to the challenge of the values and realities of the modern world.

The lack of resolution of such normative problems as these can explain not only the factionalism that destroyed the Musaddiq government – and which the Khomeini regime can hardly avoid – but also the common character of Iranian nationalism during both periods. Since the Iranians have not yet settled upon their core values, have not yet determined their basic institutions, and have not yet devised appropriate procedures for governing themselves, their exercise of the principle of national independence has been prone to xenophobic tendencies. The founding fathers of the United States, for example, are said to have sought to use national interests as a means to such higher ends and purposes as individual rights to life, liberty and the pursuit of happiness. More than a decade ago, I asked: 'What are those higher ends beyond self-interest to which Iran aspires?'[54] And now, despite the Iranian revolution, this question must be asked again for, besides anti-imperialism, neither Musaddiq's secular nationalism nor Khomeini's religious nationalism has yet provided answers about the fundamental ends and means of government and politics in Iran, at least not answers that the Iranian people can widely and freely accept. Khomeini's all-absorbing crusade against the 'Great Satan' has only replaced Musaddiq's preoccupation with British imperialism. Just as Musaddiq told the Iranian masses that 'the source of all the misfortunes of this tortured nation is only the oil company',[55] Khomeini has told them that 'the world must realize that all the difficultes faced by the Iranian nation and the Muslim peoples are because of aliens, because of America.'[56]

The lack of widely accepted answers to such normative questions can also explain the recurring cycles of emotional national convulsion followed by periods of authoritarian rule. The Constitutional Revolution was followed by Riza Shah's dictatorship, just as the promise of the Iranian revolution has been followed by the imposition of Khomeini's brand of Islam or the so-called 'jurisprudential Islam'. After each outburst of nationalist fervour, political quietude (rather than genuine political stability) reigns and there is little reason to believe that this vicious cycle can be broken until the Iranian intellectual and political elites and the public at large can reach a stage in their historical development that will enable them to come to terms with the values and realities of the modern world.

Finally, foreign powers must realize that their intervention in such third world nations as Iran will not create stable regimes in the long term, as indeed the Anglo-Russian intervention in the Constitutional period, and the Anglo-American intervention in the Musaddiq period did not. Foreign intervention will only destroy the opportunity for these nations to practise trial and error in their search for popular and acceptable political systems on which any genuine political stability must ultimately rest.

Notes

1 See Richard N. Frye, *Persia* (London, 1968) p. 113.
2 See James Alban Bill, *The Politics of Iran: Groups, Classes, and Modernization* (Columbus, 1972) pp. 138–9.
3 See George Lenczowski, 'Political process and institutions in Iran: the second Pahlavi kingship', George Lenczowski ed., *Iran Under the Pahlavis* (Stanford, 1978) p. 443.
4 See Joseph M. Upton, *The History of Modern Iran: an Interpretation* (Cambridge, Mass., 1960) pp. 90–100.
5 See Bahman Nirumand, *Iran, the New Imperialism in Action* (New York, 1969) p. 89. For somewhat similar themes see also, Faramarz S. Fatemi, *The U.S.S.R. in Iran; the Background History of Russian and Anglo-American Conflict in Iran, its Effects on Iranian Nationalism, and the Fall of the Shah* (London, 1980) p. 187, and Iranian Students Association in the USA, *U.S. Involvement in Iran: Imperialist Disguises and Liberal Illusions* (Berkeley, 1978) p. 39.
6 Bizhan Jazani, *Capitalism and Revolution in Iran*, trans. the Iran Committee, selected writings of Bizhan Jazani (London, 1980) pp. 29–30.
7 See Havadaran-i Sazman-i Vahdat-i Kumunisti, *Siyasat-i hizb-i Tudeh: Qabl az inqilab, ba'd az inqilab* (a small pamphlet which gives no place of publication or date).
8 See Sazman-i Danishjuyan-i Musulman-i Irani, *Asnad-i muntashireh-i Sazman-i Mujahidin-i Khalq-i Iran*, vol. 1 (Wilmette, Ill., 1978) pp. 14–15.
9 Rahim Gudarzi-Tabrizi, *Luzum-i hifz-i bitarafi* (Tehran, 1955) pp.1–55.
10 Homa Katouzian, *The Political Economy of Modern Iran* (New York 1981) p. 175.
11 Robert Graham, *Iran: the Illusion of Power* (London, 1978) p. 67.
12 John Marlowe, *Iran: a Short Political Guide* (London, 1963) pp. 99–100.
13 Richard W. Cottam, *Nationalism in Iran* (Pittsburgh, 1979) p. 284. See especially Cottam's chapter in this volume for a view on the character of Iranian nationalism which is different from my view discussed below.
14 See Havadaran-i Jibheh-i Milli-yi Sivvum dar Kalifornia, *Musaddiq va muvazineh-i manfi: Bahsi dar falsafeh-i Junbish-i Milli-yi Iran* (n.p., 1972). See also Husayn Kay-Ustuvan, *Siyasat-i muvazineh-i manfi dar Majlis-i Chahardahum*, vol. 2 (Tehran, 1950).
15 Muhandis Mihdi Bazargan, *Inqilab-i Iran dar daw harakat*, 3rd edn (Tehran, 1983) pp. 16–17.
16 See the sources in *n*.14 above. See also, Parsa Yamgani, *Karnameh-i Musaddiq* (Tehran, 1978).
17 See Cottam, *Nationalism*, p. 267.

18 See *Ittila'iyeh az barnameh-i inqilabi-yi Fida'iyan-i Islam* (no place or publisher 1357/1978) p. 1. This 1978 edition of the Fida'iyan manifesto mentions only Sayyid Husayn Imami as the killer of Kasravi. For a different version, see Farhad Kazimi, 'The Fada'eyan-e Islam: fanaticism, politics and terror', in Said Amir Arjomand ed., *From Nationalism to Revolutionary Islam* (Albany, NY, 1984) pp. 158–76.

19 See M. Dihnavi ed., *Majmu'eh'i az maktubat, sukhanraniha va payamha-yi Ayatullah Kashani*, vol. 2 (Tehran, 1982) pp. 145–6.

20 See the text of the Fida'iyan manifesto in the reference cited in *n.*18 above.

21 This estimate is partly based on Ervand Abrahamian's useful article, 'The strengths and weaknesses of the labor movement in Iran, 1941–53', in Michael E. Bonine and Nikki Keddie eds, *Continuity and Change in Modern Iran* (Albany, NY, 1981) pp. 181–202. See also his *Iran Between Two Revolutions* (Princeton, 1982) especially on the Tudeh Party.

22 See Muhandis Mihdi Bazargan, *Mudafa'at, asnad-i Nahzat-i Azadi-yi Iran*, vol. 3, part 1 (n.p., 1977) pp. 90–4.

23 See *n.*25 below.

24 Ali Akbar Hakamizadeh's work was published by the publishers of Kasravi's newspaper *Parcham* in 1322/1943.

25 Author's translation from Ruhullah Khomeini, *Kashf-i asrar* (Tehran, 1943) pp. 4–5.

26 See Rouhollah K. Ramazani, *Iran's Foreign Policy, 1941–1973: a Study of Foreign Policy in Modernizing Nations* (Charlottesville, 1975) pp. 181–250.

27 See Rouhollah K. Ramazani, *The Foreign Policy of Iran, 1500–1941: a Developing Nation in World Affairs* (Charlottesville, 1966) pp. 81–113.

28 See Rouhollah K. Ramazani, 'Iran's "White Revolution": a study in political development', *International Journal of Middle East Studies* 5.2 (April 1974) pp. 124–39.

29 Ramazani, *Iran's Foreign Policy, 1941–1973*, pp. 181–250.

30 See Sepehr Zabih, *The Communist Movement in Iran* (Berkeley and Los Angeles, 1966).

31 Ramazani, *Iran's Foreign Policy, 1941–1973*, pp. 181–250.

32 See the source in note 18 above.

33 Abdul Hamid Zanganeh, according to the Fida'iyan manifesto, was killed by Nusratullah Qummi. I happened to witness the assassination at the main entrance of the School of Law, Political Science and Economics at the University of Tehran.

34 See Mohammad Reza Shah Pahlavi, *Mission for My Country* (New York, 1961) pp. 82–110, 126–8.

35 Dr Musaddiq and his close associates often emphasized this point. See Ramazani, *Iran's Foreign Policy, 1941–1973*, pp. 181–250.

36 See Ramazani, *Foreign Policy of Iran, 1500–1941*, pp. 81–113.

37 See R. K. Ramazani, 'Who lost America? The case of Iran', *The Middle East Journal* (winter 1982) pp. 5–21. See also R. K. Ramazani, *The United States and Iran: the Patterns of Influence* (New York, 1982).

38 Jalal Al-i Ahmad, *Dar khidmat va khiyanat-i rawshanfikran*, vol. 2 (Tehran, 1978). I have used this volume's first printing, which will be cited hereafter as *Dar khidmat*, rather than a one-volume work under the same title, but with

the addition of the subtitle, *Matn-i kamil va munaqqah va sansur nashudeh*, published by Intisharat-i Ravaq in 1977. I thank Dr Farhang Rajaee for this information.

39   Ibid., pp. 37–8.

40   Ibid., p. 18.

41   See Ahmad Kasravi, *Dar rah-i siyasat*, 14th edn (Tehran, 1945) pp. 38–9.

42   See Ahmad Kasravi, *Shi'agari* (Paris, 1982) pp. 23–43.

43   Ibid., pp. 113–14. Author's translation.

44   See Kasravi, *Dar rah-i siyasat*, p. 71.

45   Ibid., p. 22.

46   Ibid., p. 19.

47   See Sadeq Hedayat, *Hajji Agha: Portrait of an Iranian Confidence-Man*, trans. G. M. Wickens, intro. Lois Beck (Austin, 1979). I am grateful to professor Mohammad R. Ghanoonparvar for bringing this translation to my attention.

48   Ibid., p. 107

49   Ibid., p. 102.

50   Ibid., pp. 96–97.

51   For the text of Sanjabi's statement, see *Komiteh bara-yi difa az huquq-i bashar va pishraft-i an dar Iran* 16 (day 10, 1357) 99–100. For the circumstances surrounding this declaration, see R. K. Ramazani, *The United States and Iran: the Patterns of Influence*, esp. pp. 111–16.

52   This theme has been fully developed in R. K. Ramazani, *Revolutionary Iran: Challenge and Response in the Middle East* (Baltimore and London, 1986). See also R. K. Ramazani, 'Iran: burying the hatchet', *Foreign Policy* 60 (fall 1985) 52–74.

53   Lucian W. Pye, *Aspects of Political Development* (Boston, 1966); see p. 8 from where I have borrowed the concept of 'world culture'.

54   See Ramazani, *Iran's Foreign Policy, 1941–1973*, p. 454.

55   *Ittila'at*, 22 February 1951.

56   Ibid., 26 October 1981.

Conclusion

ALBERT HOURANI

A reading of the chapters in this volume will bring vividly to mind the part played by the contingent and unexpected in human affairs. It has been said that clear lines of policy consistently pursued exist mainly in the minds of scholars; what actually happened in Iran from 1951–4 may have been a series of hasty and improvised reactions to events within an environment which was continually changing. These papers will compel a reader to ask himself questions beginning with 'If only . . .' Would things have ended other than they did if Eden had not fallen ill at a critical moment and yielded control of policy to Churchill; if a Democratic had not been replaced by a Republican Administration in the United States; and if the fragile coalition which supported Musaddiq had shifted in different ways and at different times? Perhaps it is not an accident that such questions about what might have been come to our minds when we think about this episode in history. They are signs of a widespread feeling that the way in which the episode ended ought to have been different: some kind of agreement between the British government and an Iranian government headed by Musaddiq was possible, and it would have been better than what actually happened – better at least in the long term, for it is inevitable that we should now see what happened 30 years ago in the perspective of what has happened more recently in Iran.

It may, therefore, be worthwhile to go once more over the arguments, and put the question: could there have been an agreement between the government headed by Dr Musaddiq and the British government? This is not a simple question, and it needs to be considered at three different levels.

The question may be posed first in abstraction from all considerations of policy and perosnality. Was there any way in which the essential interests of the two parties could have been reconciled? The differences between those interests, as the two parties perceived them, were complex. They were differences about compensation, about the position of British officials and technicians, about control of production and marketing, and beyond these there were also differences about power. Who was to control not only Iran's most important economic asset, but its territory and population? Whether it intended it or not, the Anglo-Iranian Oil Company was in fact the dominant power in a large part of southern Iran. It had intimate connections with local authorities and communities, in a country where the power of the central government was still precarious and the unifying force of the national idea still weak. Since the company was mainly owned by the British government, its power was in the end that of Britain.

These differences at every level raised important and difficult questions of principle and of that imponderable but important matter, *prestige*. Nevertheless, such disputes can be reconciled, given a clear understanding on both sides of what is essential and what is not, and given the will to reach an agreement. At the same time as negotiations were going on between Britain and Iran, the British government was engaged in a similar exercise in another country, the negotiations with Egypt about control of the canal zone. Control of the zone was at least as important as control of Iranian oil for British policy and strategic planning; it was an issue more deeply rooted in British imperial memories; and it raised just as many fundamental questions about who really controlled Egypt in the last analysis. Agreement was reached in the end, however, after a long and difficult process of negotiation and thanks to a certain clarity of vision on both sides and a willingness to redefine what was really essential. In Iran, the proposals associated with the name of George McGhee in October 1951, and the similar ones put forward by the World Bank early in 1952, might have served as the basis of an acceptable compromise had both parties wanted one at the same time.

To say this, however, is to pose the same question at a second level. Even if an acceptable compromise was possible in principle, did both sides have the freedom of political manoeuvre to be able to accept it, and to make it acceptable to those who supported them and to whom they were responsible?

So far as Musaddiq and his government are concerned, it is necessary first of all to remember the political context within which any Iranian prime minister had to work. As Dr Azimi has shown, there was a structural weakness in the Iranian Constitution.[1] Between the power of the Palace and that of the Majlis, it was virtually impossible to create a strong executive. The Majlis was an assembly of men of whom most had an independent social and political position. Many of them were related by kinship or marriage. They might be linked loosely with each other or with recognized leaders, but not in such a way as to make possible the creation of permanent, organized political parties. A prime minister could only acquire the independent power necessary to govern effectively if he could create and hold together an alliance of interests; but such alliances by their nature were fragile. In the years after 1945 two such attempts were made, first by Qavam in 1946 and then by Musaddiq. Musaddiq was able to bring together a coalition of educated nationalists, some of the religious leaders (although not the most important of them), and the Tudeh Party; he was able to mobilize the crowd in the streets of Tehran, and to obtain at least the acquiescence of the Shah. There were, however, dangers in such methods of political action. The coalition could easily break up; a part of it could try to impose its will upon the leader; the expectations aroused among the crowd could be disappointed. Nevertheless, in the first period of his rule Musaddiq probably had the power of manoeuvre to accept a compromise such as that put forward in the McGhee–Musaddiq proposals.

At a later stage this option may have been impossible. The coalition gradually disintegrated. The most powerful of the men of religion who had supported it, Ayatullah Kashani, began to separate himself from Musaddiq. Musaddiq's majority in the Majlis crumbled, particularly after his demand for an extension of the emergency powers that had been granted to him. The attempts to reach an agreement with the British and American governments alienated some of the nationalists. The army officers, who had not at first been hostile, became increasingly so. A potential coalition began to form around the Shah, although it is doubtful whether he would have had the strength and resolution to move against Musaddiq had it not been for the Anglo-American intervention.

The government was also running into economic difficulties because of the boycott of Iranian oil organized by the AIOC. Dr Katouzian argues in his paper that the measures taken by the government in the face of its difficulties were effective: restricting imports, expanding exports other than oil, cutting down public expenditure, increasing income from indirect taxes, and borrowing from the public and the banks.[2] The underlying assumption of such measures was that the crisis would not last long, because the boycott would be ineffective or Britain would be willing to compromise, and this might well have happened had the coup not taken place. In the short term, however, the economic situation may have eroded some of the popular support for Musaddiq.

The British government was also working under restraints. The force of public opinion had to be acknowledged. There was in England at that time a kind of delayed reaction to the changes brought about by the war, and the irrevocable loss of Britain's paramount position in the world. The withdrawal from India in 1947, that extraordinary act of statesmanship, seems in retrospect to have taken place easily and without arousing the strong feelings that might have been expected. Such a reaction was perhaps only possible in a period of deep collective fatigue after the efforts of war, and of public preoccupation with a different range of problems, those of demobilization, nationalization of industries, and financial crisis. Having withdrawn from India, the government did not draw the conclusion that the British Empire had come to an end and it should withdraw from other positions of strength in the world; on the contrary, there was a determination to cling to the positions which were left, and in particular to those in the Middle East. This goal was supported on the whole by a rather sensitive national pride; the nationalization of the AIOC concession thus aroused strong feelings.

The convictions and opinions of those who directed the company also had to be taken into account. The company's relationship with the government was not a simple one: although the government owned a major share in the company, it did not interfere in its operations, and could not easily override the opposition of the company to making major concessions. The company was generally regarded as very successful and a major national asset.

Restraint of another kind hindered the government's freedom of action. Even in a diminished form, Britain was still a world power; that is to say, it had interests and positions to defend in every part of the world. It was not able to pursue a single-minded policy in regard to any particular country or interest. The pressure of business, of urgent decisions to be made, did not cease. A prime minister or foreign secretary could not give the major part of his time to the affairs of Iran, or even to the Middle East as a whole. Moreover, when the affairs of Iran were discussed, it was not possible to think of them in isolation from what was happening or might happen in other parts of the world; it was always necessary to bear in mind the possible implications of a decision about Iran for the British position elsewhere. Because of this vast complex of interrelated interests, the government had a natural caution about making decisions that involved the abandonment of an established position. This is what was really meant when it was said, 'Our prestige will suffer if we have to leave Iran.'

In particular, what was happening in Iran and what was happening in Egypt should be seen side by side. The visit of Musaddiq to Cairo on his way back from the United Nations in 1951, and his meeting there with the Egyptian nationalist leader Nahhas Pasha, was a symbolic incident; news and photographs of it had a certain effect on British public opinion.

Considered in this context, did the government have enough freedom of action to accept a compromise? By 1951 the Labour government probably did not. It was coming to its close, and was perhaps incapable of taking new initiatives. Having taken the decision to withdraw from India, it had to show that it was not sacrificing essential British interests elsewhere in the world. There were also restraints upon the Conservative government which took office in October 1951. A considerable section of the party had not really accepted the withdrawal from India and would certainly react strongly against any line of policy that seemed to show a weakness of nerve and will. Nevertheless, the government probably did have enough freedom of action to be able to reach an agreement if it wished to. It was in a strong position, with a satisfactory majority in the House of Commons. The two dominant figures, Churchill and Eden, were political realists, and able to take difficult decisions. Churchill's own feelings had clearly been against the withdrawal from India, but once it happened he accepted it, just as later he was to accept the withdrawal from the canal zone in Egypt, and to urge it upon his supporters in parliament. Eden too appears to have behaved with intelligence and strength throughout the episode; he had not yet shown signs of the weaknesses of character, aggravated by ill health, which were to lead to the grotesque episode of Suez.

There may have been a brief moment, threfore, when both parties had the freedom to accept a compromise which would have guaranteed their essential interests. To say this, however, is to raise the same question once more, at a third level. Even if a compromise was logically possible, and even if Musaddiq probably and the Conservative government certainly had the strength to accept it, in the event no agreement was reached. This lack of resolution needs to be explained. In the western world, the explanation was usually given in terms of the personality of Dr Musaddiq. The British Ambassador, Sir Francis Shepherd, described him as a 'lunatic', and as 'cunning', 'slippery', and 'completely unscrupulous'. The British chargé d'affaires at a later stage, George Middleton, called him a megalomaniac who showed signs of mental instability. John Foster Dulles thought him 'a wily oriental'.[3] It is possible, however, to make similar indictments about some of those holding responsible positions on the British side. In official papers of the period, speeches in parliament, and articles in some newspapers, there can be found the typical expressions of an uneasy and challenged authority: obstinacy, denigration of the opponent, even hysteria. Thus, whatever questions we ask about Musaddiq we should also ask about the British, and such questions can be put in two forms, one less charitable than the other. It may be asked: was Musaddiq mad, and was Sir Francis Shepherd mad? Alternatively, it may be asked: was it possible to do business with Musaddiq, and was it possible to do business with the British?

It is difficult not to think of the whole episode in terms of the personality of Dr Muhammad Musaddiq. Certain undoubted eccentricities of personal behaviour should be discounted. When thought about carefully, the criticisms of his behaviour reduce themselves to two points: he wore pyjamas when negotiating, and he wept in public. It is typical of those who have long enjoyed wealth, power or authority that their personal idiosyncrasies can expand without being checked by consideration of what other people think of them. Mr Churchill too conducted much business lying in bed in the mornings, and was perhaps the last British politician to have the gift of tears. Musaddiq's histrionic public behaviour may also be discounted. One of the moral dangers of a political career is that it may have certain effects upon the character. In a parliamentary system, a politician has to cultivate a persona and project it, and in the end it may take him over. Musaddiq's dramatic persona and rhetoric seem to have appealed to many Iranians. Rhetoric, like humour, is not international, however, and Iranian political rhetoric may not have been appreciated in England, where twentieth-century modes of political expression are very different. (They were not always so, however; we read of Sheridan making a speech of several hours during the impeachment proceedings of Warren Hastings, and collapsing dramatically into the arms of Edmund Burke at the end of it.)

That Musaddiq was a difficult negotiator is undoubtedly true. On issues of this degree of importance, negotiation is bound to be protracted and complex, with constant changes of position as circumstances change, until final agreement is reached. When Dulles called him wily and devious in 1952, he was saying more or less what Eden would say of Dulles during the Suez crisis in 1956.

It is more profitable to set aside such matters and regard Musaddiq as a rational human being: that is to say, one whose mind worked in more or less intelligible ways on the basis of certain principles or assumptions. Such principles were derived from the thought and experience of a long life; and it might perhaps be said that in his case they were rather more fixed than in most people, or certainly most Iranian politicians of his generation.

What were the fixed principles which determined the direction of his thought, his reaction to events, and his policies? Some of them can be explained in terms of his place as an Iranian of a particular class and generation; others were common to the Middle Eastern and Asian nationalism of his time. He was not only an Iranian, he was the product of a particular milieu in Iranian society. His basic education and training, before he went to Switzerland and France for his higher studies, was the traditional training of the Treasury official, the *mustawfi*. He thus inherited the oldest continuous political tradition of Iran, older than the Qajars and Safavis, older even than Iranian Shiism: the tradition of the chancery and Treasury officials whose cumulative political and administrative understanding was set down in such manuals as that of Nizam al-Mulk. He had, it is clear, a deep sense of responsibility derived from the past to something called Iran, to the authority of the state. He was also an intellectual formed in the French legal tradition, and in this he was similar to many other nationalists of his period and age. We should not forget that he was in his seventies when he became prime minister, and his mind and political approach had been formed in an earlier time: he was not so much a nationalist of the 1950s – the age which was to be dominated by the personality of Nasser – as of the 1920s or 1930s. The closest parallel would perhaps be with Zaghlul of Egypt; he belonged to the period of the Wafd, the old Destour in Tunisia, or Congress in India (but the Congress of Motilal Nehru rather than Jawarhalal).

As Professor Cottam has pointed out, nationalism is very simple.[4] It is the idea of an attachment to an ethnic community which is or can be organized into a state. It only acquires force in so far as it serves as the fixed point around which a constellation of other ideas can gather. What were the ideas which, in the age of Musaddiq, gave meaning to the idea of Iranian nationalism? The first was that of genuine independence. This took priority over everything else in his mind, and it was for this reason that the question of the oil concession was for him a political question before anything. Those who negotiated with him complained that he could not be brought to understand the financial and commercial factors involved; was it not rather that he could understand them but regarded them as secondary, that he and Harriman, for example, were not talking about the same thing?

Coupled with this idea of nationalism was the idea of Britain as the main enemy of Iranian independence. It may be difficult for us now to remember how Britain bestrode the whole world of Asia and Africa at that time; we should think not just of the AIOC in southern Iran but of the vast extent of the British Empire stretching round the Indian Ocean, with the Royal Navy keeping guard over it, and the strength of sterling as an international currency. It might be said that Musaddiq carried this idea about Britain into an age when it was no longer true, and that he took it beyond the bounds of reason to the point of obsession. His belief in a British conspiracy against him, however, was not just irrational; in the end he *was* ousted by a conspiracy. The books written by Woodhouse and Roosevelt show clearly that the coup which finally overturned him and restored the power of the Shah was first planned by MI6 in London, and then taken over by the CIA in Washington.[5]

Musaddiq had also a certain idea of what a modern civilized state should be. The word 'secular' is sometimes used of him, but this is too simple a description. He believed, according to Dr Azimi, that 'established norms and principles should not be hastily undermined in the name of modernism.'[6] His legal dissertation, *Le testament en droit musulman*, was written within a certain tradition of 'Islamic modernism' familiar in Arabic and Turkish writing of the early twentieth century. Writing of the laws passed by the Majlis after the Constitutional Revolution, he argued that they should be based upon the principles of the *shari'a*, but that those principles should be interpreted by reason in the light of the changed circumstances of the modern world.[7]

The nationalism of Musaddiq's time was the ideology of a small group of educated people, aiming to win support at crucial moments from a larger group that did not share their ideas and aspirations beyond a certain point. This may help to explain why he was not able to form and lead a party. Working within similar limitations, Egyptian, Indian and Tunisian nationalists were able to create effective and lasting political organizations; there may have been factors in the Iranian society of the time that made this impossible. There is no doubt that Musaddiq tried to introduce certain changes in Iranian society; but it seems doubtful whether, as a nationalist of an older generation, he would have been capable of carrying out a real change in its structure, coming as he did from a rich and privileged group and having as he did unorganized and undisciplined political support.

If Musaddiq and other Iranians were moved by certain fixed ideas about

Britain and the world, the British also had certain ideas about nationalism, and particularly Middle Eastern nationalism, which helped to give a direction to British policy. In the second edition of *The Middle East: a Political and Economic Survey*, an authoritative work published by the Royal Institute of International Affairs in 1954, the basic analysis of nationalism occurs in a section called 'Xenophobia'. Its argument is that Arabs and Persians, having in the first place seized upon western innovations with open arms, have not at once found in them the touchstone that produces wealth, power and technical ability. Some of them express their frustration by reviling the western word. They damn the foreigner, who seems to them no cleverer or more efficient than they have it in themselves to be:

> The Egyptian soldier is confident that he can run the Canal Zone and the Persian that a race that developed the Persian miniature cannot fail in running an oil industry.[8]

This quotation expresses, in a slightly absurd form, an idea which was widespread at the time. British writers or speakers on nationalism would shake their heads sadly. Emotion, they would say, leads to the desire for complete independence; it is quite natural and we should sympathize with it, but rational thought would surely lead us to the conclusion that complete independence is impossible, and that the preservation of acquired western interests is also, rationally considered, in the real interests of Egyptians or Iranians.

This mode of thought was connected with a certain relationship of power. It is in the nature of this relationship that those who are subject to the power of another are always conscious of it, while those who have the power easily forget it. They accept it as the natural order of things, and come to believe that the existing situation expresses a pre-established and permanent harmony of interests. The politicians and officials who wielded the instruments of power, however, were always aware of it, and prepared to use it if necessary. The idea of armed intervention, of an ultimate use of force in order to preserve an existing position believed to be important, was generally accepted at the time, and such use of power was not regarded as morally reprehensible. Bevin was opposed to it, as Roger Louis has shown in his book, *The British Empire in the Middle East*, but his was a personal view not shared by all his colleagues and officials.[9]

This British power was a threatened power, and in some ways it was illusory. Britain's position as paramount power in the Middle East had been created after the first world war: the Ottoman, Austrian and German empires had collapsed; Russia had withdrawn into itself; France was in the region, but in a more limited way and weakened by a victory which was more like a defeat. This paramount position had been artificially prolonged after the second world war. The United States, having taken responsibility for Greece and Turkey, was prepared to leave major responsibility for the rest of the area to Britain, except for its intervention in Palestine in 1948; the USSR was more interested in other parts of the world; Britain clung to its position in the Middle East as the one part of the world where it could still, in the last resort, impose its will. This was an illusion which was finally ended by the Suez crisis of 1956, but already there were threats to the British position from different directions. Once more we should remember the meeting of Musaddiq and Nahhas in Cairo, which could be taken as a symbol of that 'revolt of the East' that had haunted the imperial imagination, a reminder to the British that the loss of a privileged position in Iran could lead to pressures and defeat elsewhere.

From another quarter, there was a threat, or at least a supposed threat, from the USSR. The negotiations concerning Iran, like those concerning Egypt, took place within a certain context: that of the discussions about the creation of a defence system for the western position in the Middle East. The USSR was not only seen as an external threat, however. A familiar theme at the time was that Middle Eastern nationalism might prepare the way for communism: it was too weak to serve as a defence against it; or it might even be a kind of communism in disguise. This thesis was put forward in a book published a few years later, and which had a certain influence, Walter Laqueur's *Communism and Nationalism in the Middle East*. 'Nationalism in the Middle East', he maintained, 'is not a force opposed to communism. On the contrary, at the present time it has paved the way for and has collaborated with it.' Most Middle Eastern countries 'do not belong to the western camp; they therefore constitute a vacuum between West and East which will hardly be tolerated in today's world'.[10]

The Iranian crisis as it developed did not give much support to this thesis. The USSR did not show any strong desire to profit from the difficulties of the British or Americans and the Tudeh Party did not appear to be gaining control over Musaddiq and his government. It may be doubted whether all British officials believed in the communist danger, although Woodhouse's book makes clear that some of them did. They did, however, use it in order to enlist American support. The Anglo-American relationship in the Middle East during this period was an ambiguous one. There was always a fear on the British side that, while appearing to support the maintenance of British power, the Americans might be acting in such a way as to undermine it, either in pursuit of their own interests or out of misguided sympathy for nationalism.

There was indeed some ground for such British fears during the early months of the crisis. The general opinion of the Truman Administration seems to have been that the Musaddiq government was one of those 'moderate nationalist' governments which should be encouraged, because they were likely to make for social and political stability, and could be

drawn into friendly relations with the western states; the nationalization of
the oil concession was an acceptable act of sovereignty, provided adequate
compensation was offered. Everything possible should therefore be done
to encourage a compromise between Britain and Iran. In spite of British
suspicions, it does not appear that the major American oil companies were
anxious to break the monopoly of AIOC over Iranian oil; the resources
under their control were adequate to their needs. Some of the independent companies may have wished to go in, but they were restrained by the
US government. (Indirectly, the American companies, assisted by the
government, cut the ground from under the negotiating position of AIOC,
by making the Fifty–fifty Agreement with Saudi Arabia.)

In 1952, however, the American position began to change. The
Democratic Administration of Truman was replaced by the Republican
Administration of Eisenhower, and the need to take strong and urgent
measures against Soviet expansion became the guiding principle of
American policy. It would not be too much to say that this became as much
of an obsession in the minds of the Secretary of State, John Foster Dulles,
and the head of the CIA, Allen Dulles, as Musaddiq's suspicion of British
policy. The US government now began to look at the Iranian situation in a
new light. The need to maintain the strength of the British position and the
western alliance became the paramount consideration. Iranian oil was seen
as a valuable resource which the West should not lose. The interests of the
major US oil companies may also have played a part at this stage, now that
it was clear that AIOC would not be able to regain its monopoly over the
production and marketing of the oil of Iran. The government of Musaddiq
was no longer seen as one of 'moderate nationalists', but as one of those
weak, neutralist, pro-Russian regimes which, to use Laqueur's words, 'will
hardly be tolerated in today's world'. As the US ambassador in Tehran,
Loy Henderson, said: 'We are confronted by a desperate, a dangerous
situation and a madman who would ally himself with the Russians.'[11]

The means to end the situation were now to hand. During the period of
Truman, the CIA had been an intelligence agency gathering information.
The Truman Administration was less willing to overturn foreign governments by stealth than its successor. In the new era, however, the danger
from the USSR was no longer seen in terms of military expansion alone,
but of 'subversion' of weak or unfriendly governments; and the adequate
response to this would involve something more than propaganda,
economic aid, and diplomatic action. As Eveland has shown, the nature of
the CIA changed: covert political operations took priority over collecting
information, and such operations were extended from the countries under
the control of the USSR to those of Asia, Africa and Latin America. The
CIA was more able to act freely because of the close relationship and
identity of views between its director and the Secretary of State.[12]

It was in these circumstances that in June 1953 the decision was taken, at the highest level of the US government, to put into operation the plan for a *coup d'état* which had previously been discussed between MI6 and the CIA. In the period when it was only a British plan, the British Foreign Secretary, Eden, had been unwilling to go further with it unless the United States were willing to co-operate. Now that it was willing, Eden might still have been cautious and hesitant, but by this time he was ill and out of action, and responsibility for foreign affairs was in the hands of the prime minister, Churchill, who had no such reluctance. So the coup was set in motion, and Musaddiq was overthrown.

The fall of Musaddiq seemed to bring to an end an isolated and even bizarre episode in the political history of Iran. He himself was never again to play a part in political life: he spent the years until his death in 1967 first in imprisonment and then in enforced residence away from the capital. For more than 20 years the Shah would hold almost unchallenged control of the government, and receive increasing support from the United States. Seen in retrospect, however, the brief years of Musaddiq's rule have had a deep and lasting significance. His was the most determined attempt to create a strong executive power in Iran, upheld by popular support, and to use it in order to obtain not simply an improved position within the imperial system but complete independence. The episode of his rule takes its place in the series of events which was carried on by the Suez episode, the Algerian struggle for independence, and the Vietnam war. It marks also a stage in the process by which the paramount influence of Britain in the Middle East was replaced by that of the United States. Inside Iran, his memory remained as a symbol of independence, and had a certain power as opposition to the Shah came once more to the surface in the 1970s, until it was obscured by new ideas and images after the revolution of 1979.

Notes

1   F. Azimi, 'The Politics of Dynamic Stalemate: Iran 1944–53' (D.Phil. thesis, Oxford, 1984).
2   H. Katouzian, 'Oil boycott and the political economy: Musaddiq and the strategy of non-oil economics' (see chapter 8).
3   R. Louis, 'Musaddiq, oil and the dilemmas of British imperialism' (see chapter 9).
4   R. Cottam, 'Nationalism in twentieth-century Iran and Dr Muhammad Musaddiq' (see chapter 1).
5   C. M. Woodhouse, *Something Ventured* (London, 1982) pp. 104–35; K. Roosevelt, *Countercoup* (New York, 1979); W. C. Eveland, *Ropes of Sand* (New York, 1980) p. 356.
6   F. Azimi.
7   M. Mossadegh, *Le testament en droit musulman (secte Chyite)* (Paris, 1914) pp. 36–88.

8   Royal Institute of International Affairs, *The Middle East: a Political and Economic Survey* (London, 1954) pp. 48ff.

9   R. Louis, *The British Empire in the Middle East 1945–1951* (Oxford, 1984).

10 W. Z. Laqueur, *Communism and Nationalism in the Middle East* (London, 1956) pp. 275, 279.

11 Roosevelt, *Countercoup*, p. 18.

12 Eveland, *Ropes of Sand, passim*.

Bibliography

English language works

Abrahamian, Ervand, *Iran Between Two Revolutions* (Princeton: Princeton University Press, 1982).
——, 'The strengths and weaknesses of the labour movement in Iran in 1941–53', in *Continuity and Change in Modern Iran*, ed. Michael E. Bonine and Nikkie R. Keddie (Albany NY: State University of New York Press, 1981).
Acheson, Dean, *Present at the Creation: My Years in the State Department* (New York: Norton, 1969).
Akhavi, Shahrough, *Religion and Politics in Contemporary Iran: Clergy State Relations in the Pahlavi Period* (Albany: State University of New York Press, 1980).
Alexander, Yonah and Nanes, Allen eds, *The United States and Iran: a Documentary History* (Frederick, Md: Aletheia Books, 1980).
Alsop, Joseph and Stewart, *The Reporter's Trade* (New York: Reynal, 1958).
Ambrose, Stephen, *Eisenhower: the President* (New York: Simon and Schuster, 1984).
Anderson, Irvine, *Aramco, the United States, and Saudi Arabia* (Princeton, NJ: Princeton University Press, 1981).
Andrew, Christopher, *Secret Service: the Making of the British Intelligence Community* (London: Heinemann, 1985).
Avery, Peter, *Modern Iran* (New York: Frederick A. Praeger, 1965).
Azimi, Fakhreddin, 'The politics of dynamic stalemate: Iran 1944–53', D.Phil dissertation, Oxford, 1984).
Baldwin, G. B., *Planning and Development in Iran* (Baltimore, Md: The Johns Hopkins University Press, 1967).
Banani, Amin, *The Modernization of Iran, 1921–41* (Stanford: Stanford University Press, 1966).
Bharier, J., *Economic Development in Iran, 1900–1970* (London: Oxford Economic Press, 1971).
Bill, James Alban, *The Politics of Iran: Groups, Classes, and Modernization* (Columbus: Charles E. Merrill, 1972).
——, *The Eagle and the Lion: the Tragedy of American–Iranian Relations* (New Haven and London: Yale University Press, 1988).
Blair, John M., *The Control of Oil* (New York: Pantheon Books, 1976).
Cairncross, Alec, *Years of Recovery, British Economic Policy 1945–51* (New York: Methuen, 1985).
Chesterton, G. K., *Robert Browning* (London: Macmillan, 1903).

Churchill, Winston S., *The World Crisis*, 2 vols (New York: C. Scribners, 1923).

Cleveland, Harlan, 'Oil, blood and politics: our next move in Iran', *The Reporter* 9 (10 November 1953) 19.

Cottam, Richard, *Foreign Policy Motivation* (Pittsburgh, Penn.: University of Pittsburgh Press, 1977).

——, 'Nationalism and the Islamic Republic of Iran', in *Canadian Review of Studies of Nationalism* 9.2 (autumn 1982).

——, *Nationalism in Iran* (Pittsburgh, Penn.: University of Pittsburgh Press, 1979).

Deutsch, Carl, *Nationalism and Social Communication* (Cambridge, Mass.: Massachusetts Institute of Technology Press, 1966).

Dorman, William A. and Farhang, Mansour, *The U.S. Press and Iran: Foreign Policy and the Journalism of Deference* (Berkeley, Calif.: University of California Press, 1987).

Eagleton, William Jr, *The Kurdish Republic of 1946* (London: Oxford University Press, 1966).

Eden, Anthony, *Full Circle, the Memoirs of Anthony Eden* (Boston, Mass.: Houghton Mifflin, 1960).

Elwell-Sutton, L. P., *Persian Oil: a Study in Power Politics* (London: Lawrence & Wishart, 1955).

Eveland, W. C., *Ropes of Sand* (New York: W. W. Norton, 1980).

Fanning, Leonard M., *Foreign Oil and the Free World* (New York: McGraw-Hill, 1954).

Fatemi, Faramarz S., *The U.S.S.R. in Iran: the Background History of Russian and Anglo-American Conflict in Iran, its Effects on Iranian Nationalism, and the Fall of the Shah* (London: Thomas Yoseloff, 1980).

Fatemi, Nasrollah Saifpour, *Oil Diplomacy: Powderkeg in Iran* (New York: Whittier Books, 1954).

Ferrier, R. W., 'The development of the Iranian oil industry', in *Twentieth-Century Iran*, ed. Hossein Amirsadeghi (London: Heinemann, 1977).

——, *The History of the British Petroleum Company*, vol. I (Cambridge: Cambridge University Press, 1982).

Ford, Alan W., *The Anglo-Iran Oil Dispute of 1951–1952* (Berkeley, Calif.: University of California Press, 1954).

Frye, Richard N., *Persia* (London: George Allen & Unwin, 1968).

Gasiorowski, Mark, 'The 1953 *coup d'etat* in Iran', *International Journal of Middle East Studies* 19 (1987).

Gellner, Ernest, *Nations and Nationalism* (Ithaca, NY: Cornell University Press, 1983).

Glazer, Nathan and Moynihan, Daniel P., *Ethnicity: Theory and Experience* (Cambridge, Mass.: Harvard University Press, 1975).

Graham, Robert, *Iran: the Illusion of Power* (London: Croom Helm, 1978).

Green, Jerrold D., *Revolution in Iran: the Politics of Countermobilization* (New York: Praeger, 1982).

Hamilton, Charles W., *America and Oil in the Middle East* (Houston, Tex.: Gulf Publishing, 1962).

Hayes, Carlton, *The Historical Evolution of Modern Nationalism* (New York: Macmillan, 1948).

Heider, Fritz, *The Psychology of Interpersonal Relations* (New York: Wiley, 1958).

Hobson, John A., *Imperialism: a Study* (London: G. Allen & Unwin, 1902.

Huntington, Samuel P., *The Common Defense: Strategic Programs in National Politics* (New York: Columbia University Press, 1961).

Jazani, Bizhan, *Capitalism and Revolution in Iran* (London: Zed Press, 1980).

Katouzian, Homa, *The Political Economy of Modern Iran 1926–79* (New York: New York University Press, 1981).

Kaufman, Burton I., *The Oil Cartel Case* (Westport, Conn.: Greenwood Press, 1978).

Kayhan Research Associates, *Iran Yearbook* (Tehran: Kayhan, 1977).

Keddie, Nikki R., *Roots of Revolution: an Interpretative History of Modern Iran* (New Haven, Conn.: Yale University Press, 1981).

Kedourie, Elie, *Nationalism in Asia and Africa* (Cleveland, Ohio: World Publishing, 1970).

Krasner, Stephen D., *Defending the National Interest: Raw Materials, Investments and U.S. Foreign Policy* (Princeton, NJ: Princeton University Press, 1978).

Krock, Arthur, *Memoirs* (New York: Funk & Wagnalls, 1968).

Kuniholm, Bruce R., *The Origins of the Cold War in the Near East, Great Power Conflict and Diplomacy in Iran, Turkey, and Greece* (Princeton, NJ: Princeton University Press, 1980).

Lambton, A. K. S., 'The Impact of the West on Persia', *International Affairs* (January 1957).

Lapping, Brian, *End of Empire* (London: Granada, 1985).

Laqueur, W. Z., *Communism and Nationalism in the Middle East* (New York: Praeger, 1956).

Lebkicher, Roy, *Aramco and World Oil* (New York: Russell F. Moore, 1952).

Lenczowski, George, 'Political process and institutions in Iran: the second Pahlavi kingship', in *Iran Under the Pahlavis*, ed. George Lenczowski (Stanford: Hoover Institute Press, 1978).

——, *Russia and the West in Iran, 1918–1948: a Study in Big-Power Rivalry* (Ithaca, NY: Cornell University Press, 1949).

Levy, Marion J. Jr, *Modernization and the Structure of Society* (Princeton: Princeton University Press, 1966).

Longrigg, Stephen H., *Oil in the Middle East: its Discovery and Development*, 3rd edn (New York: Oxford University Press, 1968).

Louis, Wm Roger, *The British Empire in the Middle East 1945–1951* (Oxford: Oxford University Press, 1984).

Mannheim, Karl, *Ideology and Utopia: an Introduction to the Sociology of Knowledge* (New York: Harcourt, Brace & World, 1936).

Marlowe, John, *Iran: a Short Political Guide* (London: Pall Mall Press, 1963).

Martin, Kingsley, 'Conversation with Dr Mossadeq', *New Statesman*, 11 January 1952.

McGhee, George, *Envoy to the Middle World: Adventures in Diplomacy* (New York: Harper & Row, 1983).

McLellan, David S., *Dean Acheson: the State Department Years* (New York: Dodd, Mead, 1976).

Mikdashi, Zuhayr, *A Financial Analysis of Middle Eastern Oil Concessions: 1901–65* (New York: F. A. Praeger, 1966).

Miller, Aaron David, *Search for Security: Saudi Arabian Oil and American Foreign*

Policy, 1939–1949 (Chapel Hill, NC: University of North Carolina Press, 1980).

Millspaugh, Arthur, 'Iran wants an "Aladdin's lamp" economy', *New York Journal of Commerce*, 10 December 1948.

Mosley, Leonard, *Power Play: Oil in the Middle East* (Baltimore, Md: Penguin Books, 1973).

——, *Dulles* (New York: The Dial Press/James Wade, 1978).

Nirumand, Bahman, *Iran: the New Imperialism in Action* (New York: Modern Reader Paperbacks, 1969).

Novak, Michael, *The Rise of the Unmeltable Ethnics* (New York: Macmillan, 1972).

Pahlavi, Mohammad Reza, *The Shah's Story* (London: Michael Joseph, 1980).

——, *Mission for my Country* (New York: McGraw-Hill, 1960; London: Hutchinson, 1961).

Philby, H. St John B., *Saudi Arabia* (London: Ernest Benn, 1955).

Pleadings, I.C.J. *Anglo-Iranian Oil Co. Case, United Kingdom v. Iran* (Leiden, Brill, 1952).

Powers, Thomas, 'A book held hostage', *Nation*, 12 April 1980.

——, *The Man Who Kept the Secrets: Richard Helms and the CIA* (New York: Pocket Books, 1979).

Pye, Lucian W., *Aspects of Political Development* (Boston, Mass.: Little, Brown, 1966).

Rabe, Stephen G., 'Energy for war: United States oil diplomacy in Latin America during World War II', in *Proceedings of the Conference on War and Diplomacy, 1976*, ed. David H. White (Charleston, SC: The Citadel, 1976).

Rajaee, Farhang, *Islamic Values and World View: Khomeyni on Man, the State and International Politics* (Lanham, Md: The University Press of America, 1983).

Ramazani, Rouhollah K., *The Foreign Policy of Iran, 1500–1941: a Developing Nation in World Affairs* (Charlottesville, Va: University Press of Virginia, 1966).

——, 'Iran: burying the hatchet', *Foreign Policy* 60 (fall 1985).

——, *Iran's Foreign Policy, 1941–1973: a Study of Foreign Policy in Modernizing Nations* (Charlottesville, Va: University of Press of Virginia, 1975).

——, 'Iran's "white revolution": a study in political development', *International Journal of Middle East Studies* 5.2 (April 1974).

——, *Revolutionary Iran: Challenge and Response in the Middle East* (Baltimore, Md and London: The Johns Hopkins University Press, 1986).

——, *The United States and Iran: the Patterns of Influence* (New York: Praeger, 1982).

——, 'Who lost America: the case of Iran', *The Middle East Journal* (winter 1982).

Rand, Christopher T., *Making Democracy Safe for Oil* (Boston, Mass.: Little, Brown, 1975).

Richard, Yann, 'Ayatollah Kashani: precursor of the Islamic Republic" in *Religion and Politics in Iran*, ed. Nikki Keddie (New Haven, Conn.: Yale University Press, 1983).

Roberts, N. S., *Iran: Economic and Commercial Conditions* (London: Overseas Economic Surveys, Board of Trade, 1948).

Roosevelt, Kermit, *Countercoup: the Struggle for Control of Iran* (New York: McGraw-Hill, 1979).

Rubin, Barry, *Paved with Good Intentions* (New York: Oxford University Press, 1980).

Sampson, Anthony, *The Seven Sisters: The Great Oil Companies and the World They Made* (New York: The Viking Press, 1975).

Schelling, Thomas, *The Strategy of Conflict* (New York: Oxford University Press, 1969).

——, *Arms and Influence* (New Haven, Conn.: Yale University Press, 1969).

Shwadran, Benjamin, *The Middle East: Oil and the Great Powers* (New York: Wiley, 1959).

Stegner, Wallace E., *Discovery: the search for Arabian Oil* (Beirut: Middle East Export Press, 1971).

Stoff, Michael B., *Oil, War, and American Security* (New Haven, Conn.: Yale University Press, 1980).

Turner, Louis, *Oil Companies in the International System* (London: George Allen & Unwin for the Royal Institute of International Affairs, 1978).

Ullman, Richard, *Anglo-Soviet Relations: the Anglo-Soviet Accord* (Princeton: Princeton University Press, 1972).

Upton, Joseph M., *The History of Modern Iran: an Interpretation* (Cambridge, Mass.: Harvard University Press, 1960).

Villiers, Gerard de, *The Imperial Shah: an Informal Biography* (Little, Brown, 1976).

Walters, Vernon A., *Silent Missions* (New York: Doubleday, 1978).

Wilber, Donald N., *Contemporary Iran* (New York: Frederick A. Praeger, 1963).

Williams, Philip M., *Hugh Gaitskell: a Political Biography* (London: J. Cape, 1979).

Williamson, Harold F. et al., *The American Petroleum Industry*, 2 vols (Evanston, Ill.: Northwestern University Press, 1959–63).

Woodhouse, C. M., *Something Ventured* (London: Granada, 1982).

Young, Arthur N., *Saudi Arabia: the Making of a Financial Giant* (New York: New York University Press, 1983).

Young, T. Cuyler, 'The race between Russia and reform in Iran', *Foreign Affairs* 28 (January 1950).

Zabih, Sepehr, *The Communist Movement in Iran* (Berkeley, Calif. and Los Angeles: University of California Press, 1966).

Persian works

Adamiyyat, Firaydun, 'Fikr-i azadi va muqaddameh-i nahzat-i mashrutiyyat-i Iran' (The idea of freedom and the constitutional movement), *Sukhan* (1340A.H.S./ 1961).

Afrasiyabi, Bahram, *Musaddiq va tarikh* (Musaddiq and history) (Tehran: Intisharat-i Nilufar, 1360A.H.S./1981).

Afrasiyabi, Bahram and Dihqan Sa'id, *Taliqani va tarikh* (Taliqani and history) (Tehran: Intisharat-i Nilufar, 1360A.H.S./1981).

Afshar, Iraj, 'Sanadha'i chand bara-yi karburd dar tarikh' (A selection of documents for use in history), *Ayandeh* 11.8 (1364 A.H.S./1985).

Afshar, Iraj ed., *Taqrirat-i Musaddiq dar zindan* (Musaddiq's life-style in prison), recorded by Jalil Buzurgmihr (Tehran: Sazman-i Kitab, 1359A.H.S/1980).

Al-i Ahmad, Jalal, *Dar khidmat va khiyanat-i rawshanfikran* (On the loyalty and disloyalty of intellectuals), vol. 2 (Tehran: Khvarazmi, 1357A.H.S./1978).

Asnad sukhan miguyand: Aya Musaddiq Feramason bud? (Documents speak: was Musaddiq a Freemason?) (Tehran: Rasa/Abu-Zar, 1359A.H.S./1980).

Ayat, Hasan, *Chihreh-i haqiqi-yi Musaddiq al-Saltaneh* (The true face of Musaddiq al-Saltaneh) (Qum: Intisharat-i Islami, 1360A.H.S./1981).

——, *Darsha'i az tarikh-i siyasi-yi Iran* (Lessons from the political history of Iran) (Tehran: Hizb-i Jumhuri-yi Islami, 1363A.H.S./1984).

——, *Fasli az tarikh-i siyasi-yi Iran: Nigarishi kutah bar nahzat-i milli-yi Iran* (A chapter from the political history of Iran: a short review of the Iranian nationalist movement) (Qum: Intisharat-i Islami, 1362A.H.S./1983).

Bahar, Mihdi, *Miraskhar-i isti'mar* (The heir apparent of imperialism) (Tehran: Amir Kabir, 1357A.H.S./1978).

Bazargan, Mihdi, *Inqilab-i Iran dar daw harikat* (The Iranian revolution in two phases) (Tehran: Nahzat-i Azadi, 1363A.H.S./1984).

——, *Mudafa'at: Asnad-i Nahzat-i Azadi-yi Iran* (Defence: the documents of the Freedom Movement of Iran), vol. 3, part 1 (n.p.: 1345A.H.S./1977).

——, *Shawra-yi Inqilab va Dawlat-i Muvaqqat* (The revolutionary council and the provisional government) (Tehran: Nahzat-i Azadi, 1361A.H.S./1982).

Buzurgmihr, Jalil, *Musaddiq dar dadgah-i nizami*, vol. 1 (Musaddiq in the military court) (Tehran: Nashr-i Tarikh-i Iran, 1363A.H.S./1984).

—— ed., *Musaddiq dar mahkameh-i nizami* (Musaddiq in the military court), book 1, vol. 1 (Tehran: Nashr-i Tarikh-i Iran, 1363A.H.S./1985).

Buzurg-Umid, Abu'l-Hasan, *Az mast keh bar mast* (All our own doing) (Tehran: Amir Kabir, 1335A.H.S./1956).

Chigunehgi-yi intikhab-i avvalin nakhust vazir-i Jumhuri-yi Islami-yi Iran (How the first prime minister of the Islamic Republic of Iran was selected) (Tehran: Daftar-i Tahqiqat va Intisharat-i Ravabit-i Umumi, 1360A.H.S./1981).

Dihnavi, M. ed., *Majmu'eh'i az maktubat, sukhanraniha va payamha-yi Ayatullah Kashani* (A collection of the correspondence, speeches and messages of Ayatullah Kashani), vol. 2 (Tehran: Chap-i Ashna, 1360A.H.S./1982).

Farhang-Qahramani, Ataullah, *Asami-yi namayandigan-i Majlis-i Shawra-yi Milli az aghaz-i mashrutiyyat ta dawreh-i 24 qanun-guzari va namayandigan-i Majlis-i Sina dar haft dawreh-i taqniniyeh az 2508 ta 2536 Shahanshahi* (A list of members of parliament from the beginning of the constitutional era to the 24th Majlis and of senators of the 7th legislative session 2508–2536) (Tehran: Chapkhaneh-i Majlis-i Shawra-yi Milli, 1356A.H.S./1977).

Fateh, Mustafa, *Panjah sal naft-i Iran* (Fifty years of Persian oil) (Tehran: n.p., 1335A.H.S./1956).

Ghani, Cyrus, *Yaddashtha-yi Duktur Qasim Ghani* (The notebooks of Dr Qasim Ghani), vol. 9 (London: Ithaca Press, 1361A.H.S./1982).

Gudarzi-Tabrizi, Rahim, *Luzum-i hifz-i bitarafi* (The need to preserve neutrality) (Tehran: Chapkhaneh-i Musavi, 1333A.H.S./1955).

Havadaran-i Jibheh-i Milli-yi Sivvum dar Kalifornia, *Musaddiq va muvazineh-i manfi: Bahsi dar falsafeh-i junbish-i milli-yi Iran* (Musaddiq and the policy of negative equilibrium: a debate in the philosophy of the Iranian national movement) (n.p., 1351A.H.S./1972).

Isma'ili, Bahman, *Zindiginameh-i Musaddiq al-Saltaneh* (A biography of Musaddiq al-Saltaneh) (Tehran: n.p., n.d.).

Istakhr, Muhammad Husayn, 'Duktur Muhammad Musaddiq ustandar-i Fars' (Dr Muhammad Musaddiq, governor general of Fars), *Salnameh-i Dunya* 11 (1334A.H.S./1955).

Ittila'iyeh az barnameh-i inqilabi-yi Fida'iyan-i Islam (A report on Fida'iyan-i Islam's revolutionary projects) (n.p., 1357A.H.S./1978).

Janzadeh, Ali, *Musaddiq* (Tehran: Hamgam, 1358A.H.S./1979).

Javanshir, M. F., *Tajrubeh-i 28 Murdad: Nazari beh tarikh-i junbish-i milli shudan-i naft* (The experience of 28 Murdad: a review of the movement for the nationalization of the oil industry) (Tehran: Hizb-i Tudeh, 1359A.H.S./1980).

Kalam-i Imam: Milligara'i (Imam's words: nationalism) (Tehran: Amir Kabir, 1362A.H.S./1983).

Kalam-i Imam: Saltanat va tarikh-i Iran (The Imam's words: monarchy and Iranian history) (Tehran: Amir Kabir, 1363A.H.S./1984).

Karubi, Mihdi, *Ifshagari darbareh-i Nahzat-i Azadi* (Exposing the Freedom Movement of Iran) (Tehran: Bunyad-i Shahid, 1361A.H.S./1983).

Kashani, Mahmud, *Qiyam-i millat-i Musulman-i Iran dar 30 Tir 1331* (The uprising of the Muslim people of Iran on 17 July 1952) (Tehran: Sitareh-i Sabz, 1359A.H.S./1980).

Kasravi, Ahmad, *Dar rah-i siyasat* (On the path of politics) (Tehran: Intisharat-i Paydar, 1324A.H.S./1945).

——, *Shi'igari* (Shiism) (Paris: Nur, 1361A.H.S./1982).

Katuzian, Humayun, *Khatirat-i siyasi-yi Khalil Maliki* (Khalil Maliki's political memoir) (Tehran: Ravaq, 1360A.H.S./1981).

Kay-Ustuvan, Husayn, *Siyasat-i muvazineh-i manfi dar Majlis-i Chahardahum* (The policy of negative equilibrium in the 14th Majlis) (Tehran: Ibn Sina, 1327A.H.S./1949).

Khomeini, Ruhullah, *Kashf-i asrar* (The revelation of secrets) (Tehran: Islamiyyeh, 1363A.H.S./1984).

Khushniyyat, Husayn, *Sayyid Mujtaba Navvab Safavi: Andishiha, mubarizat va shahadat-i U* (Sayyid Mujtaba Navvab Safavi: his views, political career and martyrdom) (Tehran: Manshur-i Barabari, 1360A.H.S./1981).

Mahmud, M., *Tarikh-i ravabit-i siyasi-yi Iran va Ingilis* (A history of political relations between Iran and Britain), 5 vols (Tehran: Iqbal, 1328–33A.H.S./1949–53).

Majmu'eh-i qavanin-i sal-i 1333 (Acts of parliament, 1333) (Tehran: Sazman-i Ruznameh-i Rasmi-yi Kishvar-i Shahanshahi-yi Iran, 1334A.H.S./1955).

Makki, Husayn, *Kitab-i siyah* (The black book) (Tehran: Sazman-i Intisharat-i Naw, 1320A.H.S./1941).

——, *Tarikh-i bistsaleh-i Iran* (A twenty-year history of Iran), vol. II (Tehran: Ilmi, 1359A.H.S./1980).

Maliki, Ahmad, *Tarikhcheh-i Jibheh-i Milli* (A short history of the National Front) (Tehran: n.p., 1332A.H.S./1953).

Maliki, Khalil, 'Sarnivisht-i tarikhi-yi libiralism' (The historical fate of liberalism), *Ilm va Zindigi* (August–September 1331A.H.S./1952); 'Alami az naw bibayad sakht' (A new flag should be made), ibid. (January–February 1332A.H.S./1953); 'Mubarizeh ba buzurgtarin khatari keh nahzat-i milli ra tahdid mikunad' (Challenging the greatest danger which threatens the national movement), ibid. (May–June 1332A.H.S./1953).

Mihdiniya, Ja'afar, *Zindigi-yi siyasi-yi Razmara* (A political life of Razmara) (Tehran: Giti, 1353A.H.S./1984).

Mujahid (pseud.), *Ayatullah Kashani va nameh-i Muhandis Hasibi* (Ayatullah Kashani and Muhandis Hasibi's letter) (Tehran: Sipihr, n.d.)

Musaddiq, Muhammad, 'Intikhabat dar Urupa va Iran' (Elections in Europe and Iran), in *Musaddiq va masa'il-i huquq va siyasat* (Musaddiq and problems of law and politics), ed. Iraj Afshar (Tehran: Zamineh, 1358A.H.S./1979).

——, 'Kapitulasion va Iran' (Capitulations and Iran), in *Musaddiq va masa'il-i huquq va siyasat* (Musaddiq and problems of law and politics), ed. Iraj Afshar (Tehran: Zamineh, 1358A.H.S./1979).

——, *Nutqha va maktubat-i Duktur Musaddiq dar dawrehha-yi panjum va shishum-i Majlis-i Shawra-yi Milli* (Dr Musaddiq, his speeches and correspondence in the 5th and 6th Majlis (Paris: Intisharat-i Musaddiq, 1350A.H.S./1971).

——, *Mukatibat-i Musaddiq: Talash bara-yi tashkil-i Jibheh-i Milli-yi Sivvum* (Musaddiq's correspondence: struggle for the formation of the Third National Front) (Tehran: 1354A.H.S./1975).

Mustawfi, Abdullah, *Sharh-i zindigani-yi man ya tarikh-i idari va ijtima'i-yi dawreh-i Qajariyyeh* (The story of my life or an administrative and social history of the Qajar period), vol. 3 (Tehran: Zavvar, 1324A.H.S./1945).

Nigarishi kutah bar nahzat-i milli-yi Iran (A short review of the Iranian nationalist movement) (Tehran: Sazman-i Mujahidin-i Inqilab-i Islami, 1358A.H.S./1979).

Pirnia, Husayn, *Dah sal kushish dar rah-i hifz va bast-i huquq-i Iran dar naft* (Ten years struggle to preserve and expand Iranian rights in oil) (Tehran: n.p., 1331A.H.S./1952).

Rahimian, Ghulam-Husayn, article in *Musaddiq, naft, kudita* (Musaddiq, oil, *coup d'état*), ed. Mahmud Tafazzuli (Tehran: Amir Kabir, 1358A.H.S./1979) pp. 161–3.

Ra'in, Isma'il, *Feramsoniri dar Iran* (Freemasonry in Iran), vol. I (Tehran: n.p., n.d.)

Ruhaniyyat va asrar-i fash-nashudeh az nahzat-i milli shudan-i san'at-i naft (The ulama and the unrevealed secrets of the nationalization of the oil industry) (Qum: Dar al-Fikr, 1358A.H.S./1979).

Ruhani, Fu'ad, *Tarikh-i milli shudan-i san'at-i naft-i Iran* (A history of the nationalization of oil in Iran) (Tehran: Jibi, 1352A.H.S./1973).

Sazman-i Danishjuyan-i Musulman-i Irani. *Asnad-i muntashireh-i Sazman-i Mujahidin-i Khalq-i Iran* (Published documents by the Mujahidin-i Khalq), vol. 1 (Wilmette, Ill.: 1357A.H.S./1978).

Sazman-i Mujahidin-i Inqilab-i Islami, *Nigarishi kutah bar nahzat-i milli-yi Iran* (A short review of the Iranian national movement) (Tehran, n.p., 1358A.H.S./1979).

Tavanayan-Fard, H., *Duktur Musaddiq va iqtisad* (Dr Musaddiq and economics) (Tehran: Alavi, 1332A.H.S./1953).

Yamgani, Parsa, *Karnameh-i Musaddiq* (Musaddiq's Record) (Tehran: Intisharat-i Ravaq, 1357A.H.S./1978).

Index